OXFORD MEDICAL PUBLICATIONS

Heroin Addiction and Drug Policy

# Heroin Addiction and Drug Policy

## The British System

Edited by

### JOHN STRANG

*Getty Senior Lecturer in the Addictions and Deputy Director
Addiction Research Unit, National Addiction Centre,
The Maudsley/Institute of Psychiatry, London*

and

### MICHAEL GOSSOP

*Head of Research, Drug Dependence Unit, National Addiction Centre,
The Maudsley, London*

Oxford   New York   Tokyo
OXFORD UNIVERSITY PRESS
1994

Oxford University Press, Walton Street, Oxford OX2 6DP

Oxford   New York   Toronto
Delhi   Bombay   Calcutta   Madras   Karachi
Kuala Lumpur   Singapore   Hong Kong   Tokyo
Nairobi   Dar es Salaam   Cape Town
Melbourne   Auckland   Madrid
and associated companies in
Berlin   Ibadan

Oxford is a trade mark of Oxford University Press

Published in the United States
by Oxford University Press Inc., New York

A catalogue record for this book is available from the British Library

Library of Congress Cataloging in Publication Data
Heroin addiction and drug policy : the British system / edited by John Strang
and Michael Gossop.
p.   cm. — (Oxford medical publications)
Includes bibliographical references and index.
1. Heroin habit—Great Britain—Prevention.   2. Heroin habit—
Treatment—Great Britain.   3. Pharmaceutical policy—Great Britain.
4. Drug abuse—Government policy—Great Britain.   I. Strang, John.
II. Gossop, Michael, 1948–   .   III. Series.
[DNLM: 1. Heroin Dependence—prevention & control—Great Britain.
2. Public Policy—Great Britain.   WM 288 H5585 1994]
HV5840.G7H47   1994   362.29'380941—dc20   93–42495
ISBN 0 19 262046 0

Typeset by Apex Products, Singapore
Printed in Great Britain on acid-free paper by
Bookcraft (Bath) Ltd, Midsomer Norton, Avon

# Foreword

# What is so special about the British System?

*Marcus Grant*

*Programme on Substance Abuse, World Health Organization, Geneva*

Probably the most remarkable feature of the so-called British System of responding to drug misuse is how much better known it is outside Britain than it is at home. Many clinicians and researchers working in Britain might be forgiven for wondering if such a thing exists at all. If any such doubters are beginning to read this book, then they might be advised first to travel across the Channel in order to avoid viewing the next 27 chapters as an elaboration of a rather elegant confidence trick. The fact of the matter is that in countries all around the world, drug experts (to say nothing of policemen and politicians) are not only convinced that something called the British System exists, but are also convinced that they know what it is.

It is this second aspect of their certainty that is the more worrying, since the story which this book tells is not of the formulation, implementation and evaluation of a coherent and self-contained policy. Rather, it is the story of a pragmatic and shifting response to a rapidly changing phenomenon.

In Britain as elsewhere, the drug scene of the late 1960s was very different from the 1990s. We have moved from a time when it was only just beginning to occur to people that illicit drugs might not after all be swept away by timely enforcement, to a time when people are beginning to question how some drugs came to be called illicit at all and whether this might not be half the problem. In between, we have had AIDS, the war on drugs and the creation of a new United Nations agency to co-ordinate global action. At the same time, in Britain as elsewhere, the range of different individuals and agencies dealing with drug misuse has expanded steadily.

Somehow, in the midst of this confusion, the British System arose. Rather like another famous British phenomenon, the Loch Ness Monster, it is more talked about than observed and better known for its mythic dimensions than for its clear authenticity. None the less, it is a plausible monster, this British System, and if it did not exist, somebody would certainly have been eager to invent it. In the history of international responses to drug misuse, it has reared above the murky waters of the United Nations Commission on Narcotic Drugs on several noteworthy occasions. Like Nessie, you may not believe in it, but you can hardly ignore it.

Dr Strang and Dr Gossop are to be congratulated on having brought together the evidence on this elusive monster, so that readers around the world can judge for themselves where the weight of the evidence lies. The presumed influence of the British System on the policies of other countries is considerable, but it is an influence which has frequently depended on hearsay evidence rather than on any objective account of the nature of the System.

As so often, we end up being able to make more useful observations on the process of developing the System than on the effects which it may or may not have produced, but that in itself is a substantial step in the right direction.

As never before, the world is ready for a radical reconsideration of how best to respond to drug misuse. There is general dissatisfaction with the poor results of supply reduction strategies, coupled with bewilderment at what demand reduction is going to mean. At the World Health Organization, where a new Programme on Substance Abuse has recently been established, there is a willingness to find ways of helping countries just beginning to experience drug problems to learn from the experiences of those who have been grappling with them for decades. It is clear that nobody has all the answers, certainly not the British. But in the story told in this book, there are lessons for us all. In a field awash with competing orthodoxies, the most important lesson of the British System is the lesson of pragmatism.

# Contents

## Part II   Clinical responses                                    149

# Contributors

**Sue Clement,** Renfrew General Acute Unit Royal Alexandra Hospital, Paisley.

**Niall Coggans,** Addiction Research Group, University of Strathclyde, Glasgow.

**Philip Connell,** Emeritus Physician, The Bethlem Royal Hospital and the Maudsley Hospital, London.

**Steve Cranfield,** Independent Trainer and Consultant. (Formerly Senior Nurse, UCH Drug Dependency Unit, London.)

**John B. Davies,** Professor and Director, Addiction Research Group, Centre for Occupational and Health Psychology, University of Strathclyde, Glasgow.

**Nicholas Dorn,** Development Director, Institute for the Study of Drug Dependence (ISDD), London.

**Charlotte Feinmann,** Senior Lecturer in Psychiatry, Academic Department of Psychiatry, University College and Middlesex School of Medicine, London.

**Michael Farrell,** Consultant Psychiatrist and Senior Lecturer, National Addiction Centre, The Maudsley, London.

**Ewan Ferlie,** Associate Director, Centre for Corporate Strategy and Change, University of Warwick, Coventry.

**Hamid Ghodse,** Professor of Psychiatry and Addiction Behaviour, St George's Hospital and Medical School, University of London.

**Mark Gilman,** Lifeline Project, Manchester.

**Alan Glanz,** Senior Research Officer, Health Education Authority, London. (Formerly: National Addiction Centre, Institute of Psychiatry, London.)

**Michael Gossop,** Head of Research, Drug Dependence Unit, National Addiction Centre, The Maudsley, London.

**Marcus Grant,** Programme on Substance Abuse, World Health Authority, Geneva.

**Paul Griffiths,** Senior Researcher, National Addiction Centre, The Maudsley, London.

**Rachel Lart,** Research Associate, School for Advanced Urban Studies, University of Bristol. (Formerly The Centre for Research on Drugs and Health Behaviour, London.)

**Roger Lewis,** Director of the Centre for HIV/AIDS and Drug Studies, Lothian Health Board, Edinburgh.

**Richard Lynch,** Assistant Warden, Oxford Probation Hostel, Oxford.

**Susanne MacGregor,** Professor of Sociology and Social Policy, Middlesex University, London.

**Martin Mitcheson,** Consultant Psychiatrist, South West Regional Drug Services, Glenside Hospital, Bristol.

**Joy Mott,** Principal Research Officer, Home Office Research and Planning Unit, London.

**Michael Murray,** Memorial University of Newfoundland, St Johns, Canada. (Formerly University of Ulster, Londonderry, Northern Ireland.)

**Edna Oppenheimer,** Demand Reduction Technical Advisor, UNDCP (United Nations International Drug Control Policy), Bangkok, Thailand. (Formerly National Addiction Centre, Institute of Psychiatry, London.)

**Geoffrey Pearson,** Wates Professor of Social Work, Goldsmiths' College, University of London.

**Martin Plant,** Professor and Director, Alcohol Research Group, Department of Psychiatry, University of Edinburgh.

**Robert Power,** Senior Research Fellow, The Centre for Research on Drugs and Health Behaviour, London.

**Roy Robertson,** Senior Lecturer (University of Edinburgh) and General Practitioner, Muirhouse Medical Group, Edinburgh.

**Susan Ruben,** Consultant Psychiatrist, Liverpool Drug Dependence Unit, Liverpool.

**Nigel South,** Lecturer, Department of Sociology, University of Essex, Colchester.

**Bing Spear,** former Chief Inspector, Drugs Branch, Home Office, London.

**Gerry V. Stimson,** Professor and Director, The Centre for Research on Drugs and Health Behaviour, London.

**John Strang,** Getty Senior Lecturer in the Addictions and Consultant Psychiatrist, National Addiction Centre, The Maudsley/Institute of Psychiatry, London.

**Paul Toon,** Director of Residential Drug and Alcohol Rehabilitation Programme, Ley Community, Oxford.

**David Turner,** Director, SCODA (Standing Conference on Drug Abuse), London.

**Cathy Walter,** Director of Children's Services, Kingston and District Community Health Unit. (Formerly AIDS Co-ordinator, Bloomsbury Health Authority, London.)

**Brian Wells,** Consultant Psychiatrist, Riverside Substance Misuse Services, London.

**Jasper Woodcock,** Director, ISDD (Institute for the Study of Drug Dependence), London.

**Part I**

---

The problem

# 1. The early years of the 'British System' in practice

*Bing Spear*

## Introduction

For nearly 40 years, until the recommendations of the second Inter-departmental Committee on Drug Addiction (1965), more usually referred to as the second Brain Committee, were implemented in 1968, the British approach to the problem of opiate abuse rested on an implicit faith in the integrity of the medical profession and a wary respect for its power and influence. This was backed by a monitoring system which was at best haphazard, and at worst, non-existent.

That a loose amalgam of statutory provisions, administrative practices and professional co-operation could apparently successfully contain the level of opiate abuse in the United Kingdom, as proponents of the 'British System' claim, whilst understandable to the British, is still a topic for continuing and at times vigorous debate, analysis, misunderstanding, and deliberate distortion in those countries which traditionally have had more serious abuse problems and where rigorous regulation of professional discretion and activity is the order of the day (Spear 1975).

Whilst accepting, for the purposes of this chapter only, that there ever was, and may even still be, a special 'British System', it is not the intention to traverse ground which has been well traversed by others. How the 'accommodation between doctors and the Home Office in which medical involvement in strategies of control was confirmed' came into existence has been described (Bean 1974; Berridge 1984) but as it will be some time before the official papers dealing with the changes of 1968 become available the personal reflections of someone closely involved with events during that period may be of some interest.

### The author's involvement

My involvement, as a member of the Home Office Drugs Branch In-spectorate, was during the period 1952–86, which saw two significant changes in the character and scale of the British drug abuse problem.

The first of these was the emergence in the early 1950s of a small group of young heroin addicts, who differed in many respects from the heroin addicts of the pre-war period (Spear 1969); the second was the development in the last decade of a criminal illicit traffic in heroin of a type hitherto unknown in the United Kingdom. It is with the first of these that this chapter is primarily concerned, a change which was linked to serious deficiencies in the 'British System'. These deficiencies, were not to be rectified until 1973 and are usually ignored by those who, for various reasons, are keen to claim that the 'British System', or what is occasionally misrepresented as the 'British experiment with the supply of heroin to addicts', has failed. This was a fascinating, if frustrating, period made even more interesting because in 1952, when I joined the Inspectorate, its two senior members, the Chief Inspector, F. R. ('FT') Thornton OBE and his Deputy A. L. ('Len') Dyke, had both been involved in drug control and enforcement before the war and knew that 'scene' intimately. 'FT' had the unique distinction of having been involved since 1917 when he was transferred to the Home Office from the Board of Trade where he had been engaged in the issue of export licences for opium and cocaine under the Defence of the Realm Regulations. On the other hand Len Dyke, who held the Chief Inspector's post from 1956, when 'FT' retired, until 1965, brought a different perspective as he came to the Home Office in 1941 from the Metropolitan Police, where, as a Detective Sergeant, he had been the force's first specialist drugs officer.

## The beginnings of the 'British System'

The philosophy of the British approach to the treatment of addiction can be said to have been set by the publication in 1926 of the report of the Rolleston Committee (officially the Departmental Committee on Morphine and Heroin Addiction), but the first tentative steps towards general drug control had been taken much earlier and it might be helpful to a clearer appreciation of the practical application of that philosophy if these were briefly described. In July 1916, in response to representations from the Metropolitan Police and the Service authorities about the abuse of cocaine by servicemen ('an evil, now rapidly assuming huge dimensions'), the Home Secretary was persuaded to use the special war-time powers provided by the Defence of the Realm Act to make it an offence to be in unauthorized possession of cocaine. This meant that anyone found in possession of cocaine who was not a member of the medical profession, who had not obtained the drug on a medical prescription or did not hold a permit issued by the Home Secretary, could be prosecuted for unlawful possession. Defence of the Realm Regulation 40B remained in force until replaced by the Dangerous Drugs Act 1920, and its subordinate Regulations of 1921, which extended the earlier controls to morphine and heroin. These established the broad framework of a control, the basic aim of which remains today, namely the restriction of general access to 'dangerous' drugs with at the same time as little interference as possible with their legitimate use.

The 1921 Regulations authorized any medical practitioner to possess and supply drugs 'as far as may be necessary for the practice of his profession or employment in such capacity', but did not qualify that 'authority' in any way. This is important. The Regulations imposed no limitation on a doctor's choice of drug or the quantities or the circumstances under which he could prescribe; but it was assumed that he would exercise that 'authority' responsibly, in accordance with his professional judgement and the basic purpose of the legislation, which was to prevent the spread of drug addiction. This was an assumption which the Home Office soon had reason to question as evidence began to appear that doctors were supplying, or prescribing, drugs to addicts. Whether this was a proper exercise of a doctor's 'authority', and whether the supply of morphine or heroin to a person who was addicted was 'medically advisable' were questions on which the Home Office needed advice and they were accordingly referred to the Rolleston Committee with results which are well known (Bean 1974 p. 57; Judson 1974, p. 19; Trebach 1982, p. 89), if still occasionally misunderstood and misrepresented. Although the Committee's recommendations on the precautions to be observed when a patient was addicted never acquired the force of law, they were included in a revised edition of a memorandum (Home Office 1929), which was distributed to the medical and dental professions to explain the various provisions of the legislation. (Nine editions of this memorandum were prepared and distributed in the period up to 1961.)

## Tribunals and scrutiny from the Home Office

Unlike Rolleston's medical recommendations, one administrative proposal, of importance in the light of the situation which was to develop 30 years later, was given legal status. This was that Tribunals should be established 'whose function it would be to consider whether or not there were sufficient medical grounds for the administration of the drugs by the doctor concerned either to a patient or to himself, and that they should advise the Home Secretary whether the doctor's right to be in possession, to administer, and to supply the drugs should be withdrawn'. The Home Secretary had had this power since 1916 under Defence of the Realm Regulation 40B in respect of authorized persons convicted of offences against the Regulations (usually of failure to maintain proper records); Rolleston proposed this should be extended to cover those medical issues which were currently causing difficulties for the Home Office.

As the argument with the recently established Ministry of Health over where responsibility for drug control should lie had been resolved in favour of the Home Office (Berridge 1984, p. 23), it fell to that Department to determine the extent to which medical practitioners were following the guidance provided by Rolleston. The primary source of information about prescribing was pharmacy records and for this the Home Office was dependent on the police. In August 1921, in a circular letter explaining the background and provisions of the recent legislation, and without apparently any prior consultation with either police, medical, or pharmaceutical interests, the Home Office requested Chief Constables to make arrangements, as part of the police's responsibility for the enforcement of the provisions relating to the supply and possession of drugs, 'for special attention to be paid to the observance of the Regulations which apply to the sales of drugs to the general public'. (The reason this responsibility was placed upon the police was quite simply that the Home Office did not itself have the resources to undertake it; in 1926, when Rolleston reported, the Home Office had only two Inspectors who were mainly preoccupied with the inspection of licensed persons and firms, the issuing of licences and the examination of statistical information about the legitimate trade.) The police were to ensure that the records and prescriptions which chemists had to keep were inspected from time to time and cases in which it was suspected that the requirements were not being observed reported to the Home Office. There was no request for regular, unusual, or large supplies to be reported, which was a serious omission not to be rectified until 1939, when a long awaited *Manual of guidance* included advice on the sort of information from pharmacy records which would be of interest to the Home Office.

## The quiet times of the 20s to the 50s

The first rumblings of discontent at this new duty surfaced at the Central Conference of Chief Constables in 1925 but were firmly rejected by Sir Malcolm Delevingne of the Home Office, who made it clear that whatever the difficulties chemists should be inspected systematically. Despite this firm statement of Home Office expectations most forces took only a perfunctory interest in this duty, a level of response which was to last for some 40 years and matched an equally low level of response to the criminal aspects of drug abuse (Freemantle 1985, p. 33). Many officers regarded the inspection of pharmacy records as an extraneous duty which bore no relation to their normal police work and felt ill equipped to deal with professional men who could so easily 'blind a police officer with science'. The inadequacy of the police response was soon recognized and in 1935 Inspectors were charged with visiting all forces periodically and systematically to make certain that each had 'a staff told off for dangerous drugs work'.

For a variety of reasons, not least of which were the limited resources of the Inspectorate, the outbreak of war and the absence of any outward signs of a drug abuse problem, police interest remained at a fairly low level until the immediate post-war years when special efforts were made to revive and improve the personal liaison between the police and the Inspectorate. These efforts were gradually rewarded with an increase in the number of reports submitted to the Home Office but when I joined the Inspectorate in 1952 the overall efficiency of the inspections was still a long way short of what was desirable or acceptable and it is only within the last decade, which has seen specialist officers appointed in many forces, that the standard of cover would justify the confidence of the first Interdepartmental Committee on Drug Addiction (1961) 'that the arrangements for recording manufacture and supply, and for inspection, continue to ensure that nearly all addicts are known to the Home Office, to the Ministry of Health and to the Department of Health for Scotland' (para 26).

The inadequate monitoring of pharmacy records probably mattered very little in the pre-war period when most of the addicts in the United Kingdom had either become addicted therapeutically and caused few problems, unlike the generation to come, or were members of the medical or associated professions, whose addiction often came to light through the Inspectorate's monitoring of wholesalers' records, as a result of their behaviour or the suspicion of a concerned pharmacist. When reports of supplies to patients were received from the police they were followed up to establish if the case was one where the drugs were required for the relief of some organic condition, in which case no further action would be taken, or if it was one of addiction, of either therapeutic or non-therapeutic origin. If the case proved to be one of addiction the rate of supply would be kept under review primarily to ensure that the prescriber was familiar with the Rolleston guidance, was not losing control of the case and was not merely pandering to the patient's addiction.

Where the supplies were ostensibly 'for practice use' it was important to confirm that they were in fact required for practice purposes and not to sustain the doctor's own addiction. Since the early days of drug control, as is shown by the unsuccessful attempt in 1922 to make it unlawful for a doctor to prescribe for himself (Berridge 1984, p. 24), the Home Office has recognized and been concerned about the special problems posed by the doctor addict. That concern was shared with the Rolleston Committee which proposed that the Home Secretary should be able to withdraw the 'authority' of such an addict on the recommendation of a medical Tribunal, which it was felt, would be better able than a court of law to judge the issues involved. Although different tactics were favoured, there was clearly agreement between the Home Office and the medical profession, as represented by Rolleston, that the strategy should be to prevent the doctor from using his privileged position to obtain supplies to support his own addiction and this has always been the primary objective of the Inspectorate's intervention in such cases. However, before the doctor addict could be persuaded, or in the extreme case forced by legal sanctions, to obtain his drugs from another doctor, an admission that his purchases were for his own use was desirable but, not surprisingly, was often difficult to obtain. Explanations for large or regular purchases of morphine or heroin have ranged from the unoriginal, and usually easily disproved claim that the purchaser was treating a number of terminal cases, to the much more imaginative injection of heroin into strawberry plants in the course of cancer research, and the use of heroin solutions as culture media. Although most doctor addicts could have been prosecuted for such technical offences as failing to keep, or properly maintain, a drugs register, and when convicted have had their 'authority' to possess and supply drugs withdrawn, this step was usually taken only where all other measures had failed or where the case was one in which such action was urgently necessary. For many years it was the practice to offer a doctor addict the opportunity to give a voluntary Undertaking, which had no legal force, that in future he would not obtain drugs for his own consumption on his own 'authority' but would obtain them from a named colleague under whose care he agreed to place himself. This worked reasonably well, as in the case of the doctor whose longstanding Undertaking came to light only when his name was put forward in 1968 for a heroin prescribing licence, but there were also many failures although perhaps none quite as immediate as the doctor who came down from Scotland for an interview with 'FT' and on his return journey through London and Glasgow made four purchases of morphine on signed orders written on the back of his copy of the Undertaking.

## New heroin addict groups begin to appear

However, in one respect the statement that nearly all addicts were known to the Home Office was correct. Since the emergence in 1951 of the new group of heroin addicts special attention had been paid by the Inspectorate to the distribution of hypodermic tablets of heroin, the form in which it was normally prescribed. This task was considerably helped by the existence in the West End of London of two pharmacies, Boots, in Piccadilly Circus and John Bell & Croyden, in Wigmore Street, each providing a 24 hour service, and therefore very popular with addicts. Frequent inspection of the records at these two pharmacies, and the excellent co-operation of their staff, ensured that most of the addicts who were receiving heroin prescriptions quickly came to notice and the expansion of this group could be closely monitored. The arrest of 'Mark'

(Judson 1974, p. 28), who had been the group's main supplier, naturally created problems. Only two of his customers had previously received prescriptions from a doctor, one used 'Mark' to supplement her prescribed supply and subsequently continued to receive prescriptions from her doctor until he decided to 'retire' in 1953. The other, a young man who had only recently come out of prison, was less fortunate as his previous prescriber, although quite willing to accept other ex-'Mark' customers, refused to take him back. However, having links with the older group of addicts he was able to persuade one of their prescribers to accept him. Only one other ex-'Mark' customer surfaced in 1951 but in 1952 eight came forward and in 1953 a further four. Given that none of these encountered any problems in finding doctors willing to prescribe for them, it is a little surprising that so many of these new addicts chose to maintain their addiction with illicit supplies, in one instance for 7 years. No doubt the understandable fear, as there is today in respect of 'notification', of becoming known to authorities, a refusal to accept that he was addicted and in need of help, which receipt of a prescription would have confirmed, and the belief of many addicts that 'you don't get hooked as badly when you're buying on the black' were partly responsible for this reluctance.

If 'Mark' had introduced heroin into the West End of London where it was not currently available, the subsequent generous prescribing of a small number of doctors ensured that he would not be missed. The doctors who became involved with addicts in these early days fell into three main groups, the genuine, the gullible, and the generous, although some qualified for inclusion under more than one heading. (Ten years later gullibility and generosity were to be associated to a hitherto unrivalled extent.) Those in the first group, usually had no previous experience of addiction, tended to have only one addict patient, to maintain a firm control over a modest dosage and to do their best to persuade their patients to undergo hospital treatment. It is interesting, in view of current attitudes about the role of private prescribers, that a number of these doctors firmly believed that addicts should not be able to obtain their drugs on National Health Service (NHS) prescriptions and that a small fee was simply compensation for the trouble which addicts invariably caused. The genuinely, as distinct from the conveniently, or diplomatically gullible, formed the smallest group at this particular period and is best represented by the doctor who unhesitatingly accepted his patient's story that before taking his discharge from hospital he had been able to convince the staff he was taking only two tablets of heroin per day, whereas he actually needed a hundred each week (shortly to rise to a hundred every other day). This addict was strongly suspected of going into hospital for a partial reduction of his dosage whenever he found that his own habit was eating into his profits!

## Who were the doctors?

A detailed review of the development of this new group, completed in April 1955, identified six doctors whose prescribing gave cause for concern. None of these ever had more than two or three addict patients at any one time and in 1955 only two, Dr E. A. Maguire of Linden Gardens, W2, who first came to Home Office attention in 1946 when he started to prescribe for one of the pre-war addicts, and Dr J. M. Rourke of Kensington Church Street, W8, were still actively involved. Each had only two heroin addicts and were said to have 'a working relationship', the exact nature of which was never established but which appeared to be designed to protect from prosecution those addicts who were obtaining prescriptions concurrently from each of them, sometimes on the same day. Of the others, one had decided to sever his hitherto quite extensive links with the addict world following a Court appearance in 1953, two others were successfully 'persuaded' to withdraw, whilst the oldest, who had qualified in 1903, had had no addict patients for nearly a year. This was surprising since the state of his practice suggested that any income from treating addicts was more than welcome and it was known he was not averse to telephoning a patient to enquire whether another prescription was not required.

As the following examples show, an addict accepted by any of these doctors could confidently expect his dosage of heroin to be increased virtually on request. In January 1954, Dr B who had no previous contact with addicts, began to prescribe heroin for C, a Nigerian, who claimed he had started using drugs in the USA. (Two other Nigerians who approached other doctors around the same time had been introduced to heroin by an American doctor since returned to the USA!) According to Dr B the dosage was two grains of heroin per day, yet in the first 10 days of January he gave C prescriptions for over 100 grains (6000 mg). When asked to explain this he admitted he had merely been supplying what the addict requested and expressed his suspicion that some of the heroin was being sold. Within a short time he was prescribing cocaine in addition to heroin, again at the patient's request, C having suggested that if he were given cocaine he would be able to reduce his dosage of heroin. (Shortly afterwards the other two Nigerian addicts also asked their doctors for cocaine.) Although Dr B's practice was in North London and C had by now moved to Pimlico, he continued to treat him as a National Health Service patient, 'out of kindness' and to visit him frequently, the cost of his petrol being met by the patient. At an interview in July 1954, after which he decided to have no more dealings with addicts, Dr B again voiced his suspicions that C was selling part of his supplies in the West End at exorbitant prices. These suspicions were based on the fact that C did not work, owned two mews flats and an expensive car, and always had plenty of money. Why, if he had these suspicions, he had continued to prescribe large quantities of heroin and cocaine he could not explain, apart from saying that C had continually asked him for supplies. That Dr B was correct to regard C with some suspicion was shown by the dramatic downturn in the latter's economic situation when he came under the care of another doctor who drastically reduced, and controlled his daily dosage.

The second example throws interesting light on the 'working arrangement' between Dr Maguire and Dr Rourke and involved another Nigerian, Broderick Walker, who in April and May 1954 endeavoured unsuccessfully to persuade six doctors that he was addicted to heroin. Nevertheless on 27 August 1954 he received his first prescription from Dr Maguire and a month later his first from Dr Rourke. Thereafter until his death in March 1955 he continued to be a patient of both doctors and in the period 27 August 1954 until 19 January 1955 received 38 NHS prescriptions from Dr Maguire for a total of 3750 tablets of heroin and 47 NHS prescriptions for a further 3005 tablets from Dr Rourke. On five occasions prescriptions were issued by both doctors on the same day. Although Walker claimed in an interview with police officers that he was taking six grains of heroin a day, he was in fact receiving between three and four times that amount. It is not known if at this period Dr Maguire was aware of Dr Rourke's involvement, and if so the extent of it, but there is no doubt that the latter knew Walker was a patient on Dr Maguire's NHS list as he signed some prescriptions 'pp Dr Maguire'. For a short time after Walker's death Dr Rourke continued to give prescriptions in his name to the woman with whom Walker had been living and who was also addicted. Details were submitted to the Director of Public Prosecutions and on 8 September 1955 Dr Rourke appeared at Marylebone Magistrates Court to answer six charges of aiding and abetting the unlawful possession of drugs. Dismissing these the Magistrate, Mr Geoffrey Raphael, explained that he was 'unable to find anything (in the Regulations) which prevents a doctor exercising his own discretion and saying, "In my view this man should have this drug" and give it to him' (*Daily Telegraph* 9th September 1955; Criminal Law Review 326, 1956) supporting a similar interpretation that the Regulations did not in any way limit a doctor's right to prescribe dangerous drugs, which had been given by Counsel in connection with the submission of evidence to the Rolleston Committee some 30 years earlier.

Surprisingly, Mr Raphael's decision was not interpreted by Dr Rourke as a 'green light' to expand his clientele and in the ensuing years he was content to deal with two addicts only. (Dr Maguire who had been called as a witness and had confirmed that he and Dr Rourke had a 'working arrangement' to treat each other's patients, decided that this was an opportune moment to withdraw.) Unfortunately the two addicts who remained with Dr Rourke were the two, A and D, whose names were most frequently mentioned as suppliers and the quantities of heroin they were receiving suggested the allegations were well founded. D had transferred to Dr Rourke from Dr Maguire in September 1953 and by January 1960, when he moved on to another doctor who was subsequently to prove even more generous, he was receiving around 20 grains (1200 mg) of heroin each day. His fellow patient, A, had been accepted by Dr Rourke in January 1954 and by July was receiving a similar dosage, considerably enhanced by supplementary prescriptions which appeared to be related more to his financial circumstances than to his physical needs. (Years later A confirmed to me that he had been paying Dr Rourke between £7 and £10 per week even though he was a NHS patient.) On more than one occasion when presenting a prescription for dispensing he would have another in his hand, which he explained was 'for midnight' and by the time he transferred to another doctor in October 1958 his relationship with Dr Rourke had reached the point where he was writing his own prescriptions, merely presenting them to the doctor for signature and dating. The departure of D marked the end of Dr Rourke's involvement with addicts and he died in September 1960.

## The need for a different type of response

That this was a thoroughly unsatisfactory and unacceptable state of affairs was obvious. The Inspectorate were virtually powerless, since for reasons which will shortly be explained the machinery which Rolleston had recommended to deal with such prescribing no longer existed. A very close watch was kept on what was happening and attempts were made in the course of numerous interviews with the doctors concerned to persuade them to exercise more care and control and although this was successful in two instances, Drs Maguire and Rourke proved to be totally impervious to such approaches. The police were in no better position. Although they could and from time to time did arrest addicts who were not obtaining their heroin on prescription, they were equally powerless to deal with addict–suppliers who were lawfully entitled to any heroin found in their possession. As the Head of the Metropolitan Police Drug Squad told a meeting of the Forensic Science Society in 1962, 'we have never found—or received reliable evidence—of heroin being trafficked in London in any other form than a tablet' (Cooke 1962). To prove an unlawful supply it was necessary for the police to witness the actual handover of drugs and whilst there were periods when it was possible to stand outside Boots in Piccadilly Circus and watch an addict pass on part of his recently dispensed supplies to someone else, one successful police operation there meant that future sales would be conducted under more secure conditions.

Responsibility for this situation has to rest firmly with the Home Office. As the following cases show, Drs Maguire and Rourke were not the first doctors since 1926 whose prescribing to addicts had been questionable, yet the machinery thoughtfully provided by Rolleston had never been used. Why there was such apparent reluctance to refer cases to Tribunals is not now entirely clear although there are some grounds for thinking the Home Office had quite early come to the view, later to be endorsed by the first Brain Committee, that the type of evidence likely to satisfy a Tribunal would be very difficult to obtain. (Experience gained since 1973 in using the reintroduced Tribunal machinery has shown these fears to be totally unjustified.) In 1935 interest centred on Dr Joseph Hirshman, who in a short space of time had acquired a small group of morphine addict patients, none of whom lived in his area of London and for whom he began to prescribe. He was interviewed by Len Dyke, then still with the Metropolitan Police, who reported that in his opinion Dr Hirshman 'was one of the worst script doctors known to us' yet the relevant Home Office papers bore the cryptic comment that the Tribunal machinery, which had been introduced to deal with precisely this sort of prescribing, 'would be of little avail in the case of a man of his stamp'. Perhaps the fact that by failing to keep proper drug records Dr Hirshman had presented the Home Office with a much simpler solution had some bearing on this thinking; in February 1936 he was convicted of the technical record-keeping offence which enabled the Secretary of State withdraw his 'authority' to possess and supply dangerous drugs. As reported in the *Morning Advertiser* of 26th February 1936

... the importance of the prosecution was that the doctor was known to be treating a number of drug addicts and it was clear from the information in the possession of the authorities that he was not dealing with these addicts as he should. The prosecution had prescriptions to show that the doctor rather than reduce the dose of drugs, had been in a number of cases increasing the dose in a short space of a few months, one grain being increased to seven or ten grains.

Such a ready solution was not offered by Dr Gerald Quinlan who was careful not to contravene the technical requirements of the Regulations. In the immediate pre-war years Dr Quinlan collected an appreciable number of the more notorious of London's addicts and prescribed for them on a 'lavish' scale. In 1941 it was decided to approach the General Medical Council to see if they would be prepared to consider dealing with him. Again why the Home Office apparently did not favour reference to a Tribunal is not clear. There is little doubt the Council would have preferred to act on the basis of a conviction under the Dangerous Drugs Act but they agreed to consider the matter if the Home Office could provide evidence that Dr Quinlan had sold drugs to patients at exorbitant prices, at frequent intervals or otherwise than as medicines in the course of his treatment of them, and that, knowing they were addicted, he continued to supply them with drugs to 'their moral and physical detriment'. The facts were collected and submitted to the Council before whom Dr Quinlan was summoned to appear in June 1942. However, the hearing was repeatedly postponed and 'FT' was informed by the President of the Council that it had been intimated to him that this was a case in which the Home Office should exercise its power under the Regulations and not employ the time of a body like the General Medical Council and that he had decided to postpone the case to the November session. Not surprisingly Dr Quinlan took advantage of this breathing space and reduced both the number of his addict patients and their dosages so that when he met Len Dyke some time later he was able to claim he had 'a good defence' as he had made good progress with the addicts and had gained experience in handling them. In the circumstances the General Medical Council were informed that the Home Office would not be unduly disturbed if the case against the doctor was dropped.

Although the General Medical Council did not erase Dr Hirshman's name from the Medical Register following his conviction and were reluctant to act against Dr Quinlan, it would be wrong to give the impression that the medical authorities were entirely disinterested in the activities of such prescribers. In 1944 and in 1945 the British Medical Association and the General Medical Council enquired about the current status of the Tribunals and whether any references were likely in the near future. In reply the Home Office doubted if any useful purpose would be served by reappointing members to the Tribunal, many of whose original members had died or retired, and expressed the view that doctors who misused drugs almost invariably committed offences which could be dealt with in the Courts. This was clearly a reference to doctor addicts and was based on a review carried out in 1944 of the practice of using the Courts in such cases. (The problems posed by 'script' doctors, whose activities raised difficult questions of medical judgement, seem to have been largely ignored.) In the course of this review it was argued that the medical profession could justifiably complain that the special problems of addicted doctors were not being dealt with as Rolleston intended, but rather surprisingly the Ministry of Health took the view that doctors would prefer to be prosecuted for a technical record-keeping offence than appear before a Tribunal where the real reason for their drug purchases would be disclosed.

Within a few years the Home Office was to regret this rather negative response. The doctor concerned, Dr Marks Ripka, had first come to notice in 1935 but it was his generous prescribing in the post-war period which led to the decision in 1950 that steps had to be taken to curtail his activities. Again the preference appeared to be for proceedings in the Court, but this foundered on the same question which had caused difficulty to Sir Malcolm Delevingne in the 1920s, whether the supply of drugs to addicts could be held to be a contravention of the Regulations. It was also felt that a Court might criticize the Home Office for not referring this very difficult medical question to a Tribunal as provided for in the Regulations. As there was no reason to suppose the General Medical Council would take a different view to that taken in the case of Dr Quinlan, details of Dr Ripka's prescribing were referred to the Home Office Legal Adviser who, in February 1951, confirmed that in his view there was sufficient evidence to place before a Tribunal. The medical authorities were informed a reference was proposed and were asked to nominate members for the Tribunal. Lengthy discussions about the admissibility of evidence and a number of procedural arrangements could not be concluded until July 1952 when it was too late to include the amended provisions in the consolidated Regulations about to be introduced and it was decided these would have to be introduced separately later. However, this was not the setback it might have been because although by January 1953 Dr Ripka had accepted two of 'Mark's' former customers, his contact with this newly emerging group of addicts was about to come to an end. In February 1953 he appeared at Clerkenwell Magistrates Court and pleaded 'guilty' to two summonses of aiding and abetting one of his patients in the unlawful possession of heroin, which she was sending to an addict then living in Malta. Dr Ripka informed the Court that he would in future accept no more addicts as patients, a welcome decision since for technical reasons the Secretary of State was unable to exercise his power to withdraw his 'authority' to possess and supply drugs (*Daily Telegraph*; *Daily Express* 12 February 1953).

With Dr Ripka's withdrawal the re-introduction of the Tribunal provisions became less urgent but by 1955, following the review of the increasing heroin problem and the doubly unsuccessful attempt to deal with Dr Rourke, it was again clear that some control over the prescribing to addicts was necessary. (Following the dismissal of the case by Mr Raphael details of Dr Rourke's prescribing were referred to the General Medical Council who confirmed their position had not changed since 1942. In their opinion such cases should be dealt with under the appropriate provisions of the Dangerous Drugs legislation, which of course did not then exist.) Unfortunately, before the revised Regulations could be introduced the Government appointed the Committee on Administrative Tribunals and Enquiries (the Franks Committee) and it was decided the Tribunal Regulations would have to be further postponed until that enquiry had been completed. By the time the post-Franks legislation, the Tribunals and Inquiries Act 1958, was on the statute book it had been decided to review the advice given by Sir Humphrey Rolleston's Committee 30 years earlier, 'in the light of more recent developments' and the first Brain Committee was appointed in June 1958.

## The first report of the Brain Committee

Their Report, published in 1961, was a classic of complacency and superficiality. The increase in the number of known addicts was simply the result of 'an intensified activity for the detection and recognition' of addiction, and there was no cause to fear that any real increase was occurring. Moreover the Committee 'were impressed' that the right of doctors in Great Britain to continue at their own professional discretion the provision of dangerous drugs to known addicts had not contributed to any increase in the total number of patients receiving regular supplies in this way. In view of this assessment of the current state of opiate abuse in the United Kingdom it is not surprising that the Committee saw no need for any significant changes in existing practices and procedures.

To criticize the Committee for their failure to recognize the change, which was then occurring is not to take advantage of the power of hindsight. The threat posed by the new addicts had been accepted in 1955 by J. H. Walker, who had administrative responsibility in the Home Office for drugs policy, and would certainly have been one of the 'recent developments' placed before the Committee had he not been transferred to other work before they began their enquiry. Whilst most of the blame for the failure to bring the emergence of this new group to the attention of the Committee, must rest with the Home Office, the Committee cannot entirely escape responsibility. It simply will not do to claim 'we were never told', as some members of the Committee did at the meeting of the Society for the Study of Addiction in April 1961 when 'Benny' Benjamin, the pharmacist at John Bell & Croyden, shattered the self-congratulatory atmosphere by announcing that at his pharmacy he was dispensing heroin and cocaine for more addicts than had apparently come to their notice (Judson 1974, p. 36).

The real tragedy of the first Brain Committee, however, was not the failure to recognize the new threat, serious though that was, but their naïvety in believing that because they had been told (incorrectly) that there had been only two 'script' doctors in the past 20 years and their own 'widespread enquiry' had not detected the existence of Dr Rourke (who continued to prescribe for D until January 1960), there would be none in the future. Unlike their predecessors in 1926, who had had the common sense and foresight to anticipate there would probably be such cases and to suggest how they should be dealt with, all this Committee could offer was the opinion that cases of excessive prescribing were matters for the General Medical Council, an opinion which the Home Office knew, if members of the Committee did not, the Council did not share. (The reason for the Council's reluctance to get involved did not become clear until 1969 when in evidence to the Amphetamines Sub-Committee of the Advisory Committee on Drug Dependence (ACDD), the President of the

Council, Lord Cohen, explained that the Council's disciplinary powers were limited to cases of 'serious professional misconduct' and that a doctor who overprescribed drugs because in good faith he regarded this as the right treatment for his patient would not be guilty of serious misconduct. (It is interesting to note that the Council are now showing a far greater willingness than hitherto to test the bona fides of practitioners prescribing to addicts or drug dependants and in the past 5 years several doctors have been found guilty of serious professional misconduct, arising from their irresponsible or non-*bona-fide* prescribing.)

## The second report of the Brain Committee

The cost of the first Brain Committee's failure can be seen in the dramatic rise in the number of known heroin addicts, from 62 in 1958, when the Committee was appointed, to 342 in 1964 when, as a result of two reports submitted by the Inspectorate, they were reconvened. At Lord Brain's insistence the terms of reference of this second enquiry, to review 'the advice they gave in 1961 in relation to the prescribing of addictive drugs by doctors', were deliberately narrow as the problem which the Committee was being asked to consider was clearly identified in the Inspectorate's reports. The first of these, in May 1962, was a detailed review of the prescribing of Lady I. M. Frankau, a psychiatrist of 32 Wimpole Street, W1, the second, in November 1963, updated the special reports on the heroin problem, prepared in 1955 and 1960, and offered a number of suggestions for tackling what Judson was later to describe as prescribing of 'lunatic generosity'.

## Lady Frankau

Whilst the main conclusions of this second enquiry are well known and need no further comment here, some statements in the Report have led to a serious misunderstanding of the problem the Committee faced and to the creation of a mythology which it now seems impossible to destroy or even dent. Far from being a problem of 'six' doctors, it was essentially a problem created by one, a fact readily acknowledged by Lord Brain, who after Lady Frankau had given evidence to the Committee on 4 December 1964, looked over his glasses at the civil servants at the end of the table and said, 'Well gentlemen, I think your problem can be summed up in two words, Lady Frankau'. Yet the final Report recorded that '... the major source of supply has been the activity of a very few doctors who have prescribed excessively for addicts' (para 11). The reality is rather different. As Kenneth Leech, who as curate at St Anne's, Soho was well placed to observe the developing problem, has commented, '... there never was a static group of six. At any one time between 1960 and 1968, you could identify between six and 12 doctors in the inner London area who were prescribing significant amounts of heroin for non-therapeutic purposes—that is, for addicts. The group changed from time to time, though some doctors remained constant throughout the period. In almost every case, the doctors were well-known to the Home Office drugs branch before the press discovered them...' (Leech 1981). In the original evidence to the Committee the Home Office referred anonymously to only four doctors who were prescribing but at one of the Committee's meetings, in reply to a member, I said I thought there were then possibly 'around six'.

This reply subsequently appeared in the Report as '... not more than six doctors have prescribed these very large amounts of dangerous drugs for individual patients ...' (para 12), a totally misleading statement as with one exception, all the 'very large amounts' had been prescribed by Lady Frankau. The exception, a prescription for 1020 heroin tablets, was given to one of the veteran Canadian addicts by his NHS doctor to cover a two week absence from London. The other 1000 tablet prescription quoted in the Report was issued by Lady Frankau and was for 1008 tablets of heroin and 252 grains (15 120 mg) of cocaine to cover a 6 week period whilst the addict was in Wales 'withdrawing'. Instead he went immediately to Paris returning after 3 days to another doctor to whom he gave a different name. Lady Frankau was also the doctor responsible for the prescribing of over 600 000 heroin tablets during 1962, another of the Committee's most frequently quoted 'findings', yet the Report made no reference to the number of patients for whom this seemingly excessive quantity of drugs had been prescribed. Statistics which Lady Frankau gave to the Brain Committee showed that in the period from 1958 to 1964 she had seen just over 500 addicts which included each year about 35 who were 'not registered', undergraduates who had just started 'to play around with heroin' and about 30 old cases. On a list which she gave me in 1966, for the purpose of a follow-up study which because of her subsequent illness was never completed, there were 374 names, the vast majority of whom were heroin addicts for whom she had prescribed and whose prescriptions had been traced. (This list showed that in 1962 she had accepted, and prescribed for, 74 new addict patients compared with 125 in the statistics given to the Brain Committee.)

As Lady Frankau's prescribing was undoubtedly the mainstay of the flourishing illicit market in heroin and cocaine in London until 1966, some comment on her treatment philosophy and methods is necessary. Her interest in the treatment of drug addiction appears to have been first aroused towards the end of 1957 when Dr P. M. Stanwell, a general practitioner who already had one or two addict patients, suggested to her in the course of a consultation about an alcoholic that she might like to try her hand with an addict, but it was not until the following summer that the extent of this interest became apparent. This was because all the prescriptions were written by Dr Stanwell with Lady Frankau providing supportive psychotherapy as a preliminary to the addicts undergoing withdrawal treatment in a nursing home under her supervision. Gradually the number of patients being accepted for treatment increased, with Lady Frankau more directly involved in the issue of prescriptions, a development which eventually led to a break with Dr Stanwell who had become very concerned at Lady Frankau's readiness to increase an addict's dosage on the flimsiest of pretexts, whilst Lady Frankau, for her part, believed that Dr Stanwell was far too firm.

The effect of the removal of such restraining influence as Dr Stanwell had been able to exercise was soon apparent as Lady Frankau's prescribing became increasingly bizarre and irresponsible. The more startling examples of her prescribing have been quoted in the second Brain report and while there are many more which could be given, it is the rationale behind this prescribing (Frankau and Stanwell 1960) which is of interest. Put simply, the essential element of Lady Frankau's treatment philosophy was that the patient had to be made independent of the illicit market, although in many instances the practical effect was merely to change the addict's role in relation to the market, from customer to supplier. One of the difficulties in achieving this independence was the addicts' inability

to say simply that they had overstepped the usual amount, instead they either augmented their supplies from the black market, or produced plausible stories of accidents or losses. Eventually they realised that it was better to state bluntly that too much had been used. Extra supplies were prescribed to prevent them returning to the black market, which would involve them in financial difficulties, and (which is even more important) would mean a return to the degradation and humiliation of contacting the pedlars ... During this phase of treatment the addicts acquired enough insight into their condition to be able to cooperate.

This was amplified in her Niagara Falls address in February 1963 when she explained that each patient (Frankau 1964)

was assured that prescriptions would always be available and, that if he could genuinely claim to have spilled or lost part of his supply, the lost drug would be replaced. If he had used too much and came and reported this, he would be given a prescription and the reasons for his lapse be discussed ...

Clearly the success of such a policy rested upon the ability to determine whether claims for additional or replacement supplies were genuine and it was in this respect that Lady Frankau clearly had a distinct advantage over other doctors since, as she frequently asserted, she could always tell if one of her patients was lying. Her willingness to entertain such claims confirmed the ingenuousness first hinted at in the 1960 paper and which no doubt partly accounted for the irregularity of her prescribing, where not only the interval between prescriptions varied widely but so also did the quantities prescribed and it was not uncommon to find two, or even three, prescriptions to the same addict dispensed on the same day. To this ingenuousness has to be added an unrivalled capacity for self-deception (typified by her statement to the Brain Committee that 'all my patients are too tightly controlled to sell drugs on the black market'), which in its turn led to an unshakeable confidence in the correctness of her methods and a haughty intolerance of other approaches and disregard for many of the normal courtesies of medical practice. These attributes are well illustrated by a case involving a patient who was convicted of obtaining 'dual supplies' of heroin concurrently from Lady Frankau and his NHS general practitioner, who had written to her for a report but had had no reply. When first told she would be required to attend Court Lady Frankau complained to the Home Office that she did not have the time as 21 patients were scheduled to come for their prescriptions between 10 a.m. and 11 a.m. on the morning of the hearing (an average of 3 min per consultation). In Court she said she had a large number of addicts as patients and had no time to write or talk to any doctor; she had asked the addict if he was still going to his general practitioner and accepted his reply that he was not. The addict's version was that when his NHS doctor went on holiday he simply went to Lady Frankau who gave him 'large supplies' ('I just asked for what I wanted and she took my word. If you spun her enough story she would believe you').

Of the many myths to which this period has given birth three of the most persistent are that the 'six' were all in private practice, that the influx of Canadian, and to a lesser extent US, heroin addicts in the early 1960s was the direct result of a lecture tour which Lady Frankau made to Canada and that her involvement with addicts was motivated entirely by financial considerations. All are wrong. Although the second Brain Report offered no information on the point, Lady Frankau was the only private prescriber at that time and the concern expressed in para 7.13 of the *Treatment and rehabilitation* Report of the Advisory Council on the Misuse of Drugs (1982) was shared by the 1960s prescribers. Their attitude to this delicate question was fairly reflected in Dr Hawes' comment that 'to have accepted any as private patients would have laid one open to the charge of having a vested interest in addiction' (Hawes 1970).

### The Canadians

As has been shown (Spear and Glatt 1971; Zacune 1971), the peak of the Canadian influx was in 1962, a year before Lady Frankau gave her paper at Niagara Falls and her own records show that in 1962 she accepted 26 new addicts from Canada but only six in the following year and 13 in 1964. Whilst her visit to Canada inevitably attracted considerable press attention, what those who have chosen to represent it as a recruiting drive have failed to appreciate is the effectiveness of the addicts' grape-vine, which had already relayed back to Canada the experiences of the first arrivals, who had found the United Kingdom, with its readily available supplies of legitimate heroin, to be the 'seventh heaven' they had been led to believe. This invasion had little effect on an indigenous situation which had been developing steadily since 1951, without trans-Atlantic help and its limited extent was predicted with remarkable accuracy by the then RCMP Liaison Officer in London.

Just as the influence of Canadian addicts on the domestic heroin scene has been exaggerated, so too has been the influence of US addicts and again it is Lady Frankau's involvement with this group which has received most attention. The number of US addicts for whom she prescribed during the period 1958 to 1966 was about 60, few of whom were long-term residents. The largest number of new cases (20) occurred in 1965 by which time, as word passed along the addicts' grape-vine, she had acquired a considerable international reputation as an unquestioning supplier of drugs. It was well known in addict circles in Paris that in times of need supplies of heroin could always be obtained by the simple expedient of visiting Lady Frankau, and admirably demonstrated by one internationally famous jazz musician who arrived at London Airport from Paris one morning in March 1962 and departed the same afternoon after receiving from Lady Frankau a prescription for heroin, cocaine, and methadone.

Of the many reasons which have been advanced to explain Lady Frankau's involvement the one for which there is no evidence is that she was financially motivated and allegations that she was can usually be traced to disgruntled addicts or to doctors unable to accept that anyone would willingly devote so much time trying to help such undeserving cases without adequate financial reward. In fact from the outset, her work with addicts was subsidized by her private psychiatric practice and it was by no means uncommon at West End pharmacies to find prescriptions endorsed 'charge to my account'. Whilst many of her critics preferred to keep their distance, those, including some of her severest, who did meet her to discuss her treatment philosophy and methods, invariably admitted afterwards that although she might be misguided, or in the words of one, be 'a well meaning fool', her sincerity and integrity could not be doubted.

That these and other myths should still exist in 1990 is regrettable as they give a misleading picture of a critical period in the development of the British drug problem, a period which saw fundamental changes in both the character and extent of that problem. Yet these changes continue to be represented as the result of the activities of a few rogue or misguided, doctors, an analysis which if understandable in the 1960s, is not today. We had moved from a reasonably comfortable situation in which the typical addict was 'a middle aged housewife whose illness was treated if not understood, with some measure of success by the family doctor', to one in which 'the known mores of pre-war surburbia were exchanged for those of a youthful minority subculture of the Western World' and in which 'the comforting solidity of expert ignorance was exchanged for the frightening limbo of a world where each expert's word contradicted that of the next' (Home Office Drugs Branch 1968). It was a situation for which we were not prepared.

It is therefore not surprising that the temptation to ignore the significance of what was really happening, and to place responsibility for these changes on a few readily identifiable scapegoats, could not be resisted. The blanket criticism of all the 1960s prescribers, apart from being grossly unfair, diverts attention from the real tragedy of the period, the unwillingness of the vast majority of the medical profession to take up the challenge which these new young addicts presented. Any doctor who ventured into this area, and most chose not to, had to be 'unusually brave, compassionate, skilful and lucky if he were to achieve success' and there is no doubt that most of those who did become involved were dedicated practitioners who were prepared to put themselves to endless trouble on behalf of the addicts (Jeffery 1970). The *Sunday Times*, on 20 February 1966, following an investigation in which the main prescribers were interviewed 'at length', concluded that

all of these doctors have some unusual quality about them—some direct element of the 'outsider' in their make-up; strong political opinions; the status of exile; or perhaps an unusual degree of professional compassion. And it is possible as a result of this that they succeed in acting as a link between the outcast addicts and normal society.

Unfortunately, the fact that only a handful were prepared to respond to the new challenge meant that they did not have the necessary time to decide which were reasonable demands and which were not. In the words of Dr Hawes (1970),

... you became a junkie doctor with one patient; if you responded to his plea you had started your career in that line, because he sent his friends and they sent their friends. Soon you would be (as I was) overwhelmed by the sheer numbers. In the past ten years I had through my hands (not treated) somewhere about a thousand addicts. I kept fairly full notes about the first three hundred, but after that time allowed no more than the bare details.

Moreover, those who were prepared to help quickly found that the kind of assistance from hospital out-patient and in-patient services, upon which general practitioners could ordinarily rely, was 'almost totally lacking' when the patients were addicts (Hewetson and Ollendorff 1964).

## Non-participation from the majority of doctors

If further confirmation was needed that the vast majority of United Kingdom doctors wanted as little contact as possible with addicts, a situation which has changed little over the past 20 years (Waller 1990), it is provided by their response to the Brain II proposals. Ten years earlier the profession had rightly, vigorously and successfully, resisted the Government's plan to ban the future production and use of heroin (Bean 1972, p. 133; Judson 1972, p. 29), yet the imminent limitation on the hitherto unfettered, and jealously guarded, right of a doctor to prescribe whatever drug he considered to be in his patient's best interest, attracted very little discussion or opposition. Reasons for this uncharacteristic response are not hard to find. First, as Glatt *et al.* (1967) have suggested there was an ideological objection because

... addicts have a very poor prognosis, and basic to the ideology of most doctors is that they should attempt to cure their patients. This of course means that the doctor must first accept the idea that drug addiction is a disease and treatable in general practice. It would seem that this idea is not yet accepted by many British doctors ...

Secondly, the new arrangements would give general practitioners in particular, protection from the kind of pressures described by Dr Hawes; a doctor who did not have the legal right to prescribe heroin was far less likely to be approached for 'treatment'. The removal of a power which had never been used was likely to excite only those doctors who saw the matter as an issue of principle and a campaign to preserve an unfettered freedom to prescribe heroin to addicts was unlikely to attract much support from a public which had been left in little doubt by the publicity given to the 'six', and to the later activities of Dr John Petro and Dr Christopher Swan (Judson 1972, p. 58; Leech 1981; Trebach 1982, p. 178; Freemantle 1985, p. 23), that the current heroin problem was largely the result of that unfettered freedom.

Whilst the negative response of the medical profession is perhaps understandable, the Brain II proposals, and their implementation have not escaped criticism entirely. If Brain II had 'narrowed the problem down to only a few doctors, why did the medical profession and the government not proceed to deal with those few?' (Trebach 1982, p. 117) and what were "the serious matters involving extensive consultation 'as professional interests' were involved" which meant that it took over 2½ years to implement the Committee's findings? (Bean 1972, p. 83). These questions will not be satisfactorily answered until the relevant Ministry of Health papers are released but it was apparent at a very early stage in the Committee's deliberations that not only did they still hold the view, expressed in their first Report (para 44) that special Tribunals would be difficult to establish, but they were very much attracted to the concept of special centres at which addicts could be treated. (The suggestion that a speedy reintroduction of updated Tribunal machinery, possibly linked to some statutory limitation on the number of addicts an individual doctor could treat, and the maximum dosage which could be prescribed without a second opinion, did not find much support). As the idea of special treatment centres had been put forward by one of the psychiatrist witnesses (Bewley 1965) and the Report suggested that such centres 'might form part of a psychiatric hospital or of the psychiatric wing of a general hospital' (para 22), the 'psychiatrizing' of addiction treatment policy in the United Kingdom was assured.

Given that this was the chosen, and accepted, solution to the problem of the over-prescriber, the delay in the implementation of the proposals was inevitable. Existing facilities were clearly inadequate and would be unable to cope with the numbers of addicts who would have to be transferred from the general practitioners currently looking after them, let alone those who, it was hoped, would be encouraged to quit the illicit market. With few exceptions most psychiatrists had successfully avoided, or had had little opportunity for contact with these young addicts and consequently had very little practical experience upon which to draw, whilst those doctors with such experience, the heavily criticized general practitioners, were to be denied further involvement. It was not surprising therefore that the influence of US thinking did not take long to surface. An early proposal, unveiled at a meeting at the Home Office, was that the prescribing of heroin would be discontinued despite the very clearly expressed view of Brain II (para 15) that addicts should be able to obtain supplies of this drug 'from legitimate sources'. Although this proposal was dropped in the face of strong Inspectorate objections, the advocates of a methadone only, and an eventual non-prescribing policy, were to obtain their objective, by other means.

Those responsible for planning the new centres had been given no detailed blueprint by Brain II but they were fortunate to be able to draw on the experience of Dr John Owens at All Saints Hospital, Birmingham, who in 1964 had established an addiction unit, which over the next 2 years attracted increasing numbers of young heroin addicts. Some of these were self, some medical, referrals, but significant numbers were referred by the police and probation services. The All Saints approach, embodying those same principles, controls on prescribing, responsible behaviour by the addicts and good relations with the community, which led Connell to exempt the Shreveport clinic of Dr Butler from his general criticism of the failed American clinics of the 1920s (Trebach 1982, p. 187), successfully contained the problem in the Birmingham area and has not received the recognition it deserves (Nyman 1969; Judson 1972, p. 88).

Whether, as is sometimes suggested, the delay in phasing out the prescribing general practitioners, and the uncertainty 'on the street' about what was going to happen contributed significantly to the way in which the United Kingdom heroin problem was to develop, is for social historians of the future to determine. What is certain is that during this period two important barriers came down. First, the reluctance of an addict population, which up until then had been almost entirely dependent on pharmaceutical heroin, to use illicitly manufactured heroin of unknown purity and strength, gradually disappeared and 'Chinese' heroin became a regular feature of the London black market. Secondly, early in 1968, largely through the efforts of Dr Petro, the amount of injectable methyl-amphetamine in the West End of London increased dramatically and, as Leech (1973) has described, 'provided the bridge between the needle culture and the kids in the clubs' making "the process of 'fixing' an integral part of the West End drug culture", and to transform it over the next few years into a multi-drug injecting 'scene'. The inadequacies of the existing legislation, and the continuing absence of effective machinery to deal with dubious prescribing, which were not to be rectified until 1973, ensured there were sufficient supplies of methadone, amphetamines, methyl-phenidate ('Ritalin'), barbiturates, and dipipanone ('Diconal'; later to become a sufficiently serious problem to justify it being placed under the same prescribing restrictions as heroin and cocaine), to supplement the dwindling supplies of heroin from the treatment centres (Spear 1982).

## Conclusion

It could be said that the 'British System', as it evolved following Rolleston, ceased to exist in 1953, when the Tribunal provisions were dropped, but it is the restrictions on prescribing which came into effect on 16 April 1968 which have been interpreted as heralding the end of the Rolleston era and the formal abandonment of the 'British System'. This is a total misreading of the situation, which firstly, overlooks the fact that the 1968 changes were a response to a specific problem, the prescribing of heroin and cocaine by one doctor. They were not intended to replace the advice given by the first Brain Committee which had reviewed the general addiction problem a few years earlier and endorsed the Rolleston concept of 'the stabilised addict' (para 36). The basic philosophy of the British approach was unaffected by the 1968 changes and in 1990 an addict to heroin, or any other drug, is as free to consult any doctor of his choice, and for that doctor to accept or reject him, as would have been the case in 1926. The only difference is that the doctor would now be unable to prescribe heroin, cocaine, or dipipanone unless specially licensed but would be perfectly entitled to give his patient any other drug for the purpose of 'maintenance', 'stabilization' or in the course of a detoxification regimen. The decision whether or not to issue a licence rests with the Home Secretary, after consultation with the Department of Health, and whilst it is current policy not to license general practitioners to prescribe heroin, there is nothing in the Regulations to prevent a general practitioner from applying for a licence, and if refused, from challenging that decision in the Courts. (A few licences to prescribe dipipanone have in fact been issued to general practitioners.)

The belief that the 'British System' has now been abandoned arises from a misunderstanding of the relationship between the law and the conduct of medical practice. As mentioned above, United Kingdom drug laws aim to provide a framework within which doctors are free to use drugs in accordance with their clinical judgement, which may or may not accord with the consensus of medical opinion at that time. Whether a particular drug is used in the treatment of a specific disease is not a matter to be dictated by the Department of Health, the Home Office, or any other government agency, a fact still not fully appreciated even in this country. What is now being interpreted as the formal abandonment of the 'British System' is merely a change in medical attitudes which Fazey (1989) has ascribed to the seizure of the moral high ground by a group within the medical establishment and psychiatry in particular,

who declared unilaterally that drug addicts should not be given drugs ....... Psychiatrists who took over treatment decided that the U.S.A. knew best, and addicts could be cured of their addiction. Abstinence became the universal goal to be enforced by only offering detoxification regimes, as in-patients or out-patients and oral methadone in a few cases.

This shifting of the goalposts away from the clearly expressed intention in 1968 that heroin should still be supplied in minimum quantities 'to avoid the development of an organized illicit traffic on a scale hitherto unknown in this country', and that the out-patient clinics would make 'drugs available to those addicts who could not be persuaded to do without them' (Ministry of Health 1967; Glancy 1972) was not based on a proper evaluation of previous policies. Moreover, this change was accompanied by pressure to conform to the new orthodoxy, which in 1984 was enshrined in *Guidelines of good clinical practice in the treatment of drug misuse* (Department of Health 1984), drawn up by a working group of doctors with expertise in the field, mainly psychiatrists, and representatives of various medical bodies. As these guidelines were distributed by the Department of Health to all doctors, it is understandable that they should be seen as 'official' discouragement to any doctor still favouring the Rolleston approach, and effectively ensure the virtual, universal acceptance of the new orthodoxy.

However, the advent of AIDS has introduced a new element into the equation and the validity of such an inflexible non-prescribing approach, in the face of a threat which has been officially recognized as posing a greater danger to public health than drug misuse (Advisory Council on the Misuse of Drugs 1988) is now being seriously questioned. The next few years may therefore see at least a partial return to principles and practices which were jettisoned for medico-political reasons before they had been properly tested or evaluated and not because they had failed. It would therefore be premature to write the obituary of the 'British System'; it has merely been under psychiatric care for the past 25 years.

# References

Advisory Committee on Drug Dependence (1970). *The amphetamines and lysergic acid diethylamide*. HMSO, London.

Advisory Council on the Misuse of Drugs (1982). *Treatment and rehabilitation*. HMSO, London.

Advisory Council on the Misuse of Drugs (1988). *AIDS and drug misuse*. HMSO, London.

Bean, P. (1974). *The social control of drugs*. Martin Robertson, London.

Berridge, V. (1984). Drugs and social policy: the establishment of drug control in Britain 1900–1930. *British Journal of Addiction*, **79**, 18–29.

Bewley, T. H. (1965). Heroin and cocaine addiction. *Lancet*, 808–10.

Cooke, E. (1962). The drug squad. *Journal of the Forensic Science Society*, **3**, 43–8.

Departmental Committee on Morphine and Heroin Addiction (1926). *Report*. HMSO, London.

Department of Health (1984). *Guidelines on good clinical practice in the treatment of drug misuse*. HMSO, London.

Fazey, C. S. J. (1989). What works: an evaluation of drug treatments for illicit drug users in the United Kingdom and Europe. *Studies of Drug Issues: Report No. 3*. Centre for Urban Studies, University of Liverpool.

Frankau, I. M. and Stanwell P. M. (1960). The treatment of drug addiction. *Lancet*, 1377–9.

Frankau, I. M. (1964). Treatment in England of Canadian patients addicted to narcotic drugs. *Canadian Medical Association Journal*, **90**, 421–4.

Freemantle, B. (1985). *The fix*. Michael Joseph, London.

Glancy, J. E. McA. (1972). The treatment of narcotic dependence in the United Kingdom. *Bulletin on Narcotics*, Vol XXIV No. 4, 1–9.

Glatt, M. M., Pittman, D. J., Gillepie, D. G., and Hills D. R. (1967). *The drug scene in Great Britain*. Edward Arnold, London.

Hawes, A. J. (1970). Goodbye junkies. *Lancet*, 258–60.

Hewetson, J. and Ollendorff R. H. V. (1964). Preliminary survey of one hundred London heroin and cocaine addicts. *British Journal of Addiction*, **60**, 109–14.

Home Office Drugs Branch (1968). The dangerous drugs legislation, 1967. *The Police Journal*, Vol LXI, 249–54.

Home Office (1929). *Memorandum as to duties of doctors and dentists*. HMSO.

Jeffery, C. G. (1970). In *Modern trends in drug dependence and alcoholism*. Butterworths, London.

Judson, H. F. (1974). *Heroin addiction in Britain*. Harcourt Brace Jovanovich, New York and London.

Leech, K. (1973). *Keep the faith baby*. SPCK, London.

Leech, K. (1981). John Petro, the junkies' doctor. *New Society*, 430–2.

Ministry of Health (1967). *The treatment and supervision of heroin addiction.* Hospital Memorandum [67], 16.

Nyman, M. (1969). Addiction unit-All Saints' Hospital. *British Journal and Social Service Review*, 1451–2.

Spear, H. B. (1969). The growth of heroin addiction in the United Kingdom. *British Journal of Addiction*, **64**, 245–56.

Spear, H. B. and Glatt M. M. (1971). The influence of Canadian addicts on heroin addiction in the United Kingdom. *British Journal of Addiction*, **66**, 141–9.

Spear, H. B. (1975). The British experience. *The John Marshall Journal of Practice and Procedure*, **9**, 67–98.

Spear, H. B. (1982). In *The dependence phenomenon*. MTP Press, Lancaster.

Trebach, A. S. (1982). *The heroin solution.* Yale University Press, New Haven.

Waller, T. (1990). Ways to open the surgery door. *Druglink*, Vol 5, No 3, 10–11.

Zacune, J. (1971). A comparison of Canadian narcotic addicts in Great Britain and in Canada. *Bulletin on Narcotics*, Vol XXIII, No 4, 41–9.

# 2. Drug trends since 1968

*Robert Power*

## Nothing new under the sun

Reaffirming the adage that there is nothing new under the sun, contemporary concern over the use of heroin and cocaine echoes the very issue that precipitated the setting up of the clinic system in the late 1960s. Referring to that period, Edwards (1981) identifies the problem of the non-therapeutic use of heroin and cocaine as a 'speedball', and the leakage on to the grey market, as a prime reason behind the revision of treatment and the control response. Consequently, one of the key objectives of the 1967 Dangerous Drugs Act, which restricted the prescribing of heroin and cocaine unless licensed by the Home Office, was to control supply and prevent an expansion of the black market by reducing over-subscribing. Since those early days the role of the clinics has expanded and diversified, and the whole prescribing debate has been reopened in light of concern about human immunodeficiency virus (HIV) disease and injecting drug use.

As Stimson (1981) notes, prior to 1968, some legitimately supplied 100 per cent pure pharmaceutical heroin was being prescribed to drug users by doctors and then resold for injecting. But it was the conclusion of the Brain Committee (Ministry of Health 1965) that not more than a handful of doctors, perhaps only six, were involved in excessive prescribing. Lewis (1984) gives the example of one private doctor who prescribed 6 kg of heroin in one year in the early 1960s. A number of cases hit the headlines, such as Lady Frankau of Wimpole Street, who was prescribing to 50 addicts. Some of these addicts were receiving 1800 mg/day, which was 180 times the therapeutic dose (Bennett 1983).

As early as 1962, notified heroin addicts exceeded morphine addicts for the first time, and by 1964 the vast majority known to the Home Office had not acquired their addiction in the therapeutic setting, signalling the development of an independent drug subculture. When the drug dependency centres opened in April 1968, less than 1000 heroin users were in treatment and only 147 of these were outside of London. The common policy of the clinics was to transfer patients from prescribed heroin to injectable methadone and then on to oral methadone. By the end of 1969, approximately 50 per cent were being prescribed methadone alone, and by 1978 this figure had risen to over 70 per cent (Stimson and Oppenheimer 1982).

An immediate effect of a decrease in the prescription of pharmaceutical heroin was an increase in its value on the 'grey market', and an added black market interest in injectable methadone which had not previously existed (Spear 1975).

In the following years, Britain would witness an unprecedented explosion in the black market for illicit drugs and an associated expansion of the grey market in pharmaceuticals.

Patterns and trends in drug use result from a range of individual, socio-economic, political, and judicial factors and will vary from region to region within any given nation state. They will also have a temporal dimension that is influenced not only by supply and demand, but also by prevailing fads and fashions. Hippies, mods, rockers, skinheads, and casuals have always had specified drugs that are part and parcel of the desired image. The Acid House parties that became so infamous during the late 1980s would not have had the same impact (either on the participants or the public) had not Ecstasy (or 3,4-methylenedioxy-methamphetamine) been an integral part of the phenomenon.

As Hartnoll *et al.* (1985) have shown, only a minority of problem drug users will turn to agencies for help. Indeed, Home Office notification statistics have consistently shown that the majority of help-seekers are heroin users, leaving a wide range of illicit substance misusers to cope, one way or another, with their drug user in the community. Blackwell's (1983) work on heroin users highlighted the way in which individuals would 'drift' along a spectrum that included both problem and recreational use, reinforcing the point that the majority of drug users function without recourse to the helping services.

Having made the caveat that the evolution of drug trends is multi-dimensional and multi-causal, there can be little doubt that the initiation of the clinic system had an important impact upon the course of events in Britain. It is the prime aim of this chapter to plot the drug trends from that time to the present day and to identify the important landmarks along the way.

## The search for alternatives: Methedrine and Diconal

Although the consumption of a range of pharmaceutical drugs was nothing new to heroin users, the demand for alternative supplies increased once it became apparent that the licensing system would decrease the availability of legitimately prescribed heroin and cocaine. In the early post-clinic days, existing drug users needed to look no further than the general practitioners. The London epidemic of methylamphetamine abuse in the summer of 1968 pinpointed flaws in the new arrangements. One general practitioner, who was a major source of heroin before the clinic system, began to prescribe Methedrine (methylamphetamine) as a substitute for the now unavailable cocaine. Although illicit amphetamine in tablet form, especially Drinamyl (amphetamine/barbiturate mixture), was prescribed through the 1960s, there was little evidence of amphetamine injecting (Connell 1964). In one month in 1968, this doctor prescribed 24 000 ampoules to 110 individuals. This was the equivalent of 46 ampoules per patient per day. By May of 1968 Drugs Branch officers recovered 35 248 prescriptions from eight private doctors for ampoules of Methedrine. This drug was subsequently controlled under the Drug (Prevention of Misuse) Act, 1971, and manufacturers agreed only to supply methylamphetamine to hospitals. The two main offending prescribers were removed: one was struck off the Medical Register and the other was convicted of serious criminal drug charges (Spear 1975).

However, and independently of the new prescribing practices, Methedrine had grown in popularity during the late 1960s as part of the growing 'hippy' subculture, in which psychedelic drugs played an integral role. Illustrating this point, Hawks *et al.* (1969), studying 84 young London methylamphetamine abusers, showed that they had been using the drug for an average of 19 months before the study, obtaining supplies from those in receipt of personal prescriptions.

One important side-effect of methylamphetamine use, which abated after the recalcitrant doctors were brought to task, was its role in popularizing, not just the use but also the injecting of amphetamines, an issue to become critical in the decades to follow. Prior to this time, amphetamine users had taken their drugs orally, with injecting remaining the province of heroin users. The two cultures had remained apart, but as Leech (1973) points out, Methedrine provided the bridge between the needle culture and the pill-popping club scene. Similarly, Glatt (1971) reported that in the wake of Methedrine had come the injecting of other stimulants, notably methylphenidate under the trade name of Ritalin.

The grey market continued to expand in other directions to encompass a new range of pharmaceutical products. Dipipanone, which was to become a favourite with polydrug injectors in the 1970s and 1980s, was marketed with the anti-nausea drug cyclizine as Diconal, in a tablet form which was easily crushed in preparation for injection. Although eventually controlled under the 1984 Misuse of Drugs Act (Amendment), its abuse emerged shortly after the initiation of the clinic system. Spear (1982) puts 1970 and the north of England as the first significant incident of Diconal abuse outside of the opiate treatment context. This was soon followed by two incidents of Diconal abuse in the next year at south coast towns, unconnected to the first incident. Doctors were discovered

to be prescribing Diconal to groups of young individuals complaining
of backache, some of whom were drug clinic patients. Diconal, an
acceptable heroin substitute for drug users, was also being obtained from
forged prescriptions and pharmacy break-ins. When police and Home
Office pressure led to the south coast doctors being forced to retire from
the prescribing scene, users moved on to alternative sources, especially
single-handed practices and elderly general practitioners.

The attraction of Diconal continued down the years, with Home Office
figures for the numbers and quantities of seizures and arrests showing
1975—84 to be the height of activity. After the restrictions on prescribing
in 1984, the Drugs Branch Inspectorate (1985), reported that Diconal
had virtually disappeared from the British illicit drugs scene, and fears
that Palfium (detromoramide) would fill the gap proved to be largely
unfounded.

Prescribing restrictions increased the illicit value of Diconal from its
pre-control price of £5 a tablet to £8 a tablet, and the Drugs Branch
Inspectorate (1986) report suggests that Diconal prescribing and subsequent availability was once more on the increase. Such was the enduring
popularity of Diconal that Gilman (1988), looking at the drug scene in
the north of England, commented that some of its afficienados, who
saw street heroin as a poor substitute, contemplated and even achieved
abstinence at times when Diconal was unavailable.

## The quest continues: barbiturates and benzodiazepines

The barbiturate range of drugs, including Tuinal (quinalbarbitone and
amylbarbitone), Nembutal (pentobarbitone), and Seconal (quinalbarbitone), along with their successors the benzodiazepines, were finally controlled for the first time in 1986 as Class C drugs, but not before a
protracted history of misuse. Although taken by heroin users since 1962,
barbiturates first became popular in the mid-1960s, especially Drinamyl,
the legendary 'purple hearts', which were a mixture of barbiturates and
amphetamines (Edwards 1981).

Prior abuse of these drugs had been largely restricted to middle-aged
and older users (Glatt 1962; Mitcheson *et al.* 1970), but were sought
after by drug users to augment the lower doses of heroin legitimately
available after 1968, leading to an expansion of abusers, particularly
injectors (de Alarcon 1969; Chapple 1969). As with Diconal, prescriptions
were forged or obtained from doctors on a casual or regular basis, along
with the customary thefts from pharmacies and wholesalers. Illustrating
the growth of the 'grey market' in pharmaceutical drugs, Mitcheson
*et al.* (1970) conducted a study of 65 heroin users, and found that 62
had taken barbiturates, 52 had injected them, and 41 had used Mandrax
illicitly. In addition, 40 had received prescriptions for barbiturates from

general practitioners (29 under the National Health Service and 18 privately), or else they bought from sellers who themselves were in receipt of a prescription. Tyler (1986) reported that Tuinal had been used by 'speed freaks' as an antidote to the stimulatory effects of amphetamine sulphate. By the early 1970s, barbiturate-related deaths in the United Kingdom had risen to 2000 per annum, resulting in something like one-half of all fatal poisonings between 1969 and 1974; and the aggressive behaviour of barbiturate abusers presenting at casualty departments was noted (Ghodse 1971; Tyler 1986).

Despite the voluntary restrictions on barbiturate prescribing amongst general practitioners from the 1970s, benzodiazepines (which were seen as new and safe tranquillizers), soon took over as prescribed drugs of major concern, not least because of the leakage on to the grey market. The peak of prescribing took place in 1975 when there were 47.5 million prescriptions dispensed at retail pharmacies. During 1975 and 1979 psychotropics such as benzodiazepines and barbiturates increased at a steady annual rate of about 43 million prescriptions; between the early 1970s and the mid-1980s, diazepam (Valium) became the largest selling drug in the world. Along with extensive tranquillizer use in general populations (Dunnell and Cartwright 1972; Williams 1983; Ashton and Golding 1989), the benzodiazepines became an integral part of the illicit drug user's repertoire.

The Drug Branch Inspectorate (1984) noted the use of Valium by illicit drug users and, 2 years later, commented that amongst certain populations temazepam had actually become the drug of choice (Drug Branch Inspectorate 1986). Official sources in the second half of the 1980s make several references to the intravenous use of temazepam as a replacement for heroin, especially in Scotland where it was the preferred drug (Drug Branch Inspectorate 1987).

The growing range and relatively free availability of pharmaceutical drugs has exposed many polydrug users to new compounds. Perera *et al.* (1987) found that 90 per cent of a sample of illicit drug users in Sheffield had used benzodiazepines in the year prior to interview. One-third claimed general practitioners as the original source, gaining prescriptions to aid sleep, reduce anxiety, and to avoid withdrawals. Over one-half said that the ease of obtaining these drugs from the 'streets' or general practitioners influenced their initial decision to use.

More recently, Gilman *et al.* (1990) have described the growth of a drug-injecting subculture in the north-west of England, centred on cyclizine, especially the travel-sickness pill Valoid. This has been encouraged by the reduction in the local availability of heroin since 1986, and the return to a polydrug culture, which has included the injection of other pharmaceuticals, such as Temgesic (buprenorphine) and temazepam. Ruben *et al.* (1989) noted the specific use of cyclizine injection in combination with oral methadone amongst a group of drug users in Nottingham. Recent research in London has highlighted the use of DF118 (di-hydrocodeine) amongst primary opiate users, where Swadi *et al.* (1990) found a 31 per cent rate of use amongst a clinic sample of 143 drug users. The work of Hammersley (1990) and Morrison (1989) reinforces earlier findings, stressing the growing and predominant trend in Scotland of injecting pharmaceuticals such as Temgesic and temazepam.

## Into the black hole: the heroin epidemic

Of even more dramatic impact than the growth of the grey market in pharmaceutical drugs, has been the dramatic expansion of the black market in a wide range of substances (most notably heroin) since the 1970s.

By the end of 1968, there were just over 1000 thousand addicts notified to the Home Office. By 1989, this had multiplied to nearly 15 000, a growth largely accounted for by the 'heroin epidemic' of the mid-1980s. This figure is partial and indicators suggest that a better estimate for heroin users for England and Wales is in the order of five times the official tally (Hartnoll *et al.* 1985). The need for drug users to find alternative supplies of heroin itself (as opposed to substitutes) soon became apparent once it was obvious that only limited supplies would be prescribed or diverted from the newly formed clinics. Indeed, in 1977, 19 per cent of addicts in London clinics were receiving some heroin, reducing to 6 per cent by 1984. Oral methadone alone was prescribed to 29 per cent of addicts in 1977, a figure rising to 70 per cent in 1984. Ampoules of methadone for injecting were prescribed to 52 per cent of drug users in 1977 and this reduced to 21 per cent by 1984 (Hartnoll *et al.* 1987).

Just as the grey market in pharmaceutical heroin pre-dated the clinic system, so also there existed an illicit market in London in the late 1960s. This comprised what came to be called 'Number Three heroin', which was smoked by drug users found within the close-knit Chinese community in Soho. Although only 30–45 per cent pure, it soon found a market amongst London's non-Chinese heroin users who felt the need to supplement the drugs emanating from the clinics. Between 1967 and 1968, only two samples of this type of heroin were sent to police forensic laboratories, but this figure rose to 60 by the end of 1969. This heroin was imported from Hong Kong where it was manufactured in a pinkish-grey powder from heroin or morphine. In the early 1970s, and especially at the end of the Vietnam war in 1973, Chinese 'Number Three heroin' was replaced by heroin from the golden triangle of South-east Asia, originating from Burma, Thailand, and Laos. Subsequent poor harvests in 1978 and 1979, coupled with successful police clampdowns on its dealers, led to a reduction in the availability of South-east Asian heroin.

The overthrow of the Shah of Iran in 1979 and the influx of Iranian refugees into Britain, many bringing with them heroin from South-west Asia, led to the drug from this source establishing itself as the market leader. South-west Asian heroin from the 'Golden Crescent' of Afghanistan, Pakistan, and India, has dominated the British illicit heroin market throughout the 1980s. This was especially so in the first half of the decade, when copious supplies led to a 25 per cent reduction in London street prices relative to inflation (Lewis *et al.* 1985).

In terms of the epidemiology of heroin use in England and Wales, available evidence suggests that the 1970s witnessed a generally stabilizing heroin-using population. Home Office notification figures increased slightly, but were countered by a levelling off of the numbers found guilty of heroin-related drug offences. Notably, there was an increase in the average age of newly notified drug users and, significantly, an increase in the age of drug offenders from 22 years in 1973 to 26 years in 1980 (Home Office 1984).

But by the 1980s, evidence emerged as to the growing extent of illicit heroin use (Ditton and Speirets 1981; Lewis *et al.* 1985; Pearson 1987; Parker *et al.* 1988). These research findings from cities and towns around Britain point to an increase in heroin use in the first half of the 1980s, a trend borne out by statistical evidence. All official indicators, including seizures, notifications, and drug offences, point to an epidemic in the years between 1980 and 1985. In 1985, 6000 individuals were newly notified, five times the rate for 1980. Figures for that year noted a fourfold increase in heroin-related drug offences compared with 1980 (Home Office 1987). Earlier in the decade, 1983 customs' seizures for heroin were double those of 1982 and six times the annual average for 1973–78. The year of 1983 also witnessed something in the order of a 50 per cent increase in re-notified addicts compared with 1982, with a similar figure for newly notified addicts (Home Office 1984). The second half of the decade showed a levelling off of incidence, with a decrease in newly notified heroin addicts, indicating that the 'epidemic' had peaked (Home Office 1990*a*).

How then do we account for the explosive growth of heroin use in the mid-1980s? Two associated factors had roles to play. First, the arrival of cheap, high-purity heroin from South-west Asia, and especially Pakistan. Secondly, the fact that heroin from this source could be smoked. This was important in making heroin accessible to those unwilling to inject drugs. A study in the early 1970s pointed to an aversion to intravenous use amongst a sample of 159 young drug users, where only 31 (16 per cent) reported to have injected drugs. Indeed, amongst the sample there was a generally held negative feeling regarding injecting as a route of administration (Plant 1975). Thus, when Parker *et al.* (1988) investigated the marked outbreak of heroin use amongst the younger sections of the population of the Wirral, which had grown from less than a hundred users in 1980 to an estimate in excess of 5000 by 1987, the researchers noted that 79 per cent of their sample smoked or 'chased the dragon', compared with only 4 per cent who were solely injectors. On the other hand, Pearson (1987), looking at various towns and cities in the north of England, and illustrating the importance of regional and local variation, found major differences in the pattern of drug use from one area to the next, noting that the route of administration of the newly-available cheap South-west Asian heroin would depend on the traditional route of administration of other drugs, especially amphetamine sulphate. Burr (1987), conducting an anthropological study of young heroin users in south London, observed that 'chasing the dragon' had spread rapidly, partly because it was freely available and relatively cheap, making experimentation more enticing and attractive.

### The cocaine issue: white tidal wave or gentle breakers?

Since the late 1960s, major concern about the supply and consumption of cocaine has only matched that regarding heroin since the last years of the 1980s. The voluntary agreement of clinics not to prescribe cocaine meant that those receiving licit cocaine decreased from 564 in 1968 to 81 by the end of 1969. Although cocaine was popular amongst certain sections of society during the 1970s, its high price of between £60 and £100 a gram was prohibitive for most people, giving it the reputation as a 'champagne drug'. From about 1983, the price has decreased in relation to inflation, yet its retail price is still approximately six times that of amphetamine sulphate, retaining the latter as Britain's most popular stimulant (Hartnoll *et al.* 1987). Although Lewis (1989) reported that by 1973 cocaine could be found without much difficulty in many parts of London, he noted that the market was restricted, and the average recreational user reserved consumption for special occasions.

Home Office figures for seizures of cocaine, and convictions for offences involving cocaine, showed a gradual increase throughout the 1970s, yet reports from the Drugs Branch Inspectorate (1984 and 1985) have consistently failed to find evidence of widespread cocaine misuse. Again, the Drugs Branch Inspectorate (1986) noted that the predicted cocaine explosion had not occurred, and although its use was increasing, it was still concentrated in the upper socio-economic groups in London, with 75 per cent of all seizures being made in the capital. Importantly, although customs seizures for cocaine during 1987 exceeded those of heroin, 200 of the 360 kg total resulted from a single shipment intercepted in transit to a European port. In that year, when cocaine seizures were increasing throughout Europe, police also seized more cocaine

(51 kg) than heroin (36 kg) for the first time since 1976 (Drugs Branch Inspectorate 1987).

In spite of much media and political concern about cocaine use, especially in its smokeable form as 'crack', the most recent official statistics have yet to track a significant problem. The 530 cocaine users notified to the Home Office during 1989 account for only 9 per cent of the total. Although this represents a 15 per cent increase in notified cocaine users over the 1988 figures, it does not match the 17 per cent overall increase in total notifications (Home Office 1990*a*). Cocaine offences continue to be low, and although 1988 figures showed a slight increase, they fell short of the 1984 peak. Numbers of 'crack' seizures increased to 138 reported during 1989, compared with the 27 recorded for 1988. But the total weight of crack seized was 250 g with only 37 instances involving seizures of 1 g or more (Home Office 1990*b*). The Home Office, with the assistance of the Department of Health, have commissioned a major research project to assess the nature and prevalence of cocaine and 'crack' use in Britain. This 3 year study, conducted at the Centre for Research on Drugs and Health Behaviour, in London, will provide both qualitative and quantitative data to inform this issue.

Notwithstanding this, available indicators still point to amphetamine sulphate as the most popular stimulant amongst British drug users. Along with high reported rates of use (relative to other illicit drugs) by a number of surveys conducted during the 1970s (see Stimson 1981), total numbers of police seizures of amphetamine sulphate at street level have consistently exceeded those for cocaine (Home Office 1990*b*). The Drugs Branch Inspectorate (1984) reported that amphetamine use was widespread in the early 1980s, especially in the Midlands, with several police forces reporting levels of usage higher than cannabis. By 1985, a serious escalation in availability was noted, particularly for use by injection, with incidence in some areas occurring at the same rate as for cannabis (Drugs Branch Inspectorate 1985). Indeed, since 1971, when amphetamines and similar stimulants were controlled under the Misuse of Drugs Act, a thriving illicit market in amphetamine sulphate has existed in Britain, often centred around specific fashions and trends, such as the 'punk' movement and northern dance circuit of the mid-1970s. A breakdown of recent amphetamine seizures by customs and police sources points to the importation of the drug in tablet form and the manufacture of powders within the country. Successful police operations against major laboratories in 1987 and 1989 highlight not only the continued manufacture, but also enduring popularity of amphetamine sulphate in Britain. This decade will also need to address the increasing use of crack cocaine and especially new patterns of drug use amongst young people. These include designer hallucinogenics and stimulants, the use of which are closely tied to emerging subcultures that are centred on music and other forms of recreation.

## Conclusions: piecing the jigsaw together

It soon became apparent, in the years immediately following the setting up of the clinics, that the system would never succeed in one of its earliest aims: the control of the illicit supply of drugs. No one could have predicted the escalation in illicit drug use that would occur in Britain and the concomitant development of a sophisticated illicit market. Even ignoring cannabis, which accounts for well over 80 per cent of all seizures and offences, and is Britain's most commonly used illicit drug, the illicit market has expanded dramatically over the past two decades. As Stimson and Oppenheimer (1982) pointed out nearly a decade ago, the rapid expansion of illicit heroin from South-east and South-west Asia made it clear that prescribing at the clinics would not undercut a black market, especially as the majority of clinics at this time were prescribing oral methadone only, which had a limited black market value. In tandem and despite legislation and controls, the 'grey market' has been augmented by a steady stream of pharmaceutical products. The pharmaceutical industry's quest for the Holy Grail of the non-addictive pain-killer or sedative has placed the relative newcomers, Temgesic and temazepam, alongside Diconal and Valium as part of the drug users' repertoire. Drug users are as adept today as they were in the late 1960s and early 1970s at securing supplies of licit drugs; and some doctors are still injudicious (if not naive) in their tendency to over-prescribe.

The vast profits to be made from the illicit drugs market, a trade estimated to be second only to armaments on the world economy, has led to a steadily increasing involvement of entrepreneurial, criminal syndicates, and even to a situation whereby certain societies are dependent upon this trade for economic stability. But, as the work of the Pompidou Group (1987) has shown in its comparison of seven European cities, any given socio-political and judicial context has an important impact upon the emerging patterns and trends of drug use. The establishment of the clinic system in the late 1960s is clearly an influential factor in the overall picture and subsequent evolution of British drug trends. But as with any specific change in clinical policy or practice, it represents but a small part of a difficult jigsaw, whose other pieces include broader structural factors such as: growing social deprivation and youth unemployment, wasting inner-cities and rising crime, highly attractive profit margins in an expanding world-wide illicit market, and desultory alternatives for many producer economies. This overall picture is framed in the context of the political and legislative setting within which drug trends emerge. Add to this the significance of regional variations, the impact of subcultural trends and fashions, and individual drug careers and proclivities, then the complexity of the issue of drug trends becomes clearly apparent. The current concern about the link between HIV infection and injecting drug use, and the concomitant renewal of the debate around prescribing policy, are two additional issues to impact upon the unfolding drug trends for the 1990s and beyond.

Much of the information on British drug trends of the last two decades or so derives from official sources and studies that have drawn samples from treatment settings. There have, of course, been notable exceptions, mainly resulting from the work of social scientists. Such valuable data have highlighted: the heterogeneity of drug using subcultures (Plant 1975; Pearson 1987; Parker *et al.* 1988); the complexity of the drug using career (Blackwell 1983); the significance of local drug markets (Burr 1987) and the need for multi-indicators of patterns of use, which include both quantitative and qualitative measures (Drug Indicators Project 1985). The introduction of a new monitoring system, that will collect data from both statutory and non-statutory services, should expand the available dataset and shift the balance away from the present emphasis on statutory agency clients and the opioids (Donmall 1990). This system will provide a highly useful backdrop, giving both a broader national picture, whilst also allowing regional comparisons. However, to work towards a comprehensive picture of the epidemiology of drug patterns, it is crucial that we dig beneath the surface and permeate the population of problem drug users who remain hidden from official sources. To achieve this we need to refine and develop appropriate research tools, such as ethnography and the use of 'indigenous' field-workers who are well known and respected in any local drug scene. Only then, by use of complementary multi-indicators, will we be able to chart with confidence new and emerging of trends in illicit substance use.

# References

de Alarcon, R. (1969). Methaqualone. *British Medical Journal*, **1**, 122.

Ashton, H. and Golding, J. (1989). Tranquillizers: prevalence, predictors and possible consequences. Data from a large United Kingdom survey. *British Journal of Addiction*, **84**, 451–6.

Bennett, J. (1988). The British experience with heroin regulation. *Law and Contemporary Problems*, **51**, 299–314.

Blackwell, J. (1983). Drifting, controlling and overcoming: opiate users who avoid becoming chronically dependent. *Journal of Drug Issues*, **13**, 219–35.

Burr, A. (1987). Chasing the dragon: heroin misuse, delinquency and crime in the context of South London culture. *British Journal of Criminology*, **27**, 333–54.

Chapple, P. A. L. (1969). Dangers of mandrax for patients on oral methadone. *Medical News*, February, **21**, 23–5.

Connell, P. H. (1964). Amphetamine misuse. *British Journal of Addiction*, **60**, 9–27.

Ditton, J. and Speirits, K. (1981). *The rapid increase of heroin addiction in Glasgow during 1981*. University Press, Glasgow.

Donmall, M. (1990). Towards a national drug database. *Druglink*, March/April, pp. 10–12.

Drugs Branch Inspectorate (1984). *Annual Report*. Home Office, London.

Drugs Branch Inspectorate (1985). *Annual Report*. Home Office, London.

Drugs Branch Inspectorate (1986). *Annual Report*. Home Office, London.

Drugs Branch Inspectorate (1987). *Annual Report*. Home Office, London.

Drug Indicators Project (1985). *Drug problems: assessing local needs*. Drug Indicators Project, London.

Dunnell, K. and Cartwright, A. (1972). *Medicine takers, prescribers and hoarders*. Routledge and Kegan Paul, London.

Edwards, G. (1981). The background. In *Drug problems in Britain: a review of ten years* (ed. G. Edwards and C. Busch), pp. 5–25. Academic Press, London.

Ghodse, H. (1971). Drug dependent individuals dealth with by London casualty departments. *British Journal of Psychiatry*, **131**, 273–80.

Gilman, M. (1988). DIY Diconal. *Mersey Drugs Journal*, **1** (5), 6–7.

Gilman, M., Pearson, G., and Traynor, P. (1990). The limits of intervention. *Druglink*, **5** (3), 12–13.

Glatt, M. M. (1962). Abuse of methylamphetamine, *Lancet*, ii, 215–6.

Glatt, M. M. (1972). Drug use in Great Britain. *Drug Forum*, **1**, 291–306.

Glatt, M. (1977). *Drug dependence. Current problems and issues*. MTP Press, Lancaster.

Hammersley, R. (1990). Buprenorphine and temazepam abuse. *British Journal of Addiction*, **85**, 301–3.

Hartnoll, R., Lewis, R., Mitcheson, M., and Bryer, S. (1985). Estimating the prevalence of opioid dependence. *Lancet*, i, 203–5.

Hartnoll, R., Daviaud, E., and Power, R. (1987). Patterns of drug taking in Britain. In *Drug use and misuse: a reader* (ed. T. Helter, M. Gott, and C. Jeffrey), pp. 13–19. Wiley, London.

Hawks, D., Mitcheson, M., Ogborne, A., and Edwards, G. (1969). Abuse of methylamphetamine. *British Medical Journal*, **2**, 715–21.

Home Office (1984). *Statistics of the misuse of drugs: addicts notified to the Home Office, United Kingdom, 1983*. HMSO, London.

Home Office (1987). *Statistics of the misuse of drugs: addicts notified to the Home Office, United Kingdom, 1986*. HMSO, London.

Home Office (1989). *Statistics of the misuse of drugs: addicts notified to the Home Office, United Kingdom, 1988*. HMSO, London.

Home Office (1990*a*). *Statistics of the misuse of drugs: addicts notified to the Home Office, United Kingdom, 1989*. HMSO, London.

Home Office (1990*b*). *Statistics of the misuse of drugs: seizures and offenders dealt with, United Kingdom, 1989*. HMSO, London.

Leech, K. (1973). *Keep the faith baby: a close-up of London's drop-outs*. SPCK, London.

Lewis, R. (1984). The illicit traffic in heroin: cultivation and production. *Druglink*, Spring, 7–14.

Lewis, R. (1989). European markets in cocaine. *Contemporary Crisis*, **13**, 35–52.

Lewis, R., Hartnoll, R., Bryer, S., Daviaud, E., and Mitcheson, M. (1985). Scoring smack: the illicit heroin market in London 1980–1983. *British Journal of Addiction*, **80**, 281–90.

Ministry of Health (1965). *Drug addiction: the second report of the Inter-departmental Committee.* HMSO, London.

Mitcheson, M. C., Davidson, J., Hawks, D., Hitchins, L., and Malone, S. (1970). Sedative abuse by heroin addicts. *Lancet*, **i**, 606–7.

Morrison, V. (1989). Psychoactive substance use and related behaviours of 135 regular illicit drug users in Scotland, *Drug and Alcohol Dependence*, **23**, 95–101.

Parker, H., Bakx, K., and Newcombe, R. (1988). *Living with heroin.* Open University Press, Milton Keynes.

Pearson, G. (1987). *The new heroin users.* Blackwell Scientific Publications, London.

Perera, K., Tulley, M., and Jenner, F. (1987). The use of benzodiazepines among drug addicts. *British Journal of Addiction*, **82**, 511–15.

Plant, M. (1975). Drug takers in an English town: factors associated with the use of injected drugs. *British Journal of Criminology*, **15**, 181–6.

Pompidou Group (1987). *Multi-city study of drug misuse in Amsterdam, Dublin, Hamburg, London, Paris, Rome and Stockholm.* Council of Europe, Strasbourg.

Ruben, S., McLean, P., and Melville, J. (1989) Cyclizine abuse among a group of opiate dependents receiving methadone. *British Journal of Addiction*, **84**, 929–34.

Spear, H. B. (1975). The British experience. *John Marshall Journal of Practice and Procedure*, **9**, 66–98.

Spear, H. B. (1982). British experience in the management of opiate dependence. In *The dependence phenomenon* (ed. M. Glatt and J. Marks), pp. 51–79. MTP, Lancaster.

Stimson, G. V. (1981). Epidemiological research on drug use in general populations. In *Drug problems in Britain: a review of ten years* (eds G. Edwards and C. Busch), pp. 51–75. Academic Press, London.

Stimson, G. V. and Oppenheimer, E. (1982). *Heroin addiction: treatment and control in Britain.* Tavistock, London.

Swadi, H., Wells, B., and Power, R. (1990). Misuse of dihydrocodeine tartrate (DF118) among opiate addicts, *British Medical Journal*, **300**, 1313.

Tyler, A. (1986). *Street drugs.* New English Library, London.

Williams, P. (1983). Patterns of psychotropic drug use. *Social Science Medicine*, **17**, 845–51.

# 3. Flexible hierarchies and dynamic disorder—the trading and distribution of illicit heroin in Britain and Europe, 1970–90

*Roger Lewis*

## Introduction

Some profound changes have occurred in heroin consumption in Britain and Europe over the past 20 years. Most traces of the 'alternative' ideology of the early 1970s have disappeared. The icon/role model of the misunderstood 'right-on' street junkie/anti-hero, surviving on his own terms against an oppressive society, has lost its attraction. By the mid-1980s heroin use had become an almost banal affair, with dwindling transgressive status. Growing awareness of the risks of human immuno-deficiency virus (HIV) infection has also affected attitudes. Yet, despite high rates of social marginalization, familial rejection, violence, arrest, prison, overdose, relapse, and seropositivity, a proportion of the addict population hang on tenaciously to their lives, their drugs, and their battered identities. Others lead relatively ordinary lives of work or study in which their drug use is secret, or known only to their families and close friends. The everyday nature of such consumption contributes to its 'invisibility'.

Generally speaking, the illicit market in heroin has remained resilient, although polydrug use tends to be the norm for most consumers. Where heroin has become hard to obtain, it has been replaced by pharmaceutical preparations, such as dihydrocodeine, buprenorphine, and benzodiazepine in cities such as Nottingham and Edinburgh. Changes in the supply and marketing of heroin and other illicit drugs cannot be understood without taking account of productive origin, trading routes, local and regional geography, and drug-related entrepreneurial crime. Similarly, demand for drugs cannot be understood if the social formation, economic situation, and cultural predispositions of the consumer population are ignored. The availability of drugs and a social network within which drug users socialize are as critical to the development of a market as the simple presence of individuals predisposed to drug use. Evidence from the United Kingdom suggests that when social and supply networks are absent such individuals are unlikely to become involved in illicit drug use, at least within their own community (de Alarcon 1973; Mott and Rathod 1976; Fraser and George 1988).

The study of illicit drug markets is still in its infancy. Most of the early work originated in the United States (Preble and Casey 1969; Redlinger 1974; Johnson *et al*. 1985). Since then a pool of epidemiological and ethnographic knowledge has evolved in several European countries. A number of studies have attempted to examine how distribution takes place, the manner in which transactions are negotiated, and the way illicit heroin markets function (Lewis *et al*. 1985; Ingold 1984; Dorn and South 1987; Fraser and George 1988; Power 1990; Arlacchi and Lewis 1990*a,b*).

## A growing market and its components

There has been an illicit market in heroin in Britain since the mid-1960s when six pharmaceutical heroin pills (64 mg) could be purchased for £1. Although so-called 'Chinese' heroin was evident in London prior to 1968 when the treatment system was restructured, a firmly rooted market in illicitly imported heroin did not develop until the early 1970s. South-east Asian 'No. 3' smoking heroin (30—45 per cent purity) and 'No. 4' or 'Thai' heroin (50—70 per cent purity) were largely supplanted in the late 1970s when illicit heroin manufactured in South-west Asia came on stream. This ranged from crudely refined, chocolate-coloured heroin from Iran, first seen in London in 1974, to beige or buff-coloured Turkish, Pakistani, and Afghan heroin. The years 1978—80 were a watershed for heroin use in Britain, and Western Europe generally. Increased availability and falling prices filled existing demand, encouraged experimentation, and generated new demand. There was a decline in subcultural taboos against heroin and a concurrent spread in consumption to provincial towns and cities (Lewis *et al*. 1985).

Retail heroin was dealt initially in the centres of major cities. In due course dealing extended beyond the centres and beyond the cities themselves. This 'shift to the periphery' in which activity radiated outwards to the suburbs (particularly those districts displaying high indices of social deprivation), was evident in Paris by 1978 (C. Olivenstein, personal communication 1978) and in Rome by 1980 (Arlacchi and Lewis 1987). Whereas some pockets of squatted and short-life housing in London were displaying high rates of consumption by the mid-1970s, the extent of heroin use on inner-city and suburban estates was not generally acknowledged until 1982. Subsequent studies in the north of England

and Scotland revealed widespread heroin use in local communities in Liverpool, Manchester, the Wirral, Glasgow, and Edinburgh. These studies revealed that heroin consumption was not uniformly dispersed through given cities or regions, but tended to be concentrated in particular districts (Parker *et al.* 1986; Haw 1985; Pearson *et al.* 1987; Haw and Liddell 1989). Small sub-markets developed in these districts which in turn attracted novitiates, who had never participated in a central drug scene.

In the initial stages of the European market in the early 1970s, couriers would bring in multiple kilos of heroin by air from the Far East. The global nature and magnitude of the traffic by the 1980s was such that large numbers of trucks and freighters began to be intercepted carrying cargoes of heroin from the Near East, the Indian subcontinent, and South-east Asia. Afghan, Pakistani, Turkish, Iranian, and Middle Eastern heroin has tended to predominate in Western Europe over the last 10 years. Production capacity in South-west Asia remains high. Seven hundred and forty-one kilos of heroin were seized in Turkey alone in the first 6 months of 1989 [International Narcotics Control Board (INCB) 1989]. In late 1990 over one-fifth of a ton was found in a single overland shipment entering Britain through the Channel ports.

With the establishment of a fully fledged market in Britain the number of heroin seizures by the police rose precipitately in the early 1980s, peaking at 3003 in 1985. They subsequently declined to 1877 seizures in 1987 and rose again in 1988. The quantity of heroin seized by HM Customs between 1980 and 1988 indicates a similar trend. Less than 50 kilos of heroin were seized by Customs in 1980, 334 kilos in 1985, 179 kilos in 1986, and 211 kilos in 1988 [Institute for the Study of Drug Dependence (ISDD) 1990]. A European decline in overdose deaths, along with a fall in seizures, raised hopes that consumption might have peaked in 1986. However, a marked rise in heroin-related mortalities in the late 1980s (INCB 1989), probably related to increased heroin purity at street level and the spread of HIV, suggests that demand remains strong and supplies are available.

The retail purity of illicit heroin in Britain and Holland has always been relatively high compared with the United States, where an organized crime presence fostered dilution practices and lowered customer expectations. The size and poverty of the United States' addict population may have resulted in larger numbers attempting 'to live off' the market by heavily diluting the product before trading it forward. In Britain long-established commercial, colonial, and cultural ties with a number of heroin-producing nations enabled illicit entrepreneurs to take advantage of favourable trading terms. Some of the benefits (lower price and higher purity) were passed on to the consumer. In the early 1980s, the purity of retail heroin in London was sometimes as high as 45–55 per cent (Lewis *et al.* 1985). Average retail purity in Britain was 39 per cent in 1985, 30 per cent in 1987, and 38 per cent in 1989 (ISDD 1990). Such purities have been consistently higher than in some other European countries, which are experiencing rising overdose rates as consumers accustomed to low quality heroin begin to encounter unpredictably higher purities following recent shifts in global trading patterns.

Retail heroin prices in Britain over the past 10 years have also been relatively constant. Just as there are variations in prevalence and modes of consumption from region to region, there are also variations in pricing. Prices are likely to be determined by proximity to ports of entry, importer/distributor connections to countries of transit or origin, the availability of bulk supplies, and the efficiency of the delivery system. The retail price of heroin in London in the early 1980s oscillated between £70 and £80 per gram (Lewis *et al.* 1985). After rising from £65 to £90 per gram between 1985 and 1986, prices steadied at £70–£80 in early 1989. Even given a relative decline in purity since the early 1980s and a tendency over time for dealers to give shorter measures in 'bags' and 'wraps' (unweighed units), these figures suggest that, in London at least, the average retail price of heroin fell in real terms between 1980 and 1990 when set against inflation. Data for Glasgow suggest that prices were relatively stable over the past 5 years at £90–£100 per gram (ISDD 1990). In Edinburgh, on the other hand, heroin cost as much as £140 per gram in 1990, despite the city's proximity to Glasgow. It may be possible to identify similar disparities between Liverpool and Manchester.

## Distribution and delivery

Preble and Casey's six-level hierarchical outline of the New York delivery system (1969) remains relevant to European markets as a point of departure rather than as a blueprint. The following distribution categories have been elaborated from empirical observation by the author, and others, of markets in Britain and Italy and, to a lesser extent, France, Holland, and Germany. They are broad approximations rather than rigid definitions:

(1) importers and importer combinations;

(2) distributors;

(3) large-scale wholesalers;

(4) small-scale wholesalers and apartment dealers;

(5) retail sales—street and appointment dealers, network suppliers, and user—sellers;

(6) end-users and street consumers.

Heroin distribution systems are composed of complex, articulated, multi-faceted series of layered networks, which individuals enter and exit according to means and circumstance. Despite restricted access to distribution levels, there are occasions when importers deliver directly to wholesalers, distributors supply house dealers, and ordinary consumers buy from wholesalers. The British national market is notably more flexible than some continental markets, which have higher barriers to entry constructed by organized crime groups that assert territorial control, exclude competitors, and demand a share of all profits.

In countries like Italy there are fewer opportunities for individual initiative in the upper-echelons of the system, where criminal coalitions tend to dominate distribution. However, there is no universally applicable 'mafia' model of control in Italy or any other country. For instance, there is easy access to a range of quality and price arrangements in the strategically placed city of Verona where mafia-type groups have been all but marginalized by local traders (Arlacchi and Lewis 1990*a*).

## Importers and bulk distributors

The development of distribution systems within Britain and Western Europe, as opposed to older-established trafficking enterprises directed at the United States, can be traced to the late 1960s and early 1970s. Heroin consumers, who were a minority within a wider pool of recreational drug users, lacked access to routine, wholesale connections. The common concern that bonded them at first found expression in long-distance 'ant-trafficking' (smuggling by individual consumers or groups in 'co-operative ventures') rather than in sustained large-scale business activity. With the perceived 'commercialization' of the drug subculture, such ventures tended to become less co-operative and more entrepreneurial. Without considerable investment, a sophisticated infrastructure, and professional organization, international initiatives were increasingly risky, expensive, and dangerous.

The arrival of bulk supplies of beige and brown South-west Asian heroin in Britain and Western Europe, between 1978 and 1980, coincided with the consolidation of a complex, high-turnover market. The size of consignments and the regularity of delivery clearly indicated that supply was being organized on a more systematic basis. Availability no longer depended upon individual journeys by ant-traffickers and user−dealers to Holland, India, or Thailand. The acquisition and distribution of large quantities of heroin constituted a major business investment. Trading ceased to be simply a means:

(1) to acquire heroin cheaply for personal consumption; or

(2) to make a relatively modest living and subsidize future personal consumption through sales to other users.

In simple models of heroin distribution, the product commences its in-country trajectory as a high-quality kilo imported 'fresh off the boat'. It then passes by stages through the delivery system, where it is diluted to varying degrees, until it reaches the consumer as a retail unit. Some cities, like London, Amsterdam, Barcelona, Paris, and Milan, function as points of importation, warehousing, and brokerage. In zones where drugs transit in bulk quantities, there is frequent leakage on to local markets. In such situations wholesale and retail prices may tend to be lower and purity proportionally higher because onward transportation and delivery costs are eliminated, and some of the intermediary stages within the distribution network are bypassed.

Bulk distributors and wholesalers are usually insulated from the street by three or four intermediary layers of distribution. In consequence, consumers and street-dealers know little about transactions at the apex of the system. Research information about the behaviour of distributors and wholesalers is normally the hardest to gather. Those involved in importation and bulk distribution are often full-time professional criminals, directly or indirectly connected in some parts of Europe to organized crime groups, which tends to make them both hostile and dangerous.

## Bulk wholesalers

Importers, distributors, bulk wholesalers, and house dealers (small-scale wholesalers), while performing different functions, all work in the wholesale sector. The bulk wholesaler bridges the middle ground between large-scale importer/distributors and low-level wholesalers and dealers. However, there are no hard and fast rules, particularly in cities where there is a high degree of mobility between layers of the market. Some independent distributors negotiate with apartment dealers. They may have narrower profit margins and no obligations to a wider organization, circumventing bulk wholesalers in order to sell directly to apartment dealers (small-scale wholesalers) or to dealers delivering directly to private elite circles.

Bulk wholesalers may purchase:

(1) directly from importers (or importer/producers who import semi-finished goods (morphine or heroin base) and convert it to finished goods (heroin) as has occurred in Italy, France, and Holland);

(2) from distributors who have bought undiluted kilo units from importers or are acting on their behalf; or

(3) travel to places of brokerage where they have their own contacts. One might normally expect wholesalers to purchase half-kilo to 100 g units and to sell diluted 100–30 g units to apartment dealers (small-scale wholesalers).

The kind of individuals involved at wholesale level can vary enormously from:

(1) drug entrepreneurs, who in the past may have operated at retail level;
(2) legitimate traders, who have developed sidelines as distributors or wholesalers (see also Dorn and South 1987);
(3) predatory professional criminals, who have found a lucrative source of income in drugs.

On the whole, distributors and bulk wholesalers tend to be in their thirties and forties and have criminal records, while retail dealers and sellers, like most heroin consumers, are commonly in their twenties. Day-labourers working at street level as runners and look-outs can be in their teens.

Bulk suppliers are at their most vulnerable when taking or making deliveries. They are particularly exposed when:

(1) collecting from large caches and fixed deposits;
(2) transporting 30, 50, and 100 g units that cannot be justified as possession for personal use; and
(3) making deliveries to customers.

Wholesalers may employ other individuals to perform such tasks. Evidence of wholesale delivery often emerges when there are seizures of gram and multi-gram quantities from house dealers and, for instance, empty 100 g bags containing traces of heroin are found on the same premises.

## Small-scale wholesalers and apartment dealers

House (or apartment) dealers perform wholesale and retail functions. They buy 30–to 100 g units from bulk wholesalers that service a number of such enterprises and, on occasions, from upper level distributors. They sell in 1–30 g lots to street, network, and user–dealers, and directly to consumers. They are usually independent, although some may be franchised by criminal groups higher up the supply chain. Unlike network and street sellers, who can change location at will, the apartment dealer operates from a fixed base. This is normally an apartment or house, but may be a place of work or a bar. Places of legitimate business provide good cover in the sense that individuals can come and go without arousing suspicion and illicit income can be recycled through legitimate channels. The drawback of a fixed site is that once the location is identified by the police or hostile competitors, it becomes a relatively easy target. This also applies to fixed caches and stockpiles in isolated or rural hiding-places.

Ingold's description (1985) of Parisian apartment dealing in many ways resembles house dealing in cities like London. Ingold reports that assistants are frequently employed to answer the telephone, to find and select customers, and to collect and deliver money and/or drugs. They may be paid in money, drugs, or both. The telephone, despite its vulnerability to interception, is an important instrument for receiving and relaying information. If the dealer is supplying both retailers and end-users, there is a possibility that the premises will become a place of consumption as well as distribution.

Dealers handling wholesale quantities of heroin also have to consider their own consumption. House dealers are normally users. If they fail to regulate personal use, they are liable to consume profits and stocks in the form of drugs. In consequence, they run the risk of exhausting their capital and resources, running into debt, going out of business, and attracting the interest of enforcement by neglecting security. Even if they avoid prison, they may be left with a 5 g/day heroin habit that they can no longer afford. Hence, there is a constant tension between acquiring immediate satisfaction by consuming heroin as desired, and longer-term considerations of controlling levels of dependence in order to stay in business and guarantee future personal supplies.

Some transactions still may retain characteristics of personalized exchange and barter that were common to illicit drug markets prior to 1976. In such situations it is important that participants share a common history, and are known and accepted by their peers. They are normally members of restricted circles of heroin users of the kind found among small, discreet groups of recreational cannabis and cocaine users. They combine together to buy high-quality grams of heroin from wholesalers for their own consumption, and sometimes pool money as 'consumer co-operatives' to buy heroin in cities of importation or travel to producer nations in the manner of ant-traffickers.

## Retail sales—street and appointment dealers, network suppliers, and user–sellers

Most retail suppliers of heroin are consumers and, hence, user–dealers or user–sellers. The term 'dealer' is used to indicate an individual who supplies drugs for a cash return. The prospect of ready supplies of low-cost heroin is a prime motivation for entering the business. The lowest level of non-sedentary retail suppliers may be composed of:

(1) appointment dealers;
(2) street dealers;
(3) network suppliers;
(4) user–sellers; and
(5) social suppliers.

Such categories serve to:

(1) distinguish such suppliers from wholesale apartment dealers, who may also engage in retail supply;
(2) emphasize that retail supply takes place in contexts other than the street or in purchases from apartment dealers;
(3) encompass the fact that some retail suppliers cater for particular consumer networks by transferring the product to consumers on the supplier's premises, by visiting network members in their homes, or by appointment in a public or semi-public place.

Some consumers work as day-labourers in the market place. They switch service roles from day to day, fulfilling a variety of functions from testing, diluting, and transporting heroin to selling, making introductions, and keeping look-out. Such tasks are determined by what is most lucrative, least demeaning, least risky, and least offensive to themselves (Johnson *et al*. 1985; Arlacchi and Lewis 1990*b*). The often chaotic way that drugs are consigned publicly to end-users means that arrests (effected as drugs change hands or soon afterwards), are a regular occurrence.

As relationships of mutual reciprocity, that were part of the earlier drug scene, broke down, transactions became progressively more detached and profit-oriented. As a result, drugs are less likely to be consumed and shared by buyer and seller in a group context. Many dealers do not wish to increase their vulnerability by employing their residence as a place of business or by dealing from a fixed location nor do they want their customers, or their potential competitors, to know where they live. The appointment system partly developed for these reasons. It normally involves one supplier and six to 10 regular customers who keep in touch on a daily basis. Some cities have reported multi-personnel enterprises involving 200–300 transactions per day. Locations are alternated or changed, according to a pre-arranged plan, although purchasers are not informed of the site until close to the time of transaction. Telephones play an important role as do pagers, which are no longer esoteric New York-style accessories. They serve an important organizational function for some south London dealer networks.

The appointment system combines some of the characteristics of both apartment dealing and of street supply. Apartment dealing of wholesale and large retail units is common to most drug markets, as are sales in public locations where the product is dealt in minimal retail units by small-time dealers and user—sellers to consumers lacking better-placed connections. Appointment dealing constitutes a more discreet form of trading than random street sales. The rotation of locations avoids the risks entailed in a fixed site. Its drawback is that appointments normally take place in public or semi-public places. Hence, appointment dealing is:

(1) planned in advance;

(2) exposed, even though locations may be changed from day to day;

(3) not suitable for prolonged negotiation or large-scale transactions that could involve the testing or weighing of the drug and, consequently, entails rapid retail trading;

(4) subject to disruption by the inadvertent arrival of third parties, or through confusion about arrangements in the mind of the buyer or seller.

In spite of precautions, an employee or a telephone placed under surveillance can make the pre-arranged appointment as vulnerable as fixed site dealing.

Some buyers try to establish relations with a regular dealer, who can be visited at home. Prior to this, an element of trust has to exist between buyer and seller. New clients normally have to be vouched for by regular customers. Apartment purchases are usually safer, cheaper, and less subject to fraud than street purchases. Both dealer and customer have an investment in the continuity of the relationship. Apartment dealing is also less precarious than street dealing, although once an apartment has been identified by the police or the public, the dealer becomes more vulnerable than the street dealer, who, if he is lucky, can disappear without trace.

On the street itself, points of refurbishment and sale tend to be in continual flux. News travels fast on illicit consumer networks. In large markets some open-air, multi-product, retail enterprises are organized in a very sophisticated fashion. Appointment dealers frequently change distribution points around the city on a day-to-day basis to avoid police surveillance. Runners, look-outs, and messengers, paid in money, drugs, or both, are systematically co-ordinated. Deliveries may be made by car, motor cycle, or public transport. In large retail enterprises, supplies are purchased directly from bulk wholesalers, circumventing apartment dealers who probably could not fulfil demand on a daily basis.

'Historic' public dealing venues such as Piccadilly in central London, the Dam in Amsterdam, the Zoo in Berlin, and the Parco Lambro in Milan tend to be places where:

(1) casual users or young initiates, unfamiliar with the market, come to buy;

(2) old-style street survivors congregate, partly to stay in touch and, partly, in the hope of obtaining drugs or cash by interposing themselves between retail dealers and potential customers; and

(3) regular consumers, whose usual points of supply have been lost or terminated, seek a temporary substitute. Quality is usually lower, prices higher, weights shorter, and theft and fraud more frequent in such a context. 'Birds of passage', surviving on the social fringes of a host country, are able to work as suppliers in such high profile locations because of their very transience. They are vulnerable as single individuals but, because of their impermanence, the dealing in which they engage is less subject to systematic police and mono-polistic criminal pressure.

The vulnerability of heroin market participants and the ability of violent criminals to intimidate them, is enhanced by:

(1) criminal domination of some illicit markets;

(2) the physical dependence of addicts and their need to expose them-selves in search of both drugs and money;

(3) the limited sources of alternative supply;

(4) the reputation and capacity of criminal entrepreneurs for carrying out their threats; and

(5) the illegality of much addict behaviour and consequent lack of recourse to the police. Some consumers argue that levels of violence may be directly proportional to the availability of heroin. The more heroin that is available, the less theft, conflict, and violence occurs at street level. When there is a heroin shortage incidents of fraud and theft increase. Frustrated demand, in other words, appears to be a major cause of violence.

The violence that occurs usually:

(1) happens between users;

(2) is imposed on users by other predatory users or as part of a puni-tive mechanism within the distribution system; or

(3) is imposed by outsiders attached to criminal and, sometimes, law enforcement bodies.

The resilience and adaptability of the heroin delivery systems described above, in the face of sustained enforcement pressure, raises questions as to the usefulness of contemporary prohibitionist models of control. It is possible that a formally regulated and taxed market might lead to a reduction in the drug-related harm, revenue-raising crime and violence that are associated with illicit heroin economies. The fact that such a taboo subject is now a matter for lively debate suggests that in Europe, if not the United States, the regulation of drug markets is being seen as a practical policy issue rather than as just one more business opportunity for moral entrepreneurs.

## References

Arlacchi, P. and Lewis, R. (1987). *Analisi del mercato delle droghe e sua influenza ai fini della determinazione della categoria giuridica della modica quantità.* Ministero di Grazia e Giustizia, Rome.

Arlacchi, P. and Lewis, R. (1990*a*). Droga e criminalità a Bologna. *Micromega*, 4, 183–221.

Arlacchi, P. and Lewis, R. (1990*b*). *Imprenditorialità illecita e droga—il mercato dell' eroina a Verona.* Il Mulino, Bologna.

de Alarcon, R. (1973). Lessons from the recent British drug outbreak. In *Proceedings of the Anglo-American conference on drug abuse.* Royal Society of Medicine, London.

Dorn, N. and South, N. (1987). *Some issues in the development of drug markets and law enforcement.* Working paper, workshop on drugs, 22–23 October. Commission of the European communities, Luxembourg.

Fraser, A. and George, M. (1988). Changing trends in drug use, an initial follow-up of a local heroin-using community. *British Journal of Addiction*, 83, 655–63.

Haw, S. (1985). *Drug problems in Greater Glasgow.* Standing conference on drug abuse, Glasgow.

Haw, S. and Liddell, D. (1989). *Drug problems in Edinburgh district.* Standing conference on drug abuse, London.

Ingold, R. (1984). La dependance economique chez les heroinomanes. *Revue Internationale de Police Criminelle*, 391, 208–13, ottobre.

ISDD (1990). *Drug misuse in Britain. National audit of drug misuse statistics.* Institute for the Study of Drug Dependence, London.

INCB (1989). *Report of the International Narcotics Control Board.* United Nations, New York.

Johnson, B. D. *et al.* (1985). *Taking care of business—the economics of crime by heroin abusers.* Lexington, Lexington, MA.

Lewis, R., Hartnoll, R., Bryer, S., Daviaid, E., and Mitcheson, M. (1985). Scoring smack—The illicit heroin market in London, 1980–1983. *British Journal of Addiction*, 80, 281–90.

Mott, J. and Rathod, N. H. (1976). Heroin use and delinquency in a new town. *British Journal of Psychiatry*, **128**, 428–35.

Parker, H., Bakx, K., and Newcombe, R. (1986). *Drug misuse in Wirral, a study of 1800 problem drug users known to official agencies. The first report.* University of Liverpool, Liverpool.

Pearson, G., Gilman, Mark. and McIver, S. (1987). *Young people and heroin, examination of heroin use in the north of England.* Gower Health Education council, Aldershot.

Power, R. (1990). Patterns of drug use and some recent research developments in Britain. In *Epidemiologic trends in drug abuse* (ed. N. Kozel), Vol. II, pp. 83–104. Proceedings. National Institute on Drug Abuse, Rockville, MD.

Preble, E. and Casey, J. J. (1969). Taking care of business, the heroin user's life on the street. *International Journal of the Addictions*, **4**, 1–24.

Redlinger, L. J. (1974). Marketing and distributing heroin. *Journal of Psychedelic Drugs*, **7**, 331–53.

# 4. Drugs and adolescence

*Martin Plant*

'Adolescence' is typically defined as the developmental period between both childhood and adulthood. This phase of life varies in onset and termination between societies and individuals. Since the emergence during the 1950s and 1960s of a distinctive 'youth culture' there has become established a widespread interest and concern about the lifestyles and behaviours of 'adolescents', 'teenagers', or 'young people'. This concern, sometimes fully justified, is at least partly attributable to the fact that certain potentially dangerous activities appear to have a particular fascination for adolescents. In addition such people, due to their powerful drives and inexperience, are perceived as being especially vulnerable.

The use of psychoactive drugs, legal and illegal, by adolescents has become firmly established as a major area of concern. Adolescent drug use must, however, be considered in the general context of the overall levels of drug use and misuse in society. In Britain, as in many other countries, psychoactive drugs are very widely used. Over 90 per cent of adults consume alcohol at least occasionally, one-third of adults smoke tobacco and hundreds of thousands are believed to be dependent on minor tranquillizers (Plant 1987). Most of those who use or misuse psychoactive drugs are adults. Accordingly 'adolescent' drug use is only part of a wider picture.

This book is largely concerned with the use and misuse of illicit drugs such as cannabis, cocaine, and opiates. These are also a major focus of this chapter. Even so it is not possible to present a balanced picture of adolescent drug use without also including the use of alcohol and tobacco. Adolescents are far more likely to drink alcohol than they are to use any other drug. In addition there is a clear relationship between legal and illegal drug use. This is important and serves as a reminder that the legality of a substance is only one criterion by which it may be judged.

## The growth of 'the drug scene'

Chapters 2 and 3 have described the upsurge of illicit drug use in the UK during the 1960s and 1970s. During this period, as noted above, a distinctive youth culture became established in Britain. This culture, avidly fostered by the mass media and by commercial interests, placed great emphasis on sensation seeking. Extensive publicity was given to the sexual and drug taking exploits real or imagined (and frequently exaggerated) of young people. A considerable number of studies into youthful drug use in Britain have been undertaken. These provide a reasonably full picture, but not a systematic or comprehensive one, of the extent and changing pattern of drug use among young men and women. In Britain, unlike the USA there have been no regular national surveys of illegal drug use. Instead studies have been largely conducted in a piecemeal and uncoordinated way. This situation has been elaborated elsewhere (Plant 1990*a*).

Binnie and Murdock (1969) carried out a survey of self-reported drug use amongst higher education students in Leicester. This indicated that 9 per cent had used some form of illicit drug. Wiener (1970) conducted a survey of drug use amongst pupils from a sample of British secondary (high) schools and concluded that 6 per cent had used drugs. Another secondary school study by Hindmarch (1972) indicated that 10 per cent of those surveyed reported having used drugs.

A survey of 305 people aged 17–24 years in Cheltenham indicated that 20 per cent had used either cannabis, LSD, or amphetamines (Plant 1973). Considerable mass media attention during this period was directed towards drug use among university and college students. This attention was reinforced by several studies, which indicated relatively high levels of drug experience amongst young people in such institutions.

A study of medical undergraduates at Glasgow University revealed that 14 per cent reported having used either cannabis, LSD, or other illicit drugs (McKay *et al.* 1973). Another Glasgow-based study examined self-reported drug use amongst 16–24-year-olds in the following groups: secondary school pupils, college and university students, casualty patients, and those attending clinics for sexually transmitted diseases. Data were elicited from 2809 people of whom 31 per cent reported to have used illicit drugs (Fish *et al.* 1974).

Kosviner and Hawks (1977) concluded that over a one-third of those surveyed in two university colleges had used illicit drugs.

## Some more recent studies

The British Crime Survey was conducted in 1981. This indicated that 19 per cent of those aged 20–24 years in Scotland and 16 per cent of those in this age group in England and Wales had used cannabis (Chambers and Tombs 1984; Mott 1985). During 1982 the *Daily Mail* newspaper commissioned a sample survey of self-reported drug use amongst people aged between 15 and 21 years. The results of this study are elaborated by Table 4.1.

**Table 4.1** Regional variations in self-reported illicit drug use amongst the 15–21 years age group in Britain

| Drugs ever used | Area | | | | |
|---|---|---|---|---|---|
| | Scotland | North of England | Midlands, East Anglia, Wales | South of England excluding London | London |
| | $(n = 57^*)$ %| $(n = 447^*)$ %| $(n = 338^*)$ %| $(n = 330^*)$ %| $(n = 153^*)$ %|
| Cannabis | 21 | 15 | 16 | 28 | 28 |
| Amphetamines | 8 | 4 | 6 | 3 | 10 |
| Glues | 2 | 5 | 1 | 2 | 4 |
| Barbiturates | 16 | 2 | 4 | 2 | 3 |
| LSD | 8 | 3 | 4 | 2 | 3 |
| Heroin | 7 | ** | 1 | 1 | 1 |
| Cocaine | 9 | 1 | 1 | 1 | 1 |

\* Weighted total.  \*\* Less than 0.5%.  *Source:* NOP Market Research Ltd (1982).

As this table shows, some marked regional variations emerged from this survey. The highest levels of drug use were evident in London and in Scotland. It must be noted that only relatively small numbers of people were surveyed in either of these areas. Accordingly these results may have been misleading. Even so this study, taken together with earlier surveys, showed that cannabis was by far the most widely used illegal drug. In most areas of Britain no more than 1 per cent of young people reported having used heroin, though in Scotland a surprising 7 per cent reported having done so (NOP Market Research Ltd 1982).

Between 1979 and 1983 a follow-up study monitored the alcohol, tobacco, and illicit drug use of a study group of young adults in the Lothian Region in Scotland. These people were aged 15 and 16 years during 1979. During that year 15.2 per cent of males and 10.7 per cent of females reported having at some time used some form of illicit drug. During 1983, when 92 per cent of the original study group had been re-interviewed, 37 per cent of the males and 23.2 per cent of the females had used drugs (Plant *et al.* 1985).

Williams (1986), in an article significantly entitled 'The Thatcher Generation' described the results of a survey of 2417 secondary school and college students in England and Wales. This indicated that 17 per cent had used cannabis, 6 per cent had used glues and solvents, and 2 per cent used heroin. Brown and Lawton (1988) described the findings of a survey of 1063 schools and colleges for students aged 11–19 years and older. This study, in Portsmouth and Havant, revealed that 5 per cent of those surveyed reported having used illicit drugs. Drug experience, as in the Lothian survey, rose with age. One per cent of those aged 11, 12, or 13 years reported drug use. Five per cent of those aged 15 and 16 years reported having used drugs. Amongst those aged between 16 and 19 years the level of drug experience rose to 12 per cent.

A survey of 1600 school pupils aged 13 years in Dyfed, Berkshire, and the Highlands of Scotland indicated that 5 per cent had used illicit drugs (Bagnall 1988, 1990; G. M. Bagnall, personal communication 1990).

Several researchers have sought to estimate the prevalence (extent) or incidence (number of new cases) of drug use or drug problems in specific areas. As noted by Pattison *et al.* (1982) such estimation is very difficult to conduct in a rigorous or satisfactory manner. Hartnoll *et al.* (1985) produced estimates of 'regular opioid use' for the London boroughs of Camden and Islington over the period 1977–1983. They concluded that in the 16–24-year age range the rate was 12 per 1000. Parker *et al.* (1988) have reported rates of such regular opioid use amongst those aged 16–24 years of 18 per 1000.

A recent non-random survey in Scotland indicated that 21.5 per cent of a study group of people aged 16–30 had used Ecstasy (MDMA) (Anderson 1992). This drug has been widely used at 'raves' or other social events.

Drug users occurs amongst young adults from all socio-economic backgrounds. As indicated by the evidence cited above, illicit drug users in Britain are mainly young, between 11 and 35 years. Even so illicit drug use is also reported by older people and, sometimes, amongst younger people. The misuse of glues and solvents, for example, has been reported among young children (for example Watson 1979). Studies uniformly show that males are more likely than females to use illicit drugs, though this difference is not always great. As elaborated elsewhere in this book, some people suffer serious adverse consequences from drug use, but the great majority of adolescents who use drugs do not appear to be harmed thereby.

## Polydrug use

The American sociologist Erich Goode (1972) advanced the following view in relation to drug use in the USA (note: *author's addition):

... people who use illegal drugs, marijuana (*cannabis**) especially, are fundamentally the same people who use alcohol and cigarettes—they are a little further along the same continuum people who abstain from liquor and cigarettes are far less likely to use marijuana than people who smoke and/or drink.

This conclusion is consistently supported by evidence related to youthful drug use in Britain. Surveys have routinely indicated that illicit drug users are more likely than other young people both to smoke and to drink heavily (for example Bagnall 1990, MORI 1990; Morrison and Plant 1991; G. M. Bagnall, personal communication 1990).

Most British adolescents drink alcohol and approximately one-third smoke tobacco (March and Matheson 1983, Marsh *et al*. 1986; Plant *et al*. 1990; MORI 1990). The recent MORI survey (op. cit.) concluded that 8 per cent of English schoolchildren had tried smoking by the age of 9 years and that by the age of 13 years 38 per cent had done so. Recent surveys have also indicated that by the age of 14 years 95 per cent of teenagers have consumed alcohol and that by the ages of 15 and 16 years approximately one-third are drinking during most weeks (Marsh *et al*. 1986; Plant *et al*. 1990). Most British adolescents who use illicit drugs also drink and a disproportionate number also smoke tobacco. Individuals who are heavy users of illicit drugs are often heavy drinkers and may also have alcohol-related problems (Morrison and Plant 1990).

Plant *et al*. (1985) followed up the legal and illegal drug use behaviours of a group of young adults between 1979 and 1983. This study indicated that teenagers who were heavy drinkers or drug users at the ages of 15 and 16 years were not necessarily still heavy drinkers or drug users 4 years later. Even so heavy alcohol use at the age of 15 and 16 years did increase the chances that an individual would be a relatively heavy drug user 4 years later. A 10 year follow-up of the original 1979 study group indicated that early alcohol and tobacco use were not significant predictors of later illicit drug use. Even early alcohol use had only a modest association with drinking 10 years later (Bagnall 1991).

## Why do adolescents use drugs?

People use drugs for a considerable number of reasons. Two reviews have concluded that many theories have been suggested as explanations for drug taking, but that none offers an adequate account of such varied types of behaviour (Fazey 1977; Plant 1981).

Many studies, conducted in Britain and elsewhere, have concluded that legal and illegal drug use is fostered by factors such as the price and availability of drugs and social pressure to use them. Davies and Stacey (1972), in their classic study of *Teenagers and Alcohol*, noted that young adults are subject to strong peer pressures to drink. The latter is widely seen as adult, sociable, and highly desirable. Young (1971) has provided a very cogent account of the 'social meaning' of drug use in Britain two decades ago. This description detailed the hedonistic, experience-seeking ethos of 'the drug scene'. Young's important work emphasized the role of drug use as part of a more general lifestyle and allied to the rejection of traditional values. Other authors have noted the positive appeal of drug use to young adults, together with the social support, status and excitement that many people derive from involvement with drug use. It is probable that initial drug use is commonly fostered by curiosity, and peer pressure. Continued drug use is often motivated by enjoyment of drug effects and by social support to use drugs. Long-term drug use and drug problems may be attributable, at least in part, to stressful life events, habit, personality, or to a host of personal experiences as well as to social, cultural, and economic factors. Several commentators have drawn attention to evidence linking the use of heroin and other drugs with unemployment and social deprivation. (Peck and Plant 1986; Pearson 1987; Dorn and South 1987; Parker *et al.* 1988). The massive rise in UK unemployment during the 1970s and 1980s was prevailed by an increase in heroin use. It is emphasized that this fact does not simply 'prove' that unemployment causes heroin use or vice versa. Even so this connection underlines the fact that drug use in linked with a number of other factors. The appeal of heroin to young unemployed people living in the next derelict urban areas is understandable. Readers are, however, reminded that young people who use drugs come from all types of backgrounds, including the most privileged and affluent.

## Drug use and 'risk taking'

Consistent with the fact that people often use both legal and illegal drugs, it has been suggested that those who engage in one form of 'problem behaviour' are also likely to engage in others. This view has been expanded and provided with empirical support by the classic study of young people in the USA by Jessor and Jessor (1977). British evidence, though limited, is at least partly consistent with the Jessors' theories of 'problem behaviour'. Heavy or dependent users of illicit drugs are more likely to drink and smoke heavily and to be delinquent. Even so there is clear evidence that the use of illegal drugs in itself is associated with other criminal behaviours (Mott 1981).

The advent of the acquired immune deficiency syndrome (AIDS) epidemic has heightened interest in the possible role of psychoactive drugs in 'unsafe' sexual behaviour. This interest is fostered by two main factors. First, in Edinburgh, Dundee, and increasingly in other areas, human immunodeficiency virus (HIV) infection has been spread through sharing infected injecting equipment (Robertson 1987). Secondly, the use of alcohol, cannabis, and cocaine have been linked with risky sexual behaviours due to the disinhibiting effects of these substances (For example Stall 1987; Plant 1990*b,c*). 'Disinhibition' has been defined thus: 'activation of behaviours normally suppressed by various controlling influences' (Woods and Mansfield 1983).

A Scottish study by Robertson and Plant (1988) examined contraceptive use and drinking amongst a study group of young adults who, atypically, married while they were teenagers. These were asked whether or not they had consumed alcohol immediately prior to their first sexual intercourse, and whether or not they had used any type of contraceptive. Those who had consumed alcohol were significantly less likely than those who had not done so to have used contraceptives of any type. This information is consistent with a growing body of evidence. This indicates that the combination of alcohol or illicit drugs and sexual activity is associated with increased rates of 'high risk sexual behaviour' (Leigh 1990; Bagnall *et al*. 1990). Even so it has *not* been shown that an individual's sexual behaviour becomes less safe after using alcohol or illicit drugs. Both sexual behaviour and, as noted below, drug use, are difficult to influence. The connection between drinking and drug use and risk taking poses a difficult problem for health educationalists and others concerned with the prevention of drug problems and AIDS risks (Plant and Plant 1992).

## Preventing adolescent drug problems

The inappropriate, heavy, or simply illegal use of psychoactive drugs undeniably causes a tragic toll of accidents, illnesses, deaths, and other adverse consequences. A considerable amount has been written on the topic of the prevention of drug problems. Before preventive strategies can usefully be considered it is important to acknowledge that, as noted earlier drug use is influenced by a bewildering array of factors. These include the price and availability of drugs, peer pressure to use them, national, regional, and local cultural influences, gender and religious (or other ideological) norms, age, affluence, socio-economic status, life events, personality, education, and family background. Some of these influences are very powerful and are difficult, if not impossible, to counter.

The upsurge of youthful drug use has understandably caused both public concern and has provided the impetus for many initiatives designed to curb or to prevent drug use or specific drug-related problems. Such initiatives have included mass media 'anti-drug' campaigns exemplified by the 'Heroin Screws You Up' exercise conducted in England and Wales and the 'Just Say No!' approach popularized in the USA. Such campaigns are doubtless often well-intentioned. Sadly there is very little to commend them. Dorn and South (1990, p. 162) have recently drawn the following sombre conclusion:

Education does not work as a means of prevention of illegal drug use. Nor do mass media communications such as television commercial street posters or newspaper announcements.

'Just Say No!' has a simple and populist appeal. High profile mass media campaigning is also politically attractive as a demonstration that something is being done. British mass media drug campaigns have seldom been properly evaluated. Marsh (1986) concluded that the notorious 'Heroin Screws You Up' campaign mounted in England and Wales was assessed in a grossly inadequate way and that the effects, if any, of this expensive initiative are unknown. Mass media campaigns are often rather exercises in propaganda or exhortation. There appears to be no persuasive British evidence that education has succeeded in exerting more than a minor impact on adolescent alcohol or drug use. This conclusion is consistent with reviews by Kalb (1979), Kinder *et al.* (1980), Schaps *et al.* (1981), Bandy and President (1983), and Bagnall (1990).

Leathar *et al.* (1985) conducted an evaluation of the Scottish Health Education Group's 1985 drug campaign. They did not, however, monitor changes attributable to this campaign nor did they employ any form of control group. This study, accordingly, did not indicate whatever effect the campaign had exerted.

Coggans *et al.* (1989) evaluated a drug education in Scotland. They concluded that package-based drug education in schools increased drug-related knowledge, but not attitudes or behaviour.

## Conclusions

A substantial minority, and in some areas probably a majority, of British adolescents use illicit drugs. Fortunately, most drug use is confined to cannabis or to only the experimental or limited use of other substances. Adolescent use of illegal drugs, like alcohol and tobacco use, is influenced by many factors, including curiosity and peer pressure. There are marked regional variations in drug use. Drug users come from all social backgrounds, but evidence supports the conclusion that there is a connection between opiate use, unemployment, and social deprivation. The complex aetiology of drug use is a powerful barrier to preventive initiatives. Health education and mass media campaigns have not been shown to discourage drug use by young people.

## References

Anderson, K. (1992). The use and misuse of exstasy (MDMA) in Scotland. *Report to SHHD (Scottish Home and Health Department), Edindurgh.*

Bagnall, G. M. (1988). Use of alcohol, tobacco and illicit drugs amongst 13-year-olds in three areas of Britain. *Drug and Alcohol Dependence*, **22**, 241–51.

Bagnall, G. M. (1990). *Educating young drinkers.* Tavistock/Routledge, London.

Bagnall, G., Plant, M. A., and Warwick, W. (1990). Alcohol, drugs and AIDS-related risks: results from a prospective study. *AIDS Care*, **2**, 309–17.

Bandy, P. and President, P. A. (1983). Recent literature on drug abuse and prevention and mass media: focussing on youth, parents, women and the elderly. *Journal of Drug Education*, **13**, 255–71.

Binnie, H. L. and Murdock, G. (1969). The attitudes to drugs and drug takers of students of the university and colleges of higher education in an English Midland City, University of Leicester, *Vaughan Papers*, **14**, 1–29.

Brown, C. and Lawton, J. (1988). *Illicit drug use in Portsmouth and Havant*. Policy Studies Institute, London.

Chambers, G. and Tombs, J. (eds) (1984). *The British crime survey, Scotland, Scottish research study*. HMSO, Edinburgh.

Coggans, N., Shewan, D., Henderson, M., Davies, J. B., and O'Hogan, G. (1989). *National evaluation of drug education in Scotland*. Centre for Occupational and Health Psychology, University of Strathclyde.

Davies, J. B. and Stacey, B. (1972). *Teenagers and alcohol*. HMSO, London.

Dorn, N. and South, N. (eds) (1987). *A land fit for heroin?* MacMillan, London.

Dorn, N. and South, N. (1990). Communications, education, drugs and HIV. In *AIDS and drug misuse* (eds J. Strang and G. V. Stimson), pp. 162–73. Tavistock/Routledge, London.

Fazey, C. (1977). *The aetiology of psychoactive substance use*. UNESCO, Paris.

Fish, F., Wells, B. W. P., Bindeman G., Bunney, J. E., and Jordan, M. M. (1974). Prevalence of drug misuse amongst young people in Glasgow 1970–1972. *British Journal of Addiction*, **69**, 231–6.

Goode, E. (1972). *Drugs in American society*. Alfred A. Knopf, New York.

Hindmarch, I. (1972). Adolescent drug use. *Synapse: Journal of Edinburgh University Medical School*, **21**, 3, April.

Jessor, R. and Jessor, S. L. (1977). *Problem behaviour and psychosocial development: a longitudinal study of youth*. Academic Press, New York.

Kalb, M. (1975). The myth of alcoholism prevention. *Preventative Medicine*, **4**, 404–16.

Kinder, B. N., Pape, N. E., and Walfish, S. (1980). Drug and alcohol education programmes: a review of outcome studies. *International Journal of the Addictions*, **15**, 1035–54.

Kosviner, A. and Hawks, D. (1977). Cannabis use amongst British University students, II. patterns of use and attitudes to use. *British Journal of Addiction*, **72**, 41–58.

Leathar, D. S., Hastings, G. B., and Squair, S. I. (1985). *Evaluation of the Scottish Health Education Group's 1985 Drug Abuse Campaign*. Advertising Research Unit, University of Strathclyde.

Leigh, B. C. (1990). The relationship of substance use during sex to high-risk sexual behavior. *Journal of Sex Research*, **27**, 1199–213.

Marsh, A. and Matheson, J. (1983). *Smoking attitudes and behaviour*. HMSO, London.

Marsh, A., Dobbs, J., and White, A. (1986). *Adolescent drinking*. HMSO, London.

Marsh, C. (1986). Medicine and the media. *British Medical Journal*, **292**, 895.

McKay, A. J., Hawthorne, V. M., and McCartney, H. N. (1973). Drug taking amongst medical students at Glasgow University. *British Medical Journal*, **1**, 540–3.

MORI (1990). *Teenage smoking*. MORI, London.

Morrison, V. and Plant, M. A. (1991). Licit and illicit drug initiations and alcohol-related problems illicit drug users in Edinburgh. *Drug and Alcohol Dependence*, **27**, 19–27.

Mott, J. (1981). Criminal involvement and penal response. In *Drug problems* in Britain (ed. G. Edwards and C. Busch), pp. 217–43. Academic Press, London.

Mott, J. (1985). Self-reported cannabis use in Great Britain in 1981. *British Journal of Addiction*, **80**, 30–43.

NOP Market Research Ltd. (1982). Survey of drug use in the 15–21 age group undertaken from the *Daily Mail*, NOP, London.

Parker, H., Bakx, K., and Newcombe, R. (1988). *Living with heroin*. Open University Press, Milton Keynes.

Pattison, C. J., Barnes, E. A., and Thorley, A. (1982). *South Tyneside drug prevalence and indicator study*. Centre for Drug and Alcohol Studies, Newcastle.

Pearson, G. (1987). *The new heroin users*. Blackwell Scientific, Oxford.

Peck, D. F. and Plant, M. A. (1986). Unemployment and illegal drug use: concordant evidence from a prospective study and from national trends. *British Medical Journal*, **293**, 929–32.

Plant, M. A. (1973). *Young people at risk: a study of the 17–24 age group*. Cheltenham Youth Trust, Cheltenham.

Plant, M. A. (1975). *Drugtakers in an English town*. Tavistock, London.

Plant, M. A. (1981). What aetiologies? In *Drug problems in Britain* (eds G. Edwards and C. Busch), pp. 248–80. Academic Press, London.

Plant, M. A. (1987). *Drugs in perspective*. Hodder and Stoughton, London.

Plant, M. A. (1990*a*). Epidemiology and drug misuse. In *Drugs research and policy in Britain* (ed. V. Berridge), pp. 170–94. Avebury, Aldershot.

Plant, M. A. (1990*b*). Alcohol, sex and AIDS. *Alcohol and Alcoholism*, **25**, 293–301.

Plant, M. A. (ed.) (1990*c*). *AIDS, drugs and prostitution*. Tavistock/Routledge, London.

Plant, M. A., Peck, D. F., and Samuel, E. (1985). *Alcohol, drugs and schoolleavers*. Tavistock, London.

Plant, M. A., Bagnall, G., Foster, J., and Sales, J. (1990). Young people and drinking: results of an English national survey. *Alcohol and Alcoholism*, **25**, 685–90.

Plant, M. A. and Plant, M. L. (1992). *Risk-takers: alcohol, drug, sex and youth*. Tavistock/Routledge, London.

Robertson, J. A. and Plant, M. A. (1988). Alcohol, sex and risks of HIV infection. *Drug and Alcohol Dependence*, **22**, 75–8.

Robertson, J. R. (1987). *Heroin, AIDS and society*. Hodder and Stoughton, London.

Schaps, E., Dibartolo, R., Moskowitz, J., Balley, C. G., and Churgin, G. (1981). A review of 127 drug abuse prevention programme evaluations. *Journal of Drug Issues*, **11**, 17–43.

Stall, R. (1987). The prevention of HIV infection associated with drug and alcohol use during sexual activity. In *AIDS and substance use* (ed. L. Siegel), pp. 73–88. Harrington Park Press, New York.

Watson, J. M. (1979). Solvent abuse: a retrospective study. *Community Medicine*, **1**, 153–6.

Wiener, R. S. C. (1970). *Drugs and schoolchildren*. Longman, London.

Williams, M. (1986). The Thatcher Generation. *New Society*, 21 February, pp. 312–15.

Woods, S. C. and Mansfield, J. G. (1983). Ethanol and disinhibition: psysiological and behavioural links. In *Alcohol and disinhibition: Nature and* meaning of the link (eds R. Room and G. Collins), pp. 4–23. NIAAA Research Monograph 12. US Department of Health and Human Services, Washington, DC.

Young, J. (1971). *The drugtakers*. Paladin, London.

# 5. Use of public health indicators of the extent and nature of drug problems during the 1970s and 1980s

*Hamid Ghodse*

## Introduction

Practical planning for problems related to drug abuse requires knowledge of the number of people involved and of the nature of their problem. Unfortunately, this information is not readily available in the UK. Those involved may not perceive that they have a problem and even if they do they may choose to conceal it, sometimes because their drug use is illegal. Because of the number of drugs that may be abused and the different problems-that ensue, no single epidemiological method is ever going to provide 'the answer'—the 'magic number' of those within a population with a problem related to drug abuse and, if it did, the information would be useless because it would say nothing about the nature of the particular problems encountered. Thus when assessing drug abuse problems, the researcher must be prepared to use a variety of methods each of which contributes a 'patch' or area of information that may or may not blend or interconnect with information from other studies, so that gradually a picture emerges of drug abuse within the community and the problems consequent upon this.

## What is a 'case'?

It is obviously essential for any epidemiological study to have a precise definition of what constitutes a 'case' for that particular study; according to the research being undertaken a 'case' might be an incident of drug overdose, a road traffic accident in which drugs were implicated, a septic complication of drug injection, or death due to drug abuse. Preliminary research is often necessary to formulate an operational definition that can be used in multicentric research. Such operational definitions can usefully include both theoretical and empirical approaches.

It is also necessary to know the total population from which such cases are drawn and to define the time period being studied. If all this information is available it is then possible to establish prevalence rates—either at a particular point in time (point prevalence), or over a defined period (period prevalence). For drug abuse problems, the incidence rate—the rate of occurrence of new problems—may be of particular interest and importance in assessing new patients and trends in drug abuse.

## Pattern of consumption of drugs

In Britain, as in other countries, one way of finding out about patterns of drug use is to investigate the supply situation by obtaining information on production (licit and illicit), importation (licit and illicit), and exportation (licit and illicit). (Bruun 1983; Ghodse *et al.* 1987; Idanpaan-Heikkila and Poshyachinda 1987). In practice, of course, reliable data can only be obtained about licit sources of supply as no official figures are kept on illicit practices. However, some information can be obtained from figures about drug seizures and purchases made on the black market for investigation purposes. These data give some idea of the availability, purity, and cost of individual drugs; further information can be obtained from sampling surveys of the general and drug-using populations, although this has problems of consistency and validity. Even if the data obtained in the ways outlined above were not absolutely accurate, its regular collection will show up changes in the supply of drugs and may, on occasion, give an indication of a developing abuse problem.

Another way of investigating patterns of drug use is to assess drug distribution by means of prescriptions. This can provide information on individual drugs or drug classes, prescribed either for the total population or for selected populations. It also, of course, allows trends and patterns in prescribing practices to be studied. Prescriptions dispensed through pharmacies and institutions and doctors' prescription records, can all provide useful and complementary data, which, if collected regularly, will again show up patterns and trends in prescribing.

Knowledge of the supply and distribution of drugs, although important, cannot say anything about which drugs are actually being swallowed either licitly or illicitly. Most studies on drug consumption, however, rely on self-report methods and therefore suffer problems of validity. Studies may be on total populations or selected populations (for example, high consumption groups such as females, youth, the elderly), by self-administered questionnaire or using interviewing techniques. In general, the investigation of illicit consumption requires less formal methods of inquiry.

Finally, all methods have advantages and disadvantages and whenever possible, more than one method should be used to investigate drug consumption so that the different results may complement each other and build up a more complete picture than if single approaches are adopted in isolation.

## Morbidity

Since direct measures of drug abuse problems are not available, other indicators are used instead. Prominent among these are studies of morbidity: the problems that arise as a consequence of drug abuse (Ghodse 1981).

These drug-related health problems, apart from acting as indicators of drug abuse are worthy of study in their own right. Awareness of such problems permits the development of more effective health and social services, and of better preventive measures.

One way of finding out about drug-related health problems is to monitor public health data on the frequency of reports of various types of pathology, such as viral hepatitis, fetal damage, etc., on the assumption that these problems are closely enough linked to drug consumption to be reasonable indicators. The advantage of this method is its simplicity and low cost, and if data are gathered promptly and routinely, they provide early information about the extent of psychotropic drug use. However, the simplicity and economy are offset by the lack of specificity of a particular morbidity for psychotropic drug use.

A particular difficulty associated with this methodology arises because the monitoring of public health data depends on the identification of cases in different centres, with an epidemiological picture being built up by multicentre reporting of fairly low frequencies. Case definition and case recognition vary from centre to centre and may vary in time with changing medical awareness. Other factors also combine to make morbidity an unreliable indicator of drug use; the proportion of casualties presenting to medical agencies may vary at different times and at different centres, and the percentage of those who take drugs and sustain a particular complication, may also vary from time to time. Hepatitis for example, at one stage in the UK, appeared to be a reliable indicator of heroin dependence, but for a variety of reasons became a much less certain marker.

Because of difficulties such as these, attempts to design indices of drug misuse, similar to those designed for alcohol, are unlikely to succeed; although specific morbidities can be useful in providing an early warning of new drugs being misused or of geographical spread to new areas or involvement of new population groups. Some examples of how specific morbidities can be and have been used to monitor substance abuse, are given below.

## Drug overdoses

The continuing epidemic of drug overdoses that is occurring in many countries is, in numerical terms, probably the most serious morbidity associated with psychotropic drug use. In London, for example, the annual prevalence rate, almost certainly an underestimation, was calculated to be 430 per 100 000 of the population. This vast number of overdoses is made up of those who take a drug overdose accidentally, those who do so deliberately in a suicidal attempt or gesture, and those who do so in the course of drug dependence in a search for heightened effect (Ghodse 1976, 1977a).

The majority of cases of drug overdose are seen in hospital Accident and Emergency departments which offer several advantages for undertaking research into drug-related problems, including drug overdose. Although their organization may vary from centre to centre and in different countries, some form of emergency facility exists in all health-care systems so that there is a ready-made and cost-effective set-up, readily available, for monitoring drug-related problems. If valid results are to be obtained, however, the monitoring procedure must be planned very carefully. All studies should be prospective in nature because notes made in an emergency situation are rarely sufficiently detailed for comprehensive data to be gleaned from them later. The conditions of a busy Accident and Emergency department must be kept firmly in mind, when the questionnaire is designed; it should elicit the maximum information but, at the same time, should be brief and simple so that the staff of the departments, whose responsibility is to the patient and not to research, can complete it easily. It should concentrate on factual rather than judgemental or descriptive data, and all responses should be in terms of defined criteria that are easily quantifiable. All definitions should be operational rather than theoretical. Uniformity in tabulating results is essential if valid comparisons are to be made; for example, a decision must be taken at the outset about a uniform system for classifying age groups and for recording and classifying the drug taken. A choice also has to be made about whether to study incidents or individual patients; the latter poses difficult problems of confidentiality which cannot satisfactorily be dealt with in a large survey while, at the same time, providing valuable information which probably cannot be obtained in any other way, about the hard core of drug misusers with a particularly serious drug problem.

One such study was carried out in London in 1975, involving 62 of the 66 Accident and Emergency departments. During the month of the survey a questionnaire was completed for each person who attended the department with a drug-related problem. It recorded the reason for the attendance, the drugs that precipitated the incident and their source of supply, the method of administration, and any previous overdoses. Demographic details were noted as well as certain physical and mental effects of the drug, such as the level of consciousness and aggressive behaviour (Ghodse 1976).

During the month of the survey there were 1706 drug-related incidents involving people aged 15–65 years, of which 1641 (96 per cent) were cases of drug overdose. More than half of these were suicidal attempts or gestures, but 20 per cent of the incidents in men and 10 per cent of those in women were due to an overdose in the course of drug dependence.

The survey continued for 1 year in seven hospitals and demonstrated that the rate of drug-related attendances in the Accident and Emergency population was 18.3 per 1000. Again, 95 per cent of attendances were for drug overdose, and although barbiturates were implicated most frequently, their use declined throughout the course of the year (Ghodse *et al.* 1981).

When the Accident and Emergency survey was repeated in 10 hospitals in 1982, there was a significant reduction in both the number of drug-related incidents and in the number of drug-dependent incidents attending, compared with 1975. Hypnotic drugs were used in a significantly smaller percentage of drug overdoses, but there was increased use of minor tranquillizers (Ghodse 1978).

The results of these related studies have been described albeit briefly, because they illustrate the potential usefulness of surveys within Accident and Emergency departments for monitoring trends in drug misuse. The methods of the 'London casualty survey' were used in a WHO multicentre study to test the validity of this public health indicator in different cultural and health service settings. It was found to be a practical and universally applicable tool. It was also a simple and cheaper method than similar methods used in North America. Unrestricted by conventional preoccupations with dependence on particular drugs or groups of drugs, studies in Accident and Emergency departments can make a valuable contribution to the total picture of drug misuse practices.

An additional major survey was carried out in the original 62 hospitals to explore the attitudes of staff working in Accident and Emergency departments towards patients who take drug overdoses. There was in general a very negative attitude towards drug-dependent individuals compared with those who took an overdose for other reasons, and it was believed that special services for the care of drug-dependent individuals should be developed. At that time (1975) about 60 per cent of staff of all disciplines supported the idea of a voluntary ban on the prescription of barbiturates. These studies were very influential in the development of services during the 1970s (Ghodse 1978, 1979).

## Drug dependence

Although dependence on opiate drugs had long been recognized it took 30 and 50 years, respectively, for the dependence producing potential of amphetamines and barbiturates to be appreciated. The severity of the dependence upon cocaine was not recognized until the epidemic of the 1980s produced increasing numbers of casualties. Stimulated perhaps by threats of litigation, awareness of the potential for dependence on other psychotropic drugs has been heightened (Ghodse and Khan 1988).

Nevertheless, the difficulties of diagnosing dependence on these drugs should not be minimized. Whereas dependence on opiates involves drugs with which the general population is unfamiliar, psychotropic drugs are well known to many people and, although some are prescribed for well-defined psychiatric illness, many are taken to mitigate personal and inter-personal problems. The difference between this type of use and use for personal pleasure is much less than in pre-psychotropic days when non-dependent individuals took drugs only for specific physical conditions. The difficulty of coming to a decision about the dependence status of a patient is illustrated by the considerable proportion (20 per cent) of patients attending an Accident and Emergency department with a drug-related problem who are assigned to the 'not known' category as regards their dependence status (Ghodse 1977a,b).

Drug dependence may be diagnosed in individuals in a variety of different settings—drug dependence treatment units, mental hospitals, prisons, remand homes, general practitioners' surgeries, Accident and Emergency departments—or by local religious and social leaders. If accurate data are to be accumulated, all of the staff involved in the above settings must be aware of their obligation to diagnose drug dependence and to record the diagnosis.

In the month long casualty survey described in the previous section, 395 drug-dependent patients were identified, who were responsible for 477 separate incidents, the majority of which were drug overdoses. When these patients were checked against the official Home Office Index of notified addicts, only 57 per cent were known to the Home Office. This demonstrates very clearly how repeated research in Accident and Emergency departments could play a valuable role in monitoring drug abuse and dependence and might produce information supplementary to that obtained from the specialized drug treatment agencies and other sources of information (Ghodse 1977b).

## Hepatitis B

Hepatitis is an example of a complication of drug-abuse due, not to any particular drug, but to the method of drug administration. It occurs because of dirty injection habits, and is usually attributed to serum types B and C hepatitis. The discovery of Australia antigen and its association with serum hepatitis has provided a more specific test. Hepatitis in addicts is an interesting example of a morbidity, the incidence of which appears to have changed with time (Ghodse 1981). It is now much less useful as an indicator of heroin dependence because jaundice, hepatitis, and gross abnormalities of liver function occur less frequently now in addicts due to the easy availability of sterile injection equipment through syringe exchange schemes. This illustrates that the percentage of people using a particular drug and suffering a particular complication may vary and emphasizes that it is very unwise to rely on one indicator in isolation for a picture of drug abuse. There are further problems in using hepatitis data. First, there are many causes of hepatitis B. In addition to drug abuse, it can be transmitted by blood transfusion or sexual contact, and increased emphasis on safer sexual practices has undoubtedly contributed to the decreased incidence of hepatitis B. Secondly, it is incompletely and irregularly reported and there may be difficulties with the sensitivity and specificity of the diagnosis of hepatitis B in some laboratories. Nevertheless, it is still worthwhile to screen drug abusing patients for hepatitis and to maintain a register of those suffering from it. Although it is an unreliable quantitative indicator of drug abuse, it is a serious drug-related health problem and if it is monitored and recorded routinely and systematically, any extension of drug injecting to new areas will be picked up more promptly.

## AIDS

The acquired immune deficiency syndrome (AIDS) can also be used as an indicator of drug abuse. Unknown before 1981 it is caused by the human immunodeficiency virus (HIV). There are three main routes of infection: by sexual intercourse, by using injection equipment contaminated with the blood of an infected individual and, for babies, by being infected from the mother before or during birth. Transfusion of contaminated blood has been implicated, notably in haemophiliacs. Because the incubation period may last several years, the disease itself is less useful as an indicator than identification of infection by HIV, using an antibody test.

As HIV is not confined to drug abusers, it is not an exclusive indicator for this condition. Indeed, as it becomes more widespread within the community as a sexually transmitted disease, it will become less useful as an indicator of drug abuse. At present, the incidence and prevalence of HIV carriers can be used as an indicator of drug abuse by injection. In Edinburgh (Scotland) for example, more than 50 per cent of injecting drug abusers are AIDS carriers and in the USA intravenous drug abusers accounted for 17 per cent of all known cases of AIDS in 1985. Sadly, the incidence of congenital infection may also serve as an indicator of drug abuse, at least until the disease becomes more widespread.

## Other infectious complications

Certain other infectious complications occur in drug abusers, characteristically as a result of non-sterile injection techniques. They include: septic injection sites, abscesses, pneumonia, septicaemia, and endocarditis. They often present atypically in addicts and, if caused by uncommon organisms, can be difficult to treat. Again, if information about these complications was recorded in a systematic and accessible fashion, it could be used to monitor injecting activity.

## Neonatal problems

Drug-related problems affecting the newborn are an area of particular concern with drug withdrawal syndromes described in infants born to mothers dependent on opiates, sedative hypnotics, and stimulants such as amphetamines and cocaine. Furthermore, LSD and cannabis, have both been implicated as teratogens, but there has been little sound systematic research into this problem, and anecdotal accounts of congenital deformities in infants born to mothers who have taken drugs in pregnancy, do not prove that there is a causal relationship, particularly if the condition is one of high background incidence.

This serious public health problem requires thorough evaluation, and all drugs taken in pregnancy should be recorded routinely. The gradual accumulation of data on psychotropic drugs would enable rational decisions to be made on drug control measures.

## Drug psychosis

Some psychotropic drugs (for example, amphetamines and other synthetic stimulants, LSD, and cocaine), when taken in excess or in combination with other drugs, can cause an acute reversible psychotic illness. Many such reactions are probably dealt with satisfactorily by companions participating in the drug-taking experience, and only the more serious ones ever come to medical attention. Even when they do, it may be very difficult to distinguish them from schizophrenia and other psychotic illnesses, and accurate diagnosis may be difficult. For all of these reasons, drug psychosis is unlikely ever to be an accurate epidemiological indicator. Nevertheless, if cases were recorded by psychiatric hospitals and outpatient clinics and by Accident and Emergency departments in a systematic and accessible way, a more complete picture of the relevant syndromes might begin to emerge.

Amphetamine psychosis is a good example of how an alert attitude to diagnosis can increase epidemiological information. Although the condition was unrecognized until 1958, large series of cases have since been reported by many physicians, probably because they were looking for them specifically, with the help of chemical tests for drug detection.

## Analgesic nephropathy

Those who misuse minor analgesics resemble, in many important ways, those who use psychotropic drugs. They often deny misuse and may go to considerable lengths to conceal it; many misuse other drugs too, and admit that they take analgesics for the feeling of well-being that they induce. Analgesic nephropathy, like amphetamine psychosis, is an example of how medical case reports may draw attention to a previously overlooked condition and thereby provide reliable epidemiological information (Murray 1972). Here again, records of cases should be kept in a systematic and accessible way.

## Notification of adverse drug reactions

Some countries are already members of the WHO system for the international monitoring of adverse reactions to drugs. A register to monitor the side-effects of drugs may be organized on a voluntary basis; although in some countries notification is a statutory requirement with physicians and dentists sending notifications when they diagnose or suspect a harmful side-effect. It is important that forms should be as brief and simple as possible, to encourage doctors to notify, and a feedback mechanism in the form of an annual summary for the reporting professionals is also helpful.

The notification of adverse drug reactions is a quick, cheap, and practical way of monitoring them; it also makes doctors more aware of the possibility of side-effects from drugs, which in turn leads to better medical practice.

In some countries, various statutory registers have been set up for a variety of conditions that are particular health problems, for example, congenital malformation registers, cancer registers, etc. It is possible to incorporate information for these registers in a special section of the adverse drug reaction form, and this has the advantage of not overwhelming doctors and other health-care workers with a multiplicity of demands and forms.

More countries should be invited to join the WHO system for the international monitoring of adverse reactions to drugs and to keep registers of such reactions.

## Mortality

Although it is difficult to arrive at a definition of a 'serious' drug problem, there can be no argument that anyone who dies as a result of drug abuse undoubtedly had a serious problem, and this is the justification for studying the mortality statistics of drug abuse. Causes of death are numerous: an overdose, whether suicidal, accidental, or homicidal, may cause fatal poisoning; side-effects of drugs, non-sterile self-injection, and functional impairment increasing the risk of serious accidents are other possible causes of death.

There are several possible ways of studying mortality due to drug abuse.

### National cause of death statistics

These statistics cover the whole population of a country and, because of this, their publication is often delayed. Changes in mortality, reflecting for example changing trends of drug abuse, cannot be recognized promptly and initiation of any response is, therefore, also delayed.

In fact, many Western European countries now regularly publish details of deaths from overdoses, mainly from opiates, as a measure of their addiction problem, but comparability of results from different countries is not always possible because of differences in the cause of death examinations (that is, autopsy/no autopsy) and differences in coding them.

### Cause of death surveys

Cause of death surveys are retrospective and information is sought from any potentially fruitful source, for example police, friends, teacher, etc., and from the medical records. Prospective studies of an epidemiological cohort of drug abusers may also be carried out.

### Forensic examination

The analysis of a series of forensically examined cases has proved to be a fairly reliable method of distinguishing trends in drug abuse; because the forensic examination is carried out by individuals familiar with the procedure, the practical details of the examination remain constant and there is little, if any, bias.

Although these results again only refer to a small and unrepresentative group they can be derived rapidly and new fatal trends in drug abuse can be pinpointed promptly. For example, a detailed examination was carried out of 134 deaths in the early 1970s recorded by coroners as being due to drug addiction. This showed that 41 per cent of the addicts were unknown to the Home Office, illustrating yet again the incompleteness of official statistics. Barbiturate overdose accounted for over half the deaths, though two-thirds of these occurred in individuals 'registered' as addicts to notifiable drugs. Since the Home Office Index is concerned with addiction to opiates and cocaine only, it fails to reflect accurately the prevalence of other serious forms of addiction. Thus for many addicts it was not the notifiable drug that finally caused their death, but the less strictly controlled barbiturates (Ghodse *et al.* 1978).

Nevertheless, the Home Office Index is a valuable source of information. A search of the file of addict deaths from 1967 to 1981 identified 1499 deaths (Ghodse *et al.* 1985). The 15 annual cohorts demonstrated a remarkable constancy in the death rate of 3 per cent during the first year after notification and 1.9 per cent for the second year, and again showed the very significant role of medically prescribed drugs as a cause of death in comparison with illicitly imported ones. The role of forensic examination as an indicator of drug abuse has also been recognized in the USA where the reports of Medical Examiners form part of the data collected by the Drug Abuse Warning Network (DAWN 1990).

It should be emphasized that an important variable that may significantly affect the results of mortality studies is the frequency with which toxicological analysis is carried out and its accuracy.

## Law enforcement indicators

Indicators taken from the law enforcement area include the amount of drug seized, its price and its purity, and the number of arrests for drug-related crimes. They can be considered as second-order indicators of drug abuse because they reflect the prevalence of drug abuse through varying levels of drug availability.

## Population surveys

A population survey is another way of assessing the extent and nature of drug use in normal populations. As it is impossible to question every individual, it is important that the sample chosen should be a representative one. Surveys can also be carried out on selected groups such as university students, prisoners, etc.

Reporting systems that use defined and systematic procedures to notify a central authority about drug problems can be used to measure trends in drug abuse on a continuous basis. Well-known examples include DAWN in the USA, which is an event-reporting system that records every drug-related problem attending a participating Emergency Room. CODAP—the Client-Oriented Data Acquisition Process, also in the USA—is a case-reporting system which permits multiple events for the same individual in the same institution to be reported as a single case. In the UK, the Home Office maintains an index of those addicted to certain, notifiable drugs; this functions as a case register because an individual is counted as just one 'case' even if reported by several institutions.

The development of the regional database in the UK in recent years will provide a more comprehensive picture of substance misuse problems. This system which in theory is very simple, could be extended to include dependence on any drug; in practice it only provides accurate information if all doctors who see/treat dependent patients remember to notify them, and it seems that some doctors, mainly those in Accident and Emergency departments, where many drug-dependent patients are seen, are unaware of their statutory obligation to notify addicts. An alternative system for maintaining an index of dependent patients is exemplified by the system in Malta, where the regulations concerning the prescription of drugs are unusual, if not unique, in that some psychotropic drugs are controlled more strictly than opiates. Any prescription for one of the controlled psychotropic substances (including Mandrax, Tuinal, Seconal, and amphetamines), requires authorization from the Chief Government Medical Officer, the patient is notified as being in receipt of these drugs, regardless of his/her dependent status, and has to be identified by both the prescriber and the dispenser. This system thus incorporates notification along with strict measures and could easily be modified to include any drug that became a drug of abuse.

It is apparent that there are many epidemiological approaches to drug abuse. Often what is needed is a co-ordinated attempt on a large scale to record in a useful and accessible way, information that is already available but often inaccessible. Many of the measures suggested here are not expensive and they need not increase the work-load of anyone involved in the care of drug-abusing individuals. Questionnaires, for example, to be used in a study of morbidity, can be designed so that it is available for comparison with the past or the future or with other centres engaged on similar research.

To establish the prevalence and incidence of drug abuse is very difficult and demands multiple research methods, all being used simultaneously. It would be naive to suggest that any research method in isolation can be the perfect indicator of drug abuse and provide all the information that is required about drug-taking. Different sources will always supply different complementary data. With a problem such as drug abuse, there is no possibility of locating a traditional 'representative' sample, and repeated or continued study of undoubtedly biased and atypical subgroups may be the only available epidemiological method for building up a picture of the drug abuse problem.

## References

Bruun, K. (ed.) (1983). *Controlling psychotropic drugs. The Nordic experience.* Croom Hill, London.

DAWN (1990). *Annual Report US Department of Health, Education and Welfare* (NIDA), Washington, DC.

Ghodse, A. H. (1976). Drug problems dealt with by 62 London casualty departments. *British Journal of Preventive and Social Medicine*, **30**, 251–6. (This article was the basis for a report to the Advisory Council on the Misuse of Drugs; Home Office—1976.)

Ghodse, A. H. (1977a). Casualty departments and the monitoring of drugs dependence. *British Medical Journal*, **1**, 1381–2.

Ghodse, A. H. (1977b). Drug dependent individuals dealt with by London Casualty Departments. *British Journal of Psychiatry*, **131**, 273–80.

Ghodse, A. H. (1978). The attitudes of casualty staff and ambulance personnel towards patients who take drug overdoses. *Social Science and Medicine*, **12**, 341–6.

Ghodse, A. H. (1979). Recommendations by accident and emergency staff about drug-overdose patients. *Social Science and Medicine*, **13A**, 169–73.

Ghodse, A. H. (1981). Morbidity and mortality. In *Drug problems in Britain. A review of ten years* (ed. G. Edwards and C. Bush), pp. 171–215. Academic Press, London.

Ghodse, A. H. and Khan, I. (ed.) (1988). *Improving the use of psychoactive drugs: educating the professionals.* WHO, Geneva.

Ghodse, A. H., Sheehan, M., Stevens, B., Taylor, C., and Edwards, G. (1978). Mortality among drug addicts in Greater London. *British Medical Journal*, **2**, 1742–4.

Ghodse, A. H., Edwards, G., Stapleton, J., *et al.* (1981). Drug-related problems in London Accident and Emergency Departments: A twelve month survey. *Lancet*, **ii**, 859–62.

Ghodse, A. H., Sheehan, M., Taylor, C., and Edwards, G. (1985). Deaths of drug addicts in the United Kingdom 1967–81. *British Medical Journal*, **290**, 425–8.

Ghodse, A. H., Baigent, B., Evans, T. C., and Anderson, S. (1987). The use of a drug utilisation index to monitor psychotropic drug use in hospitals. *International Journal of Social Psychiatry*, **33**, 21–9.

Idanpaan-Heikkila, J. E. and Poshyachinda, V. (1987). Drug utilisation studies. In *Psychoactive drugs and health problems* (ed. J. E. Idanpaan-Heikkila, H. Ghodse, and I. Khan), pp. 12–27. Government Printing Centre, Helsinki, Finland.

Murray, R. M. (1972). The use and abuse of analgesics. *Scottish Medical Journal*, **17**, 393–6.

# 6. Women drug misusers: a case for special consideration

*Edna Oppenheimer*

> I was into pain reduction and and mind expansion, but what I've ended up with is pain expansion and mind reduction. Everything hurts now, and nothing makes sense
>
> C. Fisher, *Postcards from the edge*, 1987

To-date most research, policy and treatment initatives have predominantly focused on men. The special features of women's substance misuse has in comparison received but scant attention. This neglect may be due to prevailing ignorance about the sheer numbers of women involved in drug misuse, and also to the generally unfavourable images of such women as deviant and bad and hence not deserving of special attention. Nonetheless, observers have repeatedly commented that addicts are a heterogeneous group requiring a multiplicity of responses. Women's biology, their child-bearing functions, and gender roles qualify them for special consideration. Not only are their pathways into addiction often different, but, more importantly, they often face a very different set of problems once they become addicted.

Women represent a substantial 'minority' of drug misusers—they constitute about a quarter of all opiate users in the UK but far exceed men in psychoactive drug misuse (Ashton and Golding 1989). It has been estimated that in Britain there are some 25 000–30 000 women opiate misusers, of whom half are injectors, and their numbers are said to be increasing [Institute for the Study of Drug Dependence (ISDD) 1991]. The extent of cocaine and crack cocaine use is widespread in the USA but as yet is not widespread among British women, although it was used quite heavily for a while amongst prostitutes in a number of large British cities (Mathews 1990; Patel *et al.* 1989). Early death is a serious risk for all those engaged in drug misuse, and death rates among drug misusers are 20–28 times in excess of those expected in a comparable population (Ghodse *et al.* 1978). Women are somewhat less likely than men to die prematurely from drug misuse (despite higher than expected mortality for their age and sex), but experience higher levels of medical complications during their addiction careers (Tunving 1988; Marsh and Simpson 1986).

In the last decade there has been a growing awareness of women's concerns. This was originally partly influenced by feminist thought and more recently through the advent of the human immunodeficiency virus (HIV). Women drug misusers are recognized as being in danger of becoming infected and infecting others through their work in the sex industry or because they often live with male drug users. There is also some risk of transmission of the virus to the unborn child. Much official concern has been expressed on these matters; however, the extent to which concern has been translated into action is less clear.

## The emergence of awareness of women as a 'special group'

The growing concern about women who misuse drugs has found its expression in official and semi-official documents and in the reports of expert committees set up to examine the drug problem and responses to it.

A brief résumé of some of these public statements shows that a small number of issues are repeatedly raised.

Beginning in 1982 the influential Advisory Committee on the Misuse of Drugs (ACMD 1982) examined treatment and rehabilitation for drug misusers in Britain and made recommendations on the future shape of services. In its report (1982, p. 33) it raised the issue of singling out special groups only to dismiss the idea:

In the development of services we consider it counter-productive to identify more and more specific client groups (e.g. heroin addict, amphetamine addict etc.) This can give rise to the false assumption that each category demands specific services, when experience and evidence shows that all drug misusers share similar kinds of basic problems.

It did stress, however, that treatment and rehabilitation should be directed to individual needs.

For some individuals a medical response will predominate ... for other a social work response... for yet others, an educational and counselling approach will be best.

It was the Medical Working Group on Drug Dependence reporting in 1984 on the role of medical services in the management of drug misuse which drew attention to the problems of pregnant opiate misusers, noting that pregnant opiate misusers needed a 'sympathetic understanding of the mother' and 'continuing support'.

By 1984 the ACMD (p. 23) in its report *Prevention* drew attention to the inadequacy of the provision for women drug misusers.

In 1960s and 1970s drug misuse amongst women was not considered an area of particular interest; researchers and policy makers have often assumed that hypotheses and policies drawn up in response to male drug misuse are equally applicable to women ... the women's movement has drawn attention to the need to conceptualize 'social problems' (such as the drug problem) from the point of view of women's interest and position in society ... we consider that this literature raises important issues not adequately dealt with in earlier, male-centred work.

A year later the report of the Social Services Committee of the House of Commons (1985) reporting on their inquiry about the treatment and rehabilitation of drug misusers reiterated concern at the growing number of female drug misusers, many of whom were young, pregnant or had young children. They were alarmed to hear from witnesses that pregnant women were afraid to come forward for antenatal or postnatal care for fear of the consequences for themselves and their children, and warned that '... it is essential that all agencies seeking to respond to drug misuse take greater account of this trend'.

Subsequent ACMD reports on *AIDS and drug misuse*, Parts 1, 2 (1988, 1989) have addressed themselves to issues which have arisen since dangers of HIV infection have become known. The majority of comments had been on matters relating to pregnancy and child care, urging that (ACMD 1989, para. 3.35):

counselling must be available to seropositive women who are pregnant, which addresses the implication of HIV-disease for themselves and their children, taking account of the most up-to-date knowledge of the effects of pregnancy upon women with HIV disease and the likelihood of transmission to the child.

Thus the main thrust of official concern is for the female drug misuser in her role as mother. There is less attention to the wider experiences and concerns of women outside of the mothering role.

## The special features of women's addiction

There are a number of features of women's drug misuse that are unique to their sex and gender. Most obvious is their child-bearing and mothering roles but there are other features such as pathways into addiction, the high levels of reported psychological distress and medical complications, and experiences of the criminal justice system. These issues are briefly discussed below.

### Antecedent factors

Rosenbaum (1981) noted that 'the woman addict is locked into the heroin life and out of the conventional world', but the questions are: How did she get there? How does she come to enter a 'career of narrowing options'? How can she be helped out of this hopeless 'funnel'? Maybe some of this could in part be understood by identifying women's experiences which made them vulnerable to addiction.

It is a truism that women's life experiences differ from those of men. From early childhood girls and boys are treated differently and different expectations are placed upon them. It is nevertheless difficult to determine with any certainty whether antecedent factors in women's addiction are significantly different from those of men. Some researchers have argued that women are just 'somewhat more neurotic and less psychopathic than male addicts' (Martin and Martin 1980). Others have shown that significant differences do exist.

There is no single factor which inevitably leads a person into drug misuse (Bry 1983). However, many women report widespread conflict and unhappiness in their family of origin, substance misuse by parents or siblings, and frequent and prolonged separation from parents (Stanton 1980). There is, moreover, a discernible sex difference in the perception of family problems, with women more likely than men to report negative childhood experiences, and to have noticed differences in adults' expectations of boys and girls during their own childhood. Binion (1982) concluded that initial drug use for women was closely related to interpersonal affiliation issues and that women were more likely than men to seek out an addict peer group as a reaction to an unhappy family situation. Hser (1987) has further observed that women were more likely than men to be introduced to drug use by a sexual partner. The presence of child sexual abuse in a substantial subgroup of women addicts has been reported (Rohsenow *et al.* 1988).

Most observable differences are sex and gender specific and it may be that women's addiction and its consequences are but a tragic manifestation of women's general position in society: 'Dependency is an integral part of women's daily life—use of substances is only the outward sign of it (Mefert-Diete and Soltau 1984).

## Women in the criminal justice system

There has been an overall increase in female crime in the past few decades. In Britain figures of recorded offences show that women found guilty, cautioned, or dealt with by compounding for drug offences between 1986 and 1990 has increased from 2997 to 4349 an increase of 45 per cent (ISDD 1991). This increase in female crime which has accelerated in the last few decades, has occurred mainly in what may be regarded as typical female criminal pursuits, that is crimes that are income generating (for example, drug sales and purchases, prostitution, shoplifting, and forgery). Madden *et al.* (1990) studied a random sample of 272 women serving sentences in England and Wales (one-quarter of the total female prison population). They found that in the study group one-quarter were dependent on drugs at the time of their offence, and of these nearly 80 per cent were using opiates before prison, (18 per cent of the sample) and two-thirds were injecting (15 per cent of total sample).

Prostitution has typically been viewed as the offence most often chosen by addicted women. Estimates of the proportion of female drug misusers who are also prostitutes range from 30 to 70 per cent while the proportion of prostitutes who also use drugs is reported to be higher— about 40–85 per cent (Golstein 1979). In some instances prostitution is a way to support a drug habit, sometimes drugs are seen as a way of dealing with the stresses of prostitution and other criminal activities. Thus the relationship between addiction and prostitution is complex.

Women drug misusers may also come into conflict with the law when a child custody case is at issue. There is a potential conflict between the needs of children or of the unborn child and that of the mother. In Britain, however, women have been repeatedly assured that drug misuse *per se* is not a sufficient legal reason for separating them from their children; though as has been mentioned before women are not always convinced by these assurances (ACMD 1989, para. 4.20, p. 33).

Women's experiences of the criminal justice system is mostly a function of their drug misuse and can blight their lives. Overall, however, their criminal behaviour both pretreatment and post-treatment is considerably lower than that of men (Simpson and Sells 1982), but the types of female crimes in which they engage put them in danger of violence and disease.

## Pregnancy and childbirth

Pregnancy and childbirth have increasingly occupied centre stage in considerations of the special features of women's addiction. Despite the fact that women drug misusers often lead a perilous existence, lacking economic and social supports, they often want to have children. Moriaty (1978) has observed that pregnancy gave women a sense of empowerment in contrast to their usual feelings of helplessness: 'It gave them a role as a mother to look forward to when they seemed to have nothing to live for'.

Probably 80 per cent of notified women addicts are of child-bearing age. It has been estimated that the annual incidence of birth to these women is three per 1000 births (Farrell *et al.* 1989), but for many drug misusing women pregnancy outcomes are poor. For example in a study of 12 pregnant women at two London clinics, Green and Gossop (1988) confirming research findings from the USA found that: one of the 12 pregnancies ended in stillbirth and another with the neonate dying 2 hours after birth. Seven babies were received into a special care unit with three requiring medical treatment. Nine of the 10 surviving babies were placed on the 'At Risk' register, which is monitored by the Social Services department.

Furthermore, the risks of HIV transmission by infected women to their babies is considerable and has serious implications for the management of the pregnancy.

### The effects of drug misuse on pregnancy

Different drugs or combinations of drugs when taken by a pregnant woman are likely to affect her and her fetus in different ways. It is not always easy to look specifically at the effect of one drug since many women are not only multiple drug users but are also likely to smoke tobacco and drink alcohol. However, there has been some attempt to examine specific drug effects, though many of the research findings are inconclusive. The possible effects of opiates and cocaine are described here.

*The effects of opiate misuse*   Opiate misusers are regarded as at risk for obstetric complication not only from the actual effect of the drugs but also from factors associated with poor nutrition and lack of health care. Obstetric complications may include—abruption, amnionitis, eclampsia, placental insufficiency, postpartum haemorrhage, and premature labour (Gerada *et al*. 1990). If drug taking continues during pregnancy the effects on the fetus and the new-born include low-birth rate, which is the most common complication and is believed to be a direct opiate effect (Householder *et al*. 1982). Neonatal dependence and withdrawal can take place *in utero* as well as after birth, and are characterized by central nervous system excitability, gastrointestinal dysfunction, respiratory distress, and other withdrawal symptoms including sneezing, sweating, stuffy nose, increased lacrimation, mottling, and fever (Kaltenbach and Finnegan 1986). Seizures have been reported in 2–11 per cent of neonates on withdrawal from opiates (Hertzlinger *et al*. 1977).

Research into the long-term effects on infants reported by Kaltenbach and Finnegan (1984) concluded that there are no long-term developmental sequelae that are directly associated with methadone exposure *in utero*, and that 4-year-olds who had been methadone exposed performed within the normal range for their age.

*The effects of cocaine use*   The consequences of cocaine misuse in pregnancy are not dissimilar to those of opiates. In a review of studies on cocaine abuse in pregnancy conducted in the USA, Lindenberg *et al*. (1991) concluded that cocaine misuse has been found to be associated with numerous obstetric complications such as premature labour, weight gain during pregnancy and nutritional insufficiency, though the findings about abruption, hypertension, and toxaemia in pregnancy were inconsistent. Cocaine and/or crack users have consistently been found to be less likely to receive antenatal care.

No conclusive data are available on the neonatal neurobehavioural complications in those babies exposed prenatally to cocaine and many of the findings here are also inconsistent (Brown 1991). However, exposure to cocaine has been associated with smaller head circumference and an increased risk of lower birthweight, fetal destress in labour and delivery, neonatal withdrawal, congenital malformations, and sudden infant death.

Anecdotal reports from the USA on the long-term effects on children born to mothers who misused crack cocaine have painted an alarming picture of aggressive and out of control behaviour by these children.

*The effects of HIV*   Recent figures (Department of Health 1991) suggest that 37 per cent of all women in the UK infected by the virus are intravenous drug users. The rate of transmission of the virus from mother to fetus is uncertain, but it has been estimated that 25–50 per cent of babies born to infected mothers are themselves infected (The European Collaborative Study 1988).

Studies on pregnancy outcomes conducted in the USA by Selwyn *et al.* (1989) comparing HIV-negative and HIV-positive drug misusers found no difference in pregnancy outcome; that is, in the occurrence of antenatal, intrapartum, or neonatal complications. They also found that the acceleration of HIV status during pregnancy was uncommon. But an editorial comment on this work in the same journal (Landsman *et al.* 1989) cast some doubts on this finding. Selwyn *et al.* (1989) also studied decisions to continue or terminate pregnancy among HIV-positive and HIV-negative drug misusers, and found that 50 per cent of HIV positive and 44 per cent of HIV negative chose to terminate pregnancy. Of the women drug misusers who were HIV negative 44 per cent chose termination and 56 per cent decided to proceed with the pregnancy. There were no significant differences between the two groups of women. They concluded that concerns about HIV may lead to termination in some cases but that there were other determinants of pregnancy decisions. These included a woman's previous experiences of abortion, whether the pregnancy was planned or not, religious beliefs, and family circumstances.

The information on the risks of HIV transmission and the risks to mother and fetus are as yet insufficiently known. Therefore women and their doctors are at present making decisions that are based partly on feelings and ideologies and partly on scientific probabilities.

## The needs of women drug misusers in treatment

Research from the USA indicates that drug-dependent women have treatment needs that are different from those of their male counterparts. Women do not, however, always feel able to express their needs, and tend to ask for help for medical or family problems (Brown *et al.* 1971). When entering treatment women report fewer social supports, are less likely to be employed and financially independent, and more likely to be receiving welfare and to be dependent on others (Anderson 1985).

A woman who becomes an addict is breaking many social norms and the expectations of her sex and gender roles. She is frequently blamed for her problems and is perceived as bad and deviant. The experience of depression, feelings of worthlessness, and worries about sexual inadequacy are therefore widespread. There has long prevailed a therapeutic pessimism in respect to women's drug misuse. However, research from the USA conducted on a large number of subjects showed this to be unjustified. On the whole there was no difference in treatment outcome between men and women (Simpson and Sells 1982). Others have noted that treatments which are opiate orientated are best suited to a minority of women, generally younger drug misusers, and not to the vast majority of women who experience the multiplicity of difficulties described above (Burt *et al.* 1985).

Only some of the above issues have been taken on board in Britain. A few suggestions have been made by the ACMD (1989, para. 3.32), for example that treatment personnel should refrain from passing moral judgement on women, provide women-only treatment sessions staffed by women doctors and counsellors, and that creches or child-care facilities be available to enable women to attend treatment.

## Getting women into treatment

To begin the process of helping a woman out of the 'drug' world a period of engagement in treatment is often a necessity, if only for a while. There has been some evidence that women substance misusers delay or fail to come for treatment. Studies of those who seek help for their addiction consistently report a ratio of one woman to every four men (Glanz and Taylor 1986; Sheehan *et al.* 1988), a treatment ratio believed to be an under-representation of the numbers of women drug misusers in the wider population. When they do come they often mask the real reasons by presenting with a variety of medical or somatic problems. Brown *et al.* (1971) found that 45.9 per cent of women compared with 19.4 per cent of men gave drug-related physical complication as their main reason for help seeking. Apart from the denial which may be involved, the main difficulty for women focuses on concerns about the effects of disclosure of their problems to the authorities, fears of interference by social services or medical services, and of having children put into care against their wishes.

... because they find the service off-putting and not understanding of their needs; because it is difficult to find somebody to look after their children; or because they are frightened that their children will be taken into care if they admit to having a drug problem. (ACMD 1989, para. 3.31, p. 23)

## Special treatment needs for pregnant drug misusers

At present the fear of authority is so considerable that some women choose to go through their entire pregnancy without medical care (Social Services Committee 1985). Addressing this issue the ACMD (1989, 3.32) emphasized that Social Services Departments must make it known that drug misuse *per se* is not in itself a reason for separating children from parents and that accessibility to services be improved.

The pregnant drug misuser needs skilled care. A decision about whether drug taking can safely be continued or should be discontinued has to be made. Research shows that it is safest to detoxify between the 14th and 28th week of pregnancy in order to minimize miscarriage in the first trimester, or risk precipitating premature labour and fetal distress in the last trimester (National Institute on Drug Abuse 1985). However, many uncertainties about the optimal treatment for pregnant drug misusers remain.

If the woman is also infected by the HIV virus she must decide whether to go ahead with the pregnancy. The ACMD takes the view that infected women should be advised to avoid pregnancy (ACMD 1988, para. 2.2, p. 17). However, once pregnant, it sees no purpose in advocating termination of pregnancy to all HIV-infected women since this may simply deter women from coming for antenatal care. They argue that termination of pregnancy should be an available option but not pressed upon women (ACMD 1988, para. 3.35, p. 26). Counselling should be offered to all women in order to help them reach a decision. Moreover, since knowledge on risks of pregnancy to mother and child are as yet uncertain, clinicians need to keep abreast of the latest research on the subject. The need for accessible and acceptable treatments for pregnant addicts is emphasized.

In dealing with the pregnant drug misusers it is important to foster good communication between specialist drug services and maternity services (Green and Gossop 1988). It is necessary to involve a health visitor who has been specially trained, and to offer continuing paediatric supervision and contact with the general practitioner. The importance of practical help to mother and baby is undisputed.

## Special treatment needs of women in trouble with the law

The ACMD (1991) noted the lack of appropriate treatment facilities for female drug misusing offenders and reiterated most previous recommendations, outlining ways that women drug misusers could avoid getting into trouble by making contact with treatment services. The Committee saw the need to develop motivation for help seeking, for providing services which are relevant to the special needs of this group, services that are accessible, non-threatening and which adequately disseminate information.

## Women drug misusers in Britain—a special case?

What, if anything, is singular about the way in which women drug misusers are treated in Britain? Using the ACMD as a barometer of approaches to the problem one observes that most of the structural problems inherent in women's addiction have been acknowledged in their reports and that recommendations for better and more appropriate treatments abound. In the absence of nation-wide data it is difficult to judge to what extent these statments of 'intent' have been translated into practice. To date there are few facilities which are specifically designed for women and few facilities for mothers and children. There are women-only groups in a number of treatment centres but the choice of therapist is still a luxury in drug services that are overworked and understaffed. No data exist on the consumer viewpoint: What do the women themselves feel about the services? Drug misusers as a group are a disenfranchised group whose wishes and views are rarely taken into consideration. Within this subculture women are doubly disadvantaged. Women need help to become more visible and vocal and to be enabled to express what it is they need.

## References

ACMD (Advisory Council on the Misuse of Drugs) (1982). *Treatment and rehabilitation*. HMSO, London.

ACMD (1984). *Prevention*. HMSO, London.

ACMD (1988). *Aids and drug misuse*, *Part 1*. HMSO, London.

ACMD (1989). *Aids and drug misuse*, *Part 2*. HMSO, London.

ACMD (1991). *Drug misusers and the criminal justice system*, Part 1: Community resources and the probation service. HMSO, London.

Anderson M. A. (1985). Personalized nursing: an effective intervention model for use with drug dependent women in an emergency room. In *Progress in the development of cost-effective treatment for drug abusers* (ed. R. S. Ashery). National Institute on Drug Abuse, Research Monograph 58, Rockville, MD.

Ashton, H. and Golding, J. F. (1989). Tranquillisers: prevalence, predictors and possible consequences. Data from a large United Kingdon survey. *British Journal of Addiction*, **84**, 541–46.

Binion, V. J. (1982). Sex differences in socialization and family dynamics of female and male heroin users. *Journal of Social Issues*, **38**, 43–57.

Brown, S. S. (ed.) (1991). *Children and parental illicit drug use: research, clinical, and policy issues*. Summary of a workshop. National Academic Press, Washington DC.

Brown, B. S., Gauvey, S. K., Meyers, M. B., and Stark S. D. (1971). In their own words, addicts reasons for initiating and withdrawing from heroin. *International Journal of the Addiction*, **6**, 635–45.

Bry, B. H. (1983). Predicting drug abuse: review and reformulation. *International Journal of the Addiction*, **18**, 223–33.

Burt, M. R., Glynn, T. J., and Sowder, B. J. (1985). *Psychoscial characteristics of drug-abusing women*. National Institute on Drug Abuse, Rockville, MD.

Department of Health (1991). Quarterly AIDS figures. May. Department of Health Press Release, London DHS.

European Collaborative Study (1988). Mother to child transmission of HIV infection. *Lancet*, **ii**, 1039–42.

Farrell, M., Dawe, S., and Strang, J. (1989). Obstetric liaison (letter). *British Journal of Psychiatry*, **155**, 264–5.

Fisher, C. (1987). *Postcards from the edge*. Picador Pan Books, London.

Gerada, C., Dawe, S., and Farrell, M. (1990). Management of the pregnant opiate user. *British Journal of Hospital Medicine*, **43**, 133.

Ghodse, A. H., Sheehan, M., Stevens, B., Taylor, C., and Edwards, G. (1978). Mortality among drug addicts in Greater London. *British Medical Journal*, **2**, 1742–4.

Glanz, A. and Taylor, C. (1986). Findings of a national survey of the role of general practitioners in the treatment of opiate misuse: extent of contact with opiate misusers. *British Medical Journal*, **293**, 427–30.

Goldstein, P. J. (1979). *Prostitution and drugs*. Lexington Books, Lexington, MA.

Green, L. and Gossop, M. (1988). The managment of pregnancy in opiate addicts. *Journal of Reproduction and Infant Psychology*, **6**, 51–7.

Hertzlinger, R. A., Kandall, S. R., and Vaughan, H. G. (1977). Neonatal seizures associated with narcotic withdrawal. *Journal of Paediatrics*, **91**, 638–41.

ISDD (1991). *Drug misuse in Britain: national audit of drug misuse statistics*. ISDD, London.

Hser, Y. I., Anglin, M. D., McGothlin, W. H. (1987). Sex differences in addict careers: 3 Addiction. *American Journal of Drug and Alcohol Abuse*, **13**, 231–51.

Householder, J., Hatcher, R., Burns, W., and Chesnoff, I. (1982). Infants born to narcotic addicted mothers. *Psychological Bulletin*, **92**, 453–68.

Kaltenbach, K. and Finnegan, L. P. (1984). Developmental outcome of children born to methadone maintained women: A review of longitudinal studies. *Neurobehavioral Toxicology and Teratology*, **6**, 271–5.

Kaltenbach, K. and Finnegan, L. P. (1986). Neonatal abstinence syndrome, pharmacotherapy and developmental outcome. *Neurobehavioral Toxicology and Teratology*, **8** (4), 353–5.

Landsman, S. H., Minkoff, H. L., and Willoughby, A. (1989). HIV disease in reproductive age women: a problem of the present Editorial. *Journal of the American Medical Association*, **261**, 1326–7.

Lindenberg, C. G., McDaniels Alexander, E., Gendrop, S. C., Nencioli, M., and Williams, D. G. (1991). Review of the literature on cocaine abuse in pregnancy. *Nursing Research*, **40** (2), 69–75.

Madden, A., Swinton, M., and Gunn, J. (1990). Women in prison and use of illicit drugs before arrest. *British Medical Journal*, **301**, 1133.

Marsh, K. L. and Simpson, D. D. (1986). Sex differences in opioid addiction careers. *American Journal Drug Alcohol Abuse*, **12**, 309–29.

Martin, C. A. and Martin, W. R. (1980). Opiate dependence in women. In *Alcohol and drug problems in women* (ed. O. J. Kalant). Plenum, New York.

Mathews, L. (1990). Female prostitutes in Liverpool. In *AIDS, Drugs and Prostitution* (ed. M. Plant). Routledge, London.

Medical Working Group on Drug Dependence (1984). *Guidelines of good clinical practice in the treatment of drug misuse*. DHSS, London.

Merfert-Diete, C. and Soltau, R. (ed.) (1984). *Die Altagliche Verstickung in Abhangigkeit* Hamburg: Rowohit.

Moriaty, J. (1978). The psychological understanding and treatment of pregnant drug addicts. In *Critical concerns in the field of drug abuse* (ed. A. Schecter, H. Alksne, and E. Kaufman), pp. 664–8. Marcel Dekker, New York.

National Institute on Drug Abuse (1985). *Drug dependence in pregnancy: clinical managment of mother and child*, p. 37. National Institute on Drug Abuse, Rockville, MD.

Patel, A., Merrill, J., Vidyasagar, H., and Kahn, A. (1989). *Cocaine, and crack*. *British Medical Journal*, **299**, 856.

Rohsenow, E. J., Corbett, R., and Devine, D. (1988). Molested as children: a hidden contribution to substance abuse? *Journal of Substance Abuse Treatment*, **5** (Suppl. 1), 13–18.

Rosenbaum, M. (1981). *Women on heroin*. Rutgers University Press, New Jersey.

Sheehan, M., Oppenheimer, E., and Taylor, C. (1988). Who comes for treatment: drug misusers at 3 London agencies. *British Journal of Addiction*, **83**, 311–20.

Selwyn, P. A., Carter, R. J., Schoenbaum, E. E., Robertson, V. J., Klein, R. S., and Rogers, M. F. (1989*a*). Knowledge of HIV antibody status and decisions to continue or terminate pregnancy among intravenous drug users. *Journal of the American Medical Association*, **261**, 3567–71.

Selwyn, P. A., Schoenbaum, E. E., Davenny, K. *et al.* (1989*b*). Propspective study of human immunodeficiency virus infection and pregnancy outcomes in intravenous drug users. *Journal of the American Medical Association*, **261**, 1289–94.

Simpson, D. D. and Sells, S. B. (1982). *Evaluation of drug abuse treatment effectiveness: summary of the DARP follow-up research*. National Institute on Drug Abuse, Treatment Research Report, NIDA, US printing Office, Washington, DC.

Social Services Committee (1985). *Misuse of drug with special reference to treatment and rehabilitation of misusers of hard drugs* (4th report). HMSO, London.

Stanton, D. C. (1980). A family theory of drug abuse. In *Theories of drug abuse: selected contemporary perspectives* (ed. D. Lettieri and M. Sayers *et al.*), pp. 147–57. NIDA Research Monograph, Rockville, MD.

Tunving, K. (1988). Fatal outcome in drug addiction. *Acta Psychiatrica Scandinavia*, **77**, 551–66.

# 7. The arrival of HIV

*Roy Robertson*

Since the Second World War, policy relating to management and treatment of drug abusers has been characterized by sudden upheavals followed by unplanned drifts in direction. Dramatic shifts in policy have resulted from political events changing social structures and evolving medical philosophies rather than necessarily any advance in technology or understanding of the nature of the addictive disorder. Probably the single most important determinant of interest in drug users has been the steady increase in numbers reported to the Home Office Addicts Index (Home Office 1990). Towards the end of 1985, however, events occurred which had probably the most dramatic impact on social policy in the latter half of the twentieth century—the identification of large numbers of known drug users as human immunodeficiency virus (HIV) antibody positive. This sudden discovery was brought about by the introduction of a laboratory test which could indicate the presence of antibodies in blood and, coming in the wake of the clinical epidemic of cases of acquired immune deficiency syndrome (AIDS) in homosexual men in the USA, its impact was tremendous.

Until this discovery the impact of AIDS or HIV among drug users had been minimal. In the UK only seven cases of AIDS had been reported to the Public Health Laboratory Service (PHLS) by the end of 1985, four of these were also homosexual men. Each of the three injecting drug users who were not homosexual men travelled abroad and two certainly injected in Italy and the USA. In the fourth AIDS case whose only major risk factor was injecting drug use, there was no history of travel abroad. This case had a first positive HIV test in August 1985 and developed *Pneumocystis carinii* pneumonia (full-blown AIDS) in January 1986. All these cases were men.

By the end of 1985 a total of 55 reports of newly confirmed HIV infections in injecting drug users in England and Wales had been received. Two of these 55 had their positive specimens taken in November and December 1984. The remaining 53 were all tested in 1985. There is no information in surveillance data on earlier known positives.

By the end of 1985, however, 356 positive test results attributable to intravenous drug use had been reported in Scotland (PHLS Colindale). In summary it is reasonable to conclude that when the HIV test became generally available in 1985, HIV infection was already established in injecting drug users in Scotland, England, and Wales. Transmission probably increased during 1984 and 1985 when a widespread epidemic of acute hepatitis B occurred amongst injecting drug users. (Robertson 1985; McCormick *et al*. 1987). Retrospective testing in Scotland has shown that HIV was introduced in Edinburgh drug users in 1982 (Ronald *et al*. 1993).

Unlike the epidemic in the USA where cases of AIDS emerged rapidly subsequent to its discovery in 1981 the European and British experience was of the uncovering of a potential problem still some time in the future. This had important implications for the future development of research and clinical policy. Reading accounts of the early AIDS epidemic in the USA one is impressed by this difference (Jaffe 1983; Shiltz 1987; Carrick 1989). Unlike the UK several years elapsed before absolute confirmation was available of the cause of AIDS in the USA. In retrospect, therefore, it seems likely that HIV became endemic in the homosexual community in the USA in the mid- to late 1970s and that before long substantial part of the intravenous drug-using population, at least in New York City, had become infected. This latter epidemic seems to have been greatly enhanced by the coincidental epidemic of intravenous cocaine use (Selwyn 1986). Some of this clearly extended to European centres and sporadic cases of AIDS occurred, therefore, among drug users in the UK prior to the availability of HIV antibody testing in 1985. In Scotland introduction may have been earlier and spread was certainly more rapid.

## The impact of HIV antibody testing

A test to detect antibodies to HIV was first widely available throughout the developed countries in late 1985 and was initially applied to blood transfusion donations as this represented a major threat to an otherwise low risk population. At the same time testing was carried out on samples from individuals thought to be at greater risk, including those using injecting drugs. In the UK early discoveries later confirmed pilot studies on drug users which identified widespread infection in one or two centres (Peutherer 1985; Robertson 1986; McClelland 1986). In a similar fashion testing in southern Europe identified a large problem among drug users, a clear indication of what would happen at some time in the future once the incubation period has elapsed. In most cases, certainly in the UK, large numbers of positive results came as a great surprise and those who had apparently been infected were largely still healthy and free from symptoms.

## Incubation time; the unique feature of HIV disease

Even in 1990, it is strange to imagine the importance of our current knowledge of the long incubation period of AIDS. In 1981 and 1982 it was suspected that this disease may have a prolonged incubation time, perhaps even 18 months! This was based on reported exposure times and the presence of many individuals who had clinical signs but remained well otherwise. In the early years of the AIDS epidemic no information was available to absolutely confirm that the disease was caused by a virus. Many medical people, therefore, suggested that not all those infected would become ill and that a chronic carrier state might exist without deteriorating health. As time went on it became more apparent that many of those infected would eventually become ill and that the incubation time might indeed be more prolonged than first imagined. The corollary, of course, was that infection might have been first introduced at an earlier stage and that research should look further back in time for the cause of the spread of the virus.

Even in 1985, when many Scottish drug users were found to be positive, the expectations were that 5 per cent of all those infected would eventually contract AIDS and that the remainder might remain in some chronic infected but moderately fit state. The subsequent 3 years were to rapidly eradicate this line of thought and increasingly depressing reports at subsequent World AIDS Conferences (Paris 1986; Washington 1987; Stockholm 1988) indicated the likelihood of the large majority of those with HIV antibodies to progress eventually to full AIDS. By the end of 1989 the understanding of the long incubation time was convincingly demonstrated (Moss 1989) to be about 10 years. This has been further supported by a recent report of the progress of the San Francisco cohort which found the mean incubation period to be about 11 years. Nearly 20 per cent of this group are still well, however, and will continue to be under observation. Studies in haemophiliac cohorts have confirmed these findings although the passage of further time may even prolong this incubation time. Variations depending upon so-called 'cofactors' may lengthen or shorten incubation times in individuals and one important feature associated with length of time till the onset of symptomatic disease is the age at time of infection. Several studies may have indicated that those who become infected in older years may progress more quickly (Derby 1989; Witcomb 1990; Ronald *et al.* 1993).

This, therefore, makes clear many of the previous anomalies surrounding the natural cause of HIV infection. It also explains the slow emergence in some countries and indicates the difficulties in predicting the future. By the time cases of symptomatic AIDS come to the notice of clinicians the individual is likely to have been infected for up to 10 years and not only are the events of becoming infected obscured by time, but the possible transmission to subsequent drug using or sexual contacts may be enormous. Understanding this, therefore, is essential in order to contemplate the many routes the virus may have taken in the population both among drug users and sexual partners.

## Edinburgh and Dundee

This now familiar HIV epidemic which occurred some time in the early 1980s remains the single most important source of knowledge of HIV infection in drug users. The introduction and implementation of the antibody test in Scotland rapidly indicated the presence of substantial numbers of infected drug users (Brettle 1986; Robertson 1986). Case reports and positive tests throughout subsequent years accumulated some 1000 individuals including sexual contacts and children (France 1988; Mok 1988). Individual cohorts were found to be extensively penetrated (Skidmore 1990) some 65 per cent or more being positive, comparable only with a few similarly damaged European and New York groups (Des Jarlais 1987; WHO 1988). Testing of old stored samples revealed infection present as far back as 1983, but no further and the assumption is that HIV was introduced to this group at about that time. In order for spread to be so rapid certain conditions must have been present, including extensive needle and syringe sharing; accounts of drug use in these cities at that time is of a culture in which little care was taken to avoid the injections of blood from a previous user of the injecting equipment. Since that time, however, behaviour changes have been considerable resulting in a progressive deterioration in numbers of individuals sharing equipment and a rapid increase in availability of needles and syringes from legal sources (Bath 1988; Robertson 1988).

Although the extent of transmission is the distinguishing feature of the south-east Scotland epidemic, possibly more significant is the speed with which things happened. Within the space of 18 months or 2 years a substantial proportion of those injecting drugs had become infected and after this transmissions slowed down dramatically. This maybe due to several causes including the change in behaviour but at the present time few seropositive reports are due to needle and syringe sharing (Communicable Disease Unit, Scotland 1990) and the leading cause of infection has become heterosexual contact (Ronald *et al.*, 1993, and in press).

At the present time, several years after the first introduction of the virus in both Edinburgh and Dundee, cases of full-blown AIDS are now emerging rapidly. In addition many individuals are developing symptoms both physically and psychologically related to HIV infection and these issues are dominating the available services. The advance of treatment, particularly zidovudine and its use for prophylaxis as well as in advanced cases has become a major issue for all individual health workers who have patients with HIV infection. The availability of this and other prophylactic therapies has significantly affected the counselling of patients considering testing for antibodies. It is no longer possible to say that there is no available treatment and that testing might reasonably be delayed until the onset of symptoms. Treatment with early low dose zidovudine (250 mg twice a day) has the additional advantage of having less side-effects. The headache, nausea, and anaemia associated with larger doses in more advanced cases often reduced compliance or made it necessary to stop treatment. The domination of the drug using population by AIDS has had a profound impact on the provision of services and also on the drug scene in general.

## Anecdotal accounts of the introduction of the virus to the Edinburgh drug-using population

Although the detection of the mode of introduction of the HIV agent into any population has little practical value once it has happened, there are lessons which may prevent similar spread elsewhere. There is certainly an academic interest in tracing early cases as these may be of value in the virological techniques of identifying different strains of virus and mutations as infection is transmitted. There is also an epidemiological importance attached to any study of the rapid dissemination of the virus in any population.

Several accounts have emerged of drug users travelling and sharing equipment with contacts in southern European centres. The most clearly defined example illustrates an individual known to be an early positive in Edinburgh who had used extensively in a Spanish centre (Bisset 1989). Other studies include contacts with drug-using homosexual American servicemen in England and linkage by way of a drug-injecting man known to have haemophilia. Accounts of drug-using Americans in Scotland have been unsubstantiated but extensive links with Amsterdam and occasionally Dublin raise other possibilities. An itinerant Scot who spent several years in California, including a long prison sentence, before returning to injecting drug use in Edinburgh may be the introductory contact.

Many drug users who were actively injecting during the early 1980s (when HIV is known to have been introduced into this group) remain convinced that the mode of introduction was through sexual contacts with prostitutes working in the dock area of Edinburgh. Many of these young women were drug users and this is considered by some to be the most likely mode of introduction to the drug using sub-culture of Edinburgh. Clearly many prostitutes will have contacts with itinerants and overseas visitors and this certainly could be one explanation for the presence of HIV in Edinburgh. Links with Dundee were well established drug users visiting Dundee on a regular basis to obtain quantities of heroin, some injecting in Edinburgh, and some taking drugs home to be redistributed in that city. Of some interest and importance is the position of buprenorphine (Temgesic) as a drug of injection as this emerged rapidly as a popular drug of abuse during 1984 and 1985 when it became available in tablet form via general practitioners. Prior to that this drug had been used extensively in hospital practice as a drug of injection for pain killing, usually post-operatively. After the introduction as a tablet it rapidly became widely abused (Robertson 1986) and since then has enjoyed a position of some popularity amongst drug users throughout the UK. The significance of this drug is its comparitably short action when injected intravenously and the consequent excessive use in the course of a day. Thus drug users might inject up to ten times per day a drug which has a short action rather than the two or three injections usually used with heroin. The coincidence of an epidemic of Temgesic abuse round about the time of introduction of HIV is similar to the cocaine problems reported in the United States, especially New York, which were thought to account for the rapid spread of HIV in that city (Schoenbaum 1989).

Whatever the introductory event the graphic descriptions of injecting techniques in Edinburgh at that time go a long way to explaining why transmission occurred so completely and rapidly. The abrupt closure of the most important distributor of new sterile injecting equipment in September 1982 led almost immediately to an extensive needle and syringe sharing group (Henderson 1985; personal account of the Bread Street Shop 1980–82). Repeated accounts of groups using large 10 or 20 ml syringes are recorded (Robertson and Bucknall 1986). At these times a strong solution of heroin was mixed and drawn into a syringe, serial individuals would stick the needle into a vein, draw back blood to confirm that it was in the vein, inject 2–5 ml of solution and withdraw the needle. The syringe and needle, plus increasing mixtures of blood, would then be passed on to the next user. Many individuals clearly recall the presence of 20 or 30 individuals at such sessions. It is easy to imagine transmission occurring epidemically under these conditions. Evidence suggests that these patterns of drug use largely disappeared around 1985.

## Drug services, changing priorities

The statements of the 1986 Scottish Committee and the subsequent Advisory Council on the Misuse of Drugs (ACMD) Reports (McClelland

1986; Department of Health and Social Security 1988; ACMD 1989) to the effect that the prevention of AIDS was more important than the prevention of drug injecting to a certain extent set the scene for subsequent changes in available services. Whether or not this remedicalization of drug misuse stands the test of time remains to be seen but at a stroke the attitude of the establishment had changed. Over the next few years a dramatic growth of services targeted at implementing the new philosophy emerged. Needle exchange from clinics, general practice services, mobile units, and pharmacies became regular features and prescribing substitute drugs for those dependent was transformed from a shady pastime advocated by a few to a well-supported clinical priority led by physicians and psychiatrists. Educational campaigns both national and local prioritized drug users and latterly heterosexual partners as targets for safe drug use and safe sex campaigns. Widespread media coverage made AIDS a household issue and its association with intravenous drug use unquestioned.

The rapid spread of HIV in south-east Scotland was initially thought to presage similar discoveries in other UK cities and several attempts have been made to identify the scale of the problem in other regions. Surprisingly, no such problem has yet been found in any other centre including cities with a substantially larger drug misuse problem than either Edinburgh or Dundee. These include Glasgow, Liverpool, and London where studies have included a low seroprevalence for HIV antibodies among drug users (PHLS 1990; Communicable Disease Service Unit, Scotland 1990). Additional studies of pregnant women and new-born children may supply more information shortly and Medical Research Council studies of anonymous samples from various centres are currently under way. Looking further afield, however, it becomes apparent that many other centres with large long-established drug using subcultures have low or slowly rising rates of HIV infection. These include Amsterdam, California, and London (Bunning 1986; Watters 1988). Moreover, the global AIDS epidemic is dominated in pure numerical terms by heterosexual transmission, this population obviously being the biggest risk group of all. Sexual spread among men and women seems to emerge slowly after the introduction of the infection to a population reaching large numbers after sexual years (Ancelle 1990; Chin 1990).

## Managing drug users post-AIDS

In the new climate of post-AIDS awareness by both drug workers and drug users things may or may not have changed. Drug injecting clearly continues and abusers reported to the National Surveillance System increase year by year (Home Office 1990). Neither has needle sharing vanished despite the new availability of equipment (Stimson 1989). The initial emergence of new services in the late 1980s has clearly been a positive spin-off from knowledge of AIDS by the establishment but in areas outside those known to have large numbers of infected individuals this may not be sustained and in those areas with a lot of infected individuals new services tend understandably to be dominated by clinical AIDS issues. At the beginning of this chapter the characteristics of changes in drug policy were discussed and the tendency for a shift in policy and service provision to be followed by a gradual drift in policy and slackening in enthusiasm for support. The gradual withdrawal of funds often is the key determinant of the failure of projects to work or policies to be effective. The awareness of AIDS has been associated with rapid development of new services but the most important issue for the next decade is to sustain these services. For this reason it is crucial that service provisions are not fragmented and that overlap between agencies is minimal. Drug users with or without HIV infection require therapies of various types and this is merely complicated by the presence of HIV. HIV and AIDS are here to stay and have opened up new responsibilities for drug workers and medical staff. Because of the presence of HIV infection drug misuse has undoubtedly been taken more seriously than before. Perhaps this is because those infected by drug taking represent a bridge into the general population by way of heterosexual spread. It will certainly take many years or even decades to understand the full implications of HIV infection among drug users (Friedland 1987). Those workers familiar with the emerging problems of those infected in Scotland have no doubts about the seriousness of these possibilities and already understand the devastating effect HIV and AIDS have on individuals and families.

## Non-AIDS, HIV illness

Studies in New York City (Stoneburner 1988) have illustrated the non-opportunistic infections associated with HIV infections. It seems that prior to the onset of full-blown AIDS those individuals are susceptible to a range of infectious diseases and other conditions not necessarily related to advanced immune dysfunction. Bacterial pneumonia, meningitis, tuberculosis, and other infections may cause illness or sudden death. In addition the frequency of lethal overdose seems greater in those infected. Clearly this latter cause of death is possibly deliberate (suicide) but an increased susceptibility to overdose may arise from reduced respiratory function. Mortality and ongoing illness from many causes will obviously increase in the drug-using population infected with HIV.

The new European definition of AIDS (Ancelle-Park 1993) takes in some of these HIV-related illnesses and will increase the numbers included as advanced disease. This has some importance for epidemiologists and in natural history studies.

## Developing new services to manage HIV infection in drug users

Rapidly changing events have altered the philosophical basis of delivering services to drug users and have also altered those involved in these organizations. A return to a medical model of care has required that more physicians are now influential in providing hospital care especially for those with HIV infection. General practitioners and psychiatrists are similarly increasingly in contact with drug users and encouraged to provide appropriate levels of intervention. As well as these agencies there has been extensive growth in the non statutory sector and a new imperative for liaison between agencies.

These changes in perspective caused by HIV and the involvement of a wider range of medical professionals has had different effects in different regions of the UK. A return to the abstinence model of therapy has rather unfortunately dominated much of the recent discussion and in many major drug-using centres services are available on this basis only. Regrettably the wide range of necessary services advocated by many to supply the needs of continuing drug users and those who are not able to abstain are not available in many areas despite the presence of HIV infection and AIDS. The next few years are likely to see much jostling for position among agencies trying to secure continuing funding and all those interested need to ensure the development of all agencies. The non-statutory sector is particularly vulnerable and suffers most from the pressures and stresses of short-term funding.

All agencies now becoming familiar with HIV-infected and AIDS-suffering drug users are aware of the incredible range of problems which become regular features. Moreover the prospect of large numbers of symptomatic drug users living with AIDS for many years is to say the least intimidating for those planning such services.

## Acknowledgement

I would like to acknowledge help given by Dr Noel Gill (PHLS) in preparation of the surveillance data in this chapter.

## References

ACMD (Advisory Council on the Misuse of Drugs) (1988). *AIDS and drug misuse*, Part I. HMSO, London.
ACMD. (1989). *AIDS and drug misuse*, Part 2. Report by the Advisory Council on the Misuse of Drugs. HMSO, London.
Ancelle, J. (1990). All Party Parliamentary Committee Occasional Paper No 1. London.

Ancelle-Park, R. (1993). Expanded European AIDS case definition (letter). *Lancet*, **341**, 1440–1.

Angarano, G., Pastore, G., Monno, L., Santantonio, T., Luchena, N., and Schiraldi, O. (1985). Rapid spread of HTLVIII infection among drug addicts in Italy. *Lancet*, **ii**, 1302.

Bisset, C., Jones, G., Davidson, J., Cummins, B., Burns, S., Inglis, J. M., and Brettle, R. P. (1989). Mobility of injection drug users and transmission of HIV. *Lancet*, **ii**, 44.

Brettle, R. P., Bisset, K., Burns, S., Davidson, J., Davidson, S. J., and Gray, J. M. N. (1987). Human immunodeficiency virus and drug misuse: The Edinburgh Experience. *British Medical Journal*, **295**, 421–4.

Bunning, E. (1990). The role of harm reduction programmes in curbing the spread of HIV by drug injections. In *AIDS and drug misuse* (ed. G. Stimson and J. Strang), pp. 153–61. Routledge, London.

Carrick, P. (1989). AIDS: ethical, legal and public policy implications. In *The meaning of AIDS* (ed. E. T. Juengst and B. A. Koening), pp. 163–73. Praegar, New York.

Chin, J. (1990). All Party Committee on AIDS. Occasional Paper I. House of Commons.

Communicable Disease Surveillance Unit (Scotland). (1990). Monthly report. September Ruchill. Glasgow.

Des Jarlais, D. C. and Friedman, S. R. (1987). Editorial review: HIV infection among intravenous drug users: Epidemiology and risk reduction. *AIDS*, **1**, 67–76.

France, A. J., Skidmore, C. A., Robertson, J. R., Brettle, R. P., Roberts, J. J. K., Burns, S. M., *et al.* (1988). Heterosexual spread of HIV in Edinburgh. *British Medical Journal*, **296**, 526–9.

Friedland, G. H. and Klein, R. S. (1987). Transmission of the human immuno-deficiency virus. *New England Journal of Medicine*, **317**, 1125–35.

Home Office. (1990). *Statistics of the misuse of drugs: addicts notified to the Home Office, UK, 1989*. HMSO, London.

Jaffe, H. W., Bregman, D. J., Selik, R. M. (1983). Acquired immune deficiency syndrome in the United States: the first 1000 cases. *Journal of Infectious Diseases*, **148**, 339–45.

Lazzarin, A., Galli, M., Geroldi, D., Zanetti, A., Crocchiolo, P., and Aiuti, F. (1985). Epidemic of LAV/HTLVIII infection in drug addicts in Milan: Sero-logical survey and clinical follow-up. *Infection*, **13**, 5, 216–18.

McClelland, D. B. L. (1986). *HIV infection in Scotland*. Report of the Scottish Committee on HIV Infection and Intravenous Drug Use. SHHD, Edinburgh.

McCormick, A., Tillet, H., Banniseter, B., Emslie, J. (1987). Surveillance of AIDS in the United Kingdom. *British Medical Journal*, **295**, 1466–9.

Mok, Y. J. O., Hague, R. A., Yap, P. L., Hargreaves, F. D., Inglis, J. M., and Whitelaw, J. M. (1989). Vertical transmission of HIV: a prospective study. *Archives of Disease in Childhood*, **64**, 1140–5.

Morgan Thomas, R. (1990). AIDS risks, alcohol, drugs and the sex industry: a Scottish study. In *AIDS, drugs and prostitution* (ed. M. Plant), pp. 88–108. Routledge, London.

Moss, A. R., Bacchetti, P., Osmond, D., Krampf, W., Chaisson, R. E., and Stites, D. (1988). Seropositivity for HIV and the development of AIDS or AIDS related condition: three year follow up of the San Francisco General Hospital cohort. *British Medical Journal*, **296**, 745–50.

Peutherer, J. F., Edmond, E., Simmonds, P., Dickson, J. D., and Bath, G. (1985). HTLV-III antibody in Edinburgh drug addicts. *Lancet*, **ii**, 1129–30.

PHLS (1990). AIDS Centre. Quarterly unpublished reports. No. 8. September. Colindale, London.

Robertson, J. R. and Skidmore, C. A. (1989). *AIDS in the family*. Report to SHHD, Edinburgh.

Robertson, J. R. and Bucknall, A. B. V. (1986). *Heroin users in a Scottish city*. SHHD, Edinburgh.

Robertson, J. R. (1985). Drug users in general practice. *British Medical Journal*, **290**, 34–5.

Robertson, J. R., Bucknall, A. B. V., Welsby, P. D., Roberts, J. J. K., Inglis, J. M., and Brettle, R. P. (1986). Epidemic of AIDS related virus (HTLV-III/LAV infection among intravenous drug abusers. *British Medical Journal*, **292**, 527–9.

Ronald, P. J. M., Robertson, J. R., and Elton, R. A. Continued drug use and other cofactors for progression to AIDS among injecting drug users. *AIDS*. (In press.)

Ronald, P. J. M., Robertson, J. R. Wyld, R., and Wrightman, R. (1993). Heterosexual transmission of HIV in injecting drug users. *British Medical Journal*, **307**, 1184–5.

Rutherford, G. W., Lifson, A. R., Hessol, N. A. Darrow, W. W., O'Malley, P. M. Buckbinder, S. P., *et al.* (1990). Course of HIV-1 infection in a cohort of homosexual and bisexual men: an 11 year follow up study. *British Medical Journal*, **301**, 1183–8.

Shiltz, R. (1987). *And the band played on*. Penguin. London.

Skidmore, C. A., Robertson, J. R., Elton, R. A. (1990). After the epidemic: follow up study of HIV seroprevalence and changing patterns of drug use. *British Medical Journal*, **300**, 219–23.

Stoneburner, R. L., Des Jarlais, D. C., Benezra, D., Gorelkin, L., Southern, J. L., Friedman, S. R., *et al.* (1988). A larger spectrum of severe HIV-1 related disease in intravenous drug users in New York City. *Science*, **242**, 916–19.

Stimson, G. V., Alldrit, L., Dolan, K. (1988). Syringe exchange schemes for drug users in England and Scotland. *British Medical Journal*, **296**, 1717–19.

Watters, J. K., Case, P., Huang, Cheng, Y. T., Lorvick, J., and Carlson, J. (1988). *HIV seropositivity and behavioural changes in intravenous drug users*. Poster at IVth International Conference on AIDS, June 1988, Stockholm.

Witcomb, J. C., Skidmore, C. A., Roberts, J. J. K., and Elton, R. A. (1990). Progression to AIDS in intravenous drug users, cofactors and survival. IVth International AIDS Conference, San Francisco.

# 8. Local and regional variations in drug misuse: the British heroin epidemic of the 1980s

*Geoffrey Pearson and Mark Gilman*

In the course of the transformation of Britain's drug problems as a result of the 1980s heroin epidemic, it has become clear that in spite of a substantial overall increase in the number of problem drug users, this is not truly a 'national' problem. Rather, in many respects it is better understood as a series of local and regional difficulties. The scale of heroin misuse has not only remained highly scattered and localized, but the pattern of use is also subject to local and regional variation—for example, whether the drug is smoked or injected as the dominant method of administration (Pearson *et al.* 1986; Pearson 1987*a*). The aim of this chapter is both to review some aspects of this diversity, and to attempt an understanding of its nature and its practical consequences.

Although heroin has been the substance which has justifiably attracted most concern in the 1980s, other forms of drug misuse are known in lesser or greater degrees in different parts of Britain. At the time of writing, for example, there is currently a sharp divergence between the local picture about cocaine and what is revealed by national indicators such as drug seizures. At the national level, reflecting the more general experience in Europe, there have been substantial increases in the bulk quantity of cocaine seizures by the police and customs in the late 1980s (National Drugs Intelligence Unit 1989). In spite of this, the use of cocaine and its 'crack' derivative are still relatively uncommon in most areas of Britain. There are nevertheless local pockets of concern, including parts of inner London. Research in south London has confirmed a modest increase in cocaine misuse among drug users known to agencies, including the use of smokeable cocaine. It is still rare to encounter drug users for whom cocaine is the primary drug, however, and it is mainly found within a pattern of polydrug use where heroin or another opiate is the main drug used (Strang *et al.* 1990; Mirza *et al.* 1991; Pearson *et al.* 1993).

In terms of stimulant use, there is every indication that amphetamines remain the market-leader in Britain, although again there are significant regional variations in local drug preferences. In a national survey of clients attending syringe-exchange schemes overall 79 per cent were using heroin and other opiates with only 15 per cent using amphetamine as the primary drug injected. However, in Portsmouth as many as 67 per cent were primarily amphetamine users, with 42 per cent in Carlisle and 37 per cent in Bristol (Monitoring Research Group 1988).

A further indication of this kind of diversity is that in other regions, most notably in parts Scotland, heroin misuse has given way in the course of the 1980s to Temgesic (buprenorphine) and temazepam as the primary substances of misuse (Morrison 1988 Sakol *et al.* 1989). Even so, the monitoring of two syringe-exchange schemes in the Ruchill and Easterhouse areas of Glasgow has revealed significant local differences between them in terms of the predominance of Temgesic, heroin, and other opiates (Gruer *et al.* 1990).

Our attention had first been drawn to the geographical diversity in drug misuse in the context of research for the Health Education Council on the emerging heroin epidemic in the north of England during the mid-1980s (Pearson *et al.* 1985, 1986). By way of introduction, the following are some initial indications of what this amounted to.

## Heroin use in the north of England: an initial outline

In the broadest terms, at this point in the development of the heroin epidemic, there were sharp regional differences to be found to the east and west of the Pennines, the so-called 'backbone' of England. Heroin misuse was not only found to be a much more serious difficulty to the west of the Pennines, but there were also many local variations; so that even within a city such as Manchester where there was a serious problem developing, it would be found in some neighbourhoods and not others.

One significant observation, subsequently confirmed by other research, is that the problem of heroin misuse came to settle with exceptional severity in neighbourhoods suffering from high levels of unemployment, housing decay, and other forms of social deprivation (Pearson *et al.* 1986; Pearson 1987*b*; Fazey 1987; Parker *et al.* 1988; Giggs *et al.* 1989; Fazey *et al.* 1990; Mirza *et al.* 1991). This 'urban clustering' effect will be discussed in detail at a later point.

These diverse patterns of drug use were also overlaid by other variations, principally in terms of whether heroin was smoked or injected. The heroin epidemic of the 1980s was indelibly associated with 'chasing the dragon'. Even so, there were some areas of the north of England where self-injection was the dominant mode of use (Pearson *et al.* 1986; Pearson, 1987*a*). In a novel policy context which dictates that the attempt to reduce the risks of human immunodeficiency virus (HIV) infection should be a central aim of drug services, the route of administration has become a major preoccupation [Advisory Council on the Misuse of Drugs (ACMD) 1988, 1989]. Accordingly, some observations on local and regional variations in injecting practices are in the final section of this chapter.

There were also dense folds of complexity of a more idiosyncratic nature revealed by our research in the mid-1980s. For example, in south Yorkshire to the east of the Pennines, it was reported that the use of pharmaceutical opiates accounted for approximately one-half of known heroin use, whereas in other areas it was illicitly imported 'street' heroin which predominated. In other localities, the opioid Diconal (a mixture of dipipanone and cyclizine) had become a preference drug, and in some areas this has continued to have important implications for the subsequent development of patterns of drug misuse in the form of the illicit use of travel-sickness preparations containing cyclizine (the non-opiate constituent of Diconal) (Gilman 1988*a*; Gilman *et al.* 1990).

We had been drawn to these sometimes fine-grained variations in the emerging problem of heroin misuse in the north of England because of their implications for effective health education. The government had embarked in 1985 on a series of high-profile mass media campaigns, and it was not always clear from research that these nationally conceived campaigns were relevant to the actually existing needs of drug users and their families at a local level (cf. Power 1989*b*). A recurring problem for health education is how to communicate with multiple audiences: for example, existing drug users who are already committed to their drug use and lifestyle, experimental users where the level of commitment is not so high and where informational needs are different, and not-yet-users. Geographical diversity in the heroin problem added yet one further level of complexity to this already complex picture.

## Drugs in space and time: patterns of dispersal

Having sketched in some of the issues which were forced upon our attention in the mid-1980s, we can begin to unpack what influences might have shaped these local and regional variations. The development of drug epidemics is, perhaps, invariably of an uneven nature. The experience of the north of England in the 1980s was, therefore, by no means exceptional. It merely reproduced what is more generally known about the geographical dispersal and patterning of drug problems.

Geographical patterns such as these result from the ways in which drug use and drug problems unevenly penetrate different regions and localities (Pearson 1991). Three levels of analysis can be distinguished, each with its own implications for drug control policies. Drawing upon earlier research these will be described as 'macro-diffusion', 'urban clustering', and 'micro-diffusion'.

At the broadest level, processes of 'macro-diffusion' can be identified which involve the diffusion of drug practices across time and between different regions. This process was well exemplified by the work of Hunt and Chambers (1976) which examined the North American heroin epidemics from the mid-1960s to the mid-1970s. In their study the geographical distance between towns and cities, together with the ease of communication routes between regions, proved to be a major determinant of the macro-diffusion of drug habits.

In the mid-1980s there were still widespread discrepancies in the known levels of drug misuse between the major US cities (National Institute on Drug Abuse 1987). When these variations are analysed by different substances—heroin, cocaine and PCP—the discrepancies are even more marked, with a city such as Washington showing unusually high levels of PCP use (Reuter *et al.* 1988). The east–west Pennine divide, which has already been mentioned, in the north of England is in all probability a consequence of macro-diffusion processes such as these.

At the other end of the spectrum, 'micro-diffusion' is the means by which drugs and drug practices move within friendship networks within a locality. People are invariably first introduced to drug practices by friends, rather than by 'pushers' (Hughes and Crawford 1972; Pearson 1987*a*). The spread of drug habits at this level will be encouraged or inhibited, not by environmental factors such as geographical distance and terrain, but by local subcultural preferences. Our own research in the north of England indicated that in some areas when heroin first became available in cheap and plentiful supply, although there might have been a certain degree of experimentation it did not always catch on (Pearson *et al.* 1986). In one locality, for example, a group of friends who had an established pattern of recreational drug use involving cannabis and hallucinogens found that heroin was 'too heavy a stone'. As such, it could not be accommodated within their recreational lifestyle and experimentation quickly ceased. Elsewhere, heroin was experienced as a drug which added a new edge and excitement to already existing lifestyles and was embraced as a preference drug.

A third level of analysis falls between 'macro-diffusion' and 'micro-diffusion', reflecting the ways in which some neighbourhoods (and not others) become the sites of concentration of drug problems in any given town or city. As already indicated, these will invariably be areas of high social deprivation. This is perhaps the most complex level of analysis, and involves social processes such as the mechanism of the housing market, the workings of the 'irregular economy' and the exchange of illicit goods and services, and lifestyles associated with long-term unemployment. These will be discussed in some detail in the next section.

These three levels of analysis whereby drug habits are established and generate distinct local and regional profiles—macro-diffusion, micro-diffusion and urban clustering—are not always entirely separate. In a case study from the 1960s, de Alarcon (1969) indicated the ways in which a friendship network assisted in the macro-diffusion process of heroin from London to the south coast towns of Brighton and Worthing. Under other circumstances, the process of macro-diffusion might reflect no more than the slow and seemingly haphazard drift of drug habits along communication routes. It might also be the result of a planned criminal conspiracy to introduce a drug into a region and to establish new distribution networks. Or, it could be the consequence of population movements—such as those of migrant workers who carry established patterns of drug use with them into areas where these are not yet known.

These varying mechanisms of drug diffusion have different implications for policy formulation and practical interventions. At the level of macro-diffusion, the primary intervention strategy will be that of law enforcement and drugs intelligence. In terms of micro-diffusion, on the other hand, as recognized by Moore (1977) it is extremely difficult (if at all possible) to police friendship networks. The key interventions at this level of concern will therefore involve attempts to influence drug choices and local drug cultures, through health education and health promotion strategies which are closely attuned to local circumstances, both as a generalized attempt at drug prevention and to reduce drug-related harm.

The intermediate level, which we have called 'urban clustering', must be placed within a much wider array of possible social and economic policies. These will include local authority housing allocation policies and general economic policy bearing upon the availability of affordable housing, together with local access to jobs and training. In order to explain these connections, together with the implications of 'urban clustering' for low-level enforcement strategies, we will need to expand the discussion on drugs and deprivation.

## Urban clustering: drugs, deprivation, and housing areas

The central aim in this section is to review both the evidence for the 'urban clustering' of drugs problems, and the range of mechanisms which result in the tendency for problems of drug misuse to be most heavily concentrated in areas of high social deprivation.

In North America, probably the first clear indication of this trend is to be found in a surprisingly neglected work of the Chicago School of Sociology in the inter-war years. In this study of the social ecology of opium addiction in Chicago, Dai (1937) found the problem to be densely concentrated in the city's inner zone, which was characterized by cheap rented accommodation, and also experienced high levels of delinquency, mental disorder, tuberculosis, suicide, and prostitution.

This tendency for drug misuse to be most serious in areas of multiple deprivation has subsequently been noted on many occasions in the post-war years, both in Britain and the USA. In the 1950s, Chein *et al.* (1964) in their study of narcotics and delinquency noted the concentration of these difficulties in New York's ghetto areas of socio-economic deprivation. These impressions were later confirmed for New York by Preble and Casey (1969) employing ethnographic research methods, and by Hughes (1977) and his colleagues who employed a combination of epidemiological and ethnographic methods in order to trace the onset and development of local outbreaks of heroin misuse in Chicago between 1967 and 1971. Although many areas of Chicago were touched by the late 1960s heroin epidemics, Hughes (1977, p. 75) concluded that 'the largest outbreaks occurred in economically disadvantaged communities'. Research of a different kind in Baltimore, involving an area analysis of ecological correlations, indicated the same clustering effect of levels of drug misuse, extreme deprivation and other social problems (Nurco 1972; Nurco *et al.* 1984). In the 1980s east and central Harlem continued to be the areas of New York City in which heroin problems were experienced with exceptional severity (Johnson *et al.* 1985), and the crack epidemic also came to be deeply associated with areas of urban decay and no-hope unemployment (Bourgois 1989; Williams 1989).

In the course of the 1980s, research has come to identify a similar picture to this in Britain. The first indications of a connection between increasing heroin use and levels of unemployment emerged in the mid-1980s. In her prevalence study of Glasgow, Haw (1985, p. 53) found that 'the majority of identified opiate users come from the poorer areas of the city'. A tendency for heroin misuse to be concentrated in socially deprived neighbourhoods was also found in research in the north of England (Pearson *et al.* 1986), while Peck and Plant (1986) established a correlation between unemployment and drug misuse in a study of national trends. These indications were powerfully reinforced by prevalence estimates of drug misuse in the Wirral peninsula of Merseyside (Parker *et al.* 1988) and in the city of Nottingham (Giggs *et al.* 1989). In Liverpool, a study of patients attending a drug dependency clinic established the same link between heroin use and areas of high unemployment by using newly developed techniques of geo-demographic analysis (Fazey *et al.* 1990). In the Lewisham area of south London, a survey of problem drug users known to a variety of agencies also found a growing concentration of heroin users in the poorest areas of the borough (Mirza *et al.* 1991).

Having briefly set out the evidence, how can these urban clustering effects be explained? It is certainly not the intention to advance an argument which relies upon a mechanical relationship whereby it is assumed that 'unemployment causes heroin use' (Pearson 1987*b*). This is inadequate on a number of grounds, not least that one also finds heroin misuse in the social orbit of wealthy pop stars and other members of the 'jet set'. The question which has to be addressed is not so much causal, as ecological; namely, what social forces conspire to gather together problems of heroin misuse in neighbourhoods which are already experiencing multiple social difficulties?

In approaching this question it is also necessary to guard against the so-called 'ecological fallacy' in area analysis; whereby one cannot reliably infer from established correlations at area level to the characteristics of individuals living in that area. For example, the fact that heroin use is concentrated in areas of high unemployment does not necessarily mean that individual heroin users are unemployed. In the Heroin Lifestyle Study, conducted among black men in the ghetto areas of different US cities, a surprising proportion of daily heroin users were found to be working in conventional, low-paid jobs (Hanson *et al.* 1985). Another interesting example of the ecological fallacy emerged from the Drug Information Project in south London where serious drug misuse was found to be heavily concentrated in those parts of the Borough of Lewisham which are not only the poorest, but also where Lewisham's black community lives (Mirza *et al.* 1991; Pearson *et al.* 1993). However, this did not mean that Lewisham's drug problem was a black person's problem. On the contrary, it was white heroin users living in these areas of urban deprivation which produced this potentially misleading statistical effect.

The most convenient way of approaching the urban clustering of drug problems is through the legacy of the Chicago School of Sociology. As already indicated, this programme of research in the 1920s and 1930s demonstrated that multiple social problems were densely concentrated in an inner-city transitional zone of delapidated housing and poverty. In addition to Dai's (1937) little known study of opium addiction, the celebrated work of Shaw and McKay (1942) found the highest levels of crime and delinquency in these same areas, while Faris and Dunham (1939) revealed a tendency for rates of schizophrenia to be highest in the transitional zone of the city.

In attempting to explain why high rates of mental disorder come to be associated with urban deprivation, two opposing lines of argument are commonly advanced. The first is essentially a causal argument, suggesting that the poverty and social disorganization of the 'transitional zone' had a disorienting effect on people who lived there which resulted in high levels of crime and deviance. The second, which is usually known as a 'drift' argument, suggests that the mentally ill and others were attracted to the inner-city transitional zone because it offered both affordable housing and a social milieu more tolerant of 'deviant' lifestyles. It can be noted in passing that a directly similar set of controversies — counter-posing 'causal' arguments to those of 'drift'—came to surround the interpretation of the major epidemiological study by Hollingshead and Redlich (1958), *Social class and mental illness*, which found that the highest rates of schizophrenia were among the poorest sections of the community in Social Class V, a controversy which has not been settled to everyone's satisfaction.

There is also a substantial body of research on 'criminal areas', flowing from the work of the Chicago School, which raises similar conceptual issues (Brantingham and Brantingham 1984). The link between high-crime areas and social deprivation is also clearly established by this research tradition. Most recently, in the British Crime Survey conducted by the Home Office Research and Planning Unit, the highest levels of victimization are found to be in the poorest neighbourhoods of our cities (Hough and Mayhew 1985).

In attempting to understand how high-crime areas are generated, forms of argument which resemble those of 'cause' as against 'drift' are again juxtaposed. Does poverty lead to 'social disorganization' which results in high crime rates? Or do poor neighbourhoods offer increased opportunities for crime, in whatever way, and thus attract higher levels of victimization? In order to simplify a complex argument, the most promising line of development is provided by recent research on the role of the housing market in shaping local variations in the crime rate (Bottoms and Wiles 1986; Bottoms *et al.* 1989). The outcomes of this research reflect the fact that when an area begins to develop a reputation as an undesirable neighbourhood or 'problem estate', people are unprepared to settle there unless they have the most urgent and pressing housing needs; for example, the poor, the homeless, single-parent households, discharged mental patients, and other groups who are marginal to the housing market (Reynolds 1986; Dear and Wolch 1987). It is in this way that the so-called 'problem estate' gathers together multiple social difficulties—including high rates of crime and drug misuse. Because where drug users are concerned, they also encounter a variety of social difficulties including housing problems.

The mechanism of the housing market is therefore a central means by which the phenomenon we have called 'urban clustering' is set in motion, resulting in pockets of drug misuse which then come to interact with the interlocking problems of socially deprived neighbourhoods. It is generally acknowledged, for example, that in areas of high unemployment where young people are denied legitimate opportunities to fashion meaningful identities, then other means of demonstrating status and achievement evolve. These include delinquency, gang fighting, and drug misuse (Feldman 1968). Drug epidemics can develop rapidly under such circumstances, as drug habits spread by a process of micro-diffusion through friendship networks. Equally, poor neighbourhoods generate a sustained economic demand for low-cost stolen goods, so that there is often a flourishing 'irregular economy' of illicit goods and services—perks, fiddles, favours, and 'knock-off' (Johnson *et al.* 1985). The 'irregular economy' thus acts as a further means by which residents in these neighbourhoods become familiar with the availability of drugs, since illicit drugs function as one commodity amongst many within the irregular economy (Auld *et al.* 1986; Burr 1987). Where a local demand for drugs has become established in these ways, there are tangible economic incentives for the establishment of drug dealing networks (Reuter *et al.* 1990). As Williams and Kornblum (1985, p. 59) note, in their study of young people's lives in poverty-stricken neighbourhoods of North American cities, 'the time-honoured drive to "get ahead" explains why the underground economy tend to flourish in direct proportion to decreases in regular employment opportunities and public spending for education, employment, and training'.

The 'urban clustering' effect, hereby drug problems come to be concentrated in poor neighbourhoods, can thus considerably amplify the difficulties already experienced by local residents. In Britain little attention has been paid to how drug misuse impacts on 'hard-to-let' housing estates, or the kinds of intervention strategies which might be relevant. On the more general issue of crime prevention, however, a number of possible lines of action have been recommended and implemented with varying degrees of success (Bright and Petterson 1984; Bottoms and Wiles 1986; Power 1989*a*). These include attention to housing allocation policies, environmental improvement schemes, decentralized systems of housing management, local employment initiatives, improved youth facilities, and community-oriented beat policing. The involvement of residents' organizations in initiatives such as these would appear to be essential to their success, although this is not always easy to achieve since there is considerable scope for a variety of conflicts of interest (Blagg *et al.* 1988; Sampson *et al.* 1988; Pearson *et al.* 1991).

Where drug problems are concerned, there is an urgent need to learn from the successes and failures of community-based crime prevention initiatives, and to adapt them accordingly. One additional requirement will be the development of low-threshold drug services which are more easily accessible to local people. Health education strategies also need to be closely attuned to local circumstances and local difficulties, including a sensitivity to the sometimes idiosyncratic nature of local drug subcultures (Gilman 1988*a*,*b*; Gilman *et al.* 1990). There is also a vital role for the police in developing effective low-level enforcement strategies which can provide a measure of protection and reduce the considerable harm to the wider community which can result from local drug epidemics

(Pearson 1991*a,b*; Gilman and Pearson 1991). The essential point about 'urban clustering' effects is that they involve the possibilities of significant social damage being inflicted upon already vulnerable working class communities.

## Sharing works: local and regional variations in injecting practices

The recognition that high-risk practices such as the sharing of injecting equipment by intravenous drug users might accelerate HIV transmission has had profound implications for drug control policy and service delivery (ACMD 1988, 1989; Strang and Stimson 1990; Plant 1990). This is, once more, a difficulty which exhibits many local and regional variations, both in terms of injecting practices and rates of HIV infection. This final section will sketch out some of this evidence.

Levels of known HIV infection among injecting drug users in the British Isles show marked regional variations. In England, almost two-thirds of known cases are to be found in the greater London area. Moreover, as many as 30 per cent of all English reports come from the single regional health authority area of North West Thames. The most marked regional variation, however, is that between Scotland and the rest of the United Kingdom. Of all HIV antibody positive reports in the United Kingdom among injecting drug users to the end of 1990, 44 per cent were to be found in Scotland (Table 8.1). On this basis, greater London accounts for approximately one-third of reports of HIV infection in the entire United Kingdom. By contrast, less than 1 per cent of such reports came from the Merseyside region.

Attempting to translate the established parameters of the problem into rates of HIV infection among intravenous drug users in different regions is a somewhat risky enterprise. Nevertheless, it is clear that there are considerable local, regional, and national variations in the known level of HIV infection among drug using populations, and in high risk practices (Stimson 1990). Where Britain is concerned, pronounced regional differences quickly appeared between Scotland and rest of the United Kingdom. In Edinburgh, rates of HIV infection in excess of 50 per cent had already been noted among intravenous drug users by the mid-1980s (Brettle *et al.* 1986; Robertson *et al.* 1986). By contrast, HIV infection was estimated at less than 5 per cent in Glasgow (Follett *et al.* 1986). Summarizing the position in its report on *HIV infection in Scotland*, the Scottish Home and Health Department (1986, p. 6) noted that the Scottish situation was 'markedly different' from that in England and Wales where only 11 per cent of HIV antibody tests for injecting drug users were positive. Moreover, in some areas of north-west England where the 1980s heroin epidemic had been exceptionally severe, it was reported that HIV infection

**Table 8.1**  Geographical distribution of HIV-1 antibody positive reports. Risk exposure category: injecting drug use

|  | Number | Percentage |
|---|---|---|
| United Kingdom total | 2179 | |
| Scotland | 952 | 44 |
| England | 1213 | 56 |
| Wales | 8 | |
| Northern Ireland | 6 | |
| Selected English regions | | |
| NW Thames | 361 | 17 |
| NE Thames | 179 | 8 |
| SE Thames | 192 | 9 |
| SW Thames | 35 | 2 |
| 'All London' | 767 | 35 |
| Mersey | 16 | 1 |
| North West | 69 | 3 |
| Rest of England | 361 | 17 |

Source: *Communicable Disease Report*, (1991) **1**, (6).

rates were approximating to zero. Understandably, claims have also been advanced that the extremely low levels of HIV infection in the Merseyside region are a direct consequence of the vigorous programme of harm-reduction which has been promoted in that part of the north of England (Newcombe 1989; Drugs and HIV Monitoring Unit 1990). But one obvious question is whether this might be a consequence of the marked preference in many areas of the north-west of England for 'chasing the dragon'—that is smoking, rather than injecting, the drug (and possible consequences on such injecting as does occur).

As already indicated, the 1980s heroin epidemic in the north of England involved many twists and turns, in terms of local and regional variations in the severity of the problem. Prior to the early 1980s heroin had been almost entirely unknown in many of the towns and cities where dense urban clusters of heroin misuse were to become established in the course of the epidemic. One major aspect of this local diversity was whether heroin was smoked rather than injected (Pearson *et al.* 1986; Pearson 1987*a*). In some localities, there was considerable hostility to the idea of injecting heroin. In others, it was injected from the first moment that it made its appearance.

These local differences can be largely explained according to whether or not an injecting drug subculture had already been in existence prior to the arrival of heroin in cheap and plentiful supply in the early 1980s. Where an intravenous drug-using culture had existed, previously organized around amphetamine use or various forms of polydrug use, injection emerged as the dominant preference among local heroin users. Where it did not, 'chasing' as the preferred method.

Even so, injecting practices were not unknown in those localities where 'chasing' was the dominant pursuit. Heroin smokers would sometimes experiment with self-injection, if only out of curiosity—a high-risk practice given that occasional injectors would be less likely to possess their own injecting equipment, and consequently more likely to share needles and syringes. There is also evidence of a drift towards self-injection in areas such as these. In the Wirral peninsula of Merseyside, whereas 80 per cent of known heroin users reported that they preferred to smoke heroin in 1985, this figure had fallen to 59 per cent by 1987 (Chadwick and Parker 1988, p. 12).

In spite of these worrying trends, on the basis of what is known about the injecting practices of notified problem drug users there are still substantial regional and local variations between different regions of England (see Tables 8.2 and 8.3). Where new notifications are concerned, the proportion of drug users who inject varies between 39 per cent in the Mersey Regional Health Authority and 80 per cent in Oxford, Yorkshire, and East Anglia (Table 8.2). The national average is 64 per cent of newly notified addicts and 69 per cent of re-notifications.

Regional statistics conceal even more localized variations in injecting practices. Within the Mersey region, for example, injecting rates vary

**Table 8.2** Percentage of notified drug users in England injecting and total number of notifications by Regional Health Authority, 1988 (rank order by percentage injecting)

|  | First notifications | Re-notifications |
|---|---|---|
| England | 64% (*n* = 4734) | 69% (*n* = 6847) |
| Yorkshire | 80% (182) | 81% (207) |
| East Anglia | 80% (117) | 77% (209) |
| Oxford | 80% (72) | 69% (133) |
| South Western | 79% (182) | 71% (286) |
| Northern | 79% (100) | 77% (142) |
| NW Thames | 72% (757) | 75% (1114) |
| SW Thames | 71% (253) | 75% (430) |
| W Midlands | 71% (170) | 66% (261) |
| Trent | 69% (71) | 54% (146) |
| Wessex | 67% (163) | 61% (208) |
| NE Thames | 66% (753) | 72% (1249) |
| SE Thames | 64% (552) | 81% (741) |
| North Western | 59% (576) | 58% (778) |
| Mersey | 39% (785) | 52% (957) |

*Source:* Department of Health (1989).

**Table 8.3** Percentage of notified drug users injecting by District Health Authority in the Mersey region 1988

| | First notifications | | | Re-notifications | | |
|---|---|---|---|---|---|---|
| | All methods | No injecting | % Injecting | All methods | No injecting | % Injecting |
| Mersey | 786 | 249 | 39 | 957 | 400 | 52 |
| Chester | 102 | 36 | 37 | 126 | 53 | 46 |
| Crewe | 2 | 0 | 0 | 4 | 1 | 33 |
| Halton | 15 | 5 | 36 | 55 | 28 | 52 |
| Liverpool | 259 | 87 | 40 | 273 | 124 | 55 |
| Macclesfield | 20 | 12 | 63 | 32 | 15 | 56 |
| Southport | 7 | 1 | 20 | 20 | 5 | 56 |
| S. Sefton | 91 | 22 | 34 | 65 | 15 | 29 |
| St Helens | 44 | 12 | 32 | 41 | 14 | 56 |
| Warrington | 109 | 45 | 52 | 165 | 107 | 72 |
| Wirral | 137 | 28 | 30 | 176 | 38 | 35 |

*Note:* The percent injecting figures do not equate to the 'all methods' numbers as notifications where the method of drug taking was unspecified or the notification was on old style forms are excluded from the base when calculating the per cent injecting.

*Source:* Department of Health (1989).

from 30 per cent of new notifications in the Wirral District Health Authority to 63 per cent in Macclesfield, and 72 per cent of re-notifications in Warrington (Table 8.3).

A number of tentative conclusions can be drawn from statistics of this kind. If we set to one side the experience of London with its quite unique history of drug misuse, then outside of Scotland the major impact of the heroin epidemic was in the Merseyside and Manchester regions of the north-west of England. These are also the regions of England where the overall proportion of drug users who inject remains the lowest. This confirms both that the heroin epidemic of the 1980s was a regional phenomenon, and that it was most highly developed in areas where 'chasing' was the preferred method of heroin use. Because of the large number of drug users in the north-west of England, however, and in spite of lower injection rates in this area, roughly one-half of all known injecting drug users in England living outside of London are to be found in the north-west—a formidable concentration of potential HIV risk.

The more localized variations in injecting rates among notified addicts are less easy to interpret with confidence. Undoubtedly, low rates such as those in the Wirral peninsula reflect the legacy of the 'chasing' epidemic. Equally, the high percentage of drug injectors in Macclesfield reflects the prior existence of a persistent local intravenous drug using subculture. At other times, however, high local rates of injecting among notified drug users might indicate that specialist services are locally available which cater for intravenous drug users, resulting in a 'magnet' effect: this could be what produces the unusually high rate of injecting among re-notified addicts in Warrington. Close attention to the specific circumstances of drug-using networks is an essential requirement of the highly localized nature of drug problems.

More generally, local and regional variations such as these indicate that if the effort to reduce the risks of HIV infection is to have any chance of success, the analysis of epidemiological trends must be supplemented with ethnographic research on local patterns of drug misuse and the social meanings which are attached to the practice of sharing injecting equipment (Feldman and Biernacki 1988 ; Wiebel 1988; McKeganey 1989, McKeganey and Barnard 1992). The likelihood that drug users will share needles and syringes is not solely dictated by the local availability or non-availability of sterile injecting equipment. The practice of sharing can also be a means by which drug users express a sense of fellowship and communal solidarity (McKeganey 1989).

Other little-understood cultural factors might sometimes be at work in influencing injecting practices. There is scattered evidence that black people in Britain are less likely to inject drugs (Strang *et al.* 1990; Mirza *et al.* 1991; Pearson *et al.* 1993). In Chicago and other North American

**Table 8.4** Characteristics of populations known to be HIV positive: Scotland and the rest of the UK

|                               | Scotland | Rest of UK |
|-------------------------------|----------|------------|
| Homosexual and bisexual males | 14.9%    | 51.8%      |
| Haemophiliacs                 | 5.4%     | 15.2%      |
| IVDUs                         | 57.3%    | 7.3%       |
| Male : female ratio           | 2.5 : 1  | 15.0 : 1   |

Source: Scottish Home and Health Department (1988).

cities, there are considerable variations in the likelihood that drug users will engage in high-risk practices between different ethnic groups such as white people, African-Americans and Latinos (Wiebel, 1989).

One central aspect of the future research agenda must be to identify and clarify both the potentially health promoting and potentially damaging aspects of local drug subcultures. These provide the difficulties with which we must contend, and the bedrock on which to build, effective health education and harm-reduction strategies.

# References

ACMD (Advisory Council on the misuse of Drugs) (1988). *AIDS and drug misuse, Part 1*. HMSO, London.

ACMD (1989). *AIDS and drug misuse, Part 2*. HMSO, London.

Auld, J., Dorn, N., and South, N. (1986). Irregular work, irregular pleasures: heroin in the 1980s. In *Confronting crime* (ed. R. Matthews and J. Young). Sage, London.

Blagg, H., Pearson G., Sampson, A., Smith, D., and Stubbs, P. (1988). Inter-agency cooperation: rhetoric and reality. In *Communities and crime reduction* (ed. T. Hope and M. Shaw), pp. 204–20. HMSO, London.

Bottoms, A. E., and Wiles, P. (1986). Housing tenure and residential community crime careers in Britain. In *Communities and crime, Crime and justice: a review of research*, Vol. 8 (ed. A. J. Reiss Jnr. and M. Tonry), pp. 101–62. University of Chicago Press, Chicago.

Bottoms, A. E., Mawby, R. J., and Xanthos, P. (1989). A tale of two estates. In *Crime and the city: Essays in the memory of John Barron Mays* (ed. D. Downes), pp. 36–87. Macmillan, London.

Bourgois, P. (1989). Crack in Spanish Harlem: culture and economy in the inner city. *Anthropology Today*, **5**, (4), pp. 6–11.

Brantingham, P. and P. Brantingham, (1984) *Patterns in crime*. Macmillan, New York.

Brettle, R. P., Davidson, J., Davidson, S. J., Gray, J. M. N., Inglis, J. M., Conn, J. S. (1986). HTLV-III antibodies in an Edinburgh clinic. *Lancet*, **i**, 1099.

Bright, J. and Petterson, G. (1984). *The safe neighbourhoods unit*. NACRO, London.

Burr, A. (1987). Chasing the dragon: heroin misuse, delinquency and crime in the context of south London culture. *British Journal of Criminology*, **27**, 333–57.

Chadwick, C. and Parker, H. (1988). *Wirral's enduring heroin problem: the prevalence, incidence and the characteristics of drug use in Wirral 1984–1987.* University of Liverpool, Liverpool.

Chein, I., Gerard, D., Lee, R., and Rosenfeld, E. (1964). *The road to H: narcotics, delinquency and social policy.* Tavistock, London.

Dai, B. (1937). *Opium addiction in Chicago.* University of Chicago Press, Chicago. Reprint edn., (1970). Patterson Smith, Montclair, NJ.

de Alarcon, R. (1969). The spread of heroin abuse in a community. *Bulletin on narcotics,* **21** (3), 17–22.

Dear, M. and Wolch, J. (1987). *Landscapes of despair: from deinstitutionalisation to homelessness.* Polity Press, Cambridge.

Department of Health (1989). *Data from the addicts index, January to December 1988.* Department of Health, London.

Drugs and HIV Monitoring Unit (1990). HIV infection among drug injectors in England: regional comparisons drawn from official statistics. *International Journal on Drug Policy*, **1**, 14–15.

Faris, R. E. L. and Dunham, H. W. (1939). *Mental disorders in urban areas.* University of Chicago Press, Chicago.

Fazey, C. (1987). *The evaluation of Liverpool drug dependency clinic: the first two years 1985 to 1987.* Mersey Health Authority, Liverpool.

Fazey, C., Brown, P., and Batey, P. (1990). *A socio-demographic analysis of patients attending a drug dependency clinic.* University of Liverpool, Centre for Urban Studies, Liverpool.

Feldman, H. W. (1968). Ideological supports to becoming and remaining a heroin user. *Journal of Health and Social Behaviour* **9**, 131–9.

Feldman, H. W. and Biernacki, P. (1988). The ethnography of needle sharing among intravenous drug users and implications for public policies and intervention strategies. In *Needle sharing among intravenous drug abusers: national and international perspectives.* NIDA Research Monograph 80, (ed. R. J. Battjes and R. W. Pickens), pp. 28–39. NIDA, Rockville.

Follett, E. A. C., McIntyre, A., O'Donnell, B., Clements, G. B., and Deffelberger, U. (1986). HTLV-III antibody in drug abusers in the west of Scotland: the Edinburgh connection. *Lancet*, **i**, 446.

Giggs, J., Bean, P., Waynes, D., and Wilkinson, C. (1989). Class A drug users: prevalence characteristics in greater Nottingham. *British Journal of Addiction*, **84**, 1473–80.

Gilman, M. (1988*a*). DIY Diconal?. *Mersey Drugs Journal*, **1** (5), 15.

Gilman, M. (1988*b*). Comics as a strategy in reducing drug related harm. In *Drug question: research register*, issue 4, (ed. N. Dorn, L. Lucas and N. South), pp. 125–32. ISDD, London.

Gilman, M. and Pearson, G. (1991). Lifestyles and law enforcement. In *Policing and prescribing: the British system of drug control* (ed. P. Bean and D. K. Whynes). Macmillan, London.

Gilman, M., Traynor, P., and Pearson, G. (1990). The limits of intervention: cyclizine misuse. *Druglink*, **5**, (3), 12–13.

Gruer, L., Ditton, J., Nair, G., Madigan, C. W., and Hartless, J. M. (1990). *An analysis of the demographic characteristics and frequency of clinic attendance* by all clients of the Ruchill and Easterhouse syringe exchanges up to January 1990. START (Substance treatment Agency Reporting Team), Glasgow.

Hanson, B., Beschner, G., Walters, J. M., and Bovelle, E. (1985). *Life with heroin: voices from the inner city*. Lexington Books, Lexington, Mass.

Haw, S. (1985). *Drug problems in Greater Glasgow*. SCODA, London.

Hollingshead, A. B. and Redlich, F. C. (1958). *Social class and mental illness*. Wiley, New York.

Hough, M. and Mayhew, P. (1985). *Taking account of crime: key findings from the 1984 British crime survey*, Home Office Research no. 85. HMSO, London.

Hughes, P. H. (1977). *Behind the wall of respect: community experiments in heroin addiction control*. University of Chicago Press, Chicago.

Hughes, P. H. and Crawford, G. A. (1972). A contagious disease model for researching and intervening in heroin epidemics. *Archives of General Psychiatry*, **27**, 189–205.

Hunt, L. G. and Chambers, C. D. (1976). *The heroin epidemics: a study of heroin use in the United States 1965–75*. Spectrum Books, New York.

Johnson, B. D., Goldstein, P. J., Preble, E., Schmeidler, J., Lipton, D. S., Spunt, B., and Miller, T. (1985). *Taking care of business: the economics of crime by heroin abusers*. Lexington Books, Lexington, Mass.

McKeganey, N. (1989). Drug abuse in the community: needle-sharing and the risk of HIV infection. In *Readings in medical sociology* (ed. S. Cunningham-Birley and N. McKeganey), pp. 113–37. Routledge, London.

McKeganey, N. and Barnard, M. (1992). *AIDS, drugs and sexual risk*. Open University Press, Buckingham.

Mirza, H. S., Pearson, G., and Phillips, S. (1991). *Drugs, people and services in Lewisham: final report of the Drug Information Project*. Goldsmiths' College, University of London, London.

Monitoring Research Group (1988). *Injecting equipment exchange schemes: final report*. Goldsmiths' College, University of London, London.

Moore, M. H. (1977). *Buy and bust: the effective regulation of an illicit market in heroin*. Lexington Books, Lexington, Mass.

Morrison, V. L. (1988). Drug misuse and concern about HIV infection in Edinburgh: an interim report. In *Drug questions: an annual research register* (ed. N. Dorn, L. Lucas, and N. South), pp. 111–16, issue 4. Institute for the Study of Drug Dependence, London.

National Drugs Intelligence Unit (1989). *Drug seizure statistics 1989*. New Scotland Yard, London.

National Institute on Drugs Abuse (1987). *Data from the Drug Abuse Warning Network: annual data 1986*, NIDA Statistical Series I, no. 6. NIDA, Rockville, MD.

Newcombe, R. (1989). Preventing the spread of HIV infection. *International Journal on Drug Policy*, **1** (2), 20–27.

Nurco, D. N. (1972). An ecological analysis of narcotic addicts in Baltimore. *International Journal of the Addiction*, **7**, 341–53.

Nurco, D. N., Shaffer, J. W., and Cisin, I. H. (1984). An ecological analysis of the interrelationships among drug abuse and other indices of social pathology. *International Journal of the Addiction*, **19**, 441–51.

Parker, H., Bakx, K., and Newcombe, R. (1988). *Living with heroin: the impact of a drugs 'epidemic' on an English community*, Open University Press, Milton Keynes.

Pearson, G. (1987a). *The new heroin users*. Blackwell, Oxford.

Pearson, G. (1987b). Social deprivation, unemployment and patterns of heroin use. In *A land fit for heroin? Drug policies, prevention and practice* (ed. N. Dorn and N. South). Macmillan, London.

Pearson, G. (1991). The local nature of drug problems. In *Drug misuse in local communities: perspectives across Europe* (ed. T. Bennett), pp. 67–79. The Police Foundation, London.

Pearson, G. (1992). Drugs and criminal justice: a harm reduction perspective. In *The reduction of drug-related harm* (ed. P. O'Hare, R. Newcombe, A. Matthews, E. Buning, and E. Drucker), pp. 15–29. Routledge, London.

Pearson, G., Gilman, M., and McIver, S. (1985). Heroin use in the north of England. *Health Education Journal*, **45**, 186–9.

Pearson, G., Gilman, M., and McIver, S. (1986). *Young people and heroin: an examination of heroin use in the north of England*. Health Education Council, London and Gower, Aldershot.

Pearson, G., Blagg, H., Smith, D., Sampson, A., and Stubbs, P. (1992). Crime, community and conflict: the multi-agency approach. In *Unravelling criminal justice: Eleven British studies* (ed. D. Downes), pp. 46–72. Routledge, London.

Pearson, G., Mirza, H. S., and Phillips, S. (1993). Cocaine in context: Findings from a South London inner-city drug survey. In *Cocaine and crack: supply and use* (ed. P. Bean). Macmillan, London.

Peck, D. F. and Plant, M. A. (1986). Unemployment and illegal drug use: concordant evidence from a prospective study and national trends. *British Medical Journal*, **293**, 929–32.

Plant, M. A. (ed.) (1990). *AIDS, drugs and prostitution*. Routledge, London.

Power, A. (1989a). Housing, community and crime. In *Crime and the city: essays in the memory of John Barron Mays* (ed. D. Downes), pp. 206–35. Macmillan, London.

Power, R. (1989b). Drugs and the media: prevention campaigns and television. In *Drugs and British society* (ed. S. MacGregor), pp. 129–42. Routledge, London.

Preble, E. and Casey, J. J. (1969). Taking care of business: the heroin user's life on the street. *International Journal of the Addiction*, **4**, 1–24.

Reuter, P., Haaga, J., Murphy, P., and Praskac, A. (1988). *Drug use and drug programmes in the Washington Metropolitan Area*. RAND Corporation, Santa Monica, CA.

Reuter, P., MacCoun, R., and Murphy, P. (1990). *Money from crime: a study of the economics of drug dealing in Washington, DC*. RAND Corporation, Santa Monica, CA.

Reynolds, F. (1986). *The problem housing estate*. Gower, Aldershot.

Robertson, J. R., Bucknall, A. B. V., Welsby, P. D., Roberts, J. J. K., Inglis, J. M., Peutherer, J. F., and Brettle, R. P. (1986). Epidemic of AIDS related virus (HTLV III/LAV) infection among intravenous drug abusers. *British Medical Journal*, **292**, 527–9.

Sakol, M. S., Stark, C., and Sykes, R. (1989). Buprenorphine and temazepam abuse by drug takers in Glasgow: an increase. *British Journal of Addiction*, **84**, 439–41.

Sampson, A., Stubbs, P., Smith, D., Pearson, G., and Blagg, H. (1988). Crime, localities and the multi-agency approach. *British Journal of Criminology*, **28**, 478–93.

Shaw, C. R. and McKay, H. D. (1942). *Juvenile delinquency and urban areas.* University of Chicago Press, Chicago.

Scottish Home and Health Department (1986). *HIV infection in Scotland: report of the Scottish Committee on HIV Infection an Intravenous Drug Misuse.* Scottish Home and Health Department, Edinburgh.

Scottish Home and Health Department (1988). *Health in Scotland 1987.* HMSO, Edinburgh.

Stimson, G. V. (1990). Research on behavioural change by drug users with regard to HIV infection. Paper presented to the conference on 'Assessing AIDS Prevention', Montreux, Switzerland, October 1990.

Strang, J. and Stimson, G. V. (ed.) (1990). *AIDS and drug misuse.* Routledge, London.

Strang, J., Griffiths, P., and Gossop, M. (1990). Crack and cocaine use in south London drug addicts, 1987–1989. *British Journal of Addiction*, **85**, 193–6.

Wiebel, W. W. (1988). Combining ethnographic and epidemiological methods in targetted AIDS interventions: the Chicago model. In *Needle sharing among intravenous drug abusers: national and international perspectives* (ed. R. J. Battjes and R. W. Pickens), pp. 137–50. NIDA Research Monograph 80. NIDA, Rockville, MD.

Williams, T. (1989). *The cocaine kids: the inside story of a teenage drug ring.* Addison-Wesley, New York.

Williams, T. and Kornblum, W. (1985). *Growing up poor.* Lexington Books, Lexington, Mass.

# 9. Chasing the dragon: the development of heroin smoking in the United Kingdom

*Paul Griffiths, Michael Gossop, and John Strang*

## Chasing the dragon

The image of heroin is inextricably linked in most people's minds with the paraphernalia of injection. Syringes, tourniquets, and spoons have become symbolic representations of not only heroin use but drug use *per se*. Even in some academic publications, authors have not bothered to specify the route of administration of their heroin using samples, merely referring to 'heroin addicts', confident that their audience will know that they are alluding to the injection of heroin.

At times (in the UK at least) the link between drug and route has been very close. In the 1960s all (or nearly all) heroin users in the UK used their drug by injection. In a study of opiate addicts attending a London clinic in a 12 month period between 1968 and 1969, Gardner and Connell (1971) noted that all of their patients had started their heroin use by injecting. Today, if we consider heroin use on a global scale, some form of smoking technology is likely to be the dominant technology of intoxication, with probably millions of individuals (world-wide) using heroin by such a method. In India and Pakistan, for example, it is the predominant method of drug administration for many hundreds of thousands of heroin addicts (Gossop 1989).

Patterns of heroin use have proved surprisingly fluid over time. Prior to 1979 the majority of heroin users in London first used heroin by injection, and once daily use had begun this would be almost exclusively by injecting. However, during the 1980s this changed and by the end of the 1980s almost all heroin users first took the drug by chasing the dragon (Strang *et al*. 1992*a*). Some of these subsequently moved on to intravenous patterns of use whilst others continued to use chasing as the exclusive or usual route (Griffiths *et al*. 1994).

With current concerns regarding the human immunodeficiency virus (HIV) and hepatitis infections, the *route* by which people use their drugs is now of enhanced importance. Chasing the dragon may not be risk free but it does not carry the same risks of viral transmission as injection. To tell the story of the rise in popularity of chasing the dragon, from an uncommon practice, to the dominant way in which new users are recruited into heroin use, we must turn our attention to a myriad of themes; our particular dragon has not one but many tails, and like the columns of smoke to which the original analogy refers, such themes rapidly dissipate, forming a mist of factors that allows us no simple explanation of causation.

## The history

The importance of route of administration had been noted by Wood in 1931, who argued that unlike morphine which is usually administered by a hypodermic needle, heroin can be sniffed into the system. This was an important factor in increasing its potential for abuse, as at first many people would otherwise be 'repelled by the use of a hypodermic needle' (Woods 1931, p. 14).

The growth of heroin smoking during the late 1970s and throughout the 1980s, in the UK, was not the first time the use of heroin by this method had achieved popularity. From the 1920s onwards heroin smoking had been common in Hong Kong. Many of the themes evident in the development of patterns of heroin use in the UK are also common to a consideration of the evolution of a smoking culture, some half a century earlier, in the Far East. In both cases there existed a drug-taking culture which was socialized to find smoking an 'acceptable' technology of intoxication with cultural pressures inhibiting the attractions of intravenous use. Heroin supplies were increasingly plentiful, the price was relatively low, and the product was sold in preparations which could be smoked. When heroin smoking first appeared it was seen by many commentators, in both periods, as relatively benign.

An article entitled 'The mysterious heroin pills for smoking' (Anonymous 1953) reported the introduction of 'red pills' or 'heroin pills' to the Far East. These pills contained other drugs in addition to heroin — such as caffeine, a cinchona alkaloid, strychnine, and aspirin or salicylic acid. Interestingly, this new drug, in a new form, was seen as a suitable treatment for those addicted to opium. The *North China Daily News* (Shanghai) claimed in 1925 that 5000 ounces of strychnine and 2000 pounds of caffeine were being imported into China each month for the manufacture of these heroin 'anti-opium' pills. Although taken orally at first, a smoking culture developed rapidly. The pills were smoked by the use of a small porcelain vase, into which a bamboo tube had been inserted; a small hole being drilled in the vase to hold the pill.

Once heroin smoking had become established by the smoking of pills (initially marketed as an oral medicine), the way was paved for more potent heroin preparations to enter the market. This happened rapidly and other heroin preparations superseded these 'heroin pills', which gradually declined in popularity, as had opium smoking. With these new preparations came new technologies of intoxication. A report in 1958 (Anonymous: The smoking of heroin in Hong Kong), examined the meaning of the now widely known expression 'chasing the dragon', stating that Hong Kong addicts tended to be 'shy of the needle'. The heroin employed in this new technique was cheap, crudely prepared, and 'unfit' for injection. It was reported that the majority of Hong Kong addicts could not afford high grade heroin. This smoking heroin was supplied with a base powder known as 'daai fan'. Generally, this was one of the barbiturates designed to increase or prolong the effects of the drug and aid sublimation.

The phrase 'chasing the dragon' is a translation of the Cantonese *chui lung*. The heroin and the base powder (*daai fan*) were placed about half an inch apart on a creased piece of tin foil. The base powder was then heated until it liquefied and ran, mixing at this stage with the heroin, the tin foil being tilted back and forth, whilst the flame was applied directly under the crease. The smoker would then chase the smoky tail of the liquid with a tube of some sort as it ran across the tin foil. The report noted that this 'simple' method of consuming heroin dispenses with pipes and other paraphernalia normally used in smoking opium or heroin pills.

Mo and Way (1966) noted that as well as chasing the dragon, other smoking technologies were being employed in Hong Kong at this time. For example, a lighted cigarette would be dipped into powdered heroin hydrochloride, and to stop the powder falling off the cigarette it would be smoked with the head tilted backwards; this procedure was called 'ack ack' or 'firing the aircraft gun'. It was argued that this was a less efficient method than chasing the dragon, and most users would move on to chasing in time. Intravenous patterns of heroin use had been established by 1950s in the Far East. Mo and Way (1966, p. 143) report that developing tolerance would eventually lead many heroin chasers to an intravenous habit. This was not inevitable however, as 'many addicts have been satisfied with chasing the dragon for years without any need to resort to heroin intravenously.[1]

## The market

### Early reports of heroin smoking in the UK

Prior to the late 1970s heroin smoking in the UK may have been an unusual practice, but it was not unheard of. Where communities did

---

[1] For the reader who is interested in colourful colloquialisms; if a match box was used to replace the pipe for inhaling the fumes when chasing; this procedure was called 'playing the mouth organ'.

exist who used heroin by this method, they tended to be ethnic minority populations, often with associations with the Far East. Amongst older London heroin addicts, many anecdotal accounts exist of heroin smoking in the China Town area of London. Steve, a 49-year-old Londoner who had been using heroin since 1962, was asked when he first heard about chasing the dragon:

Way back in the 70's down Gerrard street when the Chinese were dealing in pure heroin, they would say 'I smoke it' ... the heroin was always down Gerrard street, it had always been there from the early 50's, but we didn't know about it because we were getting our heroin from the doctors, although there was always the odd addict who would chase when he couldn't get a syringe. At 3 o'clock in the morning he might have to score. He might be standing in Gerrard street, sick as a dog, when a China man comes by saying 'want packet want packet', at that time in the morning can't get a syringe, so he'd get a piece of foil and chase, but the Chinese showed them how to do it.

Another example of an ethnic minority group maintaining a distinct pattern of use is the Surinamese in the Netherlands, who have maintained a heroin smoking (and more recently cocaine smoking) culture, despite widespread intravenous use among heroin users in Holland. Grund *et al.* (1991) reported how this custom grew out of their association with Chinese dealers. The process was facilitated by a strong cultural interdiction against intravenous use in Surinamese society, amongst whose members there was that is a taboo against the penetration of the body by foreign objects. Later this group has become a role model for non-ethnic minority Dutch heroin smokers.

## Diversity in the market-place

Preparations of 'Heroin Number 3' (also known as 'Chinese heroin', 'Brown sugar' and 'Hong Kong rocks'), began to appear in the Chinatown distinct of London from about 1968. Prior to this time almost all illicit heroin in the UK was pharmaceutical heroin, which had either been stolen or diverted from prescriptions. The supplies of diverted opiates began to dry up in the late 1960s and early 1970s, demand for heroin dramatically increased, and an illicit market in imported heroin became established. Heroin 'Number 3' was one of the first products in this new market-place and generally consisted of 30–40 per cent heroin hydrochloride, 40–60 per cent caffeine and small amounts of strychnine (Huizer 1987). Only occasionally did this type of heroin include free base (O'Neil *et al.* 1985).

This was increasingly replaced in the mid 1970s with South-east Asian 'Number 4' heroin (often known as Thai heroin). This was purer, more expensive and more favoured for injection (the heroin being present as heroin hydrochloride). In the mid-1970s almost all the heroin used by heroin injectors, who made up the bulk of the illicit heroin market, was of this type (H. Steed personal communication 1990). Customs seizures were predominantly of this South-east Asian heroin during this period and of high strength. It became the preferred and most common form of heroin available on the illicit market up until the period between 1977 and 1979 when supplies began to decline.

Clarke (1980) reported that since about 1975 a dark brown form of 'smoking' heroin was available in small amounts within Iranian student circles. Lewis (1989) cited 1978 to 1979 as the 'Watershed year', when Iranian heroin began to flood the British market. It was believed at the time that the political changes occurring in, what was then Persia, had resulted in many wealthy Iranians seeking some way of moving their capital out of the country. One relatively easy and profitable way to do this was in the form of heroin. Whether this was the case or not, Iranian heroin appeared in large quantities at this time in the UK market. In real terms prices fell by as much as 25 per cent between 1980 and 1983. This drop in price was not accompanied by any decrease in purity, which remained relatively high. In the 1980s South-west Asia continued to dominate the market with Iranian heroin subsequently being replaced by Turkish production and, by 1982, Pakistan had become the major supplier for the UK market.

To some extent the chemical nature of heroin seizures is determined by country of origin. Iranian and Pakistani heroin is characterized by a crude separation of morphine prior to acetylation. Samples are likely to consist of heroin in base form (for further discussion of the significance of heroin in base form, see later section on pharmacology). Between October 1978 and October 1982, all but one of the Iranian heroin seizures made by officers of Her Majesty's Customs and Excise were of heroin base; with purity ranging from 14 to 83 per cent (mean 79) (O'Neil *et al.* 1984). A number of these samples additionally contained caffeine. Heroin in this form would be particularly suitable for smoking, but not well suited for injection. It is interesting to note that Pakistani samples seized early in this period were likely to be heroin hydrochloride. This rapidly changed and the bulk of later seizures were of heroin base, these later samples being chemically indistinguishable from Iranian heroin.

South-east Asian heroin was still available during this period but was more expensive. Lewis (1989) reported how 'dark brown smoking heroin although often containing a high opiate content was crudely refined. Such heroin often caused problems when prepared for injection.' South-east Asian heroin, such as Number 4 (or Thai), however, attracted high prices, its similarity to high grade pharmaceutical heroin during the early 1980s made it suitable for injection. Heroin samples from South-east Asia, such as Chinese Number 4 and Indian samples, were likely to consist of morphine that had been more rigorously purified prior to acetylation. They were usually of high purity with heroin present as heroin hydrochloride. (Heroin as free base was found in only two samples of all customs seizures from India and South-east Asia during the period October 1978 and October 1982; O'Neil *et al*. 1984.) In 1981 Thai heroin was retailing at as much as £120 a gram compared with £70 or £80 pounds a gram for Iranian heroin. This economical, relatively strong and plentiful heroin may not have been to the taste of long term heroin injectors but to the growing army of new heroin chasers it seemed ideal.

## The pharmacology

The development of heroin smoking cultures is facilitated by the existence of pre-existing drug taking patterns which find the smoking of sub-stances a more socially acceptable behaviour than its injection. In addition, it is also necessary that the drug in question must be available in a form which can be smoked. Not only must it be smokeable, it should also be smoking efficient. That is, the individual can obtain the desired narcotic effect, for a price which is within his or her means. To explore the implications of this axiom, we must delve a little deeper into the pharmacological properties of the drug heroin itself, or to be more precise, into the pharmacology of heroin preparations.

Mick, who is in treatment for heroin addiction in London recalls that he first tried heroin in the early 1970s, by smoking the contents of a dry ampoule of heroin hydrochloride (unpublished ethnographic notes, Drug Transitions Study, London). The ampoule was purchased with the intention of injecting it, but at the last minute he had 'chickened out' and instead emptied the contents into a cigarette. This smoking resulted in no noticeable 'high' and on subsequent occasions, disappointed by his previous experience, he moved on to establish an injecting pattern of use. It may seem strange, that the pharmaceutically pure heroin in a freeze-dried ampoule had so little potency when smoked. The reason for this is due to the differing properties of different heroin compounds and preparations on heating and subsequent decomposition.

Chasing the dragon is not a simple or easy technology to master. As with injection the neophyte will have to be taught how to take his or her drugs; usually this is by instruction from an experienced user (cf. Becker 1963). The novice chaser is often the receiver of the smoke from heroin which is being heated and held by someone else, and in this respect is analogous to the first time injector receiving the injection from an experienced user. Heroin decomposes rapidly if overheated. The distance between the heat source and the foil is therefore con-stantly adjusted to produce the required temperature for a controlled sublimation. At the same time, the individual will have to chase the elusive column of vapours, constantly inhaling. Any mistake in this procedure, which is carried out under varying levels of intoxication, is likely to lead to much of the 'precious' mixture literarily going up in smoke.

All heroin mixtures can, to a certain extent, be smoked or (chased). Indeed Battersby *et al.* (1990) have even reported on a case of smoking ampoules of pharmaceutical heroin by chasing the dragon. However, the suitability of heroin mixtures for smoking varies according to the amount of heroin which becomes available to the user. As a result, the actual 'purity' of a particular sample may not match the individual's subjective experience of how 'good' it is. The form of the heroin (base or salt) and the presence of other chemicals is important. Some additives such as caffeine or barbiturate will increase the amount of heroin available to be inhaled. Other additives, such as noscapine and procaine hydrochloride, reduce heroin recovery rates. It is interesting to note that both caffeine and barbiturates were added to smoking heroin in the Far East, caffeine was added to smoking pills and the base powder *daai fan* used in chasing was a barbiturate.

A sample of 100 per cent heroin base, and one of 100 per cent heroin hydrochloride (the commonest salt of heroin), could both correctly be referred to as 'pure heroin'. However, they would not be equally suitable for injection or smoking. Drugs, such as heroin, can exist in two forms, as a base and as a salt. In both cases the core part of the drug is pharmacologically identical, as are its effects. However, the salt dissolves in water and has a high melting point; as a result the chemical is likely to decompose rather than become volatile on heating. The base chemical on the other hand is fat soluble. It does not dissolve in water and is not suitable for injection in the base form. It is more volatile, and on heating, the chemical tends to form a vapour rather than decomposing. The heroin base requires a chemical transformation, commonly involving the addition of an acid such as lemon juice or acetic acid, to transform it into heroin salt, before it can be dissolved and injected. (Base + acid = salt + water). The heroin salt, on the other hand, is likely to decompose on heating, therefore rendering it inefficient for smoking.

Huizer (1987) reported recovery rates on heating samples of heroin and heroin mixtures. These varied from only 17 per cent for pure heroin hydrochloride to nearly 80 per cent for a one to one base heroin and caffeine mixture. In general, heroin base produces a recovery rate three to four times better than that found with heroin hydrochloride.

Table 9.1 shows the varying recovery rates for different preparations of heroin (Huizer 1988). An example of the interplay of factors here is the case of 'heroin number 3', which is commonly regarded as suitable for smoking. The heroin is usually present as a salt in this product; however, the mixture also usually contains caffeine and strychnine. Both

**Table 9.1** Heroin recovery rates after chasing the dragon

| Compound | Recovery (%) |
|---|---|
| Heroin hydrochloride | 17 |
| Heroin hydrochloride + caffeine (1 + 1) | 36 |
| Heroin hydrochloride + caffeine (1 + 4) | 51 |
| Heroin hydrochloride + barbital (1 + 1) | 33 |
| Heroin hydrochloride + procaine hydrochloride (1 + 1) | 12 |
| Heroin (base) | 62 |
| Heroin (base) + caffeine (1 + 1) | 76 |

*Source:* Huizer (1988).

of these substances increase the amount of heroin which becomes available to the user on heating rendering this product smoking efficient.

Thus, for a heroin smoking culture to develop, one or more of the following factors are likely to apply:

(1) the heroin must be of relatively high purity (and/or);

(2) It must be present in base form (and/or);

(3) other chemicals must be present in the sample that allow it to volatize easily.

The best smoking heroin may have all of these characteristics. Arguably, the efficiency of injection as a technology of intoxication means that drug injectors are less likely to be influenced (or deterred) by the chemical composition of heroin preparations. On the other hand, heroin smoking cultures may be more dependent on the availability of smoking efficient products. Des Jarlais *et al*. (1991) has suggested that this may explain the failure of a smoking culture to develop in the USA where heroin is usually at such low purity at street level that it is considered 'not worth' smoking. The average retail purity of heroin, at street level, was about 4 per cent, in 1981, in America, as compared to between 40 and 50 per cent in the same year in the UK (Gossop 1982; Anonymous 1984).

## Analysis of the heroin 'epidemic' in the 1980s

The massive escalation in heroin use which occurred over the first half of the eighties cannot be attributed solely to the arrival of this new heroin preparation in the UK. Nor can the relatively small numbers of culturally isolated intravenous heroin addicts, who filled the clinics in 1968, be seen as the forerunners of the new wave of heroin chasers. Rather we must turn our attention to the development of a far larger polydrug using culture which grew up during the 1970s. Mass illicit drug use became increasingly common as the 1970s progressed. Cannabis was the mainstay of this emerging culture, but the casual use of a range of other drugs, such as amphetamines, cocaine, and LSD, was also common. Despite this pattern of polydrug use, strong cultural breaks continued to exist preventing individuals moving into injecting drug use.

## The significance of an established smoking culture

Throughout the 1970s broader and more culturally diverse groups of individuals began experimenting with drugs; the smoking of cannabis became as common on building sites as it was in college rooms. Drug use became dissociated from any particular subcultural identity and became associated with youth culture in general. With the arrival of large quantities of cheap pure and smokable heroin, many of the negative social connotations of the drug were removed in a period characterized for many by mass unemployment and social alienation.

The absence of injecting paraphernalia made chasing the dragon an apparently 'safe' and familiar mode of administration for these new users. '... Compared to injecting, it doesn't feel addictive, it's clean, easy. You can use it occasionally, keep clean and have a nice trouble free time. In fact, after you first use, particularly if you don't inject it, you'll probably wonder what all the fuss was about'. (O'Bryan 1989). The ease with which this new drug use settled into existing cultural patterns was echoed by Stewart (1987, p. 19) talking about his own experiences of heroin addiction 'Tubes and foil are passed from user to user in the way joints used to be passed around by Hippies. Everyone gets in on the act and feels they are having a good time'. *Time Out*, the London listing magazine, published in 1980 a report on this new drug use commenting 'At the margins of the leisure drug market — particularly where dealers have got used to handling a range of drugs and consumers accustomed to using them — people are now experimenting with heroin who wouldn't have dreamed of doing so even a year ago' (Clark 1980, pp. 8–9).

This smoking 'craze' did not immediately spread to all parts of the UK. Some areas, such as Edinburgh, have maintained an almost exclusively injecting subculture. It is unclear what factors are responsible for this. Some authors have suggested that the existence of an established injecting culture for other drugs, such as amphetamines, encouraged new heroin users to adopt this route with heroin (Pearson 1987a; Power 1990).

## Other influences

Pearson (1987b) has suggested that 'there is an important and significant relationship between the problem of mass unemployment and Britain's

new heroin problem'. Auld *et al.* (1986) have also suggested that the
new heroin users are more culturally diverse and include more women
than has previously been the case. To some extent, heroin in the early
1980s had become another commodity in an 'irregular economy' characterized by 'illegal patterns of thieving, dealing and exchange involving
a variety of commodities and centred primarily on streets and housing
estates'. (Auld *et al.* 1986, p. 172).

Auld *et al.* (1986) argued that the combination of an increase in
supply of heroin, and fall in relative cost, taken together with a new,
and widely acceptable mode of administration (chasing) facilitated the
development of casual and episodic patterns of use. This change in
pattern of use has been accompanied by a change in scale. The increase
in numbers of heroin users has been balanced somewhat by a decrease
in the likely harm accruing to them by adopting an episodic, non-injecting
mode of use, or in their own words ... 'Britain has acquired rather
more of a slightly less bad thing' (p. 176).

## Rather more of a less bad thing?

As the decade went on this 'less bad thing' began to look less benign.
Many 'episodic' users developed daily habits and began to approach
treatment agencies. It is unclear what proportion of heroin smokers
did, and indeed do, retain unproblematic episodic patterns of use though
levels of dependence reported by heroin chasers have been found to be
significantly lower than those for heroin injectors (Gossop *et al.* 1992).
However, as the second half of the decade approached, agencies began
to come into contact, in increasing numbers, with these 'new users'.
Parker *et al.* (1987) documenting the heroin 'epidemic' that occurred
on the Wirral, Merseyside, described predominantly young, family-based,
unemployed, and socially deprived users with a strong preference for
smoking heroin. The rate of heroin use on the Wirral was reported to
be 4.4 per 1000. Individuals were starting the habit between 16 and
18 years, and finding their way into treatment services after smoking
heroin for about 1–3 years. The area had an unemployment rate of
20 per cent, unemployment amongst heroin users was 86.5 per cent. In
south London, Gossop *et al.* (1988) reported that 43 per cent of the
clients attending a community drug team were primarily using their heroin
by chasing the dragon. The chasers were younger than injectors and
had started using heroin earlier. Again patterns of use were daily and
dependent, rather than episodic.

More worrying still, some chasers have moved to injection as a route
of administration. This may have been only as an occasional practice
for some, but others moved on to an exclusively intravenous mode of
use (Griffiths *et al.* 1992). With the advent of HIV infection in the
1980s and the large numbers of drug takers who injected drugs at least

occasionally, it might be suggested that by the end of the decade, Britain had in fact ended up acquiring rather more of a much worse thing.

## Conclusion

The development of a heroin-chasing culture in the UK has profoundly influenced the drug taking culture(s) we find ourselves facing today. Issues surrounding HIV and hepatitis infections direct attention to the way in which people take their drugs as much as, or perhaps even more than the type of drugs that they are taking. Further study is required of the influence of the differing cultural attachments to differing routes of use and the different health care implications of differing technologies of drug administration. Interventions, at all levels, must take into account the likely consequences for established patterns of use. It is encouraging that patterns of drug use have been found to be changeable. Although transitions between chasing and injection are more common, many individuals have also been able to move away from injecting to chasing (Strang *et al.* 1992*b*). The encouragement of such transitions for individuals and for drug taking subcultures should be seen as a worthy aim for today's harm reduction policies and treatment services.

## References

Anonymous (1953). The mysterious heroin pills for smoking. *Bulletin of Narcotics*, April-June, 49–54.

Anonymous (1958). Chasing the dragon. The smoking of heroin in Hong Kong. *Bulletin of Narcotics*, **10**, (3).

Anonymous (1984). Narcotics intelligence estimate. The supply of illicit drugs to the United States from foreign and domestic sources in 1984 (with near term projections). The National Narcotics Intelligence Consumers Committee, Washington.

Auld, J., Dorn, N., and South, N. (1986). Irregular work, irregular pleasures: Heroin in the 1980's. *Confronting crime*, pp. 166–87. Sage, London.

Battersby, M., Farell, M., and Strang S. (1990). Pharmaceutical heroin and chasing the dragon. *British Medical Addiction*, **85**, 151.

Becker, H. S. (1963). *Outsiders: Studies in the sociology of deviance*. The Free Press, New York.

Charman, P. (1984). Frontlines junk city. *Time Out*, 22–28 March, 8–9.

Clark, D. (1980). Smack in the Capital. *Time Out*, 15 February, 11–13.

Des Jarlais, D., Courtwright, D., and Joseph, H. (1991). The transition from opium smoking to heroin injection in the United States. *AIDS and Public Policy Journal*, **6**, 88–90.

Gardner, R. and Connell, P. H. (1971). Opioid users attending a special drug dependence clinic 1968 to 1969. *Bulletin of Narcotics*, **23**, 9–15.

Gossop, M., Griffiths, P., Powis, B., and Strang, J. (1992). Severity of dependence and route of administration of heroin cocaine and amphetamines. *British Journal of Addiction*, **87**, 1527–36.

Gossop, M. (1982). *Living with drugs*. Temple Smith, London.

Gossop, M., Griffiths, P., and Strang, J. (1988). Chasing the dragon: characteristics of heroin chasers. *British Journal of Addiction*, **83**, 1159–62.

Gossop, M. (1989). The detoxification of high dose heroin addicts in Pakistan. *Drug and Alcohol Dependence*, **24**, 143–50.

Griffiths, P., Gossop, M., Powis, B., and Strang, J. (1992). UK Transitions Report; Extent and nature of transitions of route among heroin addicts in treatment. *British Journal of Addiction*, **87**, 145–51.

Griffiths, P., Gossop, M., Powis, B., and Strang, J. (1994). Transitions in patterns of heroin administration: a study of heroin chasers and heroin injectors. *Addiction* **89**, 321–9.

Grund, J.-P. C., Adriaans, N. F. P., Kaplan, C. D. (1991). Changing cocaine smoking rituals in the Dutch heroin addict population. *British Journal of Addiction*, **86**, 439–48.

Hartnoll, R. (1985). *The drug situation in Greater London, Drug Indicators Project*.

Hartnoll, R. and Grey, R. (1986). *The drug situation in Greater London*. Drug Indicators Project London, Report prepared for the expert epidemiology working party in the Pompidou group in the Council of Europe.

Huizer, H. (1987). Analytical studies on illicit heroin V. Efficacy of volatization during heroin smoking. *Pharmaceutisch Weekblad Scientific Edition*, **9**, 203–11.

Huizer, H. (1988). Efficacy of volatilization during heroin smoking. *Analytical studies on illicit heroin*, pp. 107–26. Netherlands Ministry of Justice.

Lewis, R. (1989). Serious business—the global heroin economy. *Big deal. The politics of the illicit drug business*, pp. 1–49. Pluto Press, London.

Mo, B. P. and Way, E. L. (1966). An assessment of inhalation as a mode of administration of heroin by addicts. *Journal of Pharmacology and Experimental Therapeutics*, **154**, 142–51.

Moss, T. (1984). Chasing the dragon. *The Sunday Times*. 8 April.

O'Bryan, L. (1989). The cost of Lacoste—drugs, style and money. *Big deal. The Politics of the illicit drug business*, pp. 50–62. Pluto Press, London.

O'Neil, P. J., Baker, P. B., and Gough, T. A. (1984). Illicitly imported heroin products: some physical and chemical features indicative of their origin. *Journal of Forensic Sciences*, **29**, 889–902.

O'Neil, P. J., Phillips, G. F., Gough, T. A. (1985). The detection and characterization of controlled drugs imported into the United Kingdom. *Bulletin on Narcotics*, XXXVI, 17–33.

Parker, H., Newcombe, R., and Bakx, K. (1982). The new heroin users: prevalence and characteristics in Wirral, Merseyside. *British Journal of Addiction*, **82**, 147–57.

Pearson, G., Gilman, M., and McIver, S. (1986). *Young people and heroin. An examination of heroin use in the north of England*. Health Education Council, Report No. 8, London.

Pearson, G. (1987*a*). Social deprivation, unemployment and patterns of heroin use. In *A land fit for heroin? Drug policies prevention and practice* (ed. N. Dorn and N. South), pp. 62–95. Macmillan, London.

Pearson, G. (1987*b*). *The new heroin users*. Blackwell, Oxford.

Power, R. (1990). Drug-using trends and HIV risk behaviour. In *Aids and drug use* (ed. J. Strang and G. V. Stimson), pp. 67–76. Routledge, London.

Strang, J., Griffiths, P., Powis, B., and Gossop, M. (1992*a*). First use of heroin: Changes in route of administration over time. *British Medical Journal*, **304**, 1222–3.

Strang, J., Des Jarlais, D., Griffiths, P., and Gossop, M. (1992). The study of transitions in the route of drug use: the route from one route to another. *British Journal of Addiction*, **87**, 485–91.

Stewart, T. (1987). *The heroin users*. Routledge and Kegan Paul. Pandora Press, London. pp. 12–31.

Woods, A. (1931). *Dangerous drugs, The world fight against illicit traffic in narcotics*. Yale University Press, New Haven.

# 10. Use of illegal drugs in Northern Ireland

*Michael Murray*

Amongst the many problems that beset Northern Ireland the use of illegal drugs does not seem to be of much importance. Indeed, when compared with the extent of poverty, unemployment, social deprivation, as well as the continuing civil disturbance—all of which have attracted considerable political and academic debate—interest in the extent of illegal drug use in the region would seem to be deservedly slight.

A review of the literature reveals scant empirical research into the issue. Admittedly there has been some, although surprisingly little, research into the related issues of excessive alcohol consumption and misuse of prescribed drugs. Research into alcohol consumption has commented on the large proportion of total abstainers and the concentrated drinking style of many of the drinkers. The most recent evidence on drinking practices is that derived from two government surveys conducted in the late 1980s (Sweeney *et al.* 1990). These found that the proportion of drinkers was only 68 per cent in 1987 and 69 per cent in 1989. There were certain marked sex and age differences with 38 per cent of the women being non-drinkers compared with 23 per cent of the men in 1989, and 15 per cent of those aged 25–19 years being non-drinkers compared with 54 per cent of those aged over 65 years. Religion, which is an important demographic variable in studies of Northern Ireland, was not related to the overall prevalence of drinking. Protestants and Catholics were equally likely to be drinkers, although Catholics drank slightly more frequently.

However, although the overall prevalence of drinking is comparatively low there is a large proportion of 'heavy' drinkers (those whose alcohol consumption is more than 21 units per week for men and 14 units for women). The 1989 survey found that 26 per cent of the male drinkers and 11 per cent of the female drinkers were classified as heavy drinkers. These figures were higher among the younger drinkers reaching 36 per cent among male drinkers aged less than 30 years. Overall these figures, which were a decline on the 1987 estimates, indicate that whilst there is a large proportion of total-abstainers among adults in Northern Ireland there is also a large proportion of heavy drinkers.

The extent of the use of prescribed psychotropic drugs in Northern Ireland has been examined by King *et al.* (1982). They considered prescribing patterns for the period 1966–80 and found that throughout this period benzodiazepine tranquillizer prescriptions were 20–30 per cent higher than in the rest of the UK whereas prescriptions for benzodiazepine hypnotics were consistently lower. On analysing all the data available for the year 1978 they found that compared with Great Britain there was greater prescribing of minor analgesics, anti-emetics and tranquillizers, but less prescribing of hypnotics and anti-depressants. When these figures were compared with those from other European countries it revealed that in the period 1966–76 there was a steady rise in tranquillizer prescriptions such that by 1976 it was second only to Iceland. Subsequently there was a decline. It was estimated that in 1975 12.5 per cent of the adult population was being prescribed some form of psychotropic drug. There are conflicting explanations for this high rate of psychotropic drug use (see Cairns and Wilson 1985).

However, the concern of this chapter is illegal drug use in Northern Ireland. The limited research interest in this topic would seem to reflect its low prevalence. It is possible that consideration of some of the potential explanations for this situation, in a world context of increasing drug use, may contribute to a greater overall understanding of the issue. The aim of this chapter is to outline the extent of illegal drug use in Northern Ireland and then to consider some of the possible explanations for its apparent unpopularity.

## Extent of illegal drug use

The main sources of information are the official statistics on seizures of drugs and of arrests for drug offences, the number of people who are officially registered as drug addicts, and survey evidence. All of these, of course, have their limitations.

The most comprehensive estimate of illegal drug use is that obtained from the official statistics on seizures and arrests compiled by Northern Ireland's police force—the Royal Ulster Constabulary (RUC). Table 10.1 gives details of drug seizures, Table 10.2 details of drug-related offences and arrests since 1982, and Table 10.3 details drug convictions for the period 1984–87. When it is realized that the population of Northern Ireland is approximately 1.5 million these figures would tend to confirm the impression that illegal drug use in the region is comparatively low. The figures also indicate that, as in the rest of the UK, cannabis is the most popular illegal drug. According to the police it is the most readily available and remains relatively low in price. It is the illegal drug

**Table 10.1**  Drug seizures in Northern Ireland

| Year | Seizures | | | | |
|---|---|---|---|---|---|
| | Cannabis (kg) | LSD | Heroin | Cocaine | Amphetamines |
| 1982 | 1.7 | 4    doses | 7.9 g<br>31  tablets | 3.8 g | 3.1 g<br>81  capsules |
| 1983 | 3.1 | 17  doses | 2  tablets<br>2  ampoules | 2.0 g | 890  g<br>101  tablets |
| 1984 | 6.0 | 6.5 doses | 20  ml<br>24  mg | 5.1 g | 10.8 g<br>40  tablets |
| 1985 | 15.8 | 903  doses | 89  g<br>375  ml | 6.0 g | 50  g<br>17  tablets |
| 1986 | 17.5 | 558.5 doses | 7  tablets | — | 164  g<br>9  tablets |
| 1987 | 6.0 | 500  doses | 196  g | 98  g | 620  g |
| 1988 | 12.8 | 917  doses | 365  mg | 251  mg | 466 g |
| 1989 | 21.7 | 17.8 g<br>485  doses | 25.4 g<br>1052  tablets | 52.4 g | 659 g |
| 1990<br>(to Nov.) | 35.2 | 573  doses | 2750  tablets | — | 94  g |

*Source:*  RUC (1990).

**Table 10.2**  Drug-related offences and arrests in Northern Ireland

| Year | Offences | Arrests |
|---|---|---|
| 1982 | 837 | 288 |
| 1983 | 640 | 217 |
| 1984 | 511 | 253 |
| 1985 | 557 | 316 |
| 1986 | 483 | 317 |
| 1987 | 441 | 223 |
| 1988 | 494 | 432 |
| 1989 | 550 | 440 |
| 1990 | 552 | 420 |

*Source:*  RUC (1990).

**Table 10.3**  Persons convicted of drug offences in Northern Ireland

|  | 1984 | 1985 | 1986 | 1987 |
|---|---|---|---|---|
| Opiates | 1 | 4 | 1 | 5 |
| Amphetamines | 4 | 6 | 9 | 16 |
| Cannabis | 123 | 121 | 173 | 108 |
| LSD/Psilocybin | 3 | 6 | 5 | 8 |
| Cocaine | — | — | 1 | 3 |
| Forgery | 5 | 4 | 3 | 10 |
| Burglary of chemist shops | 7 | 9 | 1 | 2 |
| Other connected offences | 7 | — | 3 | 7 |
| Total | 150 | 150 | 196 | 159 |

Source:  RUC (1990).

preferred by young people. It is also the drug which is implicated in most drug convictions.

Although detailed research evidence is not available, information from the police would indicate that cocaine use is confined to more affluent youth. Its price would tend to put it out of the reach of the unemployed. Police convictions have revealed several cases of cocaine users being young business people.

The figures in Table 10.1 might also suggest that the use of illegal drugs has increased in Northern Ireland over the past 2 years. However, this is disputed by the police who argue that the increase in drug seizures is primarily due to an improvement in 'the professionalism and efficiency of the Drugs Squad' (Sheehy 1990). More recent reports from local community workers would dispute this. For example, one community worker in a Protestant inner city area of Belfast commented 'This area is awash with drugs. They are being sold in pubs, clubs and on street corners. Its disgusting but people are simply too frightened to campaign openly' (*Belfast Newsletter*, 19 February, 1991).

Another estimate of the use of illegal drugs is provided by the number of officially registered drug addicts. According to the Misuse of Drugs (Notification of and Supply to Addicts) (Northern Ireland) Regulations 1973, doctors are required to notify the government's Chief Medical Officer in the region of persons 'whom they consider, or have reasonable grounds to suspect, to be addicted to certain controlled drugs'. Table 10.4 summarizes the number of such persons registered over the past 5 years. According to the government office "doctors in Northern Ireland generally comply well with the notification requirements and ... numbers on the register do therefore give a useful indicator of the amount of 'hard' drug abuse" (P. J. Sloan, personal communication

**Table 10.4** Number of notified drug addicts
in the Northern Ireland register

| Year | Number |
|------|--------|
| 1985 | 35 |
| 1986 | 35 |
| 1987 | 36 |
| 1988 | 42 |
| 1989 | 37 |
| 1990 | 48 |

*Source:* DHSS (1991).

1991). The drug most frequently used by these drug addicts is heroin
(diamorphine). Overall, the figures are very low although there has been
a slight increase in the past 3 years.

Although there have been numerous surveys of illegal drug use in
Britain only one such survey seems to have been conducted in Northern
Ireland. Details of this have yet to be published but J. Craig (personal
communication 1991) has indicated that it confirms the impression of
very low prevalence.

## Availability of illegal drugs

One important explanation for the increased usage of illegal drugs in
any particular region of the world is an increase in their availability. It
is known that changes in the global distribution patterns of particular
drugs has been followed by upsurges in the use of drugs in related areas.

In Northern Ireland the availability of illegal drugs is limited. The
main explanations put forward for this have been the activities of the
police and the paramilitaries and the absence of an organized criminal
network in the region.

### Policing activities

As a result of the political disturbances in Northern Ireland over the
past 25 years there has been a substantial buildup of police and military
personnel. These forces have established sophisticated techniques for
close surveillance of the population. They also maintain a high visible
presence not only along the border with the Republic of Ireland and at
the main ports of entry but also in foot and mobile street patrols and
at checkpoints on the major roads. At all times these forces are heavily
armed and to outsiders, in particular, can present a very intimidating
demeanour. The RUC claim that this high policing profile has acted as
a deterrent to any non-residents who would consider the importation

and distribution of illegal drugs (Sheehy 1990). Admittedly, this would not seem to have been the case in other countries such as South America where an intensive military campaign against drug production and distribution has met with only limited success. This would suggest that other factors besides a large and visible police/military presence is also of importance.

In addition to the buildup of general policing, the RUC has also established a relatively large Drug Squad. This currently has a staffing of 40 located at four different centres in the region. The squad has adopted a very active role in the control of illegal drugs. They have developed a computerized intelligence system which keeps detailed records on all drug seizures and offences. This has enabled them to build up a comprehensive picture of the extent and character of drug misuse in the region.

With regard to the detection and seizure of drugs being imported, the Drugs Squad works closely with the Customs and Excise Service and with their counterparts in the Republic of Ireland. This enables them to monitor traffic in transit which could potentially be involved in the importation of illegal drugs. The Customs and Excise Service are also well equipped with sniffer dogs and X-ray equipment to help them detect drugs. Their close surveillance of incoming traffic has led to the detection of quantities of drugs.

The high profile of the Drug Squad would seem to be an important factor in reducing the availability of drugs. Sheehy (1990) has reported that the relatively high price of drugs and low purity levels would confirm that the current supply is limited. The Drug Squad has worked to maintain this situation by intervening rapidly when there is any attempt to develop a trafficking network. For example, they have reported how in 1989 a number of chemist shops were burgled and a large quantity of heroin and opiate-based substances, with an estimated street value of £119 000, was stolen. A prompt series of arrests and seizures of much of the drugs led some of the thieves to move to Dublin to dispose of the rest. However, information passed to the Drugs Squad there led to further arrests.

There have also been recent reports that criminal gangs from Dublin, which have been actively involved in selling drugs, have attempted to develop links in Belfast. These activities have been closely monitored by the Drugs Squad who have not hesitated to publicize any possible paramilitary involvement in these links (see later).

The Drugs Squad has a policy of investigating all, even the smallest, drug offences. This has enabled them to build up information on the character of drug misuse and of the persons involved. However, they have a policy of avoiding the criminalization of those who are minor users. Generally those who are first offenders and are found in possession of small quantities of illicit drugs are only cautioned. A substantial proportion of those cases which proceed to court will only receive a formal warning from the bench and thus avoid a criminal conviction/record. However, if these individuals re-offend then this formal warning would increase the likelihood of a subsequent conviction. It is the policy that habitual offenders and traffickers will be prosecuted.

Taken together, these activities of the Drugs Squad and of the Customs and Excise Service would seem to have played an important role in restricting the supply of illegal drugs in Northern Ireland. However, even they themselves would accept that other factors, particularly the role of paramilitary organizations and the absence of an organized criminal network, have also ensured that drugs remain in relatively short supply.

## Paramilitaries

In general, both the loyalist paramilitary (who support the maintenance of political union with Britain) and republican paramilitary (who oppose the union with Britain and support demands for a United Ireland) organizations are publicly opposed to the use of illegal drugs. This is for a variety of reasons but would include concern that involvement in drugs would reduce their potential support in the local communities and also concern that drug addicts who became associated with them would be more likely to inform on their activities.

It is known that the IRA, the main republican organization, has taken action against those selling drugs. For example, in August 1990 the local IRA in Derry handed a package of cannabis, with estimated street value of £3000, to a drug misuse clinic which in turn handed it over to the RUC. In an accompanying statement the IRA claimed to have 'smashed a local drugs syndicate' and proceeded to warn people against selling drugs. 'We warn them to cease these activities altogether or face serious consequences' (*Derry Journal*, August 1990).

However, it should be noted that many young people adopt a cynical attitude to those warnings. Further, when punishment action has been taken against young people by the IRA for their involvement in certain other activities it has not always led to any reduction in their involvement in the activities. For example, a recent report on joyriding found that paramilitary efforts to stamp out the activity were largely ineffective. It noted that

a scale of punishments ranging from warnings to severe gunshot wounds became commonplace. Kneecapping became a normal punishment for repeated offenders. All this attention did not have the effect of dampening the enthusiasm for joyriding. On the contrary the injuries sustained simply added to the mythology of the crime. Young men who had been shot or imprisoned grew in stature in the eyes of their contemporaries. (McCullough *et al.* 1990)

There is also evidence that while the paramilitary organizations may publicly denounce drug-taking, individual members may not be as opposed to it. Sheehy (1990) has noted that where local commanders of these organizations become actively involved in gangsterism and racketeering, especially among the loyalist paramilitaries in Belfast, they are not adverse to profiting from the distribution of drugs.

According to recent police reports trade in illegal drugs earned paramilitary organizations more than one million pounds in 1990. Although this is impossible to verify the police also claimed that loyalist and republican organizations were actively collaborating with each other to assist in the development of a drug distribution network. Specifically these reports claimed that 'people who have served long prison sentences for serious terrorist crimes and who are out to make a lot of money' have turned their attention to drugs. However, all the groups named by the police quickly issued denials of such claims describing them as 'a Colin Wallace-type sinister smear campaign' and 'a serious slur' (*Irish News*, February, 1991). It would seem that while individual members of these organizations, especially those on the loyalist side who tend to recruit more from criminal elements, may have a personal interest in the distribution of drugs the organizations themselves are less involved.

Admittedly, there are reports from outside Northern Ireland, which indicate that supporters of the various paramilitary organizations have been involved in the smuggling of drugs in North America and Europe as a means of raising money.

In general, it would seem that the paramilitary organizations have contributed to the limited availability of drugs in Northern Ireland although recent evidence would suggest that certain elements within these organizations or individuals associated with them may, as part of their involvement in wider criminal activities, becoming involved in the distribution of drugs or are profiting from the sales of such drugs within their areas. However, the influence of the paramilitaries is concentrated in certain areas, particularly working class districts of Belfast and Derry. Outside these districts, particularly in student and more affluent areas of Belfast, their influence is minimal and drugs would be more available.

Commentators have argued over the relative importance of the police and paramilitaries in controlling the availability of illegal drugs. It is best to consider it an interactive process. While the paramilitaries may deter pushers in their locality their terrorist activities have also led to the development of a large and intensive policing operation which has ensured close surveillance of any attempts to introduce illegal drugs into the region.

## Organized criminals

Throughout the world there are large criminal organizations involved in the manufacture and distribution of illegal drugs. Within Northern Ireland there is no real network of professional criminals who could become involved in drug trafficking. Indeed, despite the media image, Northern Ireland is a generally law-abiding society where the incidence of major crime, excluding those connected with political/paramilitary organisations is relatively low. According to government figures, in 1981 the crime rate in the region was lower than that recorded in 40 of 42 police force areas in England and Wales (see Cairns 1987).

The police have accepted that this characteristic distinguishes Belfast from Dublin and explains the rapid spread of drugs in the latter:

A major factor in the development of a drugs problem in Dublin was the availability of a network of professional criminals throughout the city who provided a ready-made system of distribution for heroin.

They have also commented on the failure of these Dublin criminals to extend their operations to Belfast:

Leaders of this gang came to Belfast [from Dublin] in the early 1980's with the intention of extending their network. The high level of policing by the R.U.C. and the opposition by paramilitary groups forced the gangsters to abandon their plans.
(Sheehy 1990).

However, over the past 20 years the various paramilitary organizations, especially in Belfast, have become involved in a range of legal and illegal financial activities. In an attempt to combat these activities the police developed a special Anti-Racketeering Unit. It is possibly the success of this unit which has led some paramilitaries to consider involvement in selling drugs. As already mentioned, recent police reports have claimed that members of these organizations have met criminal elements from Dublin who have been involved in drug dealing there. Although, these police reports received considerable publicity in the press and media the extent of their veracity is difficult to estimate. However, it would not seem unlikely that those elements within the organizations which previously profited from other criminal activities may become involved in drug dealing.

Finally, it would seem that outside criminal networks have considered Northern Ireland to be too small a market and too risky an endeavour to be a worthwhile proposition. For this reason there has been little attempt to organize the sale of illegal drugs in Northern Ireland from outside the region.

## Socio-cultural characteristics of Northern Ireland

Although part of the UK, Northern Ireland has a separate social and political history which has given rise to particular social mores and traditions. Consideration of some of these may help explain further the relatively low rate of illegal drug use there. The interested reader who would want further details of the historical and political factors which have contributed to these traditions are referred elsewhere (for example, Whyte 1990).

### Conservative and law-abiding culture

Despite the image sometimes conveyed by the media Northern Ireland remains a rather conservative society. The importance of this factor in explanations of drug misuse has been recognized by Sheehy (1990) who has commented that 'the population in Northern Ireland tends to be conservative in outlook. As a result new trends in society usually develop more slowly here than elsewhere'. An example of the traditional moral values of teenagers in Northern Ireland is the evidence from a study conducted by Greer (1984). He asked a sample of 18–19-year-olds to indicate their attitudes towards a range of socio-moral issues. In general, the teenagers held a very conservative outlook.

However, recent evidence from the Social Attitudes survey which was extended to Northern Ireland in 1989 suggests that this conservative orientation may be declining. Cairns (1991) compared the attitudes to a range of social issues of Northern Ireland residents with residents in Britain. He found only limited differences and concluded that 'it can no longer be argued that it [N.I.] is without qualification a conservative society'.

While differences in attitudes may be declining available crime statistics indicate that Northern Ireland remains one of the most law-abiding regions of the UK. Heskin (1985) decided to investigate the image that society in Northern Ireland was disintegrating. He examined the extent of reported crime in the region over a 14 year period (1969–83) and found that while there was a steady increase during this period, overall the crime rate remained well below that for England and Wales.

Figures on juvenile crime also indicate the law-abiding nature of Northern Ireland people. Jardine (1989) compared rates per 1000 for juveniles convicted of crimes in Northern Ireland with those convicted in England and Wales and Scotland. Although there are difficulties in making regional comparisons the overall picture is of a much lower rate of juvenile crime in Northern Ireland (see Table 10.5).

Such figures would indicate a reluctance of people in Northern Ireland to become involved in illegal activities such as the use of illicit drugs.

**Table 10.5** Juveniles found guilty or cautioned (England and Wales, Northern Ireland) or subject to police reports (Scotland) per 1000 of juvenile population

|                   | 1979 | 1980 | 1981 | 1982 | 1983 | 1984 | 1985 | 1986 |
|-------------------|------|------|------|------|------|------|------|------|
| England and Wales | 38   | 41   | 41   | 42   | 41   | 42   | 45   | 33   |
| Scotland          | 46   | 48   | 50   | 48   | 54   | 54   | 57   | 59   |
| Northern Ireland  | 20   | 24   | 24   | 22   | 23   | 23   | 26   | 25   |

Source: Jardine (1989).

## Religion

One important force which has helped to shape the attitudes and behaviour of residents in Northern Ireland is religion. The historical division which has developed between Catholics and Protestants there has reinforced and been reinforced by the power of the different churches. Unlike the remainder of the UK Northern Ireland remains a strongly church-going community. In a regional survey conducted by Rose (1971) it was found that 96 per cent of Catholics and 64 per cent of Protestants reported attending church for services or prayer at least monthly. In a later more localized survey Hickey (1984) found very similar estimates of attendance. These figures led Rose (1976) to comment that if church attendance was taken as a measure of religious conviction then 'Northern Ireland is probably the most Christian society in the western world except for the Republic of Ireland'.

The Northern Ireland version of the Social Attitudes survey which was conducted in 1989 provided evidence that this high rate of church attendance is continuing. In that year 51 per cent of the British sample reported that they did not attend church compared with only 10 per cent of the Northern Ireland sample (Cairns 1991).

However, the churches do not exert their influence merely through religious services but through a whole network of social activities. Barritt and Carter (1962) commented on how the Protestant churches 'support a wide range of ancillary activities, such as women's guilds, youth groups, badminton clubs, and men's discussion fellowships'. Similarly, Darby (1976) noted 'Catholic associations like the St. Vincent de Paul Society, the Legion of Mary and parish youth groups have received considerable support'.

These organizations have enabled the churches to exercise control over the social activities of their members. Evidence today would suggest that these organizations still remain strong, and the clergy still remain influential particularly in rural areas but also in the larger urban areas such as Belfast and Derry. Thus, not only have the churches had a strongly negative attitude towards drugs use which is conveyed to its members in church services but its control over a proportion of social activities reduces the opportunities for easy distribution of drugs.

## Family and neighbourhood structure

Another possible explanation for the low rate of illegal drug use is the close family and neighbourhood network which exists throughout Northern Ireland. The use of illegal drugs within this close network would be quickly identified and lead to action by the older and more established members.

This family and neighbourhood closeness is exacerbated by the considerable residential segregation on grounds of religion (Poole 1982). This is particularly so in areas of Belfast where physical barriers have been constructed to separate one neighbourhood from another. Although these barriers were erected partly in response to demands from local residents who feared sectarian assassination they have also contributed to the creation of small inward-looking communities in which it would be difficult to conceal the use of illegal drugs.

The importance of close family and neighbourhood ties was indicated in some of the findings from the YTP (Youth Training Programme) Cohort Study (McWhirter 1989). This study surveyed young people about their views on Northern Ireland and various other issues. It found that the most popular reason given by these young people for living in Northern Ireland was the people, their friendliness, and friendship (52 per cent) followed by family ties (17 per cent).

Although figures are not available it would seem that unlike in Britain many young people in Northern Ireland remain resident in the family household until they marry or emigrate. Several studies have indicated that it is young single people who are not resident in the family home who are particularly at risk of developing a drug habit. For this reason drug misuse is higher in large urban centres to which young single people would move in search of employment.

In the case of Northern Ireland, the net effect of a high rate of emigration would be to export a large proportion of those young people who would potentially become drug users. On average 6000 people of working age have left Northern Ireland each year since 1983. Most of these would be expected to be young people moving to Britain in search of employment. This high rate of out-migration is matched only by Scotland in the UK. It has been estimated that the net out-migration from the region since 1971 has been equivalent to one in eight of the working population (Northern Ireland Economic Research Centre 1990).

Such figures would suggest that Northern Ireland is exporting its potential drug using population. Anecdotal evidence would suggest that some young people from Northern Ireland who have emigrated to London have become involved in illicit drug use, but more research is needed to quantify this impression.

## Alternatives to illegal drug use

Although the use of illicit drugs in Northern Ireland would seem to be low this is not to suggest that people there, in particular young people, do not indulge in a variety of other hazardous activities which would be considered alternatives to drug use. Three of these are briefly considered here: alcohol, solvent abuse, and joyriding.

### *Alcohol*

As already mentioned, although there is a large number of non-drinkers among adults in Northern Ireland, there is also a large proportion of heavy drinkers. A recent survey of teenagers produced similar findings (Department of Health and Social Services 1989). This found that among the adolescents surveyed experience of alcohol was much less than in the rest of the United Kingdom. For example, 48 per cent of 13 year old boys and 76 per cent of 13 year old girls in Northern Ireland had never had a whole drink compared with 18 per cent of boys and 24 per cent of girls in England and Wales (Marsh *et al.* 1986). However, among the drinkers there was evidence of a higher consumption among the Northern Ireland youth. According to a diary record 60 per cent of all the boys and 32 per cent of all the girls who drank consumed more than 10 units of alcohol in a week compared with 38 per cent and 13 per cent of boys and girls in England and Wales. The survey concluded that this 'suggests that young drinkers in Northern Ireland follow a very similar pattern of consumption to their elders—gravitating around the extremes of abstinence and over-indulgence'.

The wide acceptance of alcohol misuse could be said to have displaced the need for other drugs. It has been suggested by one drug misuse worker (J. Hoolahan in Counterpoint 1988) that in any society where alcohol dependency has become accepted there is a lesser use of illegal drugs. He compared the position of Northern Ireland with that of Norway which also has a low reported use of illegal drugs but a substantial alcohol problem.

### *Solvent abuse*

Over the past 10 years and more there have been a variety of reports detailing the abuse of solvents—glue sniffing. This behaviour would seem to be largely confined to adolescents and to vary rapidly in intensity according to time and place such that there would seem to be outbreaks of glue sniffing associated with a school or a housing estate 1 year and not the next. Although there is no detailed information on this phenomenon in Northern Ireland the pattern would seem to be not dissimilar. According to figures from the Juvenile Liaison scheme the number of teenagers cautioned for such behaviour, which is not illegal, has varied from year to year and from area to area. In 1982 there were 741 such referrals but these dropped to 290 in 1984. According to figures from the General Registrar's Office a total of 16 people died between 1981 and 1989 due to the inhalation of Tipp-ex, glue, or aerosols. Lurid newspaper reports also confirm that glue-sniffing does go through bouts of popularity among youth in Northern Ireland.

## Joyriding

Finally, it is interesting to note one risky activity which has grown in popularity among Belfast young in the past decade—joyriding. This activity is defined as the theft of cars for pleasure rather than for profit. While this crime exists in other parts of the UK in Belfast it has taken on a more life-threatening form with young joyriders becoming involved in incidents with the police and army. As a result of such incidents a large number of young people have been seriously injured and at least 13 have been killed in the past 10 years. Some of these deaths have been due to car accidents and others when the driver or passengers were shot dead by the police or army.

In an excellent description of this phenomenon McCullough *et al*. (1990) draws many comparisons with the psychology of the drug taker. They describe the typical joyrider as a bored teenager who is seeking thrills and identity in an otherwise bleak society. They note that 'such an exhilarating activity can become obsessional. Everything else seems boring by comparison. Like the drug addict they can find no satisfactory substitute'.

## Conclusion

Undoubtedly, Northern Ireland is a region of considerable social deprivation. In comparable regions of the United Kingdom there has been a growth in the use of illegal drugs. The fact that this has not occurred in Northern Ireland would seem to be due to a variety of factors. These include the current political situation which has acted as a deterrent to those who would try to supply the drugs, the cultural climate which is generally unreceptive to drug-taking, and the high rate of emigration which ensures that many potential drug-users migrate elsewhere.

In recently reviewing the situation the police have concluded that one can be 'cautiously optimistic that a drugs problem will not develop in Northern Ireland in the foreseeable future' (Sheehy 1990). However, when attention is shifted to related activities, especially excessive alcohol consumption, there is less room for complacency.

# References

Barritt, D. P. and Carter, C. F. (1972). *The Northern Ireland problem* (2nd edn). Oxford University Press, Oxford.

Cairns, E. (1987). *Caught in crossfire: children and the Northern Ireland conflict*. Appletree, Belfast.

Cairns, E. (1991). Is Northern Ireland a Conservative society? In *Social attitudes in Northern Ireland* (ed. P. Stringer and G. Robinson), pp. 142–56. Blackstaff, Belfast.

Cairns, E. and Wilson, R. (1985). Psychiatric aspects of violence in Northern Ireland. *Stress Medicine*, **1**, 193–201.

Counterpoint (1988). *Pills and pot*. Ulster Television, Belfast.

Darby, J. (1976). *Conflict in Northern Ireland*. Gill and Macmillan, Dublin.

Department of Health and Social Services (1989). *Drinking amongst school children in Northern Ireland*. DHSS, Belfast.

Greer, J. E. (1984). Moral cultures in Northern Ireland. *Journal of Social Psychology*, **123**, 63–70.

Heskin, K. (1985). Societal disintegration in Northern Ireland: A five-year update. *Economic and Social Review*, **16**, 187–200.

Hickey, J. (1984). *Religion and the Northern Ireland problem*. Gill and Macmillan, Dublin.

Jardine, E. (1989). Trends in juvenile crime. In *Growing up in Northern Ireland* (ed. J. Harbison), pp. 93–106. Stranmillis College, Belfast.

King, D. J., Griffiths, K., Reilly, P. M., and Merrett, J. D. (1982). Psychotropic drug use in Northern Ireland 1966–80: prescribing trends, inter- and intra-regional comparisons and relationship to demographic and socioeconomic variables. *Psychological Medicine*, **12**, 819–33.

Marsh, A., Dobbs, J., and White, A. (1986). *Adolescent drinking*. HMSO, London.

McCullough, D., Schmidt, T., and Lockhart, B. (1990). *Car theft in Northern Ireland*. Extern, Belfast.

McWhirter, L. (1989). Longitudinal evidence on the teenage years. In *Growing up in Northern Ireland* (ed. J. Harbison), pp. 66–92. Stranmillis College, Belfast.

Northern Ireland Economic Research Centre (1990). *The Northern Ireland economy: review and forecasts to 1995*. NIERC, Belfast.

Poole, M. A. (1982). Religious residential segregation in Northern Ireland. In *Integration and division: geographical perspectives on the Northern Ireland problem* (eds. F. W. Boal and J. N. H. Douglas), pp. 281–308. Academic Press, London.

Rose, R. (1971). *Governing without consensus: an Irish perspective*. Faber and Faber, London.

Rose, R. (1976). *Northern Ireland: a time of choice*. Macmillan, New York.

Sheehy, K. (1990). *Assessment of drug misuse*. Royal Ulster Constabulary, Belfast.

Sweeney, K., Gillan, J., and Orr, J. (1990). *Drinking habits in Northern Ireland 1987–1989*. Policy Planning and Research Unit, Belfast.

Whyte, J. (1990). *Interpreting Northern Ireland*. Oxford University Press, Oxford.

# Part II

Clinical responses

# 11. The fall and rise of the general practitioner

*Alan Glanz*

A constant theme in the evolution of the British system during the twentieth century has been the shifting balance in policy and service provision between the roles of the the specialist and the generalist in responding to drug misusers. Over this period the position of the general medical practitioner (GP) has undergone major transitions as policy has developed in response to perceived changes in the character of the drugs problem. Several distinct phases are identifiable, during which the GP first becomes established in addiction treatment, then is displaced by the specialist, and finally re-emerges in a key role. These changes in the role of the GP in the treatment of drug misuse can also be viewed against the background of changes in the standing of the GP within the wider system of medical care.

## Emergence of the GP in addiction treatment

The role of GPs in the treatment of drug misuse emerged with the disease concept of narcotic addiction in the latter part of the nineteenth century. It has been suggested that the elaboration of the disease theory of addiction and treatment structures was part of the process of professional self-affirmation on the part of a medical profession gaining in confidence and prestige (Berridge and Edwards 1981). By this time the GP was a well-established medical figure. While its precise origins are uncertain, it has been established that the term GP was unknown before 1800, came into use increasingly between 1810 and 1830 and was firmly established by 1840 when GPs formed over 80 per cent of the medical profession (Loudon 1983). These GPs arose to meet a demand from the growing middle classes of Victorian Britain for a personal or family doctor.

It was morphine habituation among the middle classes rather than opium consumption among the lower classes that formed the clinical basis of the disease theory of addiction, for its formulation and application was limited to the class of patients doctors were likely to treat at this time (Berridge 1979). No consensus was established, however, on the best method of treatment. In general the role of the GP was to devise and supervise a gradual withdrawal regime. The method implemented varied widely and for certain cases involved institutional care.

In the early part of the twentieth century the system of medical management of addiction was threatened by the extension to the civilian population of the drug control regulations covering members of the armed forces which were passed during the First World War. Possession of opiate drugs and cocaine was restricted to authorized persons. Under regulations of the Dangerous Drugs Act of 1920, a medical practitioner was authorized to possess and supply drugs only so far as was necessary for the practice of his profession (Bean 1974).

Some GPs with addict patients interpreted this as permitting them to' continue prescribing regular maintenance doses. However, the Home Office was not satisfied with this situation and wanted to restrict the scope for interpretation of the Act. In order to secure an authoritative statement on the professional legitimacy of supplying opiate drugs to addicts, a committee chaired by Sir Humphrey Rolleston was appointed in 1924 (Berridge 1984). The Committee's Report of 1926 is a landmark in the evolution of British policy on addiction, forming the basis of the 'British System' (Departmental Committee 1926). The recommendations of the Report were implemented under further regulations of the Dangerous Drug Act. The approach adopted by the Rolleston Committee—composed entirely of medical men—rested squarely on their acceptance of the disease nature of addiction. The outcome amounted essentially to the preservation of the right of medical practitioners to prescribe opiate drugs not only for withdrawal treatment but also in 'non-diminishing doses' for certain patients. The case for the prescribing role of the medical practitioner was made by the Committee on grounds of patient welfare, but the impulse to protect professional medical control also played a part (Berridge 1980).

It is worth noting the contrast with the contemporary scene in the USA. As Trebach has shown, the Harrison Act of 1914 contained very similar language to the Dangerous Drugs Act in restricting dispensation of controlled drugs by a doctor to the 'course of his professional practice only'. The difference was in the interpretation of this phrase in the USA where a large number of doctors were prosecuted during the 1920s for prescribing to addicts as this was viewed as beyond the scope of their legitimate role (Trebach 1982).

For some 40 years the position of the GP in the treatment system established by the Rolleston Committee remained undisturbed. Over this period British society underwent profound social changes and the social structure of the drugs scene underwent a transformation of its

own. The addicts of the Rolleston era were never likely to constitute
a social problem. They were a relatively small number of largely professional and middle class individuals who formed no kind of social
network. By the mid-1960s the social circles of doctors and addicts,
which in the Rolleston era had to some extent overlapped, now became
firmly detached and distant from each other as the social characteristics
of drug users were rapidly changing. The consequence was a radical
restructuring of the treatment system and the effective removal of the
GP from the treatment system.

## Removal of the GP from addiction treatment

Some awareness of emerging changes in the drugs scene is registered by
the appointment in 1958 of an Interdepartmental Committee on Drug
Addiction under the chairmanship of Sir Russell Brain. The conclusion
of the Committee's Report in 1961 was that the Rolleston system should
remain intact as there was no evidence that the right of doctors to provide drugs of addiction in the treatment of addict patients had led to any
increase in the number of addicts (Interdepartmental Committee 1961).

However, the changing nature of the drugs scene could not be ignored
for long. In 1954 there were 57 known heroin addicts and in 1959 there
were 68, but by 1964 there were 342 heroin addicts known to the
Home Office (Spear 1969). The Brain Committee was reconvened in
1964 specifically to consider the need for revising policy on the prescribing
of addictive drugs. The Committee's Report identified the source of
the unprecedented growth in addiction as 'the activity of a very few
doctors who have prescribed excessively for addicts' (Interdepartmental
Committee 1965).

The solution which the Committee recommended was to circumscribe
for the first time the ability of medical practitioners to prescribe drugs
according to their own professional judgement. The Dangerous Drugs Act
of 1967 gave legislative effect to the Committee proposals. The power
to prescribe heroin and cocaine in the treatment of addiction was removed from ordinary medical practitioners and placed in the hands of
doctors granted a special licence from the Home Office. These doctors
were very largely consultant psychiatrists in charge of hospital-based
special centres which were now set up to treat addicts.

The incursion into clinical autonomy represented by the proposals of
the Second Brain Committee was greeted with protests by some sections
of the medical profession. In particular a Working Party of the British
Medical Association (BMA), a body mainly representing the interests
of GPs, was highly critical (Smart 1985). These objections were not,
however, vigorously pursued. As Smart has noted, the BMA made it clear
that drug addicts were not popular patients and GPs were probably

glad to be relieved of the responsibility for dealing with them (Smart 1985). The restriction on prescribing did not apply to supply of heroin for medical treatment other than addiction. The curtailment of clinical freedom was thus accepted.

It is apparent that to a certain extent doctors treating addicts were being made scapegoats for a problem which was emerging as the result of far more complex social forces. A leading article in the *British Medical Journal* complaining at the threat to clinical freedom contained in the Committee's recommendations certainly had a point in arguing that it was 'a grave step to take in order—it would appear—to control the over-prescribing habits of only a handful of doctors' (*British Medical Journal* 1965).

The establishment of a new treatment system towards the end of 1960s was linked to a new understanding of the nature of the drugs problem. While, as in the Rolleston period, addicts remained an individually isolated set of mainly middle class and therapeutically addicted persons, it was appropriate that treatment should remain in the hands of individual general and private medical practitioners. When addiction came to be seen, in the words of the second Brain Committee, as a 'socially infectious disease', with the heroin users now constituting a distinct subculture within society, individual medical practitioners no longer offered an adequate response. The system needed to be strengthened. The new addiction treatment centre, located within a hospital framework and staffed by a multidisciplinary team headed by a consultant psychiatrist, was far less vulnerable to the pressure and demands of addicts. As Stimson and Oppenheimer (1982) have put it: 'The new element introduced in the rethinking of policy in the 1960s was the emphasis on the social control of addiction'.

## The decline of general practice within medicine

The removal of the GP from the addiction treatment system can also be set within the context of developments in the status of general practice within the wider system of medicine.

Throughout the 1920s and 1930s there was a rapid acceleration of a process of change within medicine that had already been under way during the nineteenth century. The 'division of medicine'—the separation of general practice from hospital care—accentuated, with hospital medicine becoming increasingly dominant (Honigsbaum 1979). Advances in medical knowledge, in diagnostics and laboratory-based investigations, and in technological applications in treatment meant that specialization became inevitable (Stevens 1966). A number of long-standing functions of the GP were transferred to hospital-based specialists. The status of the GP declined.

During the 1950s and most of the 1960s general practice remained an unattractive career option for qualifying doctors. National surveys of medical students in 1961 and in 1966 showed that only around one-quarter of final year students gave general practice as their first choice of career (Martin 1984). Indeed, the total number of GP was declining and so was the ratio of GPs to patients (Jefferys and Sachs 1983). The view of the medical establishment was summed up in the statement in 1966 of Lord Moran, President of the Royal College of Physicians, that general practice medicine was an occupation for those who 'fall off the ladder' and failed to become specialists (Hart 1988). GPs themselves complained that they were operating merely as signposts to the specialists, wasting their training on attending to trivialities rather than doing 'real medicine' (Cartwright 1967). The mid-1960s probably represented the nadir of general practice within the medical system. It was in this climate that the new hospital-based specialist addiction treatment infrastructure was devised, which effectively eliminated the GPs from the system.

## The reinstatement of the GP in addition treatment

The creation of the specialist hospital-based addiction treatment centres together with the licensing system effectively marginalized the role of the GP in addiction treatment for more than a decade. It is unlikely that substantial numbers of GPs had in any case been involved in treating the metropolitan concentration of addicts in the 1960s. The effect, however, was to limit the variety of treatment opportunities as the drugs problem evolved during the 1970s and the drug clinics remained a largely mono-polistic and somewhat monolithic service for addicts.

There was some awareness during this period that addicts were seeking alternatives to what they regarded as narrow prescribing policies practised by the drug clinics. The private practitioner emerged as the 'unacceptable face' of addiction treatment (Bewley *et al.* 1975; Bewley and Ghodse 1983). The opiate-focused hospital treatment centres lacked the flexibility to respond to the developing drugs problem characterized by polydrug abuse involving barbiturates, tranquillizers, amphetamines, and opiates (*Lancet* 1979). Private and general practitioners, together with voluntary drug agencies were increasingly in contact with drug misusers whose treatment needs or demands left them outside the clinic system.

However, it was the rapid change in the scale of drugs problem rather than changes in its form which led by the early 1980s to the return of the GP as a major agent in the treatment framework. This re-entry of the GP was first recognized at an official level in the 1982 Report on *Treatment and Rehabilitation* from the Advisory Council in the Misuse of Drugs (ACMD). The ACMD had been established under the 1968

1971 Misuse of Drugs Act as an independent committee of experts serviced by the Home Office. Their 1982 Report noted 'the fact that over the last few years an increasing proportion of drug misusers is being treated not in the hospital based treatment clinics, but by doctors in general practice (both NHS and private)' and referred to this as 'an unplanned development' (ACMD 1982). The ACMD raised the issue of the role of GPs as a policy question for the first time since the second Brain Committee Report of 1965. According to the ACMD—in some respects echoing the Brain Committee—the principal problem of this 'unplanned development' was the 'extent to which controlled drugs are prescribed injudiciously' (ACMD 1982). Of course GPs were still entitled to prescribe any drugs, including opiates other than heroin and excluding cocaine, in the treatment of drug dependence.

The ACMD expressed concern about a number of aspects of the GPs position in relation to drug taking patients—their lack of specialized knowledge and limited training opportunities, their relative isolation leaving them vulnerable to pressure from drug misusers, and inadequate access to support staff and appropriate facilities for full patient assessment. Nevertheless, the ACMD was prepared, providing there were 'strict safeguards', to accept 'a possible role for some doctors outside the specialist services to play a part in the treatment of problem drug takers' (ACMD 1982).

The subject of safeguards regarding prescribing was soon tackled by the issue to all doctors in 1984 of *Guidelines of good clinical practice in the treatment of drug misuse*, drawn up by a Medical Working Group on Drug Dependence set up by the Department of Health in response to the recommendations of the ACMD Report (Medical Working Group 1984). The guidelines expressed encouragement to GPs 'to play a major role', and stated that 'it is the responsibility of all doctors to provide care for both the general health needs and drug related problems' of drug misusers (Medical Working Group 1984).

Clearly policy was now about reinstating the GP as a key actor in the response to drug misuse. In 1985 the Minister of State with responsibility for drugs policy expressed the view that it was the 'duty' of every GP to provide a service for drug misusers (Social Services Committee 1985). A Health Circular on services for drug misusers issued in 1986 by the Department of Health described the Department's policy as encouraging GPs 'to play a major part in the care and treatment of drug misusers' (Department of Health 1986).

In what circumstances did this fundamental shift in policy come about? The answer can be indicated by contrasting the introductions to two Government publications on the prevention and treatment of drug misuse issued 6 years apart. The earlier document of 1979 stated that 'the United Kingdom appears at present to have a relatively stable situation as far as narcotic dependence is concerned' (Central Office of Information 1979). The second in 1985 stated by contrast that 'In Britain ... the rapid rise in the misuse of drugs ... has emerged as one of the most serious social problems of the 1980s' (Central Office of Information 1985). The statistics on addicts notified by all doctors to the Home Office illustrate this dramatic change in the dimensions of the British drugs problem: 1979, 2385 addicts notified; 1985, 8819 addicts notified (Home Office 1989). These figures reflect the rapid spread of heroin use among young people in diverse areas of the country. For many of these young people a hospital treatment centre was inaccessibly distant or the waiting time for an appointment was unacceptably long as the prevalence of drug misuse outstripped the capacity of the specialist services to respond.

The GP on the other hand is an accessible and to many a natural source to turn for help. The growth in the involvement of GPs is also illustrated by Home Office statistics. In 1970 GPs were responsible for 15 per cent of notifications made by all doctors, in 1975 for 29 per cent and in 1984 for 55 per cent (ACMD 1982; Home Office 1989). An indication of the extent of GP involvement was provided by the results of a national survey of GPs in mid-1985, showing that about one in five GPs throughout England and Wales would see at least one opiate drug misuser in a given 4-week period and GPs as a whole would deal with some 40 000 new cases of opiate drug misuse over a 12 month period (Glanz and Taylor 1986).

Policy in the early and mid-1980s reflected the urgent need to respond to the growing drugs problem. GPs were now seen as a valuable resource in strengthening the framework for managing that problem.

## The changing ideological context of policy

In respect of the role of GPs, the policy response to an escalating drugs problem in the early and mid-1980s was clearly very different from the response to that of the early and mid-1960s. The ideological context of drugs policy formation had changed significantly.

Within the drugs field a change had occurred over this period in the definition of the problem at which policy was directed. The earlier disease-based notion of addiction gave way to the notion of 'problem drug taking' as formulated by the ACMD in its 1982 Report *Treatment and rehabilitation*. The idea of the problem drug taker involves a broader perspective, moving away from a substance focus and recognizing the personal, social, and medical (including dependence) difficulties which may be associated with use of a range of drugs (ACMD 1982). This reconceptualization of the drugs problem offers scope for professionals other than drug dependence specialists to play a role.

Linked to this formulation of the problem drug taker is the perception of the 'normalization' of the drug misuser. Heroin and other drug use in the 1980s was on a far greater scale and had a wider geographical distribution than in the 1960s. From the point of view of service provision, the implication is that 'as notorious drugs (such as use of heroin) become more widespread in a population the people using them are likely to be more normal (statistically and in other senses) than the abnormal population who presented originally' (Strang 1984). As a consequence the view that drug misusers need to be dealt with by specialists is undermined: 'if some of the drug-takers are becoming more normal, then perhaps some of the drug services should do likewise' (Strang 1989).

A further element in the changing ideological context of policy is the rise of the 'community' response to drug problems (Stimson 1987). As in the wider field of health and social services, provision of drug misuse services in the 1980s had been developing a community care approach, aiming to deal with the individual's problems within the social setting which they inhabit rather than offer an institutional response. 'Community drug teams' have been widely established, as in the 'model service' in the North Western Regional Health Authority (Strang 1989). These multidisciplinary groups operate outside of institutional frameworks to facilitate direct access to help and work to mobilize generic services in the community, particularly GPs, to respond to drug problems. (See also Chapter 15).

## The rise of general practice within medicine

These changes in the construction of the nature of the drugs problem and its management have promoted the GP to a prominent position as a focus for policy development and service planning. To some extent the shifts in the drugs field described above have been special applications of broader developments in health and social care. The trend towards community care and 'de-institutionalization' has had a wide impact on service provision; for example, in the case of alcohol services where the problem orientation (rather than substance orientation) initially developed (Stockwell and Clement 1987). The role of GP was widely enhanced by these developments. Indeed the status of general practice had been rising steadily for some years.

Leaders within general practice had been aware for many years of the need to rebuild a sense of professional self-esteem. General practice slowly but successfully established its credentials as a speciality in its own right following the publication of the *Report of the Royal Commission on Medical Education* (Royal Commission on Education 1968), with medical schools setting up academic departments of general practice and vocational training becoming mandatory (in 1982) for entry into general practice (Wilkin *et al*. 1987).

Cognitive foundations for the professional development of general practice required a specialist body of knowledge for a distinct specialism. This emerged with the formulation of an alternative model of medicine to that of hospital medicine, the approach of 'biographical medicine' (Armstrong 1979). Here the emphasis is on the patient as a whole, and an interpretation of signs and symptoms is given in the context of the patient's biography and environment. The holistic approach was represented in the widely influential work of Balint, who identified a particular role for the GP in dealing with the many patients presenting with symptoms which apparently had no organic basis (Balint 1966).

The increased self-confidence of general practice was supported by and reflected in improvements in conditions of service, the growth of large group practices and health centres, and the emergence of the primary health-care team. In contrast to the position in the 1960s, by 1984 general practice had become the most popular career choice of British medical students (*Lancet* 1984). Thus, the whole position of general practice had been vastly strengthened and the GP could meaningfully be called upon to play a significant role in the treatment of drug misuse.

## The advent of AIDS and the future role of the GP

The threat of human immunodeficiency virus (HIV) and acquired immune deficiency syndrome (AIDS) associated with use of contaminated injecting equipment has brought general practice even more firmly into a key position in the strategy for responding to drug problems. According to the recent *AIDS and drug misuse* Report of the ACMD, 'the network of general practitioners offers an unrivalled system of health care provision with great opportunities for intervention with drug misusing patients' (ACMD 1988). The Report noted, however, that the opportunities for GP intervention 'have not yet been adequately seized', and went on to emphasize that 'the advent of HIV makes it essential that all GPs should provide care and advice for drug misusing patients to help them move away from behaviour which may result in them acquiring and spreading the virus' (ACMD 1988).

The extent to which GPs will respond to the challenge of HIV in the context of drug misuse is at the present moment an open question. There is no doubt that GPs remain widely involved with drug misusers. Home Office figures show that a total of 7947 addicts were notified by GPs during 1989, representing 54 per cent of notifications from all doctors (Home Office 1990). Furthermore, a survey of 10 per cent of all GPs in England and Wales undertaken in early 1990 found that an estimated 19 000 drug misusers—covering use by injection and by other routes of heroin, other opiates, cocaine/crack or amphetamines, and use by injection of other drugs—are currently under the care of GPs, with around one in four GPs having at least one drug misuser currently under their care (Glanz and Friendship 1990). However, despite this extensive contact, evidence from several studies indicates that GPs are not responding with enthusiasm to the prospects of working with drug misuser patients.

The model extensively promoted in the North Western Regional Health Authority in which GPs and general psychiatrists were encouraged to provide the bulk of services to drug misusers, with specialists operating as sources of advice and teaching, has been deemed a qualified failure by those who implemented and monitored the policy (Strang 1991; Strang *et al*. 1991, 1992). The conclusion they draw from this experience is that the likely effectiveness of such a strategy for combatting HIV infection in drug misusers (which presumes that a widespread contribution will be forthcoming from the generalist, in particular the GP) must be open to considerable doubt (Donmall *et al*. 1990; Strang *et al*. 1991; Strang 1991).

Studies of the role of the GP in relation to broad issues and of HIV and AIDS have found the area of drug misuse to be particularly problematic. A survey of two groups of GPs, one group of GP trainers and one non-trainer GPs, found that both groups were reluctant to care for intravenous drug misusers and that the drug abuse problems of many patients were seen as the single greatest deterrent to caring for AIDS (Sibbald and Freeling 1988). An interview study among London GPs concerning management of problems relating to HIV found that over one-quarter would not accept known intravenous drug users as patients and a further 11 per cent would accept them only under defined conditions (King 1989). In the Parkside Health District in London a recent survey found that only 29 per cent of the GPs in the area were willing to care for HIV antibody positive intravenous drug users, compared with 60 per cent willing to care for heterosexuals and 47 per cent for homosexuals with HIV (Roderick *et al*. 1990).

Findings from the 1990 national postal questionnaire survey referred to above, covering a 10 per cent random sample of GPs in England and Wales, throw some light on the prospects for GP involvement with drug misusers (Glanz and Friendship 1990). Just under one-half (47 per cent) GPs agreed that they would undertake treatment of drug misusers as willingly as they would any other type of patient in need of care, while 41 per cent disagreed with this position. Many GPs are prepared only to have a minimal involvement—43 per cent agreed that they would refer any patient consulting for drug misuse to a specialist service and make no further appointment to see the patient for this problem. On the other hand, 80 per cent agreed that they were willing to collaborate with a specialist service in joint management of drug misusers.

In its Report on *AIDS and drug misuse* the ACMD stated that 'the spread of HIV is a greater danger to individual and public health than drug misuse' and hence there was a need 'to work with those who continue to misuse drugs to help them reduce the risks involved in doing so, above all the risk of acquiring or spreading HIV' (ACMD 1988). To what extent would GPs accept this role? The findings of the national survey are that 39 per cent of GPs expressed agreement and 41 per cent disagreement in respect of their own willingness to work with drug misusers in this way (Glanz and Friendship 1990).

A further recommendation of the ACMD is that 'all GPs should accept their responsibility for the ongoing health care of drug misusers with HIV disease' (ACMD 1989). In the national survey just under two-thirds (63 per cent) were in agreement that they would be willing to do this, with one-fifth (21 per cent) disagreeing. However, the relative aversiveness of drug misusers as patients in this context emerges in the finding that only about one-half of GPs (53 per cent) agreed that they would accept on to their list an HIV antibody positive drug misuser as willingly as they would any other HIV antibody positive patient seeking care, while 30 per cent disagreed (Glanz and Friendship 1990).

The national survey clearly revealed that GPs hold a range of negative opinions about drug misusers. Most GPs believe that drug misusers would present more severe management problems than any other type of patient (79 per cent), would make unmanageable demands on their time (71 per cent), and would not comply with any treatment regimen (55 per cent). Furthermore GPs feel that working with drug misusers was unlikely to be rewarded by satisfying results (62 per cent) and would expose them and others in the surgery to aggressive and threatening behaviour (73 per cent) (Glanz and Friendship 1990). It may be the case that there is a fundamental difficulty for the GP in dealing with patients who apparently violate so many of the standard expectations of the doctor−patient relationship (McKeganey and Boddy 1988).

The imperative of AIDS prevention requires GPs to perform a more demanding role than previously. The new model for the GP has been set out by Robertson, describing an Edinburgh general practice: 'our own policy revolves around the philosophy of risk reduction and therefore prescribing becomes a device used if it is seen as a method of prevention of greater dangers' (Robertson 1989). This involves an assessment of the complex options opened up by the 'hierarchy of goals' approach elaborated by the ACMD (1988). Such an approach would perhaps require the GP to undertake a more sophisticated assessment and response than that described for a standardized methadone detoxification regimen (Medical Working Group 1984).

Local evidence suggests that the prescribing option in the context of risk reduction will not be readily taken up. In a survey in one inner London area, only 15 per cent of GPs were prepared to undertake methadone withdrawal and 10 per cent methadone maintenance of narcotic users (Bell *et al.* 1990). The 1990 national survey shows that GPs do not regard themselves as properly equipped to handle these patients—only 15 per cent agreed that their knowledge of the clinical aspects of drug misuse was sufficient for meeting the needs of patients who may present with this problem (Glanz and Friendship 1990). Indeed Robertson and colleagues have themselves revealed the extent of the burden which drug misusers might place on GP services. They found from an analysis of practice records over a 2-year period in 1986–87 that a sample of 25 HIV antibody positive drug misusers made a total of 1485 surgery visits and that a second sample of 25 non-HIV drug misusers made a total of 1130 visits (Roberts *et al.* 1989).

If GPs are to be recruited to a sustained involvement with drug misusers in the AIDS era it is vital to guard against the phenomenon observed in the course of the heroin 'epidemic' in the Wirral area of north-west England in the early 1980s, in which, after initial high levels of involvement, GP 'burn-out' led to their wholesale disengagement from treating heroin user patients (Parker *et al.* 1988). One possible way of sustaining the involvement of GPs would be to offer a financial incentive for treating these patients—a proposal which the ACMD (1988) recommended should be explored. Indeed, one GP with experience of drug misusers has recently argued that a small payment for each drug misuser treated per year would be a very cost-effective inducement to GPs and would 'achieve a substantial increase in the nation's drug treatment workforce' (Waller 1990). However, such an approach certainly has considerable cost—and ethical—implications, and its potential effectiveness is open to doubt. In the 1990 national survey, only about one-quarter of GPs (27 per cent) agreed that some financial incentive would encourage them to extend their involvement with drug misusers.

How can GPs be effectively encouraged to overcome the numerous obstacles they identify as inhibiting their willingness to work with drug misusers? The national survey points to several possible approaches. One-half of GPs in the survey agreed that provision of training opportunities in the management of drug misuse would encourage them to extend their involvement with these patients. The availability of further human resources would be an equal incentive for GPs. About one-half of GPs (49 per cent) agreed that additional staffing resources for the primary health-care team would encourage them to extend their involvement with drug misusers.

The most effective strategy for promoting GP involvement emerging from the 1990 national survey is the provision of greater access to specialist back-up services. More than two-thirds of GPs (68 per cent) agreed that this would encourage them to extend their involvement with drug misusers. This fits with the finding reported above of the very high proportion of GPs in the survey (80 per cent) who expressed willingness to collaborate with specialist serv:ces in joint management of drug misusers.

## Conclusion

The future role of the GP within the system of provision for drug misusers is an uncertain one. The changes in policy which have brought about the fall and rise of the GP in this system have been, like so much of drug policy, largely reactive and pragmatic rather than planned and strategic. The current policy of promoting GP involvement has not been implemented within a framework of specific measures designed to secure favourable conditions for a successful outcome. Indeed recent developments in broader health service policy concerning the contractual responsibilities of GP may have a counterproductive effect in this respect (Robertson and Witcombe 1990). For GPs, HIV adds a new complication to the already difficult task of dealing with drug misusers, and yet at the same time their role within the system of provision becomes more significant than ever before. Without active steps to secure their involvement the next phase in the history of the role of GPs in the treatment of drug misuse is likely to be one of detachment and disengagement.

## References

ACMD (Advisory Council on the Misuse of Drugs) (1982). *Treatment and rehabilitation*. HMSO, London.
ACMD (1988). *AIDS and drug misuse. Part 1*. HMSO, London.
ACMD (1989). *AIDS and drug misuse. Part 2*. HMSO. London.
Armstrong, D. (1979). The emancipation of biographical medicine. *Social Science and Medicine*, **13**, 1–8.
Balint, M. (1966). *The doctor, his patient, and the illness*. Pitman, London.
Bean, P. (1974). *The social control of drugs*. Martin Robertson, London.
Bell, G., Cohen, J., and Cremona, A. (1990). How willing are general practitioners to manage narcotic misuse? *Health Trends*, **22** (2), 56–7.
Berridge, V. (1979). Morality and medical science: concepts of narcotic addiction in Britain, 1820–1926. *Annals of Science*, **36**, 67–85.
Berridge, V. (1980). The making of the Rolleston Report. 1908–1926. *Journal of Drug Issues*, Winter, pp. 7–28.
Berridge, V. (1984). Drugs and social policy in the establishment of drug control in Britain, 1900–1930. *British Journal of Addiction*, **79**, 17–29.

Berridge, V. and Edwards, G. (1981). *Opium and the people: opiate use in nineteenth-century England*. Croom Helm, London.

Bewley, T. H. and Ghodse, A. H. (1983). Unacceptable face of private practice: prescription of controlled drugs to addicts. *British Medical Journal*, **286**, 1876–7.

Bewley, T. H., Teggin, A. F., Mahon, T. A., and Webb, D. (1975). Conning the general practitioner—how drug abusing patients obtain prescriptions. *Journal of the Royal College of General Practitioners*, **25**, 654–7.

Brain Committee (1965). See Interdepartmental Committee (1965).

*British Medical Journal* (1965). Control of drug addiction. *British Medical Journal*, **2**, 1259–60.

Cartwright, A. (1967). *Patients and their doctors: a study of general practice*. Routledge, London.

Central Office of Information (1979). *The prevention and treatment of drug misuse in Britain*. HMSO, London.

Central Office of Information (1985). *The prevention and treatment of drug misuse in Britain*. Central Office of Information, London.

Department of Health (1986). *Health Service development. Services for drug misusers*. Health Circular HC(86)3.

Departmental Committee (1926). *Report*. Departmental Committee on Morphine and Heroin Addiction. HMSO, London.

Donmall, M. C., Webster, A., Strang, J., and Tantam, D. (1990). *The introduction of community-based services for drug misusers: Impact and outcome in the North-West, 1982–1986*. Report to the Department of Health, England. (Available from ISDD (Institute for the Study of Drug Dependence) Library, London.)

Glanz, A. and Taylor, C. (1986). Findings of a national survey of the role of general practitioners in the treatment of opiate misuse: extent of contact. *British Medical Journal*, **293**, 427–30.

Glanz, A. and Friendship, C. (1990). *The role of general practitioners in the treatment of drug misuse. Findings from a survey of GPs in England and Wales, 1989*. Report to the Department of Health (unpublished).

Hart, J. T. (1988). *A new kind of doctor*. Merlin, London.

Home Office (1989). *Statistics of drug addicts notified to the Home Office, UK 1988*. Statistical Bulletin 13/89. Home Office, London.

Home Office (1990). *Statistics of the misuse of drugs: addicts notified to the Home Office, UK 1989*. Statistical Bulletin 7/90. Home Office, London.

Honigsbaum, F. (1979). *The division in British medicine: a history of the separation of general practice from hospital care 1911–1968*. Kogan Page, London.

Interdepartmental Committee (1965). *Second Report*. Interdepartmental Committee on Drug Addiction. HMSO, London.

Jefferys, M. and Sachs, H. (1983). *Rethinking general practice: dilemmas in primary medical care*. Tavistock, London.

King, M. B. (1989). Psychological and social problems of HIV infection: interviews with general practitioners in London. *British Medical Journal*, **299**, 713–17.

*Lancet* (1979). Drug addiction: time for reappraisal. *Lancet*, **ii**, 289–90.

*Lancet* (1984). Towards better general practice. *Lancet*, **ii**, 1436–8.

Loudon, I. S. L. (1983). The origins of the general practitioner. *Journal of the Royal College of General Practitioners*, **33**, 13–18.

Martin, F. M. (1984). *Between the Acts: community mental health services 1959–1983*. Nuffield Provincial Hospitals Trust, London.

McKeganey, N. P. and Boddy, F. A. (1988). General practitioners and opiate abusing patients. *Journal of the Royal College of General Practitioners*, **38**, 73–5.

Medical Working Group (1984). *Guidelines of good clinical practice in the treatment of drug misuse*. Report of the Medical Working Group on Drug Dependence. Department of Health, London.

Parker, H., Bakx, K., and Newcombe, R. (1988). *Living with heroin*. Open University Press, Milton Keynes.

Roberts, J. J. K., Skidmore, C. A., and Robertson, J. R. (1989). Human immunodeficiency virus in drug misusers and increased consultation rate in general practice. *Journal of the Royal College of General Practitioners*, **39**, 373–4.

Robertson, J. R. (1989). Treatment of drug misuse in the general practice setting. *British Journal of Addiction*, **84**, 377–80.

Robertson, R. and Witcombe, J. (1990). Drug problems and primary health care. *British Journal of Addiction*, **85**, 685–6.

Roderick, P., Victor, C. R., and Beardow, R. (1990). Developing care in the community: GPs and the HIV epidemic. *AIDS Care*, **2**, 127–32.

Royal Commission on Medical Education (1968). *Report*. HMSO, London.

Sibbald, B. and Freeling, P. (1988). AIDS and the future general practitioner. *Journal of the Royal College of General Practitioners*, **38**, 500–2.

Smart, C. (1985). Social policy and drug dependence: an historical case study. *Drug and Alcohol Dependence*, **16**, 169–80.

Social Services Committee (1985). *Misuse of drugs*. Fourth Report from the House of Commons Social Services Committee. HMSO, London.

Spear, H. B. (1969). The growth of heroin addiction in the UK. *British Journal of Addiction*, **64**, 245.

Stevens, R. (1966). *Medical practice in modern England: the impact of specialisation and state medicine*. Yale University Press, New Haven.

Stimson, G. V. (1987). British drug policies in the 1980s: a preliminary analysis and suggestions for research. *British Journal of Addiction*, **82**, 477–88.

Stimson, G. V. and Oppenheimer, E. (1982). *Heroin addiction: treatment and control in Britain*. Tavistock, London.

Stockwell, T. and Clement, S. (ed.) (1987). *Helping the problem drinker: new initiatives in community care*. Croom Helm, London.

Strang, J. (1984). Changing the image of the drug taker. *Health and Social Service Journal*, October 11, 1202–4.

Strang, J. (1989). A model service: turning the generalist on to drugs. In *Drugs and British society* (ed. S. MacGregor), pp. 143–69. Routledge, London.

Strang, J. (1991). Service development and organisation: drugs. In *International handbook on addiction behaviour* (ed. I. Glass), pp. 283–91. Routledge, London.

Strang, J., Donmall, M. C., Webster, A., Abbey, J., and Tantam, D. (1991). *A bridge not far enough: Community Drug Teams and doctors in the North Western Region, 1982–1986*. (Research monograph no. 3). Institute for the Study of Drug Dependence (ISDD), London.

Strang, J., Smith, M., and Spurrell, S. (1992). Community Drug Team: goals, methods and activity analysis. *British Journal of Addiction*, **87**, 169–78.

Trebach, A. (1982). *The heroin solution*. Yale University Press, New Haven.
Waller, T. (1990). Ways to open the surgery door. *Druglink*, **5** (3), 10–11.
Wilkin, D., Hallam, L., Leavey, R., and Metcalfe, D. (1987). Anatomy of urban general practice. Tavistock, London.

# 12. The creation of the clinics: clinical demand and the formation of policy

*Philip Connell and John Strang*

The 1960s were a time of great social upheaval and change—particularly amongst the newly-emergent youth culture and their relationship with the establishment. Their iconoclasm found expression in various ways including, for some groups, the use of illicit drugs. In some ways this drug use can be seen as paralleling the search for new identities, new ways of living, and the search for chemical shortcuts to higher planes of enjoyment and self-discovery. But it was not just the significance of the drug use which was changing—major changes occurred in the substances being used, in the manner in which they were being used, and in the characteristics of the drug takers themselves.

For several decades up to the 50s, the UK drug problem had been notable by its absence (see Chapter 1), and a similar picture was seen across Europe—in contrast to the situation in the USA. No significant drug problem existed to test the adequacy or appropriateness of UK drug policy, and no significant clinical demand existed to test the adequacy and appropriateness of the treatment response. Perhaps the most clear demonstration of these changes is evident by looking at the ages of addicts in the UK. As Spear has described (1969; Chapter 1), the number of opiate addicts in the UK had been fairly constant between 400 and 600 during any year, of whom half were deemed to be therapeutic addicts who had become addicted to the drug during the course of treatment for pain associated with a physical disorder. A substantial number of the remainder were physicians or other professionals who had unusual access to pharmaceutical supplies of the drug. Of this number there were less than a hundred who were addicted to heroin, and these addicts were nearly all middle aged or older. Indeed the first known case of a heroin addict under the age of 20 years was not until 1960. Yet by 1967 there were 381 known cases of heroin addiction who were aged less than 20 years, and 827 aged between 20 and 34 years and the annual numbers of heroin addicts had increased from about 50 to a 1967 figure of 1299.

This chapter is a synthesis of various perspectives given at the time of the creation of the clinics in 1968. New perspectives were emerging on the phenomenon itself, new services were being created, and new methods of dealing with the problem of drug dependence were starting. A new analysis was evidently required.

## The new analysis

The first report from the Brain Committee (Interdepartmental Committee) had appeared in 1961 and was generally reassuring—the drug problem was small, static, and no special measures needed to be taken; it was predominantly a medical, not a criminal, problem. However, in view of the changes of the early/mid-1960s, the Committee was hastily reconvened in 1964 and published its influential Second Report (Interdepartmental Report 1965). The phenomenon itself (drug use) was seen as socially infectious, and indeed various studies of heroin use traced the chain of transmission of local spread by peer group 'infection' (de Alarcon and Rathod 1968; Kosviner *et al.* 1968; de Alarcon 1969). Sweeping recommendations were made by the Second Brain Committee: these recommendations stand as the output of a major new reconsideration of the UK drug problem, which had continued largely unaltered (and indeed largely unchallenged) since the Rolleston Report (1926). Thus the Second Report of the Brain Committee recommended: the introduction of limits on the rights of doctors to prescribe heroin or cocaine (so that only those doctors holding a special licence could prescribe either of these drugs to addicts); the setting up of specialist out-patient clinics with back-up in-patient provision (especially in London); the introduction of compulsory notification of addiction (along the lines of infectious diseases notification, but managed by the Home Office); encouragement of research into drug addiction; and the creation of a Standing Advisory Committee to look over developments in the problem and the response.

The pace of change at the time was such that urgent action was required. Over the course of 4 years (1964–68) UK policy and practice moved from an unspecified and individually determined response to less than a hundred heroin addicts in 1964 through to a network of specialist drug treatment clinics (mainly in the London area) as part of mental health services for about 2000 heroin addicts. For the first time, by 1961, Frankau and Stanwell were able to describe extensive experience of private treatment of heroin addicts, some of whom had recently arrived from Canada (see Zacune 1971), and some of whom were an indigenous population (Frankau and Stanwell 1961); and by 1964 Hewettson and Ollendorf were able to describe their General Practitioner (GP) experience of 100 heroin addicts in south London (Hewettson and Ollendorf 1964). And yet the majority of the medical profession was not involved and did not wish to be involved. In the words of one GP active in the drug field, the proposal for new services '... was flying in the face of established medical opinion in this country, which regards the prescribing of narcotic drugs as incorrect for the treatment of addiction. This dilemma is still present—namely that the majority of doctors question prescribing as a policy in this treatment' (Chapple 1967).

The pace of contemporary debate was fast, with a series of perspectives published in the *British Medical Journal*, supporting community initiatives, specialist services, primary health-care work, and the need for a research base (Bewley 1967; Connell 1967; Chapple 1967; Owens 1967). There was general agreement on the need for treatment to be available in the community. As Owens said 'narcotic addiction must be regarded primarily as a problem of community mental health' (Owens 1967). Indeed the whole focus of the *British Medical Journal* contribution from Chapple was on treatment in the community (Chapple 1967). However, as both Connell and Bewley pointed out (Bewley 1967; Connell 1967) there was a reluctance on the part of medical colleagues to be involved in provision of treatment and hence there was a strong argument for the establishment of special centres, which should be located in areas with established addiction problems, and based in teaching hospitals with back-up laboratory and in-patient facilities. Indeed, treatment should extend beyond these centres so that experimental hostels might be set up 'to provide support and supervision for the addict, and gradually to introduce him to and integrate him into the community and to prevent him going back to the addict sub-culture' (Connell 1967).

Addict voices appeared for the first time in the popular press (*Sunday Times* 1966; Trocchi 1965); public interest was considerable and included concern at the excessive prescribing by a small number of doctors, to such an extent that television was the new medium for the cross-examination and 'trial' by David Frost of prescribing doctors such as Dr John Petro (described in Judson 1974).

## The new response

Through 1967 the Ministry of Health was preparing plans for the creation of the new treatment centres. As Stimson and Oppenheimer (1982) were subsequently to comment, the new clinics were required to walk a prescribing tightrope, with the dangers of overprescribing (and hence feeding the black market) on the one hand, and the danger of under-prescribing (and hence failing to capture and contain the problem) on the other side. The blueprint for the new clinics was contained within the memorandum from the Ministry of Health (1967) entitled *Treatment and supervision of heroin addiction* in which there was a recognition of the need to achieve this balance on the prescribing tightrope. The aim of the new clinics was 'to contain the spread of heroin addiction by continuing to supply the drug in minimum quantities where this is necessary in the opinion of the doctor, and where possible to persuade addicts to accept withdrawal treatment' (Ministry of Health 1967). Edwards (1969) later described how clinicians aimed to '... with one hand give the addict heroin, while with the other hand build his motivation to come off the drug'. There was a determination to see the new clinics as providing something much more than just the hand-outs of drugs. A *Lancet* editorial (1968) conveyed the strong determination that the clinics should be adequately staffed so as to be able to practise an energetic and comprehensive approach—not just the dispensing of drugs. In similar vein, Edwards (1967) outlined how vitally important it would be that staff of the new clinics

... should he concerned with and involved in the total treatment programme, should have as their aim to woo the addict off drugs, and must have immediately available facilities for detoxification and later rehabilitation, so that, when the addict shows interest in treatment, treatment can be provided. The doctors staffing these clinics cannot be part-time clinical assistants unsupported by psychiatric training.

## The rationale of the new approach

In an account written in the months leading up to the opening of the new treatment clinics, Connell (1969) summarized the rationale of the new approach as follows:

(i)   the addict is a sick person and properly comes within the ambit of medical practice: his dependence on the drug and his craving are so strong that he is unable to behave rationally;

(ii)  heroin would be provided free at special treatment centres: this would obviate the necessity for acquisitive crime to pay for the drug from the blackmarket which was not yet criminally well organised;

(iii) NHS staff in the new treatment centres were less likely to over-prescribe, and could use the opportunity of contact with the addict to cultivate motivation towards eventual withdrawal from the drug: regular contact between the addict and the doctor of the treatment clinic would provide the opportunity for a relationship to be built-up which may eventually lead to the addict requesting to be taken off the drug;

(iv)  the prescribing of heroin by the treatment centres should so undercut the blackmarket as to prevent its development or consolidation;

(v)   a more careful approach would be taken to matching dose prescribed to dose needed so that there would be much less 'spare' heroin circulating to involve less committed individuals;

(vi) punitive detention of the addict under a penal system has not been shown to be successful in curing addiction in other countries.

Thus it was intended that a safe middle path would be trod between the two extremes of prescribing, so as to achieve adequate impact at the levels of both individual care and social control.

In a later commentary on the new clinics, Edwards (1969) put forward three hypotheses relating to the treatment being provided:

(i)   Addicts are taken on by the clinics not for the continuing handouts of drugs, but for treatment: the patient may not initially be motivated to accept withdrawal but, through contact with clinic staff, motivation will gradually be built, dosage gradually reduced, and the offer of admission for withdrawal finally accepted.

(ii)  Since successful treatment ultimately depends on the patient's own motivation, there is no place for the use of compulsory admission procedures.

(iii) There are believed to be some patients who cannot—or cannot for the time being—function without the drug, but who on a regular maintenance dose can live a normal and useful life as a 'stabilized addict': such patients will be maintained on heroin rather than have their drug withdrawn.

One further recommendation had been put forward in the Second Report from the Brain Committee—the only recommendation not to be implemented. It had been proposed that doctors should be given the power to detain addicts compulsorily in hospital (under, for example, a new provision of the Mental Health Act). However, despite attracting occasional support (for example Bewley 1967), other more sceptical voices prevailed (for example Connell 1967; *Lancet* 1968) and no such powers were agreed, for fear that too hasty provision of such compulsory powers might lead to widespread use of these powers where not necessary or likely to be ineffective or even counter-productive.

## The new services

Fifteen out-patient clinics were opened in London, most of them attached to teaching hospitals. Additionally, a smaller number of clinics were opened in towns in the Home Counties. Very few specialist clinics were set up elsewhere in the UK. Some were open every weekday whilst others were only open part-time. Almost overnight, working policies and practices needed to be developed. During the first year of operation regular meetings were arranged by the Ministry of Health of the doctors in charge of the new treatment centres across the country. Accounts of the practice of individual clinics were published at the time (for example Gardner and Connell 1970) and a contemporary account summarizing the first year has recently been published (Connell 1991). A degree of control was introduced—for example addicts now had to attend a weekly or fortnightly out-patient appointments and were usually required to collect their drugs on a daily basis from a local pharmacist. Such developments were viewed by many addicts as 'an absolute bore' (quote from Christina Boyd, interviewed by Stimson and Oppenheimer 1982), even though the degree of individual freedom, with take-home supplies, injectable drugs and fixing rooms, and free equipment in many of the clinics was still a world apart from the more controlled treatment approaches of most other countries.

## The dangers of the new approach

From the very outset it was recognized that considerable navigational skill would be required in negotiating a safe passage between the dangers of over-control and under-control which lay on either side. Concerns were voiced—for example in the *British Medical Journal*: 'One has fears for treatment centres—for example, one dreads that they will merely become prescribing centres ....' (Owens 1967). Contemporary accounts (Connell 1969; Edwards 1969) are clear illustrations of the awareness of the brinkmanship in which they were engaged. It was necessary to identify and face these dangers in order to '... avoid a drift into disaster and a breakdown of the new approach' (Connell 1969). Amongst others, the following weak points in the system were identified by Connell (1969):

(i)   It had already been demonstrated that a very small number of over-prescribing doctors could encourage an epidemic of drug taking when it coincided with a socio-cultural demand.

(ii)  The new 'experts' did not have tools for precise measurement of the dose required for each patient.

(iii) All professional classes contain weaker bretheren.

(iv)  The new planned response had required the recruitment of many more doctors into the practice of prescribing heroin to addicts.

These conflicts were graphically illustrated at the time by various commentaries. For example Edwards (1969) cited two cases to illustrate the difficulties facing the prescriber:

A 17 year old girl who was on 30 mg of heroin and 40 mg of methadone per day was in physiological balance but insisted that she wanted a bigger prescription: an increased dose was refused, so she went to the blackmarket and built her dose up to 120 mg of heroin per day, as was confirmed when she was admitted for stablisation. Because her story had not been believed, she had meanwhile certainly been receiving an insufficient script for maintenance and had been driven into criminal activities in a way which the legalised prescribing system is supposed to circumvent. The second case was an addict on 90 mg of heroin per day who complained bitterly on Monday of the clinic's callous underprescribing which, she stated, was making any sort of social adjustment impossible; later the same week she was arrested for selling the drug.

## The development of safeguards

In his contemporary analysis, Connell (1969) identified two main strategies for cutting down the pool of surplus heroin which might influence the uninitiated or uncommitted heroin user. First, it was proposed that doses of drugs already being prescribed to addicts should be reduced gradually down to more moderate levels (daily doses for some addicts had climbed astronomically—to doses many times greater than the maximum doses found necessary in other more experienced countries). By this approach, the absolute quantity of drug involved in any small diversions of supplies would represent less unit doses for the novice or uncommitted user. Secondly, the practice of clinics should be such as to promote downward rather than upward changes to the dose prescribed. Previous independent doctors had been caught in a spiralling increase of dose as tolerance developed. The downward perspective involved a recognition that addicts have two needs: a physiological need to prevent withdrawal symptoms and a psychological need to obtain the 'high' associated with increased dose: the former should be adequately addressed by stable or even slowly reducing dose, whereas attempts to satisfy the latter need would lead to continuing dose escalation. Gradually an informal code of practice was established (for 1969 account which has recently been published; see Connell 1991), although this was not a static code of practice but represented the consensus or prevailing view based on practice and experience as it was accrued. More recently, in the early 1980s, when interest in the provision of care to opiate addicts again became a subject of public and medical interest, a later code of practice was published from the London clinics (Connell and Mitcheson 1984) and was followed shortly afterwards by *Guidelines of good clinical practice* from the Department of Health (Medical Working Group on Drug Dependence 1984).

This 1969 informal code of practice included recommendations for weekly or fortnightly interview/assessment of the patient; the posting of prescriptions to a local community pharmacist by prior arrangement; the dispensing of 1 day's supply of drugs at a time by this community pharmacist; the dispersal of addicts over as large a number of chemists as practical so as to prevent the congregation of addicts at key pharmacies. Once the dust had settled from the transfer of care of the established addicts who had been in receipt of private prescriptions, a more cautious approach was adopted for assessment of the new patient prior to the commencing of prescribing heroin or cocaine—and indeed cases were identified in which the initial enthusiasm (on the part of the prescriber as well as the patient) for commencement of the prescription had led to the prescribing of opiates to non-addicted individuals (Gardner and Connell 1970).

During the first year of operation many of the doctors in charge of the treatment centres formed the view that the continued prescribing of injectable cocaine was unnecessary due to the absence of a recognized withdrawal syndrome. When addicts presented in an emergency in opiate withdrawal, the withdrawal syndrome should be managed with linctus methadone in a dose sufficient to cover the patient until his next appointment—a policy adopted partly in order to prevent the development of such emergency presentations as a loophole for obtaining extra supplies of heroin. Agreement was also reached between the treatment centres about consultation before transfer of patients between clinics so as to prevent patients from 'shopping around' solely to obtain the highest offer of a prescribed dose.

During their first few months, the clinics took over the care of all the heroin addicts who had been obtaining their supplies from the private and National Health Service GPs. From 16 April 1968 onwards, supplies of heroin or cocaine to addicts were all funnelled through the new treatment centres. It seems likely that during the transition period there was considerable overprescribing, in that most patients were taken on with a dose of drugs similar to their previous care. Gradually individual cases and individual dose requirement could be assessed by the clinics so as to identify grosser abuses of the system. Even during the first 18 months, one particular clinic had experienced something of a local epidemic which appeared to stem from internal traffic of patients within the clinic system towards the more liberal prescribing policy of this clinic.

For a while, an additional problem occurred with the prescribing of injectable amphetamine. By mid-1968, once the new clinics had taken over care of the heroin addicts, two private doctors began '... prescribing quantities of the drug (methylamphetamine ampoules) to an extent which contributed directly to the growth of the illicit market' (Hawks *et al.* 1969). A brief experiment of prescribing supplies of methylamphetamine ampoules seemed to be '... largely a record of therapeutic failure' (Mitcheson *et al.* 1976), and by the end of 1968 agreement was reached between the Department of Health and the pharmaceutical manufacturers so that the drug was withdrawn from supply to retail chemists. This intervention would appear to have been highly effective and successfully aborted the growing intravenous amphetamine problem (for analysis, see de Alarcon 1972).

At the end of this interim period, it was evident that both addicts and the clinics had survived the transition period, but there remained fundamental issues which still needed to be addressed (data collected in 1969—recently published in Connell 1991). To what extent should the clinics look for more evidence of use and dependence prior to commencing a prescription? What approach should be adopted to the new methadone ampoules (for which a special licence to prescribe was not required)? What policy should be adopted for the increasing number of primary methadone addicts (those who have never taken heroin before their methadone use)? And what should be the policy with those individuals dependent on other drugs (such as amphetamines, barbiturates, etc.) or with non-injecting drug addicts—should they be treated within the same service, in parallel services or in separate services?

## The challenge

The new drug problem undoubtedly represented a major challenge to the quiet British System. What was the nature of the challenge faced by the new clinics? In a paper written at the time of their opening of these new clinics, Connell (1969) identifies four particular challenges:

(1) the challenge to doctors in the new treatment centres to work together and adopt a reasonably uniform approach (and hence accept some restrictions on the practitioner's hallowed independence);
(2) the challenge to the biochemist to develop more rapid qualitative tests for drugs of abuse, and to develop methods for quantitative assessment of drug dosage;
(3) the challenge to medical practitioners to produce hard data relating to the different treatment programmes in order that effectiveness may be measured;
(4) the challenge to epidemiologists and sociologists to produce data relating to the causes, method of spread, and options for prevention of drug taking.

## Conclusions

Without doubt, the opening of the clinics on the 16 April 1968 was a major point of change in the relationship between the addict and the doctor in the UK. Addicts themselves had changed rapidly (in epidemiological terms) from the middle-aged addicts of the previous decades (predominently therapeutic addicts and health-care professionals) to the new young addicts born of the 1960s revolution. The change in the treatment response was a result of revision of policy over a similar time-span of a few years, and was implemented virtually overnight. As Bill Gregor said (addict patient interviewed by Stimson and Oppenheimer,

1982): 'When the clinics started, the heyday, if you can call it that, was over'. Certainly the scope for the more excessive abuses of the British freedom to prescribe had been curbed, but what was the nature of the being which grew in the new climate? Within a health-care context, a complicated script had been written for the new clinics which involved simultaneous concern about broader social and public health perspectives on the one hand and treatment of the individual patient on the other. The struggle to reconcile these two seemingly contradictory goals formed the basis of work and evolution of the British clinics during the next decade (see Stimson and Oppenheimer 1982; and Chapter 13, this volume), and the debate about the balance between these two goals has re-emerged during the late 1980s and 1990s with the new analysis required in the wake of HIV/AIDS (see Advisory Council on the Misuse of Drugs 1988; 1989; Strang and Stimson 1990; Power *et al.* 1991). Much of the rhetoric, policy consideration and clinical practice of today is strongly reminiscent of the events around the time of the creation of the clinics—and yet, sadly, scant regard is paid to perspectives from yester-year. Perhaps the ignorant must be condemned to repeat the agonies, the considerations, and the errors of history without reference to previous journeys through similarly turbulent waters.

## References

Advisory Council on the Misuse of Drugs (1988). *AIDS and drug misuse. Part 1.* HMSO, London.
Advisory Council on the Misuse of Drugs (1989). *AIDS and drug misuse. Part 2.* HMSO, London.
de Alarcon, R. (1969). The spread of heroin abuse in a community. *Bulletin on Narcotics*, **21**, 17–22.
de Alarcon, R. (1972). An epidemiological evaluation of a public health measure aimed at reducing the availability of methylamphetamine. *Psychological Medicine*, **2**, 293–300.
de Alarcon, R. and Rathod, N. H. (1968). Prevalence and early detection of heroin abuse. *British Medical Journal*, **1**, 549–53.
Bewley, T. (1967). Centres for the treatment of addiction: advantages of special centres. *British Medical Journal*, **2**, 498–99.
Chapple, P. A. L. (1967). Centres for the treatment of addiction: treatment in the community. *British Medical Journal*, **2**, 500–1.
Connell, P. H. (1967). Centres for the treatment of addiction: importance of research. *British Medical Journal*, **2**, 499–500.
Connell, P. H. (1969). Drug dependence in Great Britain: a challenge to the practice of medicine. In *Scientific basis of drug dependence* (ed. H. Steinberg). Churchill Livingstone, London.
Connell, P. H. (1991). Treatment of drug-dependent patients 1968–1969 (Document). *British Journal of Addiction*, **86**, 913–16.
Connell, P. H. and Mitcheson, M. (1984). Necessary safeguards when prescribing

opioid drugs to addicts: experience of drug dependence clinics in London. *British Medical Journal,* **288**, 767–9.

Edwards, G. (1969). The British approach to the treatment of heroin addiction. *Lancet*, **i**, 768–72.

Edwards, G. (1987). Relevance of American experience of narcotic addiction to the British scene. *British Medical Journal*, **3**, 425–7.

Frankau, I. M. and Stanwell, P. M. (1961). The treatment of heroin addiction. *Lancet*, **ii**, 1377–9.

Gardner, R. and Connell, P. H. (1970). One year's experience in a drug dependence clinic. *Lancet*, **ii**, 455–8.

Hawks, D. V., Mitcheson, M., Ogborne, A., and Edwards, G. (1969). Abuse of methylamphetamine. *British Medical Journal*, **2**, 715–21.

Hewettson, J. and Ollendorf, R. (1964). Preliminary survey of 100 London heroin and cocaine addicts. *British Journal of Addiction*, **59**, 109–14.

Interdepartmental Committee on Drug Addiction (The Brain Committee) (1961). *Drug Addiction: report.* HMSO, London.

Interdepartmental Committee on Drug Addiction (The Brain Committee) (1965). *Drug Addiction: second report.* HMSO, London.

Judson, H. (1974). *Heroin addiction in Britain.* Harcourt Brace Jovanovich, New York.

Kosviner, A., Mitcheson, M. C., Myers, K., Ogborne, A., Stimson, G. V., Zacune, J., and Edwards, G. (1968). Heroin use in a provincial town. *Lancet*, **i**, 1189–92.

*Lancet* (Editorial) (1968). Addiction new style. *Lancet*, **i**, 852–3

Medical Working Group on Drug Dependence (1984). *Guidelines of good clinical practice in the treatment of drug misuse.* HMSO, London.

Ministry of Health (1967). Treatment and supervision of heroin addiction. Health Circular 67/16. Ministry of Health, London.

Mitcheson, M., Edwards, G., Hawks, D., and Ogborne, A. (1976). Treatment of methylamphetamine users during the 1968 epidemic. In *Drugs and drug dependence* (eds G. Edwards, M. Russell, D. Hawks, and M. McCafferty), pp. 155–162. Saxon House/Lexington, Farnborough.

Owens, J. (1967). Centres for treatment of drug addiction: integrated approach. *British Medical Journal*, **2**, 501–2.

Power, R., Stimson, G. V., and Strang, J. (1991). Drug prevention and HIV policy. *AIDS 1990*, **4** (suppl. 1), S263–7.

Rolleston Committee (Departmental Committee on Morphine and Heroin Addiction) (1926). *Report.* HMSO, London.

Spear, H. B. (1969). The growth of heroin addiction in the United Kingdom. *British Journal of Addiction*, **64**, 245.

Stimson, G. V. and Oppenheimer, E. (1982). *Heroin addiction: treatment and control in Britain.* Tavistock, London.

Strang, J. and Stimson, G. V. (1990). The impacts of HIV: forcing the process of change. In *AIDS and drug misuse: the challenge for policy and practice in the 1990s* (ed. J. Strang and G. V. Stimson), pp. 3–15. Routledge, London.

*Sunday Times* (1966). Heroin addiction. *Sunday Times*, March 6th.

Trocchi, A. (1965). Why drugs? *New Society*, **5 (138)**, 1–2.

Zacune, J. (1971). A comparison of Canadian narcotic addicts in Great Britain and Canada. *Bulletin on Narcotics*, **23**, 41–9.

# 13. Drug clinics in the 1970s

*Martin Mitcheson*

Specialist drug clinics came into being as a response to the numerically small, although in percentage terms startling, increase in the number of young adults injecting heroin during the 1960s. Their supply of heroin came from the diversion of heroin prescribed to established addicts by a small number of independent doctors (Brain Committee 1965). These doctors never numbered more than six in London and were mostly working in private practice. An unknown proportion of their patients sold some of their prescribed drugs on the 'grey market' thus initiating others into the habit. In the absence of other means of controlling the prescribing of these doctors, and the subsequent diversion of heroin, the prescribing of heroin and cocaine to addicts was restricted to specially licensed doctors who worked at the new clinics which had been instituted at selected hospitals, mostly in London and including one private clinic. Effectively they became the only source in the UK of a heroin prescription for an addict.

## The early days

The staff at the clinics had varied experience in working with drug misusers. Some had no previous experience. Regular meetings of the doctors in charge of clinics were instituted for sharing information and agreeing informal policies on such matters as appropriate assessment or what procedures should regulate the transfer of patients from one clinic to another (Connell 1991). Statistical information was provided at these meetings, regarding the number of patients receiving prescriptions at each clinic and the total quantity of heroin and methadone prescribed from each clinic. Even prior to the advent of cheap pocket calculators it was relatively easy for doctors attending these meetings to calculate a mean dose of opioids per patient for each clinic (Fig. 13.1.). Given the overt reason for the establishment of clinics, which was to restrict the diversion of heroin to the grey market while allowing a sufficient continued 'ration' to established addicts, it was possible to see these meetings as typically English, discreet peer group pressure tending to

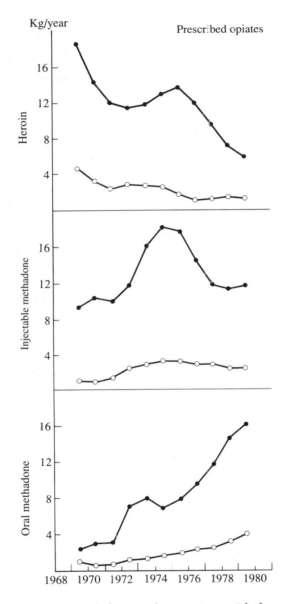

**Fig. 13.1** Information provided to regular meetings with drug clinic doctors. Source: Clinic return to DHSS. ( ● ) London; ( ○ ) elsewhere.

moderate the prescribing of heroin. The alternative drug considered more acceptable by clinic staff was methadone—a longer acting synthetic opiate—which had a respectable image resulting from Dole *et al.* (1966)

advocacy of methadone for maintenance in New York City. However, London addicts were accustomed to collecting supplies of injectable drugs from a retail pharmacy for self-injecting in private and they expected this practice to continue. Thus ampoules of methadone (Physeptone) injection were requested and prescribed. These were used in a manner very different from the USA, where clinics supervised consumption of oral methadone on the premises.

## Client contact and expectations

The early months of the clinics saw a rush of customers, who, correctly, anticipated that the initial launch of the clinics presented an opening offer to sign up for a maintenance prescription that might not be repeated. At the same time members of the street subculture rightly suspected that amounts prescribed by salaried clinic staff might be less generous that the prescriptions of independent practitioners. On the day that the new restrictive regulations came into force the *The Times* carried a report from a self-styled addiction specialist, with dubious qualifications, that the grey market price of diverted heroin had doubled from £1 to £2 for a grain of heroin—approximately 64 mg. Heroin was dispensed as one-sixth of a grain (approximately 10 mg) hypodermic tablets for injection. These were subsequently replaced by freeze dried ampoules in the late 1970s. Expressed as pence per mg, the price of diverted heroin increased from 1.5 p/mg, at which it had been traded between heroin users over the previous decade, to 3 p/mg.

From 1968 many clinics substituted ampoules of methadone for injection (supplied under the trade name Physeptone) instead of the heroin previously prescribed by independent doctors. It was not initially attempted to substitute oral methadone, as would then have been normal practice in the United States.

Initial customer reaction to 'Phy. amps' (ampoules of injectable methadone) was that they were only good for rinsing out one's 'works'. This rapidly gave way to a general realization that intravenous methadone was a rapid acting drug with euphoriant properties and the price of 10 mg units of injectable heroin and methadone rapidly achieved parity.

During the following 5 years the price of heroin rose to between 30 and 50 p/mg, the high price being charged to casual purchasers, the lower to regular safe customers. Given the average street purity of 10–20 per cent for illegally imported heroin in the 1990s, the price from the 1970s is comparable to that of 1993 (Fig. 13.2).

## Staffing of the clinics

The clinics were sparsely staffed with part-time doctors, with varying supporting staff, including nurses, perhaps a social worker and receptionist/

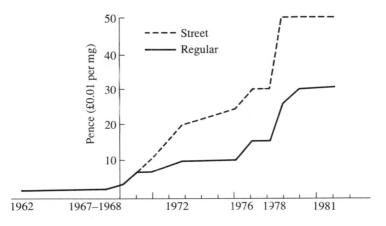

**Fig. 13.2** Price of diverted heroin and injectable methadone.

secretarial support. Psychologists worked part-time in two London clinics during this period. The clients' initial perceptions of clinics were principally as a legitimate controlled source of drugs—and a cynical comment on the parsimonious staffing would be that perhaps this view was shared by the funding authorities. However, the staff, being mainly doctors and nurses, strove to offer a more curative regimen. They offered, where possible: in-patient as well as out-patient detoxification (although one London health region then had no designated in-patient specialist drug unit and, indeed, in 1992 still had none); medical care; counselling; and social support, in several cases developing specific links with non-statutory 'street agencies' as a form of outreach foreshadowing the later development of Community Drug Teams. Nevertheless an inordinate and wearisome amount of time was spent in (usually polite) mutual manipulation between staff and patients regarding type of drug and dose. Many clinics provided a room where patients could inject the prescribed drugs with a degree of care, rather than lock themselves in the lavatory to inject (Stimson 1973).

## Questioning the therapeutic goal

By 1970 it was apparent to many clinic staff that for the majority of out-patients attending clinics their physical health and social functioning was not converted by the receipt of a legitimate supply of heroin to the behaviour exhibited by the traditional middle class therapeutic addict who had been the mainstay of the traditional British System (Schur 1963).

It should be noted that Schur's description of the British System to which he attributed the relatively low level of criminal activity by English drug users was based on his experience in the late 1950s when he undertook his research during a period at the London School of Economics. At that time young heroin users were rare compared with the older patient wholly addicted to other opiates in the course of medical treatment. He did, however, comment that in north London there was already a subcultural use of heroin, with associated drug argot, which was more akin to the American experience and had the potential for developing a different style of drug use. A contrary view to that of Schur who advocated the 'British System' as maintaining a low level of criminality was that presented by Larrimore and Brill (1967). They made several visits to the UK, and suggested that it was the bourgeois middle class, and previous non-criminal character of the traditional British prescribed addict, which enabled the 'British System' to distribute legitimate injectable heroin on medical prescription without the development of a social drug problem.

## Questioning the prescribing of injectable drugs

To examine the consequences over 1 year of a prescription of injectable heroin by comparison with a refusal to prescribe injectable drugs while offering oral methadone maintenance, a random controlled study was undertaken by this author at University College Hospital—the subjects being followed independently in the community by R. Hartnoll. (Mitcheson and Hartnoll 1978; Hartnoll *et al.* 1980). In brief this research reported that while heroin-prescribed patients attended the clinic more regularly and showed some reduction in the extent of their criminal activity, nevertheless they showed no change in their other social activities, such as work, stable accommodation or diet, nor did they differ significantly in the physical complications of drug use from those denied such a prescription. These are all areas where proponents for legal prescribing of drugs of self-injection, then and now, believe there should be a harm reduction effect. While the majority of those who were refused a heroin prescription continued to inject illegally acquired supplies and only attended the clinic when they needed a specific service, a significant minority (one-fifth) of those refused heroin stabilized on oral methadone, and another one-fifth stopped all drug use. Although approximately two-thirds of both groups continued with some criminal activity the severity of this was, however, greater in those refused heroin, and this was reflected in a higher proportion of arrests and more time spent in custody (average 1 week heroin prescribed and 2 weeks for those refused, during a 12 month period).

In the context of this chapter on clinics, the reception that this research received in 1976 when presented to the staff of other clinics was as significant as the findings. The authors were clear and categorical that these findings could be regarded as a useful source of information on which to base more rational policies, and repeatedly stated that the findings were not a clear indication that one treatment was superior to the other. Nevertheless, research was perceived by many staff in London clinics as clear evidence for replacing injectable heroin maintenance with oral prescribing. In this author's opinion this probably reflected the already formulated clinical opinion that the policy of prescribing injectable drugs was, either or both, unhelpful to the patient and/or insupportable to therapeutically inclined staff. However, the research findings formed the focus for a prolonged debate between colleagues working within clinics and in street agencies. The latter by and large acknowledged that the continued prescribing of injectable drugs was not achieving significant change or harm reduction in the individual clients who attended their service. Following this debate many clinics made a considered decision in 1976/77 to move towards a more interventionist therapeutic approach with a refusal to prescribe injectable drugs to new patients.

## Not just opiates

At the commencement and the end of the 1970s, the overwhelming majority of patients seen by drug clinics and street agencies were primarily dependent upon opioids. However, the majority were also secondary polydrug abusers (Bewley 1967; Hawkes *et al.* 1969; Mitcheson *et al.* 1970). There have been other periods before, during, and after the 1970s when perhaps other drugs were more frequently used. For example, in the mid-1960s oral dexamphetamine (often stolen from manufacturers) has been a major primary drug of misuse. With increasing control the price of dexamphetamine tablets increased, and when in 1968 two independent doctors switched from prescribing cocaine to prescribing injectable methylamphetamine there was a fusing between members of the oral tablet culture and those with injection knowledge. When methylamphetamine was withdrawn from the retail pharmacy market by the manufacturer, in agreement with professional organizations, a proportion of these primary amphetamine users transferred to injecting methadone.

## The injecting barbiturate epidemic

Next came the brief period of heavy misuse of methaqualone, under its trade name of Mandrax in 1968 (prior to the vogue for Quaaludes in the USA and Australia). This rapidly passed out of favour with intravenous drug users on account of its relative insolubility in water. The drug was also more strictly controlled under the Dangerous Drug Acts and it was replaced by the injection of barbiturates. Thus, during the early 1970s a combination of relatively easily available capsules of barbiturates, combined with the relative decrease in availability of injectable heroin as a result of clinic policies, the ending the of the Vietnam war in 1973, and several years of drought in the Golden Triangle, facilitated the development of a primary barbiturate injecting drug problem, especially in central London. Barbiturate capsules were so readily available from diverted pharmaceutical and prescription supplies, that attempts at controlled prescribing by clinics were rapidly abandoned in the face of continuing complications.

Barbiturate misusers were frequently intoxicated, alternating with withdrawals typical of alcohol sedative withdrawals and often with *grand mal* epileptic fits occurring on clinic premises. Abscesses from intravenous injection were common, producing characteristic punched out 'sterile' ulceration on the forearms and legs. Some users developed gangrene of hands and legs following accidental intra-arterial injection. The differential development of tolerance to the therapeutic or intoxicating dose on the one hand and to respiratory depression on the other, resulting in a narrowing of the therapeutic lethal ratio, gave rise to successive serious overdoses.

The inability of the out-patient clinics to assist the street agencies and hard pressed accident and emergency departments of central London hospitals to cope with the casualties of this style of drug user, eventually resulted in the Department of Health funding a short-stay residential crisis intervention centre in London—known as City Roads. This service provided a welcome respite both to services concerned with intravenous barbiturate misuse and their clients. The CURB campaign, organized by the medical profession, to reduce barbiturate prescribing reduced availability of the drug on the black market. But the problem drug users did not fade away and City Roads had to modify its protocols in order to service the same rootless inner-city drug users, who were presenting the same acute medical and social problems but were now injecting relatively poor quality South-west Asian heroin which became available at the end of the 1970s.

## Moving away from prescribing injectables

As indicated above, there was an initial drop in prescribing of heroin between 1967 and 1972 followed from 1976 by a further move away from injectable prescribing. Figures 13.3 and 13.4 and/or Tables 13.1—13.4.

By the end of the decade there was a further modification of policy with an attempt to replace indefinite prescribing with contractual programmes. A limited stabilization period was followed by reducing prescriptions, linked contractually with the requirement to attend for either individual

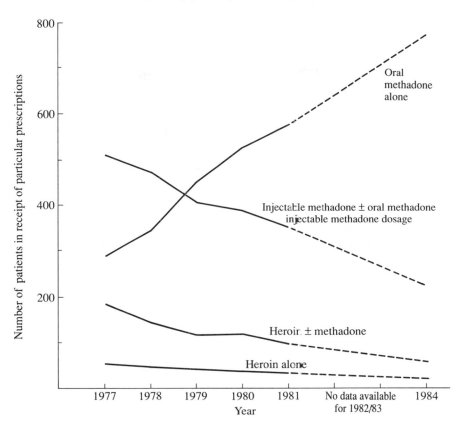

**Fig. 13.3** Numbers of patients receiving different drugs or combinations of drugs for all clinics (London).

*Source*: prescribing data collated for London Clinics meeting.

**Table 13.1** Heroin abuse

| Year | No. at clinics | No. receiving heroin alone | % | Average dose (mg) |
|------|----------------|----------------------------|-----|-------------------|
| 1977 | 982 | 53 | 5 | 250 |
| 1978 | 962 | 47 | 5 | 219 |
| 1979 | 979 | 41 | 4 | 244 |
| 1980 | 1037 | 38 | 4 | 249 |
| 1981 | 1032 | 32 | 3 | 243 |
| 1984 | 1081 | 23 | 2 | 181 |

**Table 13.2**  Heroin ± methadone (oral or injectable)

| Year | No. at clinics | No. receiving heroin ± methadone | % | Average dose heroin (mg) | Average dose total opiate (mg) |
|------|------|------|------|------|------|
| 1977 | 982 | 186 | 19 | 158 | 199 |
| 1978 | 962 | 147 | 15 | 142 | 178 |
| 1979 | 979 | 120 | 12 | 178 | 218 |
| 1980 | 1037 | 121 | 12 | 150 | 189 |
| 1981 | 1032 | 99 | 10 | 138 | 169 |
| 1984 | 1081 | 59 | 5 | 130 | 170 |

**Table 13.3**  Injectable methadone ± oral methadone (but not heroin)

| Year | No. at clinics | No. receiving injectable ± oral methadone | % | Average dose injectable methadone | Average dose total opiate |
|------|------|------|------|------|------|
| 1977 | 982 | 510 | 52 | 59 | 76 |
| 1978 | 962 | 473 | 49 | 59 | 69 |
| 1979 | 979 | 406 | 40 | 60 | 73 |
| 1980 | 1037 | 390 | 38 | 63 | 78 |
| 1981 | 1032 | 353 | 34 | 60 | 76 |
| 1984 | 1081 | 226 | 21 | 49 | 69 |

**Table 13.4**  Oral methadone alone

| Year | No. at clinics | No. receiving oral methadone | % | Average dose |
|------|------|------|------|------|
| 1977 | 982 | 286 | 29 | 39 |
| 1978 | 962 | 341 | 36 | 41 |
| 1979 | 979 | 451 | 46 | 37 |
| 1980 | 1037 | 526 | 51 | 43 |
| 1981 | 1032 | 578 | 56 | 48 |
| 1984 | 1081 | 774 | 72 | 36 |

or group therapy targeted at individual change towards specific social changes and a drug-free goal. It was the policy of many clinics to offer a series of such therapeutic interventions in the expectation that, over time, a significant proportion of drug users would accept such assistance towards a more stable and drug-free life. Certainly clinicians were not

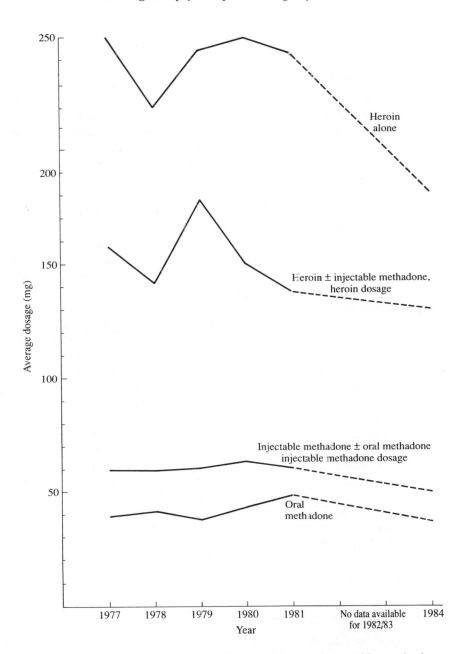

**Fig. 13.4**  Average dosages, for all clinics, of heroin, injectable methadone, and oral methadone; alone or while in combination.

so naive to believe that the majority of patients would immediately stop drug use.

## Diversity in the changes

The summated data in Tables 13.1–13.4 demonstrate a general overall policy change shared by the vast majority of London clinics, but there were of course, exceptions. There always had been considerable variations between clinics in terms of the number of clients attending and their prescribing policies. Thus, for example, in 1977 the number of patients varied between 159 at the largest clinic and eight at the smallest. In the same year the percentage of clients receiving a heroin prescription varied from 0 per cent at a clinic with 89 patients and 1 per cent at the largest clinic then prescribing for 159 to 68 per cent of the 28 patients attending one of the smaller clinics. A clinic with 111 patients in 1977, of whom 48 per cent were receiving injectable prescriptions, had by 1979 144 patients, of whom only 20 per cent were receiving injectable prescriptions. That clinic's experience would suggest that a refusal to prescribe injectable drugs had not deterred patients from seeking help.

There were large variations in the average dose of heroin prescribed which in part reflected the previous prescribing policy of that independent doctor who had transformed the initial group of patients to a particular clinic 10 years previously. The average dose of heroin in 1977 at the clinic with the highest proportion (68 per cent) of patients receiving heroin was 85 mg (range 10–150). In a larger clinic where 40 per cent were receiving heroin the mean daily dose was 224 mg (range 30–650) and another clinic recorded a top dose of 850 mg of heroin per day and a mean dose of 588 mg. By contrast the range of injectable methadone doses in 1979 was much smaller, individual doses ranged from 10 to 240 mg and clinic means ranged from 25 to 104 mg. For oral methadone the range was narrower still, with individual doses of between 1 and 200 mg and clinic means below 64 mg. Overall therefore, while recognizing that the informal discussions at meetings induced movement towards a uniform practice, there were still very considerable variations both within and between clinics which were entirely at the clinical discretion of the staff concerned.

## Why did the changes occur?

The changes during the 1970s were, in the main, a considered response by clinic workers who had acquired experience of the consequences of attempted stabilization with self-injectable prescriptions. Most of the clinics were anxious to continue to attract into a therapeutic environment those who could be assisted. There was concern that even when it was policy to offer a regular prescription of injectable drugs that there had generally been a lapse of 2–4 years between the time that someone was initiated into regular self-injection and the time they presented for treatment. Research into the epidemiology of syringe transmitted hepatitis demonstrated that, by the time most patients presented for initial treatment, they had already been infected by syringe transmitted hepatitis (Weller 1984). It was, therefore, felt that the correct emphasis was to develop outreach work and look to the availability of services and their image with the drug user, rather than rely on prescribing injectable drugs as a bait to bring in the customers.

It should be emphasized that at the time the changes in opioid prescribing were implemented there had not been a significant increase in the number of new patients presenting to clinics. The changes were based on clinical judgement in relation to the physical and social state of patients and their continued injection of a range of dangerous drugs. Increasing number of new referrals only began to present to treatment facilities at the end of the 1970s decade following the influx of Southwest Asian heroin after the Iranian Revolution. The prior introduction of time limited prescribing may, however, have subsequently enabled clinics to respond to the increased number of new referrals, without necessitating increasing staff and budgets. Although this chapter refers specifically to the 1970s it is appropriate to note that the additional funding provided from Central Government sources (first made available in 1984) was to cope with the increase in numbers presenting to clinics and particularly to enable services to be set-up outside of London where illegal heroin was becoming increasingly available. Only more recent increase in funding has been specifically linked to policy changes aimed at retaining patients in treatment for harm reduction in relation to reducing the spread of the HIV through needle sharing.

## Conclusion

The insistence that these changes were initiated on clinical judgement and not financial expediency is not a rhetorical argument. It is important to document and recall the experience of even the recent past. The uncontrolled prescribing of heroin by independent doctors between 1959 and 1968 was accompanied by a geometric increase in the number of new addicts to prescribed heroin, but a stable and low price for diverted heroin. The 1970s saw the erosion of the capacity of therapists to tolerate a numerically stable, but disorganized and distressing long-term regular clinic clientele who were persistent in their continued misuse of drugs, so that the clinics collectively swung the pendulum away from maintenance and towards confrontation of continued misuse of drugs, with active intervention and emphasis on facilitating change. Quite apart from the significant cost of funding prescriptions for long-term controlled stabilization, there will also be a cost to be paid in terms of the burnout and disillusionment of dedicated staff, both in the statutory Community Drug Teams which have replaced the drug clinics, and in the non-statutory services which provide counselling and social support. The latter by and large acknowledged that the continued prescribing of injectable drugs was not achieving significant change or harm reduction in the individual clients who attend their service.

Clearly, the experience of the 1970s is highly relevant to the necessary continuing debate in the 1990s as to the appropriate form that drug services should take. It is tempting when confronted with an intractable problem to initiate radical changes in policy unsupported by systematic outcome studies. It is important therefore, first, to remember that a drug solution to the drug problem simply by prescribing injectable drugs is unlikely to be successful, and secondly that workers in drug services are not immune from the aphorism that 'the majority of the human race prefer the certainty of irrational conviction to the uncertainty of logical doubt'. There never has been, and never will be a simple solution to the problem of substance misuse. And none of the range of services that must be provided come cheap in terms of cash or human resources.

## References

Bewley, T. H. (1965). *Lancet*, **i**, 808.
Bewley, T. H. (1967). *British Medical Journal*, **3**, 603–5.
Brain Committee (Interdepartmental Committee on Drug Addiction, chaired by Sir Russell Brain) (1965). *Second report*. HMSO, London.
Connell, P. H. (1991). Treatment of drug dependent patients 1968–69. *British Journal of Addiction*, **86**, 913–90.
Dole, V. P., Nysvander, M. E., and Kreek, M. J. (1966). Narcotic blockade. *Archives of Internal Medicine*, **118**, 304–9.
Dorn, N. and South, N. (1985). *Helping drug users*. Gower, Aldershot.
Hartnoll, R. L., Mitcheson, M. C., *et al*. (1980). Evaluation of heroin maintenance in controlled trial. *Archives of General Psychiatry*, **37**, 877–84.
Hawkes, D., Mitcheson, M., Ogborne, A. and Edwards, G. (1969). Abuse of methylamphetamine. *British Medical Journal*, **2**, 715–21.
Larrimore, G. W. and Brill, H. (1967). Epidemiological factors in drug addiction in England and USA. *Public Health Reports*, **77**, 555–60.
Mitcheson, M. C. and Hartnoll, R. L. (1978). Conflicts in deciding treatment within drug dependency clinics. In *Problems of drug abuse in Britain* (ed. D. J. West), pp. 74–7. Cambridge University Institute of Criminology.
Mitcheson, M. C., Davidson, J., Hawkes, D., Hitchens, L., and Molone, S. (1970). Sedative abuse by heroin addicts. *Lancet*, **i**, 606–7.
Schur, E. M. (1963). *Narcotic addiction in Britain and America*. Tavistock, London.

Stimson, G. V. (1973). *Heroin and behaviour: diversity among addicts attending London clinics*. Irish University Press, Shannon, Ireland.

Weller, I. V. D., Cohn, D., Sierralta, A., Mitcheson, M., Ross, M. G. R., Montano, L., Scheuer, P., and Thomas, H. L. (1984). Clinical, biochemical, histological, and ultrastructural features of liver disease in drug abusers. *Gut*, **25**, 417–23.

# 14. Prescribing heroin and other injectable drugs

*John Strang, Susan Ruben, Michael Farrell, and Michael Gossop*

## Introduction

For years, prescribing injectable heroin to opiate addicts has been unique to the UK. Indeed prescribing any injectable agonist as part of the treatment for opiate addiction occurs only in the UK, apart from a few experimental schemes with injectable morphine which have been mooted (Goldstein 1974) and implemented in The Netherlands (Derks 1990*a,b*) and three patients who are the rump of 27 heroin addicts who were started on injectable methadone in 1977 in Queensland, Australia (Reynolds, A., personal communication, 1993).

At first glance (and for some, at second and third glance also) there is something inherently paradoxical in an approach which involves the prescribing of the very drug of addiction as part of the treatment of addiction. For any consideration of this approach, a particular clarity is required with regard to the goals of treatment. Is it the containment of the 'epidemic' to those already 'infected'? Is it the overcoming of the dependence? Is it the protection from, or muting of, the associated harm? These options will be considered in more detail later in the chapter.

The prescribing of injectable heroin is perhaps the most famous characteristic of the 'British System'. And yet, at the time of writing, it is probably only 1 or 2 per cent of the estimated 75 000–150 000 heroin users who receive a prescribed supply of any injectable drug—and only a small proportion of these will be receiving injectable heroin. In 1990, the total number of addicts who received a prescribed supply of injectable heroin was approximately two hundred, with a few thousand receiving injectable methadone. In truth, although this practice may attract considerable local and international attention, the prescribing of injectable drugs is numerically of small significance in the overall UK response—even though the continuity or cessation of the practice may be a subject of great concern to the practitioners and patients for whom it forms the basis of a current treatment.

## 'Each physician is a law unto himself'

Commentators from abroad, and perhaps especially the USA, are fascinated by the extraordinary clinical freedom which is given to the medical practitioner in the UK with regard to the prescribing of drugs to the opiate addict. As Connell (1975) commented in his review of methadone maintenance schemes, 'each physician in charge of a special drug dependence clinic is a law unto himself as to how he treats and manages patients'. Whilst the prescribing of heroin, cocaine, and dipipanone (Diconal) is now restricted to those doctors who hold a special licence (in practice, the doctors who work in National Health Service (NHS) drug treatment centres), any qualified medical practitioner can prescribe oral or injectable methadone, morphine, or any other available pharmaceutical drug. However, despite this extraordinary clinical freedom, the majority of general practitioners choose not to exercise this right so that, paradoxically, the average UK doctor is extremely conservative in their prescribing to the addict, with three-quarters of a recent national sample of general practitioners reporting that they would not be willing to prescribe oral methadone—even if provided with shared care and support from a local specialist team (reported in Advisory Council on the misuse of Drugs, 1993). Thus a strange situation has developed, where a small number of general practitioners develop a degree of quasi-specialist expertise in the management of opiate addicts (e.g. Robertson 1987; Banks and Waller 1988; Dally 1990), whilst many other general practitioners react hostily to the more modest proposals in guidelines from the Department of Health (1984, 1991) that they should be involved in the prescribing of oral methadone for at least the purposes of detoxification. A similar opposition can also be seen in the hostile response from police surgeons (who are mostly general practitioners who do additional sessional work visiting police cells) who reacted angrily (Davis *et al.* 1992) to the suggestion [in the Department of Health (1991) guidelines] that they should be willing to give oral methadone to established opiate addicts who are detained in custody (Department of Health 1991; Strang 1992*a*; Ghodse 1992; Green and Drennen 1992).

Great variability in prescribing habits results from this lack of central direction and the accompanying individual clinical freedom of medical practitioners in the UK. There is probably no prescribing whatsoever of any injectable drugs to addicts in the whole of Scotland, Wales, Northern Ireland, and much of England, whereas some other areas (most famously Liverpool and other parts of the Mersey Region, and also to a lesser extent parts of London) have NHS drug specialist doctors and other doctors who include the prescribing of injectable heroin or methadone as part of their overall prescribing response. Nevertheless, despite periodic calls for the introduction of controls, the prescription of the injectable drug of main use (or an injectable substitute) continues to exist as a tool within the armamentarium of every doctor in the UK.

## The early history of injectables

The hypodermic syringe was extensively developed by Alexander Wood in Edinburgh in the middle of the nineteenth century. However, its early use was for intramuscular administration of drugs. In his account of the history of injecting, Kane (1880) describes accounts from his colleagues of some of the first few intravenous administrations of opiates—which had occurred inadvertently during an intended intra-muscular administration. Although it was initially thought that the habit-forming nature of such drug use might be avoided by circumventing the oral route, it soon became clear that injectable drug use might also be habit-forming, as had become the case for many soldiers who had regularly used their supplies of injectable morphine during the American Civil War.

By the early twentieth century, the international anti-narcotics move-ment was becoming influential, and, with the lead taken by the USA, both national and international legislation was passed. After a period during which injectable opiates were prescribed in the USA, the Harrison Act was passed and all prescribing of pharmaceutical opiates to addicts was soon stopped. In contrast, the UK establishment chose not to cri-minalize but to 'medicalize' the problem, following guidelines from the influential Rolleston Report, which had been prepared as an inter-ministerial report under the chairmanship of Sir Humphrey Rolleston (Ministry of Health 1926). In essence, this report established the right of the medical practitioner in the UK to prescribe regular supplies of an opiate drug to an addict in the following circumstances:

(i)   where patients were under treatment by the gradual withdrawal method with a view to cure;

(ii)  where it has been demonstrated after a prolonged attempt to cure that the use of the drug could not be safely discontinued entirely on account of the severity of the withdrawal symptoms produced; and

(iii) where it has been similarly demonstrated that the patient, while capable of leading a useful and normal life when a certain minimum dose was regu-larly administered, became incapable of this when the drug was entirely discontinued.

Thus it was established that the doctor might legally prescribe injectable opiates to an addict provided this was '... "treatment" rather than the "gratification of addiction" '.

The next 30 years were a period during which there was no significant problem of injectable opiate use in the UK (for further discussion see Chapter 1). However, although some commentators have eulogized about the effectiveness of the British System during these years, the direction of causality between policy and lack of problem is not clear.

The date when intravenous injecting became established in the UK is not documented. It would appear that the injectable opiate use under consideration by the Rolleston Committee (1926) was subcutaneous or intramuscular, whereas the new opiate injectors in the 1960s (see next section) were using the drug intravenously. In the US, over this period, there had been a steady spread of the intravenous habit, and this diffusion has been described in some detail (O'Donnell and Jones 1968).

As cracks began to appear in the 'British System' during the 1960s, there was a temptation to look back on what appeared to be the success of the previous decades, identifying characteristics such as the absence of any illicit traffic in drugs, the absence of an addict subculture, and the absence of any young users. However, other commentators suggested that the previous decades had merely been 'a period of non-policy' (Smart 1984) in which '... there was no system, but as there was very little in the way of misuse of drugs, this did not matter' (Bewley 1975). As Downes concluded, the British System had perhaps been '... well and truly exposed as little more than masterly inactivity in the face of what was an almost non-existent addiction problem' (Downes 1977).

## Injectable prescribing and the growth of a modern day problem

In the late 1950s and early 1960s, there was an influx of a new type of opiate addict to the UK—a North American (mainly Canadian) addict with an established criminal history. Several hundred such addicts entered the UK during these years, attracted by the accounts of prescribed supplies of injectable pharmaceutical opiates—alongside a lack of immigration restrictions. Some caught the boat to Liverpool and then a train straight to London. For others, the transfer was more direct: 'I got a taxi from the airport to a GP in the Holloway Road, and got an immediate prescription for heroin and cocaine.' (For further discussion see Chapter 1.) Up until this time, the opiate addict population in the UK had been substantially middle-aged and middle class, with a high representation of doctors and of patients who became dependent on their analgesic drugs. Thus, as a result of the prevailing patterns of prescribing of analgesics, heroin itself was rarely prescribed. For example, during the 1940s and 1950s, the total number of known opiate addicts in the UK never exceeded 500, of whom only about 10 per cent had been using (i.e. were prescribed) heroin.

The interpretation of the events during the 1960s varies greatly, with some observers concluding that the growth of a new drug culture was caused largely by the overprescribing of a handful of doctors (Second Brain Report (Interdepartmental Committee on Drug Addiction) 1965) whilst others suggest that the lax regulations and generous prescribing potential of UK doctors was a system waiting to be bust open by the newly arrived North American junkies (Blackwell 1988). Whatever the explanation, a youthful hedonistic drug using culture became established in the UK during the 1960s—particularly in London. The use of injectable opiates involved prescribed pharmaceutical opiates (particularly heroin) which was prescribed by a small number of doctors in or around London, and from whom the daily doses prescribed rose steadily: for example, some of the opiate addicts steadily increased their daily intake from about one to 40 grains of injectable heroin daily (60–2400 mg daily). The dependent status of some of the high dose users was confirmed by occasional clinical observation of them as they injected these large amounts (Gossop 1987).

## Prescribing injectable drugs from the new clinics (1968 onwards)

NHS drug clinics were established for the first time in 1968. They were expected to address multiple agenda, which included the need to provide treatment to the new addicts, and the need to contain the spreading 'epidemic'. More immediately, there was a need for them to take over the care of more than 1000 addicts who had been receiving their heroin (and sometimes cocaine) from doctors who were no longer allowed to prescribe either of these two drugs. In practice the majority of these patients were taken on by the clinics on prescriptions very similar to those which they had previously been receiving—at least in the first instance. (For further details on the changes at this time, see Connell (1991) and Chapter 12.)

During the early months of operation of the new drug clinics, the new NHS heroin prescribers also took over responsibility for prescribing injectable cocaine—almost exclusively to a population of injecting drug users who were taking both heroin and cocaine. For patients who received both drugs, doses of cocaine were either equal or lower than the dose of heroin prescribed. However, within a year, an informal agreement was reached amongst London doctors working in the drug clinics to stop the practice of prescribing injectable cocaine: this practice subsequently stopped abruptly for most such patients, since which time only a handful of addicts in the UK have received prescribed supplies of injectable cocaine.

After 18 months of operation, some degree of stability had developed in day to day clinic practice. Home Office data are available on the drugs being prescribed to the 1466 known addicts at the end of December 1969—499 were receiving prescribed supplies of heroin (of whom 295 were also receiving methadone), 716 were receiving methadone, and 251 were receiving other opiates (usually morphine or pethidine). (Note: Most methadone prescribed to addicts in the UK at this time was in the form of injectable methadone ampoules, with only small amounts of oral methadone linctus being prescribed—see Chapter 13; however, the exact breakdown of the prescribed drug by route of administration is not provided in the Home Office data.)

## Confusion and conflict in the clinics: what purpose behind injectable prescribing?

During the late 1960s and early 1970s, the new drug doctors (the NHS doctors in the drugs clinics) began to switch their prescribing habits from injectable heroin to injectable methadone (see Chapter 13). Nevertheless, returns to the Department of Health showed the continued dominance of injectable opiates in the prescriptions to addicts attending NHS hospitals in England and Wales. Examination of the total quantities of injectable heroin, injectable methadone, and oral methadone (the three main forms of opiates prescribed to addicts) prescribed reveals a gradual change during the decade after the opening of the clinics, with annual figures of 17, 11, and 3 kg, respectively, being prescribed in 1970; 15, 21, and 8 kg, respectively, in 1974; and 9, 14, and 17 kg respectively, by 1978 (Department of Health data published by Edwards 1981).

Prescription of injectable methadone steadily increased to a mid-1970s peak, after which the trend appears to have been away from any injectable prescribing, with an increased reliance on oral methadone. These data accord with the findings of Blumberg *et al.* (1974*a,b*) who reported on the slightly greater obtainability of injectable methadone than injectable heroin in the early 1970s. It is also interesting to note from Blumberg's work that injectable methadone and heroin are accorded similar scores by the addict for liking and need as measured on a five-point and four-point scale respectively (Blumberg *et al.* 1974*a*).

This potential conflict is explored by Stimson and Oppenheimer (1982). If clinics were to be given the twin aims of medical care and social control, could these aims always be met together, or might they sometimes be in conflict? 'For example, the social control of addiction might be best pursued by a maintenance-prescribing approach, but this might not be the best treatment for an individual patient ...'. The social control of addiction was usually seen as the primary task of the clinics. This conflict was also considered by Mitcheson and Hartnoll (1978) in one of the early considerations of their study of prescribing injectable heroin versus oral methadone. They observed that

... overall, prescribing heroin can be seen as maintaining the status quo with the majority of heroin-maintained patients continuing to inject heroin regularly: prescribing heroin is not associated with an improvement in social functioning or a reduction in consumption of illegal drugs, as is sometimes claimed. It may reduce the degree of involvement in criminal activity, especially in terms of arrests and conviction rates. Refusal to prescribe heroin, while offering oral methadone, constitutes a more confrontational response by the clinic and results in a higher abstinence rate. On the other hand this treatment is less acceptable to the client and the clinic fails to maintain a regular contact with the group of clients who continue to use illicit drugs ...

What was behind the move from prescribing injectable heroin to injectable methadone? No doubt it was partly influenced by the increased public and professional anxiety about prescribing heroin (in the public's eyes, a drug of abuse) compared with methadone (in public and professional eyes, a medicinal drug). However, other reasons were also articulated. The long half-life of methadone meant that it might be a drug which was more conducive to social and occupational stability, as it need only be administered once or twice a day.

There were also concerns about the safety of injecting heroin: pharmaceutical heroin was prescribed in the 1960s and 1970s in the form of tablets known as pills or jacks, which the addict (or nurse or doctor) would then dissolve in water to make the solution ready for injecting. As Bewley (1975) said

We tend to prescribe methadone because it comes in an ampoule and it won't be mixed with water from the kitchen sink or whatever: also because it's a more long-acting drug. There is no evidence that it is better than heroin in one way or another but because it is more long-acting and because people can inject it in a cleaner way, we believe that there is an advantage.

In the same proceedings, Haastrup reports on interview research with heroin users in England which showed that '... in one week, half of the addicts used normal water from the kitchen and one in ten had used water from the lavatory' (Haastrup 1975). Bewley went on to explain how clinical practice in his own clinic in London included not only the provision of clean needles and syringes, but also advice from the clinic nursing staff so that patients can be instructed on how to inject themselves. The study to which Haastrup referred may well have been the study by Stimson who reported on the extent to which addicts mixed up their heroin with either Apyrogen (ampoules of sterile water), liquid methadone (Physeptone ampoules), boiled water, tap water, or lavatory water; whilst only 12 of the 111 subjects reported use of lavatory water the majority of use was of uncertain cleanliness status (Stimson 1973).

## Injectable heroin and injectable methadone

Methadone has a hedonistic appeal and black market value which is similar to heroin when both drugs are compared in their injectable forms (see Blumberg *et al.* 1974*a*). Internationally, methadone is often considered only in its oral form, and observers mistakenly attribute properties to the drug itself when they are in fact confusing the drug with the formulation. In clinical practice with the prescribing of these drugs to opiate addicts, the committed injector seeking a prescribed supply of injectable drugs would usually be quite amenable to moves between heroin and methadone in injectable form—in sharp contrast to the determined opposition which may be encountered to suggestions of moving from injectable methadone to its oral form. In an interview with one such addict receiving injectable methadone in Amsterdam, the addict is quoted as follows: 'I have been taking it for half a year now, it's far out: they can take anything from me, my beer, my wife—so long as they keep their hands off my injectable methadone' (Kools 1992).

## Not just the opiates

The debate about prescribing of injectable drugs to addicts is usually dominated by consideration of prescribing opiate drugs. However, other drugs of dependence have also been prescribed in injectable forms, although this practice has become extremely rare.

When the new NHS drug clinics were established in 1968, many of the patients who were taken on from the private practitioners were already receiving prescribed supplies of intravenous cocaine alongside their prescribed intravenous heroin. Initially the doctors in the new drug clinics continued this prescribing of cocaine—up until a consensus was reached amongst these doctors to cease all such cocaine prescribing (in late 1968), which appears to have been implemented extensively with little or no evidence of the promotion of a black market in imported cocaine. A small number of doctors continued to prescribe injectable cocaine to extremely small numbers of addict patients (usually in conjunction with injectable opiates), but only a handful of such cases continued through to the 1980s. More recently Marks and Palombella (1990) have argued for the prescribing of cocaine 'reefers' as a possible 'harm reduction' approach, with the cocaine being added by the pharmacist to herbal cigarettes. However no useful data have yet been presented on this practice, and it is not even clear whether the drug is effectively or reliably absorbed from these 'reefers'.

An intravenous methylamphetamine epidemic occurred during 1967/68, when a small number of private doctors (whom the new regulations banned from prescribing heroin or cocaine) began to prescribe methylamphetamine ampoules (Methedrine) with a resulting epidemic of chaotic use (James 1968; Hawks *et al*. 1969). One London centre began an experimental programme of prescribing injectable amphetamines to these drug users, but this was soon abandoned when an agreement was reached between the Ministry of Health and the manufacturers to withdraw supplies of the drug to retail chemists (hence closing off its availability via private doctors) (Mitcheson *et al*. 1976).

Whilst the interruption of cocaine prescribing (see previous paragraph) might have been linked to the development of this methylamphetamine abuse (in that the methylamphetamine was being prescribed by many of the same private doctors who were no longer able to prescribe cocaine), the co-ordinated control strategy of removal of supplies of the drug from retail pharmacists would appear to stand as an example of a successful control-based intervention.

## AIDS breathes new life into the injecting debate

The debate about the appropriateness or otherwise of prescribing injectable drugs continued as a background debate during the early 1980s, but shifted from being a debate within specialist clinic practice to being the battleground between NHS and private doctors. However, it remained an extremely rare form of clinical practice in most areas, so that by the mid to late 1980s there were probably still less than 1000 addicts in receipt of injectable drugs (mainly injectable methadone) from amongst the estimated 75 000–150 000 opiate addicts (ACMD 1988).

Acquired immune deficiency syndrome (AIDS) brought a fundamental re-examination of drug policy and the goals and methods of drug treatment in the UK (Advisory Council on the Misuse of Drugs (ACMD) 1988, 1989; Strang and Stimson 1990; Department of Health 1991). The prescribing of injectable drugs was back on the main agenda—not necessarily as a recommended practice, but certainly as an option to be considered. Prescribing of any drugs to the drug user was reformulated as a possible '... useful tool in helping to change the behaviour of some drug misusers either towards abstinence or towards intermediate goals such as a reduction in injecting or sharing' (ACMD 1988). A hierarchy of acceptable goals was identified:

(1) the cessation of sharing of equipment;
(2) the move from injectable to oral drug use;
(3) a decrease in drug use; and
(4) abstinence.

For this consideration, any prescribing could be judged and compared according to its effectiveness/ineffectiveness in bringing about the desired changes.

The prescribing of injectable drugs was included in this consideration, but with the caveat that such cases should not be managed by the general practitioner and required input from specialist drug services. The ACMD (1988) went on to state that

In some cases—a small minority—prescribing of injectable drugs may be necessary to keep the individual in treatment and/or to ease the change from injecting the drug of dependence to taking a substitute orally. Where this is so, such prescribing of injectables should normally be undertaken for short periods only (rarely more than three months) ... the prescribing of injectable drugs in this way will be an important element in helping some injecting drug misusers to move gradually away from injecting. Such cases will be exceptional ... (and) should be managed by, or with guidance from, the District or Regional specialist team.

Thus the ACMD endorsed the view that interim prescribing of injectable drugs might be considered legitimate medical practice if it was found to bring about a move to oral-only use which might otherwise not have occurred: in these circumstances, the end would have justified the means. There has been insufficient study of this approach for robust conclusions to be reached, but preliminary reports show a disappointing lack of evidence of extensive achievement of these intermediate goals: rather, what is seen is a drift away to another source of prescribed or black market injectable drugs as the change over to oral drugs begins (see, for example, Battersby *et al.* 1992). The issue remains unresolved at the time of writing, but as various commentators have observed, the potential for serious error is much greater in view of the direct physical complications and supply to third parties (the black/grey market) if injectable drugs are prescribed when oral drugs would have been sufficient (Strang 1990; ACMD 1993). This debate re-emerged in the 1990s in the UK, with arguments about the relative importance that should be assigned to the debate on oral methadone versus injectable methadone (Brewer, Marks, and Marks 1992; Strang and Farrell 1992). As Dole has recently observed, whilst UK practitioners may see great advantage to the preservation of their considerable clinical freedom, there may also be disadvantages of the 'cafeteria approach' to drug treatment for the opiate addict who wishes to exercise freedom of choice when he/she may otherwise have been satisfied with a single available product (namely oral methadone) (Dole 1992).

## Doctors as healers, or doctors as grocers?

The introduction and spread of needle-exchange schemes in the UK since 1987 (Stimson *et al.* 1988, 1990) represents not only a new service to the actual or potential clientele of the drug clinics, but it also provokes a widening of the constituency of concern. The needle-exchange schemes may provide needles and syringes to the established addict (who may or may not be known to drug treatment services), but they may also provide needles and syringes to the non-dependent injector.

What should be the response of drug treatment services to this new wider constituency—the non-dependent injector? Although some drug doctors and drug workers would argue that the next logical step is to provide free supplies of the pharmaceutical drugs to put into the free needles and syringes, this could be seen as a naive and ill-considered position which fails to appreciate the fundamentally different nature of the strategies behind drug treatment services and needle and syringe services. At the heart of the debate is a different view on the role of the doctor (or other health-care worker) in providing drugs to the drug addict. Certainly the recent considerations of the ACMD have seen prescribing as a treatment for the individual—admittedly an unusual treatment by medical standards, but a treatment nevertheless—which is provided in order to bring about benefits in physical and psychological well-being of that individual which would not have been accrued (at least, not to the same extent) if the treatment had not been given. On the other hand, the case for considering the public health and individual health needs of the wider constituency of injectors is evident in the encouragement of over-the-counter sales of needles and syringes from pharmacies (Glanz *et al*. 1989) as well as the needle-exchange schemes.

But should the doctor then feel obliged to prescribe the drugs to fit inside the needle and syringe? If they were to do so, it would be far from clear whether the doctor was still providing medical treatment to the individual, or might alternatively be an overpaid grocer whose only task was to provide the products as requested (perhaps with some safety cut-off limits). Self (1992) has described this as doctors acting as 'dealers by appointment to H.M. Government'. This confusion between the availability of drugs as treatment and the availability of drugs as commodities is evident in some of the calls for legalization of drugs, where many of the points made relate to the provision of treatment to addicts (and could hence be considered in a different context). However this concerns an altogether different legitimizing ideology behind the provision of drugs to drug users, and is not considered further within this chapter.

## Conclusion

The option of prescribing heroin or other injectable drugs has long been a distinctive feature of the 'British system'. In practice, this authority to prescribe injectable drugs is rarely exercised—at the level of the specialist, as well as the generalist doctor. Nevertheless the very existence of this prescribing tool within the armamentarium has a profound influence on both policy and practice: it may well be simultaneously good and bad—good in so far as it may draw the reluctant or ambivalent drug addict into treatment at an earlier stage, and bad in so far as it may obstruct progress to a non-injectable treatment option which would have been acceptable in the absence of an injectable alternative.

Perhaps a new discipline is now required in re-examining the role of injectable prescribing. Since the advent of HIV, an old perspective has re-appeared in a new form, with the new attention to 'harm reduction' strategies. In this context, the debate about injectable prescribing has to be re-examined. Can the prescribing of injectable drugs lead (at least on some occasions) to a reduction in risk or harm? If so, what harm, and experienced by whom? And if harm is reduced in the short term, then what will be the overall effect on cumulative harm accrued over a longer period of time (Strang 1992b, 1993)? Moral positions may need to be swept aside so as to permit unobstructed scrutiny of the extent to which injectable prescribing has a beneficial and/or aggravating effect on overall harm.

Regrettably there has been an extraordinary lack of properly conducted studies of injectable prescribing so that any opinions which are formed must rely on partial anecdote in the absence of either proper research or monitoring. As a result, no reliable conclusions can be reached about such prescribing, and the issue is open to hijack by those who wish to reinforce their pre-selected position within the prescribing debate. Despite the media and public fascination with the prescribing of injectable drugs, it is probable that the greatest benefits will be accrued from the prescribing of oral substitute drugs (such as oral methadone), especially when one bears in mind that this form of the drug is prescribed to at least ten times as many heroin addicts in the UK and at least one hundred times as many heroin addicts across the world.

# References

ACMD (Advisory Council on the Misuse of Drugs) (1988). *AIDS and drug misuse report, Part 1*. HMSO, London.

ACMD (1989). *AIDS and drug misuse report, Part 2*. HMSO, London.

ACMD (1993). *AIDS and drug misuse report, Update*. HMSO, London.

Banks, A. and Waller, T. A. N. (1988). *Drug misuse—a practical handbook for GPs*. Blackwell Scientific Publications, Oxford.

Battersby, M., Farrell, M., Gossop, M., Robson, P., and Strang, J. (1992). 'Horsetrading': prescribing injectable opiates to opiate addicts. A descriptive study. *Drug and Alcohol Review*, **11**, 35–42.

Bewley, T. H. (1975). Evaluation of addiction treatment in England. In *Drug dependence: treatment and treatment evaluation* (ed. H. Bostrom, T. Larsson, and N. Ljungstedt), pp. 275–86. Almqvist and Wiksell, Stockholm.

Blackwell, J. (1988). The saboteurs of Britain's opiate policy: over-prescribing physicians or American-style junkies? *International Journal of the Addictions*, **23**, 517–26.

Blumberg, H., Cohen, S., Dronfield, B., Mardecai, E., Roberts, J., and Hawks, D. (1974a). British opiate users: I. People approaching London drug treatment centres. *International Journal of the Addictions*, **9**, 1–23.

Blumberg, H. H., Cohen, S., Dronfield, B., Mordecai, E., Roberts, J., and Hawks, D. (1974b). British opiate users: II. Differences between those given an opiate script and those not given one. *International Journal of the Addictions*, **9**, 205–20.

Brewer, C., Marks, J., and Marks, J. (1992). Methadone maintenance. *British Medical Journal*, **304**, 1441–2.

Connell, P. H. (1975). Review of methadone maintenance schemes. In *Drug dependence—treatment and treatment evaluation* (ed. H. Bostrom, T. Larsson, and N. Ljundstedt), pp. 133–46. Almqvist and Wiksell, Stockholm.

Dally, A. (1990). *A doctor's story*. Macmillan, London.

Davis, N., Bott, E. C. A., Carne, S., Davies, H. de la H., Knight, M. A., and Roberts, R. (1992). Drug misusers under police custody. *The Times*, February 10th, p. 10.

Department of Health, Scottish Home and Health Department, and Welsh Office (1991). *Drug misuse and dependence: guidelines on clinical management*, pp. 35–6. HMSO, London.

Department of Health and Social Security (1984). *Guidelines for good clinical practice in the treatment of drug misuse*. DHSS, London.

Derks, J. T. M. (1990a). The Amsterdam morphine dispensing programme: a longitudinal study of extremely problematic drug addicts in an experimental public health programme. Report from Erasmus University, Rotterdam.

Derks, J. (1990b). The efficacy of the Amsterdam morphine-dispensing programme. In *Drug misuse and dependence* (ed. A. H. Ghodse, C. Kaplan, and R. Mann), pp. 85–108. Parthanon, Carneforth.

Dole (1992). From laboratory to public health application: putting what we know into practice (the 6th Okey Memorial Lecture).

Downes, D. (1977). The drug addict as folk devil. In *Drugs and politics* (ed. P. Rock). Transaction Books, New Jersey.

Edwards, G. (1981). The Home Office Index as a basic monitoring system. In *Drug problems in Britain: A review of ten years* (ed. G. Edwards and C. Busch), pp. 25–50. Academic Press, London.

Ghodse, A. H. (1992). Care of addicts in police custody. *The Times*, February 25th, p. 11.

Glanz, A., Byrne, C., and Jackson, P. (1989). Role of community pharmacies in prevention of AIDS among injecting drug misusers: findings of a survey in England and Wales. *British Medical Journal*, **209**, 1076–9.

Goldstein, A. (1974). New approaches to the treatment of heroin addiction: STEPS (Sequential Treatment Employing Pharmacological Supports). *Archives of General Psychiatry*, **33**, 353–8.

Gossop, M. (1987). *Living with drugs*. Wildwood, Aldershot.

Green, P. G. and Drennen, P. C. (1992). Care of addicts in police custody. *The Times*, February 25th, p. 11.

Haastrup, S. (1975). The traditional follow-up technique in additional treatment. In *Drug dependence—treatment and treatment evaluation* (ed. H.

Bostrom, T. Larsson, and N. Ljungstedt), pp. 237–56. Almqvist and Wiksell, Stockholm.

Hawks, D. V., Mitcheson, M., Ogborne, A., and Edwards, G. (1969). Abuse of methylamphetamine. *British Medical Journal*, **2**, 715–21.

Interdepartmental Committee on Drug Addiction (Brain Committee) (1965). *Drug addiction; second report*. HMSO, London.

James, I. P. (1968). A methylamphetamine epidemic. *Lancet*, **i**, 916.

Kane, H. H. (1880). *The hypodermic injection of morphia*. Chas L. Bermingham and Co., New York.

Kools, J.-P. (1992). Injectable methadone: policy for supplying methadone. *Mainline: Drugs, Health and the Street* (special edition), p. 5.

Marks, J. and Palombella, A. (1990). Prescribing smokable drugs. *Lancet*, **335**, 864.

Ministry of Health (1926). *Report of the Departmental Committee on Morphine and Heroin Addiction (Rolleston Report)*. HMSO, London.

Mitcheson, M. and Hartnoll, R. (1978). Conflicts in deciding treatments within drug dependency units. In *Problems of drug abuse in Britain* (ed. D. J. West), pp. 74–9. Institute of Criminology, Cambridge.

Mitcheson, M., Edwards, G., Hawks, D., and Ogborne, A. (1976). Treatment of methylamphetamine users during the 1968 epidemic. In *Drugs and drug dependence* (ed. G. Edwards, M. Russell, D. Hawks, and M. MacCafferty), pp. 155–62. Saxon House, Farnborough.

O'Donnell, J. A. and Jones, J. D. (1968). Diffusion of the intravenous technique among narcotic addicts. *Journal of Health and Social Behaviour*, **9**, 120–30.

Robertson, R. (1987). *Heroin, AIDS and society*. Hodder and Stoughton, London.

Self, W. (1992). Drug dealer by appointment to H. M. Government. *Sunday Observer*, September 13th.

Smart, C. (1984). Social policy and drug addiction: a critical study of policy development. *British Journal of Addiction*, **79**, 31–9.

Stimson G. V. (1973). *Heroin and behaviour: diversity among addicts attending London clinics*. Irish University Press, Shannon.

Stimson, G. V. and Oppenheimer, E. (1982). *Heroin addiction: treatment and control in Britain*. Tavistock, London.

Stimson, G., Alldritt, L., Dolan, K., and Donoghoe, M (1988). Syringe exchange schemes for drug users in England and Scotland. *British Medical Journal*, **296**, 1717–19.

Stimson, G., Donoghoe, M., Lart, R., and Dolan, K. (1990). Distributing sterile needles and syringes to people who inject drugs: the syringe exchange experiment. In *AIDS and drug misuse: the challenge for policy and practice in the 1990s* (ed. J. Strang and G. Stimson), pp. 222–31. Routledge, London.

Strang, J. (1990). The roles of prescribing. In *AIDS and drug misuse: the challenge for policy and practice in the 1990s* (ed. J. Strang and G. Stimson), pp. 142–52. Routledge, London.

Strang, J. (1992a). Care of addicts in police custody. *The Times*, February 25th, p. 11.

Strang, J. (1992b). Harm reduction for drug users: exploring the dimensions of harm, their measurement and the strategies for reduction. *AIDS and Public Policy Journal*, **7(3)**, 145–52.

Strang, J. (1993). Drug use and harm reduction: responding to the challenge.

In *Harm reduction: from faith to science* (ed. N. Heather, A. Wodak, E. Nadelman, and P. O'Hare), pp. 3–20. Whurr Publishers, London.

Strang, J. and Farrell, M. (1992). Maintenance treatment with methadone. *British Medical Journal*, **305**, 182.

Strang, J. and Stimson, G. (1990). The impacts of HIV: forcing the process of change. In *AIDS and drug misuse: the challenge for policy and practice in the 1990s* (ed. J. Strang and G. Stimson), pp. 3–15. Routledge, London.

# 15. The introduction of Community Drug Teams across the UK

*John Strang and Sue Clement*

The introduction of Community Drug Teams (CDTs) in many parts of the UK must surely stand as one of the most significant changes in recent years to the organization of UK treatment services for drug abusers. Since the appointment of staff for the first CDT in 1983, there has been a rapid expansion in the number of such CDTs. This expansion has mainly been within England with the most rapid period of growth being during the mid-1980s. By 1987 there were already 62 CDTs, by 1990 the number had grown to 75 (MacGregor *et al.* 1991; also see Chapter 21) and by 1991 a CDT had been established within more than half the 192 District Health Authorities in the country.

## The end of an era?

The introduction of CDTs across the country went hand-in-hand with a fundamental shift in planning strategy in which it was envisaged that much of the care provided to drug users would be provided from within the mainstream of care delivery. The blueprint was contained within the *Treatment and rehabilitation* Report from the Advisory Council on the Misuse of Drugs (ACMD 1982) which was heavily influenced by work done done several years previously in the alcohol field (Maudsley Alcohol Pilot Project 1975; Shaw *et al.* 1978; Advisory Committee on Alcoholism 1978). Thus the 1975 report by the Maudsley Alcohol Pilot Project had already outlined an approach in which the Community Alcohol Team (CAT) 'mobilised and integrated the potential skills of a variety of services, generic and specialist, at both primary and secondary levels'. This enabling role of the community team, with its emphasis on providing training and support to generic workers, was in sharp contrast to what had gone before.

In many ways the new strategy of CDTs and consultancy heralded the end of an era with the death of the exclusive and excluding specialist. No longer was the problem of drug misuse seen as one for which a referral to the specialist was the only appropriate action. It was not that CDTs themselves represented an alternative—rather it was that they were to be the agents for the mobilization of generic services so that the management of drug misusers became but one additional client group in the rich tapestry of casework which forms the work of the generalist. It was a move from the specialist model to an integrated model of care delivery, in which the avenue of referral had become a two-way street (Strang 1989, 1991).

## Concerns around the concept of community care

At one level, care in the community is self-evidently a good idea. However, as various specific proposals have come under greater scrutiny it has become evident that there are major difficulties, not only with definition and terminology, but also with strategy and delivery. It has been observed that contrasting policies may lay claim to the title 'community care'. As Baldwin (1987) points out 'Pluralistic policies of expansion, diversity and increased costs have been successfully juxtaposed with policies of contraction, homogeneity and decreased costs', and both have been afforded the status of 'community care'. Concern about the organization of care in the community has also been raised in a more general context by the House of Commons Social Services Committee (1985) and by the Audit Commission (1986).

## The composition and setting of the CDT

Policy documents relating to the establishment of community teams for various client groups (mentally handicapped people, the mentally ill, alcohol, and other drug misusers) have all advocated multi-disciplinary membership to the teams and responsibilities to geographical catchment areas. However, the reality is that under the rubric of the 'community drug team' are gathered together a hotchpotch of different types of service, with much variation in size, disciplinary and skills mix, population served, etc., so that it is far from clear what are the common qualities of these various community teams. Thus some teams have only one member (and it is difficult to see how a single community psychiatric nurse can really be regarded as a team!) while other CDTs have at least half-a-dozen full-time staff.

The different CDTs vary considerably in their position within the structure of local services. Most typical is an arrangement in which they stand with one foot in the primary health-care setting and the other foot in the secondary service of the District Health Authority or local authority. Many CDTs are active in promoting 'shared care' work with local general practitioners whilst at the same time attempting to identify those more complicated cases which should be referred on to the 'special needs services' described by Baldwin (1987).

The original CDT model relied heavily on the consultancy role (ACMD 1982). However, it is now becoming clear that the extent to which general practitioners (GPs) and other non-specialists have responded to the clarion call has been disappointing (see Donmall *et al.* 1990; Strang *et al.* 1991; Tantam *et al.* 1993). Whilst in some areas up to one-third of GPs may be willing to contribute valuably to this work, there are still other districts in which more than 90 per cent of local GPs are unwilling to be involved to any substantial extent with drug users (McKeganey 1988; King 1989; Bell *et al.* 1990). It takes two to tango, and in the absence of a partner it now seems that many CDTs are abandoning their major commitment to a consultancy and are reverting to the direct delivery of care to drug users—thus recreating the concept of the specialist at the District level. A similar point was made in a recent audit of CDTs practice (Strang *et al.* 1992) when they observed that 'at the end of the day it seems that drug workers just want to be drug workers'.

The staffing and skills mix of the typical CDT is described by MacGregor *et al.* (1991) as being multi-disciplinary across health and social services—the average CDT is staffed by four full-time and two part-time workers (most typically two community psychiatric nurses, one social worker or worker in a non-statutory agency, one secretary, and one co-ordinator). In their survey MacGregor *et al.* (1991) found that there were 269 full-time and 119 part-time members of staff in the 73 CDTs who responded to their questionnaire.

One common characteristic of all CDTs is their clear geographical brief—the CDT serves the population living in the health district. Thus all CDTs have a clear understanding of a people whom they serve and of a geographical plot which is their responsibility. From this standpoint they are well positioned to be able to consider possible areas of unmet need to which services might be more specifically targeted— either geographical areas in which there is poor service access or uptake, or groups within the population who appear not to be using the services for which they would appear to have a need.

## The need for local adaptation

Many of the CDTs established in recent years have come into existence prior to the development of a clear operational policy. Thus, for many of these CDTs, they have found themselves involved in attempting to work out the nature of their contribution—as well as actually doing it. Despite the broad brush strokes available in the picture painted from policy documents (for example, ACMD 1982) there was little detail provided by central government or local planners as to the precise operation of the services.

The following factors have been identified (Clement 1987; Stockwell and Clement 1988) from a survey of CATs as influencing their structure and aim and would appear to be equally applicable to CDTs:

(i)   Amount and nature of existing service provision—for example the Salford CAT (Clement 1987) concentrated on a consultancy and support service to primary workers whereas the Exeter CAT (formed following closure of the local alcohol treatment unit) focused on direct provision of care from a community base.

(ii)  Available resources in the real world—the strategy adopted will be influenced by the number of full-time and funded staff, and the extent to which sessional workers may be seconded to the community service.

(iii) Locally identified needs of both clients and agencies—how is the constituency of concern defined; and what criteria of 'caseness' are used. Thus some CDTs may go for a broad constituency (for example see Schneider *et al*. 1989) whilst others have presented a rationale for concentration of resources on drug users who have or may inject.

(iv)  The priority attached to multi-disciplinary team development—this will be influenced substantially by the pre-existing relationship between health and local authorities and the historical position of non-statutory/voluntary organizations: likewise the extent of previous collaboration with probation officers and specific groups of personnel such as clinical psychologists is likely to influence the eventual skills mix seen in the new CDT.

(v)   Philosophy and professional background of service innovators— in that little central guidance was given on the detailed working of these teams, the development of the teams was sometimes part of an orchestrated expansion of services (for example the network of CDTs in every district in the North Western Region (see Strang 1989, 1991; Donmall *et al*. 1990; Strang *et al*. 1991), whilst elsewhere the development was more parochial and was influenced almost exclusively by the attitudes and inclinations of the local groups of workers themselves (for example see Schneider *et al*. 1989).

## Identification of service goals

Attention has already been drawn to the diversity of activities seen in the work of the CDT. Whilst acknowledging the considerable variation from one team to the next, it is nevertheless possible to identify a number of different broad spheres of activity.

## Direct work with clients

The architects of community teams foresaw the impracticality of trying to offer a specialist service to everybody with drug- or alcohol-related problems; the number would be just too large for any specialist service to handle, nor would it always be appropriate (Advisory Committee on Alcoholism 1978; ACMD 1982). As described in the previous section, the builders of individual CDTs have also sometimes been aware of this impracticality; whilst elsewhere it has been overlooked. However, the workers in the CDT (who might be regarded as the occupants of the buildings in this analogy) have soon found themselves dealing directly with substantial numbers of drug takers despite the recommendations to the contrary from the architects. For some teams this has been a conscious decision resulting from evident local need in the absence of any adequate service, whilst with other teams it appears to have occurred by drift or default in the absence of direction within clear operational guidelines.

It is interesting that a similar drift into direct casework was seen with community mental handicap teams in the report from Wistow and Wray (1986) when they described how external pressures on Community Mental Handicap Teams (CMHTs) were exerted by other professionals and clients, alongside internal pressures resulting from the interests, commitment, and career development needs of the team members themselves. External pressures from other professionals varied according to the degree of organizational closeness between team members and others within their professional group. Thus team members with the same line managers as non-specialist members of their own profession seemed to come under greatest pressure to engage in direct client work—either pressure from the managers or pressure from their non-specialist colleagues to whom they represented such a convenient avenue of referral for an unpopular clientele.

Such pressures were particularly difficult for team members to resist when it seemed to the team member that a greater degree of help could be provided by the CDT itself; this argument seemed particularly seductive to team members from casework-orientated backgrounds.

Many CDT workers give another explanation (either additional or alternative) as the reason for taking on direct client work—the need to establish credibility or to build bridges between the team and their generic colleagues. Indeed Clement (1989) concluded that 'there is no evidence that any community team has been successful in providing a well-utilized consultancy service to primary care workers unless they have also engaged in casework with clients'. However, there is a real danger for teams who take on direct work with clients that they will be overwhelmed with this clinical work and will thus be unable to meet other priority aims, unless they have some mechanism for controlling the amount of direct client work in which they engage. Unless prior clearly defined boundaries are agreed upon, teams can find themselves with insufficient time available to engage in the other intended areas of CDT activity.

## Provision of advice, support, and training to generic/ non-specialist others

It is disappointing how little reference has been paid by CDT architects, builders, and occupants to the earlier and continuing experience with CATs. Regardless of the client group, there is always consensus on the need for better basic training, ongoing in-service training, and the need for a higher priority to be given to the particular client group. The result is that yet another special case is heaped on the mixed caseload of the primary care worker; and it is perhaps not surprising that these primary care workers respond less and less enthusiastically to the demands for special input for yet one more special group.

In their original report, the Maudsley Alcohol Pilot Project (1975) identified three major factors underlying the inadequate response of primary care worker:

(1) anxieties about role adequacy (that is, not having the information and skills necessary to recognize and respond to the relevant cases);

(2) anxieties about role legitimacy (that is, uncertainty as to the extent to which drinking problems formed a proper part of their professional responsibilities); and

(3) anxieties about role support (the fear that there would be nowhere from which to obtain help and advice when they were unsure how or whether to respond).

These three factors conspired to create 'role insecurity', which might eventually be resolved unsatisfactorily by the emergence of 'low therapeutic commitment'. Thus the obvious response would seem to be the provision of training in the areas of identification and responding to alcohol and drug problems. However, an examination of the different possible inputs identified that the provision of clinical information and training in counselling had no impact on the persistence of role insecurity; it was only when role support was added that the development of therapeutic commitment was facilitated—at least in studies of CAT input to alcohol services (Cartwright 1980). Clement (1987) has further argued that the support of generic workers and line managers is a crucial factor in determining whether the worker sees intervention into alcohol or drug problems as being appropriate and indeed in determining whether participating in training is seen as a priority area.

In the drug field the responsibility for provision of the training of generic workers was placed largely with the newly emergent Regional Drug Training Units, established in several regions during the 1980s (Cranfield and Dixon 1990; Glass and Strang 1991). However, in reality the main recipients of training from these Regional Training Units have been the newly created drug workers themselves. GPs, despite being the group who may well have the most extensive opportunities for identification and intervention, are scarcely reached at all by these new drug training unit—for example forming less than 2 per cent of the workers attending courses or seminars run by one such Regional Drug Training Unit (Glass and Strang 1991). This separation of the training function from the provision of client services could be argued to increase the problem experienced by CDT members in adopting a consultancy role. The priority given to training generic workers by CATs, who have a clear remit to do so, cannot be mirrored by the Regional Drug Training Units faced with a variety of demands upon their resources. The inter-relationship of these two recent developments has not yet been adequately considered.

## Co-ordination of services

There are almost universal calls for better co-ordination of pre-existing diverse services. For some community teams (in particular CMHTs), this has been an explicit and high priority item within their brief. Brown (1986) has described how this service co-ordination might occur at three different levels: co-ordination so as to avoid service duplication, co-ordination to fill service gaps, and co-ordination to resolve value conflicts. A practical approach to this problem which appears to address all three levels is the individual programme plan (IPP) system for co-ordinating responses to the needs of mentally handicapped people—described by Humphreys (1986). Although no such structured approach has been developed for CDTs work, the IPP system would seem to represent an organization of the various *ad hoc* inputs provided by the typical CDT worker. The IPP system comprises three elements: preparation, the IPP meeting and follow-up, and review. Each client is allocated to a specific key worker who is responsible for undertaking initial assessment and then organizing a meeting at which the various workers already involved with the client can identify their current and possible contributions to the identified needs of the client. A written plan is prepared outlining:

(i)   how the identified needs are to be met;

(ii)  who is responsible for which components;

(iii) a specified review date; and

(iv) identification of unmet need.

There would appear to be much to commend this structured approach, which could be seen as a consolidation of the better components within CDT work: it addresses the realities of what resources are actually available at the primary care level and also helps in the identification of tasks which generic workers are either able or unable to take on in a structured fashion. Perhaps if such a system were to be backed up by a policy document accepted by relevant agencies, then the likelihood of participation from generic workers would be substantially increased.

The reality of much CDT work is that the worker is more likely to be involved in some ephemeral activity which may be grandly titled 'liaison' but does not constitute 'co-ordination'. Brown (1986) has argued that a team's ability or inability to co-ordinate services will be reflected in the number of service resources which the team itself controls: teams with limited control over resources become involved in liaison rather than co-ordination because they are predominantly involved in mediation between client and services rather than actual direction of clients to available services.

## Development of services

For different community teams, the areas of active debate have themselves been different. For CATs, the main debate has been on the competing demands for direct casework or consultancy and training to primary workers; whilst for CMHTs the debate has revolved around the dominant role of either service delivery or service development. The position of CDTs is perhaps closest to that of CATs (but with responsibility for training compartmentalized as the responsibility of 'others'— for example regional training units).

Other responsibilities relating to service development have been specified. The National Development Group recommended that CMHTs should endeavour to promote the 'facilitation of joint working between professionals in the actual delivery of services' (National Development Group for the Mentally Handicapped 1980). More specifically, the 'development of service infrastructure' was specified in the brief of CMHTs in Nottinghamshire (Wistow and Wray 1986)—although it is rare for this to be included so explicitly. It might be expected that the mobilization of informal care would exist as a service development responsibility for CDTs—especially when one bears in mind the significant historical input of self-help in the addictions field (see Robinson 1979) and the rapid growth during the 1980s of the self-help movement in the UK (see Wells 1987; see also Chapter 19). This would then be in line with the recommendations from the Barclay Report (1982) about the role of social service departments, although it should be borne in mind that even in the area of generic social service provision, the criticism was subsequently made that the 'informal network of carers' (to which the report refers) is a largely illusory concept because, in reality, informal care is most usually provided by family members rather than the true broader community (Allen 1983).

## Problems encountered by the CDT

There is a strange reluctance to recognize the poor response of generic colleagues (notably general practitioners) to the exhortation to become more involved in providing care to drug users: the response to the clarion call has been at best modest. As yet surprisingly little attention has been paid by service planners and managers to this major strategic flaw. Whilst there have been a small number of CDTs who have obtained greater co-operation from the broad mass of local GPs (for example one of the CDTs described by Strang *et al*. 1992) the majority of CDTs have taken the easy route of exploiting to the full the goodwill of a small handful of local GPs who have then become local 'specialist' GPs whose caseload is likely to grow as their colleagues off-load their drug-using patients. This is hardly the development envisaged by the original architects.

CDT workers were intended to act as key gatekeepers to the different available services, fulfilling assessment and directing functions. Thus they might operate at a point where the process of triage might be applied, with a sorting of the presenting caseload according to need and suitability for different services. In practice this sorting exercise is all too often neglected and there is a danger that the CDT worker will become little more than the supermarket attendant, putting the drug user in touch with the commodity of their choice, with little intermediate assessment of the appropriateness of the different responses.

A distinctive feature of the evolution of the CDT concept has been the dominant position held by prescribing—thus putting it in sharp contrast to the debates about the CAT, the Community Mental Health Team and the Community Elderly Team. The original blueprint for the CDT in the 1982 ACMD report regarded prescribing as but a small part of the broader response; and whilst this more holistic approach still receives lip service, there is widespread evidence that the dominant activity and area of influence of the CDT worker is with regard to the provision or non-provision of substitute drugs to the opiate addict. Indeed the lack of substitute prescribing responses is frequently cited by the CDT worker as the reason why they appear to do so badly in making contact with, and holding contact with, users of non-opiate drugs such as amphetamines or cocaine.

During the late 1980s, harm minimization emerged as a specific style of work (Buning 1990; see also Chapter 20). Although it drew in large part from pre-existing styles of work, the prominence of harm minimization within clinical activity has become marked in recent years in contrast to the previous decade. The harm minimization approach involves attempting to reduce the harmful nature (to both individual and society) of the continued drug use: concerns about a possible implicit acceptance of continued use have led to a degree of controversy surrounding this style of work. Arguments exist about the extent to which harm minimization can co-exist with other forms of drug work, although many CDTs have found it straightforward to incorporate harm minimization within their eclectic work and are not particularly bothered by the mixed messages which they may give—indeed many observe that such mixed messages are an essential part of working at different levels with the same drug user.

A major change has thus occurred in the method of working by the CDT. Over the years there has been a drift away from the original consultancy role into more traditional direct provision of care. Perhaps, when confronted by a lack of willingness to co-operate on the part of their colleagues, the CDT worker reverts to type and goes back to their roots—face-to-face casework and the direct provision of care. If so, then this may well be the future for the CDT—at least in the near future whilst the intransigence on the part of colleagues is still so pronounced. However, it must be recognized that this constitutes a failure in application of the original consultancy model and is in fact a recreation of the specialist at the local level—and that this is likely to reinforce the present minimal involvement from generic colleagues. The recommendations of a consultancy role related not only to a more appropriate location of services but also to the large scale of the problem to be tackled; hence the plan to involve the broad mass of workers in health and social services. The move back to a specialist model is likely to result in an endorsement of the present insufficient provision of care to this group, and no clear options exist for ways of tackling this if the consultancy approach is abandoned.

The human immunodeficiency virus (HIV) has had a profound impact on this debate. Not only has it prompted the debate around harm minimization and the centrality or otherwise of prescribing, but it also introduces a sense of urgency into the debate. Thus waiting for the gradual change in the prejudiced attitude of one's colleagues may be too slow a process of change in an HIV-conscious environment. The CDT planners, managers, and workers are at a point where hard decisions must be made about the proportion of time invested in the longer-term goal of generic involvement or the shorter-term expedient of direct provision of care.

## Discussion

The involvement of generic workers, particularly GPs, in the provision of services to drug users, the direct provision of services themselves, and the co-ordination and development of the overall pattern of service provision, have all been seen as part of the remit of the CDT. In practice the majority of teams spend the majority of their time in face-to-face contact with clients.

Many of the reasons for this have already been discussed and are common to all community teams. One factor unique to CDTs is the dominant role that prescribing has played in the generic/specialist debate. The original blueprint for the CDT in the 1982 ACMD report regarded prescribing as but a small part of the broader overall service response. In practice, there is widespread evidence that the dominant activity and perceived area of influence of the CDT worker is in regard to the provision or non-provision of substitute drugs to the opiate addict. The lack of substitute prescribing for the users of non-opiate drugs such as amphetamines or cocaine is frequently cited by CDT workers as the reason they appear to do so badly in making contact with, and maintaining contact with, these groups of users. CDTs have therefore frequently seen it as crucial that GPs should become involved in prescribing for their drug-using patients.

Harm minimization approaches and the impact of HIV have brought the prescribing issue into even greater prominence. While there have been a small number of community drug teams who have obtained good co-operation from the broad mass of local GPs (for example one of the CDTs described by Strang et al. 1992) the majority of CDTs have only been able to identify small numbers of local GPs willing to work with their clients. These GPs have then become seen as local 'specialists' whose case-loads have grown as colleagues have off-loaded their drug-using patients. The failure of GPs to respond to the various 'clarion calls' to get involved has resulted, in combination with the variety of other pressures, in the majority of CDT members reverting to their roots—face-to-face casework and the direct provision of care in conjunction with small numbers of 'specialist' GPs and other 'specialist' services. This recreation of the specialist service, albeit in more accessible and 'user friendly' form than previously, is a failure of the original plan.

The scale of the unmet need is such that no specialist service can meet that need. No clear options exist for creating comprehensive and adequate services that do not include generic worker involvement. At the same time, many drug workers feel that waiting for a gradual change in the attitudes of GP and other generic colleagues may be too slow a process in an HIV conscious environment.

In this area, as in many others, CDTs have been slow to draw on the experience of other community teams. Nearly 20 years have passed since the Maudsley Alcohol Pilot Project noted that providing generic workers with an account of the size of the problem and exhorting them to respond was not enough. The reasons for their failure to respond have to be understood and worked through.

Successful consultancy is based on a clear and empathetic understanding of the problems that the worker has in engaging with the client. In seeking to involve generic workers it is crucial that each CDT has a clear understanding of the reasons for reluctance to become involved and develops strategies to overcome them. Very few appear to have done so. One reason for this may be that to maintain this kind of approach requires a great deal of support to be offered to team members themselves. The frustration of attempting to meet current client need can easily lead to the development of negative attitudes towards GPs and others who are less than immediately helpful. This can cloud long-term strategic thinking and lead to a consultancy approach being written off as a pipe-dream. Only when teams have the consistent support of managers and planners in continuing to pursue a consultative remit in the context of a theoretical understanding of the problem will they come to feel more comfortable with the pursuit of generic worker involvement. The CDT planners, managers, and workers are at the point where hard decisions must be made about the proportion of time invested in the longer-term goal of generic involvement or the shorter-term expedient of direct provision of care.

The role of the CDT in service co-ordination and development also requires re-examination. CDT workers were intended to act as key gate-keepers to the different available services, fulfilling assessment and directing functions. One way of containing the demands of direct client contact is the model where the teams operate at the point where the process of triage might be applied, with the sorting of the presenting case-load according to need and suitability for different services. Where gaps in the overall pattern of services become apparent these should be flagged up by the team to managers and service planners. In order for this model to work, other services are required to be highly responsive to the needs identified in the assessment process, both in terms of individual client work and on the level of service planning. Unless the centrality of the role of the CDT in the overall pattern of services is acknowledged and valued, the danger exists that the CDT worker will become little more than a shop assistant, putting the drug user in touch with the drug or service of their choice, with little intermediate assessment of the appropriateness of the different responses and little influence over what is produced or the quality of the product.

If these issues are not tackled by managers and planners there is little doubt that, with perhaps a few exceptions, the policy of drift towards recreating specialist services at a local level will continue: if so, then opportunities will have been missed to plan and deliver a comprehensive pattern of services that are truly responsive to client need. The increasing spread of HIV introduces a sense of urgency to the debate. The cost of getting it wrong may be high.

# References

ACMD (Advisory Council on the Misuse of Drugs) (1982). *Report on treatment and rehabilitation.* HMSO, London.

Advisory Committee on Alcoholism (1978). *The pattern and range of services for problem drinkers.* Department of Health and Social Security and Welsh Office, London.

Allen, G. (1983). Informal networks of care: issues raised by Barclay. *Journal of Social Work*, **13**, 417–33.

Audit Commission for Local Authorities in England and Wales (1986). *Making a reality of community care.* HMSO, London.

Baldwin, S., Baser, C., and Pinker, A. A. (1986). The emperor's new community services. *Nursing Times—Community Outlook*, 12 February, pp. 6–8.

Baldwin, S. (1987). Old wine in old bottles: why Community Alcohol Teams will not work. In *Helping the problem drinker: new initiatives in community care* (ed. T. Stockwell and S. Clement), pp. 158–71. Croom Helm, Beckenham, Kent.

Barclay Report (1982). *Social workers: their role and tasks.* Bedford Square Press, London.

Bell, G., Cohen, J., and Cremona, A. (1990). How willing are general practitioners to manage narcotic misuse? *Health Trends*, **22**, 56–7.

Brown, S. (1986). *Community mental handicap teams: organisation, operation and outcomes.* Report to DHSS. Department of Health, London.

Buning, E. (1990). The role of harm-reduction programmes in curbing the spread of HIV by drug injectors. In *AIDS and drug misuse: the challenge for policy and practice in the 1990s* (ed. J. Strang and G. V. Stimson), pp. 153–61. Routledge, London.

Campaign for Mental Handicap (1982). *Teams for mentally handicapped people.* Campaign for Mentally Handicapped People, London.

Cartwright, A. (1980). The attitudes of helping agents towards the alcoholic client: the influence of experience, support, training and self-esteem. *British Journal of Addiction*, **75**, 413–31.

Clement, S. (1987). The Salford experiment: an account of the Community Alcohol Team approach. In *Helping the problem drinker: new initiatives in community care* (ed. T. Stockwell and S. Clement), pp. 121–44. Croom Helm, London.

Clement, S. (1989). The Community Drug Team: lessons from alcohol and handicap services. In *Treating drug abusers* (ed. G. Bennett), pp. 171–89. Routledge, London.

Cranfield, S. and Dixon, A. (1990). *Drug training, HIV and AIDS in the 1990s: a guide for training professionals.* Health Education Authority, London.

Donmall, M., Webster, A., Strang, J., and Tantam, D. (1990). *The introduction of community-based services for drug misusers: impact and outcome in the North West 1982–1986*. Report to Department of Health. Available from the library at the Institute for the Study of Drug Dependence (ISDD), London.

Glass, I. B. and Strang, J. (1991). Professional training in substance abuse: the UK experience. In *International handbook of addiction behaviour* (ed. I. B. Glass), pp. 333–40. Routledge, London.

House of Commons Social Services Committee (1985). *Second Report from the Social Services Committee—Community Care with special reference to adult mentally ill and mentally handicapped people*. HMSO, London.

Humphreys, S. (1986). Individual planning in NIMROD. In *Community mental handicap teams: theory and practices* (ed. G. Grant, S. Humphreys, and M. Macgrath). British Institute of Mental Handicap Conference Services.

Incichen, B. and Russell, J. A. O. (1980). *Mental handicap and community care—the viewpoint of the general practitioner*. Mental Handicap Studies Research Report No. 4. University of Bristol, Department of Mental Health.

King, M. (1989). Psychological and social problems in HIV infection: interviews with general practitioners in London. *British Medical Journal*, **299**, 713–17.

MacGregor, S., Ettore, B., Coomber, R., Crosier, A., and Lodge, H. (1991). *Drug services in England and the impact of the Central Funding Initiative*, ISDD research monograph no. 1. Institute for the Study of Drug Dependence, London.

McKeganey, N. (1988). Shadowland: general practitioners and the treatment of opiate-abusing patients. *British Journal of Addiction*, **83**, 373–86.

Maudsley Alcohol Pilot Project (1975). *Designing a comprehensive community response to problems of alcohol abuse*. Report to the Department of Health and Social Security, London.

National Development Group for the Mentally Handicapped (1980). Improving the quality of services for mentally handicapped people: a checklist of standards. Department of Health and Social Security, London.

Robinson, D. (1979). *Talking out of alcoholism: the self-help process*. Croom Helm, London.

Schneider, J., Davis, P., Nazum, W., and Bennett, G. (1989). The community drug team: current practice. In *Treating drug users* (ed. G. Bennett). Routledge, London.

Shaw, S., Cartwright, A., Spratley, T., and Harwin, J. (1978). *Responding to drinking problems*. Croom Helm, London.

Stockwell, T. and Clement, S. (1988). Community Alcohol Teams: a review of studies evaluating their effectiveness with special reference to the experience of other community teams. Report to Department of Health, London.

Strang, J. (1989). A model service: turning the generalist on to drugs. In *Drugs and British society* (ed. S. MacGregor), pp. 143–69. Routledge, London.

Strang, J. (1991). Organization of services: drugs. In *International handbook of addiction behaviour* (ed. I. B. Glass), pp. 283–91. Routledge, London.

Strang, J., Donmall, M., Webster, A., Abbey, J., and Tantam, D. (1991). *A bridge not far enough: community drug teams and doctors in the North Western Region 1982–1986*. ISDD Research monograph No. 3. Institute for the Study of Drug Dependence (ISDD), London.

Strang, J., Smith, M., and Spurrell, S. (1992). The community drug team: data and analysis. *British Journal of Addiction*, **87**, 169–78.

Tantam, D., Donmall, M., Webster, A., and Strang, J. (1993). Can general practitioners and general psychiatrists be expected to look after drug misusers? Results from evaluation of a non-specialist treatment policy in the northwest of England. *British Journal of General Practice*, **43**, 470–4.

Wells, B. (1987). Narcotics Anonymous (NA): the phenomenal growth of an important resource. *British Journal of Addiction*, **82**, 581–2.

Wistow, G. and Wray, K. (1986). CMHTs service delivery and service development: the Nottinghamshire way approach. In *Community Mental Handicapped Teams: theory and practice* (ed. G. Grant, S. Humphreys, and M. Magrath). British Institute of Mental Handicap Conference Services.

# 16. The development of the Voluntary Sector: no further need for pioneers?

*David Turner*

The British response to emerging drug problems was remarkably similar to the response to any other social problem. Having determined that there was no problem one year, (HMSO 1961) a couple of years later the same Committee was hastily being reconvened to make recommendations on how to respond to the problem which had now been discovered HMSO (1965). Although the report emerged with reasonable speed, its recommendations took several years to be enacted. In the meantime, a very small problem had grown rapidly.

An equally characteristic British response was the emergence of a number of voluntary organizations, in advance of statutory provision, designed to respond to the growing drug problem.

## Early non-statutory drug services

The first non-statutory services were almost exclusively linked to Christian churches. Most began with work with drug users in central London, providing befriending, some basic welfare work, and counselling. In many ways they represented the classic missionary role of the Church, reaching out to those in distress. Thus Kenneth Leech at St Anne's, Soho, Barbara Ward, youth workers from the Salvation Army's Rink Club, Barbara Henry, Vic Ramsey at the Orange Street Mission, amongst others, began working in the streets, cafés, and clubs of the West End, the theatre and entertainment centre of London, attempting to reach young drug users. Although each one was largely working alone, from their work a spate of new initiatives developed, emerging in the late 1960s into two distinctive groups. At one end, the first residential rehabilitation services were developed in Life for the World, the New Life Foundation, and the Coke Hole Trust. At the other end, the first community drug services developed with the Soho Project and the Blenheim

Project. The Community Drug Project stood out as a service which developed as a response to a local problem, inspired to a large extent by Griffith Edwards at the Addiction Research Unit.

By 1968, a new phase developed with services emerging from parent action, from concerned individuals and inspired by the experience of the United States. The Association for the Parents of Addicts, later renamed the Association for the Prevention of Addiction, was set up by Molly Craven in response to a family crisis. This spawned groups in many parts of the country, established a day centre in Covent Garden, and led to a number of services being established, many of which are still operating. In Hertfordshire, just to the north of London, Elizabeth Cory-Wright established the Hertfordshire Standing Conference on Drug Misuse, which despite a number of changes, still continues. In the second category, Terry Tanner and Ben Harrison set up ROMA (a residential rehabilitation project whose names derives from the acronym of their function of Rehabilitation Of Metropolitan Addicts) in response to the Advisory Committee on Drug Dependence report, Lord Longford established New Horizon, Eric Blakebrough opened Kaleidoscope, Peter Chapple set up CURE, Institute for the Study of Drug Dependence (ISDD) was opened and the 'alternative society' was represented by the establishment of Release to offer a legal and counselling service to those caught by the drug laws and by BIT. In the final category came the 'concept based' therapeutic communities. The leading ones were Alpha House in Portsmouth, Phoenix House in London, and slightly later Suffolk House in Iver Heath and the Ley Community in Oxford. Three of these were inspired by local consultant psychiatrists and were closely linked with a hospital-based service. Alpha House transferred to Hampshire Social Services Department and continued to be a statutory service provision well into the 1970s, although it moved out of St James' Hospital within a couple of years of opening.

## The Voluntary Sector in the new drug services

By 1970, the pattern of voluntary and non-statutory services was established. They were almost the sole providers of drug-free residential rehabilitation, with many employing former drug users on the staff seeking to provide a role model to residents. They provided the only accommodation specifically designed for drug users. And they offered day centres, outreach and detached work, advice and counselling services. The majority of these services employed paid staff, a few were exclusively provided by volunteers and many combined volunteer and paid staff.

A description of the history of voluntary organizations' work with drug users thus shows that they were at the heart of responses to drug problems in the 1960s. Whilst the haggling over the recommendations of the Brain Committee was continuing, they were opening services which have now become established approaches adapted over recent years by services provided by non-statutory and statutory organizations.

## What service was provided?

As importantly, the work undertaken by these services was a precursor to the services which are now commonly offered. In 1972, Ken Leech categorized the roles of the voluntary organizations as casualty caring, after care, education, and agitators (Leech 1972). Those roles have barely changed, just the descriptors.

### Casualty caring

Casualty caring included a wide range of activities, many now reintroduced under the rubric of 'harm reduction'. Detached and outreach work were common means of reaching drug users, as was the provision of peripatetic counselling and advisory services held in a variety of premises. The day centres provided kitchen and laundry facilities—I well remember the ingenuity which went into using up 1000 cans of donated celery soup—found emergency accommodation, provided first aid and, perhaps more interestingly in light of modern developments, supplied needles and syringes whilst three out of the four had 'fixing rooms' where prescribed drugs could be injected in a relatively sterile and safe environment.

### Aftercare

Aftercare was a broad concept. It included work with the probation service, prison visiting, preparation for release, and the development accommodation and employment services. ROMA was designed to accommodate chaotic barbiturate and opiate users through a number of housing stages as stability developed leading on to independent flats, often for a family. AREA (Addict Rehabilitation Employment Agency), set up by Alec Reed, acted as an employment agency for drug users and those leaving rehabilitation. The range of residential services provided was in itself remarkable. As well as the concept-based therapeutic communities and the Christian houses, there were differing community models such as Par House, Cranstoun and Elizabeth House, and alternative communities such as the Patchwork Community, White Light, the Kingsway Community, and Walnut Cottage. Perhaps it was inevitable that the alternative communities, so representative of an era, should not survive, but there loss was a loss of variety and opportunity which has never adequately been replaced.

## Education

Education was represented in a variety of ways. A number of organizations provided information about drugs and addiction. Initially this was too close to propaganda and too far from accurate information. The emergence of ISDD, dedicated to non-partisan, accurate information and education and of TACADE (the Teachers' Advisory Council on Alcohol and Drug Education) as a resource for school-based education had an increasing influence on the quality of the published material. In pre-video days, the production of films was also a common means of providing education. Project Icarus in Southampton was a major producer of education films whilst James Ferman, now Secretary of the British Board of Film Censors, was responsible for the production of the first comprehensive set of drug education films. It is in the area of drug education that the greatest changes have occurred. In the 1960s and 1970s education was almost exclusively concerned with limiting the likelihood of young people engaging in drug use. Now it has added limiting the likelihood of harm arising as a consequence of drug use.

## Agitation

It was the role of voluntary organizations as agitators which Ken Leech feared was most likely to be lost as services became established. He had himself been one of the great agitators, almost achieving the same heartfelt cry from Kenneth Robinson, the then Minister of Health, as Thomas à Beckett caused Henry II to make. His fears proved groundless. It was the voluntary organizations who found and exposed the corruption in the Metropolitan Drug Squad. They were at the heart of agitation for services in response to the needs of barbiturate users. They were advocates for their clients in court and with the treatment centres. Sometimes naive, they nevertheless were unquestionably on the side of their clients.

## Change and consolidation during the 70s

The 1970s was largely a period of consolidation and retrenchment. Few new services developed and a number closed. As public, political, and press concern diminished and the impression was gained that drug use was declining, so the local action groups faded away and the army of volunteers disappeared. Many of the alternative communities closed or were forced to change to survive. The day centres also faced major challenges. As treatment centres changed to prescribing oral drugs, the day centre clients who continued to inject were using illicit drugs and barbiturates. Staff were forced increasingly into policing the centres managing overdoses and administering first aid. The fixing rooms were no longer viable when those who most needed them had to be denied because their drug use was illicit and overdose a common consequence. By 1975, all the fixing rooms had closed and needles and syringes were no longer supplied. It was ironic that the agitation for a crisis service for barbiturate users which began at the start of the 1970s did not result in a service, City Roads (Crisis Intervention), until the barbiturate problem was rapidly declining and the new problems of the 1980s beginning to emerge. For the residential services it was also a time of change. The concept-based therapeutic communities threw off the shackles of their American genesis and began to develop a British identity, with some of the more extreme aspects of the programme, such as the shaving of heads and the wearing of placards announcing the residents' faults, being abandoned. ROMA closed, transferred ownership, and reopened as a compact version of its original vision. By 1981, the total number of specialist drug services operated by non-statutory organizations was 40, with about the same number of specialist hospital services.[1]

## The formation of SCODA

In 1971, the non-statutory organizations had agreed the need for improved co-ordination and co-operation and as a result established SCODA, the Standing Conference on Drug Abuse, which acted as an umbrella organization for voluntary sector projects, and which employed its first staff in 1972. By 1978, its members were reporting an increasing number of young heroin users approaching them seeking help. Once more the role as agitators came to the fore as efforts were made to achieve a commitment of resources so that drug services could be expanded to meet a growing need. The response was not dissimilar to that in the 1960s. First denial, then a call for more information and finally, in 1982, publication of *Treatment and rehabilitation* (Advisory Council for the Misuse of Drugs 1982) with the announcement of additional central funding.

## Rapid growth during the 80s

The 1980s saw non-statutory drug services develop rapidly, not only in the number and variety of services they offered, but also as influencers of policy. They produced their own critique of the *Treatment and rehabilitation* report and a framework for the development of services

---

[1] Although many more hospitals were listed as 'known to be providing some facilities for the treatment of drug addiction' the majority only offered general psychiatric outpatient appointments or in-patient detoxification in a general psychiatric ward. Some 45 hospitals had specialist treatment units.

(SCODA 1983). They challenged the draft circular on the Central Funding Initiative and submitted an alternative, which was adopted by the Department of Health almost unchanged. They prepared the guidance for monitoring services funded under the initiative. They prepared the first advice note on AIDS and drug use and developed guidance for services. They developed quality standards for service provision which have become a benchmark against which services can be measured. They campaigned for the exclusion of drug addiction as a sole basis for compulsory admission to a psychiatric hospital and for the inclusion of residential drug services within the terms of the Residential Homes Act.

The Central Funding Initiative, undertaken by the Department of Health, made dedicated funds available which provided the basis for the rapid growth of drug services throughout England. There were separate initiatives undertaken by the Welsh Office and the Scottish Office. The two main strands of service provision were community-based services and residential services. The former were subdivided between statutory provision, commonly referred to as Community Drug Teams and non-statutory provision of advice, counselling, and information services. The residential services continued to be the exclusive provision of non-statutory organizations, with an increasing number of fee-paying services being established.

## So what promotes voluntary sector growth?

There were a number of similarities to the development of drug services in the 1960s and early 1970s, although the differences may be more significant. The services of the 1960s and 1970s were primarily centred on London, concerned with a small but significant number of people with acute drug problems. Their clients had multiple problems with many who had migrated to London,[1] had been in care, were homeless and unemployed. By the 1980s, drug problems were reported throughout the country and services were opened to respond to this development. Moreover, the new drug users were predominantly smoking heroin rather than injecting, were still living at home or in their home area and were relatively young.[2] The older services, developed to work with a very different pattern of drug use, had difficulty in responding to this change.

[1] For instance, in 1972 New Horizon reported that some 50 per cent of their clients were from Scotland, primarily from the west coast. Similar experiences reported from other London services resulted in the Scots Group being established to develop links with organizations in Scotland and to seek means to reduce this migration.

[2] By 1983, almost 50 per cent of new addict notifications were under 25 years of age although the percentage of addicts under 25 years recorded as receiving notifiable drugs in treatment at the end of the year remained stable at about 19 per cent.

A number of new services emerged as a result of community and parent action. This often led to conflict with established services, both statutory and non-statutory. They were, in many ways, replicating the development process of the 1960 services which challenged the perceived complacency and inaction of the 'authorities'. There were two strands to parent action. One was concerned with direct service provision, leading to services such as CADA (Committee Against Drug Abuse; who set up a drop-in centre in South London) and Drugline in south London, Drugline in Birmingham, and the Place in Glasgow. The other was concerned with self-help and mutual support with the establishment of Families Anonymous and ADFAM and a range of local groups. Even here, there were echoes of the 1960s and the work of the APA (Association for the Prevention of Addiction).

In the mid-1980s the increased awareness of HIV infection and its possible consequences led to a further flurry of pioneering activity. Innovations in providing health information to drug users, such as *Smack in the Eye* produced by the Lifeline Project in Manchester and *Drug Alert*, broadcast by BBC Radio One[1] based on ideas developed by SCODA, represented a move away from prevention as an absolute— don't start, and if you have, stop, to an understanding of prevention in personal and public health terms where avoiding or reducing harm was important and relevant to drug and non-drug users. There were also reinventions of past practice with the development of needle and syringe exchange schemes and the reintroduction of outreach and detached work. The difference between the 1960/70s and the 1980/90s was that in the former, the pioneers were innocents who tried new approaches with little experience to go on, with no clear outcome identified as the goal and with no evaluation of the approaches they tried. In the latter, the majority were less often pioneers and more often drug worker professionals who were cautious of taking too many risks but were willing to push the boundaries of accepted practice to the limits without over-stretching the mark. This caution was re-enforced because of the threats to funding and to services observed when drug services were regarded as having gone too far, for instance by publishing leaflets which did not outrightly condemn drugs or particular drugs, or in promoting safer injecting where a drug user was unwilling to stop injecting altogether.

## The drive towards professionalization

This caution perhaps reflected some of the changes which have occurred and will continue to occur in the 1990s. The specialist drug services are

---

[1] Radio One is the popular music channel in the UK with a weekly audience reach of about 17 million people, the vast majority under 30 years of age.

now a professional group seeking to be recognized as such. The demand for formal qualifications as a basis for being employed in drug services is increasing, as is the demand for post-qualification training which will lead to a further qualification in addiction counselling, or addictions or some similar title. The internal pressure for status has been matched by the external pressure arising from changes in the way services are funded and the controls which will be put on them.

New legislation affecting health, social, and probation services, changes in charity law and in the regulations of other statutory funding sources is in danger of enforcing a new orthodoxy. Professional standards of management, detailed case recording and assessment procedures, quality assurance, performance measurement, service audit, all these are beginning to appear within contracts for service as they replace grants as the main source of funding for non-statutory services. Whilst there can be no doubt that drug users, like any other service user or customer, have the right to high quality services, there is the danger that the variety of services will be lost and that a smaller number of services will become excellent for the few who wish to use them. Pioneering will revert to the under-resourced outsiders, the agitators as the distinction between statutory and non-statutory services continues to blur.

However, this gloomy picture may be challenged by another glance at the 1960s and early 1970s. Non-statutory services have been at the forefront of developments for quarter of a century and they have the opportunity to develop that role within the new legislation. Community care and health-care planning requires that customers of services are consulted in the development of plans and that services respond to the needs of the community. Already there are developing support and action groups of drug users to some extent modelled on the Junkiebond in The Netherlands. The role of agitator, or in the new language of the 1990s, advocate, for drug users, their right to services and to services which are relevant to their needs has re-emerged as a key function.

## Conclusion

There will inevitably be conflicts between the objectives of public policy in responding to drug problems. The demand for increased international action, for improved enforcement and for deterrence will at times be in conflict with public health, social and health-care needs. There will be conflict with those who wish to establish orthodoxy and the blandness of a uniform approach. For non-statutory services, their future mission must be to be agitators for services based on and supported by an assessment of the needs of their customers.

There is still a need for pioneers. The roles identified by Kenneth Leech 20 years ago remain as valid now as then. The difference is that those roles can be pressed as insiders where drug users have rights within the broad citizens charter and within the framework of service planning and where non-statutory services can be partners as agitators and advocates for service.

## References

Advisory Committee on Drug Dependence (1969). *The rehabilitation of drug addicts*. HMSO, London.
Advisory Council on the Misuse of Drugs (1982). *Treatment and rehabilitation*. HMSO, London.
HMSO (1961). *Drug addiction*. Report of the Interdepartmental Committee. HMSO, London.
HMSO (1965). *Drug addiction*. The Second Report of the Interdepartmental Committee. HMSO, London.
Leech, K. (1972). The role of the voluntary agencies. *The British Journal of Addiction to Alcohol and other Drugs*, **67**, 131–6.
SCODA (1983). Response of SCODA to the Report of the Advisory Council on the Misuse of Drugs: Treatment and Rehabilitation. SCODA, London.

# 17. Changes in therapeutic communities in the UK

*Paul Toon and Richard Lynch*

The need for a re-evaluation of the therapeutic community (TC) approach to drug addiction has been long overdue. In 1986 Donellan and Toon highlighted the problems and suggested that a gentler, more client-orientated approach was needed, but at that time this was difficult for the TCs to accept. A major rethink was brought about mainly in response to the human immunodeficiency virus (HIV)/acquired immune deficiency syndrome (AIDS) and the introduction of Community Care legislation in the early 1990s, and all TCs are now re-evaluating their techniques and changing their strategies.

## The history of the therapeutic community

The term 'therapeutic community' originated from the work of Tom Main (1946); he developed a democratic forum in a National Health Service hospital which allowed patients to organize their own constructive activities, and social processes involving both staff and patients became the catalyst for therapeutic development within this community. The therapeutic process consisted of a sharing and understanding of the problems of others, and the interaction proved for many to be more beneficial than the established medical model which made patients passive recipients of a doctor's 'expert' treatment. This 'democratic' style of rehabilitation is quite different from, and can be contrasted with, TCs which deal with problem drug takers, which have been described by Maxwell Jones as programmatic TCs (Jones 1984).

The Concept House Model of a TC started in quite a different way. Originating in the USA, a small group of drug and alcohol abusers met regularly to discuss their own rehabilitation along the lines of Alcoholics Anonymous. From this group emerged the foundations and philosophy upon which Synanon evolved (Yablonsky 1965). Although this community later became discredited (Gerstel 1982), the concepts and philosophies spread throughout the USA and into Europe in the late 1960s and 1970s.

The Concept House approach to TCs came to Britain in the late 1960s onwards and differed from the more democratic approach already established by Maxwell Jones and others by concentrating solely on the rehabilitation of drug misusers (Alpha House in Portsmouth and Phoenix House in London; Kennard 1983). This American model of TCs imported a strong American culture into the programmes. Dr Ian Christie (a psychiatrist) spent 3 months in the USA experiencing both Phoenix House and DayTop Village in New York (both derived from Synanon), and it was from this knowledge that he based the Alpha House programme. At the same time, two graduate staff of Phoenix House in New York started the Phoenix House programme in London. Residents entering the therapeutic programme not only had to give up and learn to live without drugs, but also had to adapt to a different and alien culture. This may go some way to account for the high drop-out rate experienced in the early days.

The Ley Community in Oxford was established as a TC in 1971 by Dr B. Mandelbrote and John McCabe. Dr Mandelbrote's background was in psychiatry and traditional TCs, and this combined with John McCabe's experience as an ex-addict and staff member of both Phoenix House in London and New York. This combination of approaches had a moderating effect on the development of the programme established in Oxford.

## Three types of programme

Christian-based groups have subsequently adopted similar models and developed religious houses for the treatment of drug users. In more recent years shorter treatment programmes based on the 'Minnesota Model' have developed, and these provide a basis for rehabilitation and ongoing support through links with Narcotics Anonymous.

The term TC now covers three types of organizations:

(1) community-orientated houses, concept houses and religious houses;

(2) concept houses; and

(3) religious houses.

All have common attributes: a communal atmosphere, group meetings, a shared work-load running the TC and the encouragement of residents to take on increasing responsibility for themselves and others (Kennard 1983). The authors' experience is of a Concept House TC and here the central idea is that drug use is not an illness but rather a problem of behaviour. An individual is encouraged to take responsibility for their own drug-free life by understanding their common reactions to situations and people. The Concept House approach has always had, as its main tool, a hierarchically structured environment in which individuals may gain confidence by giving and receiving directions thus building self-esteem and confidence. Through confrontation therapy (encounter groups) negative behaviour is challenged by the peer group and relationships are encouraged based on trust and caring for each other. For many participants these structures provide the framework for people to grow and develop and gain the confidence in preparation for re-entering the real world without reverting to drug abuse. However, for others, it can provide an affirmation of their failure and a confirmation of their poor self-perceptions. Nevertheless, various studies have shown that length of stay in a TC is the greatest single indicator of a positive post-treatment outcome (De Leon 1984).

## Criticisms of the TC orthodoxy

There have been a number of criticisms of the concept house approach. Donellan and Toon (1986) highlighted the main points and criticized the assumption by TCs that residents entering the TC were incapable of taking responsibility for the management of their own lives. It was assumed that they could only achieve abstinence and happiness by submission to the therapeutic community philosophy. Secondly, staff (especially ex-addict staff) were often not qualified in the techniques they used, some of which were designed to break down the personality structure of the individual. The 'images' of all residents were confronted, whatever their nature, with the use of confrontation (often seen as harsh by a vulnerable client group and their advocates). Extra work duties and public humiliation for transgressions of community rules were often seen as punitive. In a predominantly male environment, women were confronted with male stereotypes and culture which did little to realize their potential, and former members of the community subsequently found problems re-adjusting to normal society. It was hard for them to relate to people in a non-emotional way and they tended to be over-critical of others and themselves because of their own experience in the TC. Staff, particularly ex-addict staff wielded considerable power over a vulnerable client group and this was open to abuse, as residents were expected to have blind faith in the community and not to question the philosophy of rehabilitation or the methods used.

These criticisms, however powerful, do not undermine the value of the TC approach to problematic drug users: rather they point to the way ahead. The techniques, particularly of confrontation, which have given rise to many of these criticisms have undoubted value: negative and destructive behaviour is attacked and models for substitute behaviour are provided. However, adapting the techniques to suit the British culture is now not enough (Donellan and Toon 1986): significant factors have arisen which TCs must face, of which the most significant is HIV/AIDS.

## The impact of AIDS

HIV and AIDS are not problems faced only by TCs. Society itself is coming to terms with the nature of the virus and its consequential effects on social behaviour patterns. Infection with the virus is not fatal but the effects may be. For the client groups whose pre-treatment lifestyles have exposed them to the risk of HIV infection, the TC has a major role in prevention and harm reduction. (Eighty per cent of the residents undergoing rehabilitation in the authors' Community have a history of intravenous drug abuse and needle sharing, and 93 per cent have criminal convictions.) A former resident, diagnosed as being HIV positive while undergoing rehabilitation, claimed to have shared a single syringe with 70 other inmates whilst in prison. It must follow therefore that TC has a major role to play in combating the spread of HIV infection, and total abstinence from illicit drug misuse is the most effective form of harm reduction. The most effective means of achieving this goal is long-term rehabilitation—the TC movement has not been slow to respond to these new demands although the process has been painful. The TC is not just preparation for a drug-free lifestyle: for residents infected by the HIV/AIDS virus, it must also be an environment in which their own grief will be experienced, and the Community as a whole will inevitably share this (Biase 1987).

HIV is an issue which impinges upon the ideal of a drug-free lifestyle. It affects relationships between everyone in the Community—staff and residents, and those connected with the TC share the impact of HIV infection. On one level this is carefully managed with stringent hygiene practices and educational initiatives: at another level, it forces the objectives and goals of a resident's stay to be questioned. Whilst the goal of total abstinence from drug misuse continues to be the ultimate aim, it must also be recognized that harm reduction and safer drug use are also worthy objectives (Advisory Council on the Misuse of Drugs (ACMD) 1988). The use of ex-addict staff as role models, living a drug-free life 'happy ever after' may no longer be an appropriate model for HIV-infected clients. The carrot of 'do this now and in 5 years you can have this' may no longer be realistic.

## Government

Despite the government's longstanding interest in finding solutions to drug misuse, sufficient resources have not always been provided to existing agencies to deal with the problem. However, with the implementation of Community Care and transfer of funding from Income Support to Local Authorities and consequent implications to Poll Tax payers, unpopular groups such as drug abusers have to compete directly for scarce public money with other more immediate and popular groups, such as children, the disabled and the elderly—thus echoing statements from an earlier era (Jenkins 1980). What government has provided, however, is a regulated framework in which the standards of TCs can be assessed and monitored. Social Service inspections take place regularly; in addition Fire, Health and Safety, and Hygiene regulations apply in the daily running of a TC. These controls, however necessary, have added bureaucracy to the problems which a TC must face. A danger with this bureaucracy is that it may stifle the creative principle of the TC: techniques have evolved and developed in the spirit of innovative care (Kennard 1989). A drug-free lifestyle cannot be legislated for, nor should a functional TC be legislated against. With the onset of the new government framework in 'Care in the Community', TCs are now to be in competition with other support and rehabilitation agencies for resources. Their reputation and credibility are vital. In the new competitive and more economically orientated environment, TCs must show that they are a cost-effective and significant response to problem drug taking. More poignantly, with the spread of HIV, the potential economic cost of chaotic problematic drug taking with its associated subculture of promiscuous sexual behaviour and sharing of injecting equipment may be set against the TC's success in responding to difficult HIV-related issues.

## The changing clientele

Another factor which has brought about change in the TC is the change in the client group. Many problem drug takers no longer live in isolated subgroups in society, but inhabit areas of our larger cities where drugs, crime, violence, bad housing, and unemployment are the norm. Second-generation drug users are born into environments where despair and depression are inherent and there are few role models in this subculture which provide any hope of something different. To remove users from this setting is often necessary. Should this be to a TC, then there remains a problem with loved ones being left behind. The TC's rule that residents should not attempt to contact users may mean that contact with partners and relatives is problematic. Consequently, the ideal of a drug-free lifestyle for the post-TC resident may seem less credible. Unemployment and bad housing may be the only perspective some problem drug takers have on society. These factors mirror, or may exacerbate, the depression in residents who are HIV positive. Ideals for a post-TC life may seem limited not just by society but also by a reminder of one's own mortality.

## Factors promoting change

The factors described so far show that change in TCs is necessary if not inevitable. Possible barriers to change require consideration. The assumption was always that residents of the TC were incapable of taking responsibility for the management of their own lives. They could achieve abstinence and happiness only by submission to the TC. This practice was reinforced by 'therapeutic phrases' such as 'if you are not part of the cure, you are part of the problem'. The philosophy has often been the mainstay of community life. To a certain extent it has become entrenched. Questioning techniques creates a fear that reaching the goal of abstinence will not be maintained. In practice, barriers to change have been overcome. The idea that the community is always changing as the residents change is prevalent. The first change affects prospective entrants to the TC. Enquirers are now no longer 'inducted' into the TC; rather they are assessed. The nature of problem drug taking is recognized as being diverse. The clients' needs are considered and where appropriate they are directed to other agencies. This allows easier access for clients who may benefit from the TC therapeutic process. More importantly, it signifies a recognition by the TC that their special form of rehabilitation is just one response to problem drug taking.

## Health promotion

Amongst many major changes in the TC is the introduction of health education programmes. Within the community, information about, and discussion of, HIV/AIDS are promoted. Formal workshops and seminars take place regularly given by staff and outside bodies. Safer sex and the dangers of intravenous drug use are among the topics discussed. More generally a healthier lifestyle is encouraged and a beneficial diet is promoted and efforts are made to introduce stress-reducing techniques into the programme, as well as a wide range of physical and recreational activities including yoga, volleyball, swimming, and caving.

The TC staff also train other health professions in methods of coping with drug abusers and provide information on many aspects of drug taking and treatment. The TC itself holds events such as fêtes and firework parties where local residents can see the TC for themselves, and senior residents often undertake local voluntary community work. The TC no longer regards itself as self-contained; it now works in partnership with statutory and voluntary agencies as well as its local community.

## A total or partial solution?

A significant shift in the TC's attitude is its recognition that it may be only part of the solution to a resident's problems. In the same way that prospective entrants are referred to other agencies, residents may be given the opportunity to seek outside support. HIV counselling is a particularly important example of this approach, as those with HIV may feel isolated from the majority of residents. Moreover, special health care may be needed which is only available through hospital out-patient departments. The TC is still the central feature of a resident's life; it is his/her home and forum for rehabilitation, but it is not the sole provider of support.

## The problems of re-entry into society

The problem of readjustment to normal society has also been confronted by the TC. One approach has been on earlier reintegration through voluntary work and socializing. This starts after 6 months with residents spending a significant and increasing time away from the TC. Part-time education is also encouraged. Recreational or vocational pursuits often lead to interests which continue after a resident has left the programme.

Staff are available to give support to residents who encounter problems when they leave the programme. In some communities this has taken the form of links with Narcotics Anonymous (see also Chapter 19). Although the NA philosophy differs in significant respects from that of the programmatic TC it shares the goal of abstinence and as such has proved useful to many ex-residents. Other communities have a relapse programme where former residents can return to the community. All TCs encourage the use of outside bodies such as the Regional Drugs Team, Probation Service, and drugs counsellors.

## Changes in staff attitudes

The biggest change that has taken place in the TC is the attitude of staff to the clients. The TC 'philosophy' is not now seen as the panacea for all residents' problems. The client is regarded as having the ability to give direction for their own rehabilitation. Their experience of problems, be they drug abuse, HIV, or long-term deprivation, give an insight into what is needed to overcome them. Staff can identify with a background culminating in problem drug taking, but many will not be able to relate to problems of HIV and a background of whole family involvement with drugs. With the change in the nature of clients, experienced therapeutic workers recognize that they must listen to residents who have a greater knowledge of their own problems. The TC cannot take the HIV virus away from a resident and cannot change society. What it can do is help a client find the path to achieve solutions to their own particular set of problems. This process of rehabilitation is paradoxically a return to the origins of the Concept House model of a TC. When drug abusers gave up the medical model in favour of self-help they looked to their own experiences and understanding to provide treatment. This approach now allows for different paths to the goal of abstinence since new problems require innovative responses. It may be too early to assess the full effects of a changed attitude in a TC, but one study suggests that a more democratic regime enhances post-treatment outcomes (Norris 1988).

## New objectives

The changes described in TCs have inevitably brought about a recon-sideration of goals and objectives. The primary goal of the TC is to enable residents to live a lifestyle free from problem drug taking. With financial pressures on the TC being strong, the TC must maintain a 'full house' of residents. This inevitably affects the treatment programme. Techniques which enable residents to achieve the primary goal of the TC may be dropped because some residents find them unpalatable and leave. Moreover, in a 'competitive care environment', where TCs must vie with other agencies for resources, the significant early leaver rate may be seen as a mark of inefficiency rather than an inevitable response from problem drug takers to the rehabilitation process. An important goal which is readily compatible with the primary goal of abstinence is that of promoting a healthier lifestyle. The ACMD (1988) saw HIV as a more significant health issue than drug use, and the TC provides an ideal environment for promoting HIV-related health issues. Early leavers benefit from this although their tendency to 'self-destruct' may remain.

Perhaps the most significant change in relation to the primary goal of abstinence is an acceptance that safer drug use is worthwhile as a 'second best' goal. Although within the TC total abstinence must be the objective, it is necessary in the brave new world of HIV to accept that where drug abuse restarts it should at least be carried out in a safer way. Since sexual practices are a major area of transmission any change adopted here by early leavers is also worthwhile. Moreover, should residents return not to problem drug taking but recreational use, this must be considered when evaluating the success of the TC approach.

HIV awareness is an important function in the TC and developments have followed the recommendations of the ACMD (1988, 1989) in rela-tion to HIV and may take place as early as the assessment stage, with staff providing information and counselling. Practical steps in the form of primary health care will have already been undertaken, ranging from the early availability of condoms to the employment of HIV specialists with a medical background. In the authors' Community there is a house avail-able for residents or ex-residents who have become ill through HIV, and similar houses have been proposed elsewhere in the UK (Cooke *et al*. 1990). Communities have undertaken outreach work in conjunction with local voluntary and statutory organizations. The employment of staff with personal experience of HIV is also taking place and this may be a key factor in developing the TC response to HIV. Certainly it follows closely in the tradition of the TC—albeit with a latter-day twist.

## References

ACMD (Advisory Council on the Misuse of Drugs) (1988). *AIDS and drug misuse, Part 1*. HMSO, London.

ACMD (1989). *AIDS and drug misuse, Part 2*. HMSO, London.

Biase, D. V. (1987). AIDS and the Therapeutic Community; response issues, policy and practices. In *Euroconf 87*, Conference Proceedings of the European Federation of Therapeutic Communities, 1987, pp. 63–7. Coolemine Therapeutic Community, Dublin.

Cooke, L., Barrett, A., and Tomlinson, D. (1990). HIV positivity and health in the therapeutic community. In *AIDS and drug misuse: the challenge for policy and practice in the 1990s* (ed. J. Strang and G. Stimson), pp. 248–60. Routledge, London.

De Leon, G. (1984). *The Therapeutic Community: a study of effectiveness*. Treatment Research Monograph 84–1286. National Institute of Drug Abuse, Rockville, MD.

Donellan, B. and Toon, P. (1986). The use of therapeutic techniques in the Concept House model of Therapeutic Community for drug abusers. For whose benefit—staff or resident? *International Journal of Therapeutic Communities*, **7**, 183–9.

Galea, R. P., Lewis, B. F., and Baker, L. A. (1988). AIDS education in the therapeutic community: implementation and results among high risk clients and staff. *International Journal of Therapeutic Communities*, **9**, 9–30.

Gerstel, D. U. (1982). *Paradise incorporated: Synanon*. Presidio Press, Novato, California.

Jenkins, P. (1980). Speech at Annual General Meeting, Phoenix House, quoted in Annual Report, Phoenix House, London.

Jones, M. (1984). Why two therapeutic communities?. *Journal of Psychoactive Drugs*, **16**, 23–6.

Kennard, D. (1983). *An introduction to therapeutic communities*. Routledge and Kegan Paul, London.

Kennard, D. (1989). The therapeutic impulse—what makes it grow? *International Journal of Therapeutic Communities*, **10**, 155–63.

Main, T. (1946). The hospital as a therapeutic institution. *Bulletin of the Menniger Clinic*, **10**, 66–70.

Norris, M. (1988). A follow up study of drug abusers in a therapeutic community during periods of change. *International Journal of Therapeutic Communities*, **9**, 249–61.

Yablonsky, L. (1965). *The tunnel back: Synanon*. Macmillan, New York.

# 18. Narcotics Anonymous (NA) in Britain

*Brian Wells*

## History

The 12-step fellowships originated in May 1935 when Bill Wilson and Dr Robert Smith, both chronic alcoholics, met in Akron, Ohio, and founded Alcoholics Anonymous (AA). The first 100 members collectively wrote the 'Big Book', the 12 steps and the traditions of AA. AA has always insisted that it exists to provide a recovery programme for those suffering from the illness of 'alcoholism'. Those suffering other disorders have been encouraged to go elsewhere, leading to a plethora of self-help organizations based upon the 12 steps, including Gamblers Anonymous, Emotions Anonymous, Over-eaters Anonymous, and Paranoids Anonymous (the latter being somewhat difficult to find).

Narcotics Anonymous (NA) began in California, in July 1953 when a group of motorcycle riding, middle-aged heroin addicts were ejected from their local AA meeting with some acrimony. They altered the first step from 'We admitted that we were powerless over alcohol ...', to 'We admitted that we were powerless over our addiction ...', but otherwise retained the steps, the traditions and the entire programme of recovery, applying them to the 'illness of addiction', thus offering the same to persons suffering problems relating to the whole spectrum of mind altering chemicals.

In the UK, NA was born in 1979 when an ex-drug using AA member started the first meeting at St Georges' Hostel, Worlds End, Chelsea. This weekly meeting continued for a year with a gradually increasing attendance. Then a second meeting was started, then a third. Three 'delegates' flew to Memphis and attended an NA Literature Writing and Service Convention. Upon their return in 1981, NA meetings began springing up all over London and in scattered parts of the country, notably Bristol and Weston-super-Mare. Growth was sporadic and appeared to depend upon local attitudes to 12-step fellowships and in particular the presence of 12-step based (Minnesota Model) treatment centres, the first of which was Broadway Lodge in Weston-super-Mare.

By 1984 Weston-super-Mare had become an interesting microcosm. There were at least eight NA meetings per week, some of which had mushroomed and just as rapidly folded, largely attended by ex-problem drug users who had left treatment and decided to remain in the area (either resident in a half-way house or living and working locally). At the same time a number of addicts had left treatment prematurely (or been thrown out) who also decided to live locally and continue to use drugs. The town became something of a national centre for drug taking and recovery, to the extent that users would travel from Wales, Bath, and Bristol to Weston-super-Mare in order to buy heroin. Many of these 'addicts' had friends who were in the recovering community (perhaps from their treatment peer group) and subsequently 'cleaned up', moving from the using camp to join their companions in recovery.

Elsewhere in the country attitudes, towards the fellowships were more cynical within both 'using' and professional cultures. Thus in Manchester, NA struggled to survive and blamed local professional attitudes as a major cause of the problem. In Liverpool, NA still does not exist, whilst a strong meeting has been flourishing for some 5 years, across the river in Birkenhead. As other treatment centres opened (mainly in southern England), so local NA flourished.

A London office was acquired, the service structure (quite different from that of AA) was developed and NA spread throughout the UK during the mid-1980s, so that by 1991 there were 223 weekly meetings attended by 'recovering addicts' in Britain. This reflects a relatively even distribution of NA throughout the UK whilst it remains predominant in southern England and in odd locations close to treatment centres and half-way houses. Within NA itself there is a tendency towards subcultures and 'cliques'. For example some members prefer to avoid the Chelsea meetings, feeling more comfortable, say, in the East End. In general, mature members are happy to attend anywhere at any time. As with AA, there is a 'life force' to the meetings, which changes in atmosphere as years go by, some becoming too big, or possibly as the result of a personality clash, members starting a new meeting of differing format nearby.

In the USA, NA grew as a classless structure with a small college-attending periphery, whereas in the UK, early NA was largely perpetuated by the energies of young people from socially advantaged backgrounds, many of whom had been through fee-paying 'Minnesota Model' treatment programmes. Thus early NA in Britain was viewed as for the privileged and hence unattractive to many problem drug users, whilst professionals in the field, many of whom had never considered AA as a useful treatment resource, became concerned over what they saw as 'a resource for the private sector', in 'a self-help group for rich people'. Alarm was expressed over such notions as 'the disease concept' and the need for a 'higher power' whilst workers felt that strategies such as 'tough love' and 'total abstinence' were tantamount to 'brain-washing'. Many such opinions persist today amongst British drug working professionals.

## The ideology

NA subscribes to the view that once recreational drug use has become compulsive, the 'addict' has crossed a thin line into a physical, psycho-logical, and spiritual illness that can only get worse with continued drug use. The illness is seen as progressive and eventually fatal unless it is arrested by daily abstinence allowing a process of recovery to begin. 'Addicts' are seen as not responsible for their illness, but 100 per cent responsible for recovery, via the maintenance of abstinence (from all mood altering chemicals including alcohol) and active work done on the suggested programme of recovery.

## Alcohol

Recovery doesn't stop with just being clean. As we abstain from all drugs (and yes this means alcohol and marijuana too) we come face to face with feelings that we have never coped with successfully. (NA 1989).

Many 'addicts' have had serious problems with alcohol as well as other forms of polydrug taking. Alcohol is seen as 'just another sedative drug' and is frequently referred to in meetings, to the extent that many 'alcoholics' who have had no apparent difficulty with other drugs, prefer the atmosphere of NA to AA meetings. They tend to be more youthful, more energetic and lively, whilst some would say less stable and less mature. The main factor is probably the age and life experience of the members involved, so the young drinker is often more attracted to NA. This is, however, not always the case. NA contains many 'elder statesmen' who have had problems with, say, alcohol and benzodiazepines, and who are able to identify more with NA than their local AA counterpart.

## The family

The illness is seen as affecting the entire family. Where there has been 'active addiction' over a number of years, family members (including children) often experience distress, unpredictability, violence, and legal consequences.

The self-help groups Al Anon and Families Anonymous (FA) exist for family members of 'alcoholics' and 'addicts', respectively. They are also 12-step fellowships in which family members are encouraged to work their own programme, placing responsibility for recovery from addiction upon the shoulders of the active alcoholic/addict. They are not organizations for people to attend in order to complain about their using/drinking spouse, but rather they exist to offer a programme of recovery to family members whose lives have become 'dysfunctional'.

## The programme

The suggested programme of recovery involves attendance at NA meetings. These are numerous in urban areas, to be found in hospitals, prisons and other institutions as well as in the community. Meetings vary in their format (speaker meetings, step meetings, topic meetings, etc.) but generally consist of a main speaker sharing his or her experience of addiction and recovery, possibly in relation to a particular topic (relationships, spirituality, etc.) or on one of the 12 steps. The meeting is then opened up for sharing from the floor. Typically members introduce themselves as 'I'm Fred/Jane, I'm an addict' and then refer to the main speaker, or the topic in question. Sometimes, however, sharing simply involves an account of what has happened that day, good times, difficulties, 'here and now' events. There is frequently much gratitude expressed towards the fellowship, and at times, newcomers may be forgiven for thinking that they have walked into a room full of fanatics.

Sharing is, in general, supportive, non-judgemental and includes personal identification with the main speaker and his or her subject. Visitors are often surprised at the degree of humour that abounds in meetings. Many members are articulate and psychologically sophisticated, whilst others are shy and less forthcoming. All are supported by the group.

Members are encouraged to attend frequently in the early days in order to become familiar with the jargon, the other members, and the various formats, but in particular in order to 'flood' the new member with a process that is likely to be unfamiliar, strange, and sometimes frightening. Many new members feel they have entered into something akin to a religious sect, while sharing about personal issues in public is often an alien experience. Relatively few newcomers (or indeed professionals) are able to embrace this programme with enthusiasm if they visit only a few times.

Members are encouraged to get involved, to acquire a sponsor (someone with whom they can discuss their difficulties and perceptions on a one-to-one basis) and to begin to absorb the fundamental NA message which clearly states, 'We support each other in remaining drug free, just one day at a time'.

Telephone numbers are exchanged, post-meeting rendezvous take place, conventions and fund-raising events are held. Dances, parties, and 'service events', all exist to offer the newcomer a support system within a true fellowship of recovering people that collectively retains the clear focus of daily abstinence.

## The 12 steps of NA

1. We admitted that we were powerless over our addiction, that our lives had become unmanageable.

2. We came to believe that a power greater than ourselves could restore us to sanity.

3. We made a decision to turn our will and our lives over to the care of God as we understood him.

4. We made a searching and fearless moral inventory of ourselves.

5. We admitted to God, to ourselves, and to another human being the exact nature of our wrongs.

6. We were entirely ready to have God remove all these defects of character.

7. We humbly asked Him to remove our shortcomings.

8. We made a list of all persons we had harmed, and became willing to make amends to them all.

9. We made direct amends to such people wherever possible, except when to do so would injure them or others.

10. We continued to take personal inventory, and when we were wrong promptly admitted it.

11. We sought through prayer and meditation to improve our conscious contact with God, as we understood Him, praying only for knowledge of His will for us, and the power to carry it out.

12. Having had a spiritual awakening as a result of those steps, we tried to carry this message to addicts and to practice these principles in all our affairs.

NA chose to retain the steps in their original form as written by the early AA members. Some of these members came from the religious Oxford movement and much early AA literature contains a strong religious overtone. It was felt, however, that the steps had stood the test of time and should therefore not be altered.

Much criticism is levelled at NA for its 'quasi-religious' orientation. Reference to God appears in six of the 12 steps, and prayer and meditation are encouraged. NA, however, is not a religious organization. There is a spiritual component based upon the personal understanding of a 'Power greater than oneself'. This may be the power of the group, the power of nature, love, collectivity, or some force connected with truth and honesty. Feelings of well-being engendered by the process of collective personal growth are often referred to as 'spiritual'. Whilst some members eventually do become involved with 'organized religion', others experiment with forms of meditation, martial arts, yoga, physical exercise, etc., or completely ignore the spirituality suggested by the programme.

The steps encourage a deep understanding of the need for daily abstinence, as well as insight into self. The making of restitution to self and others and the development of a spiritual direction lead to the spread of the recovery message to the still suffering addict: 'We keep what we have by giving it away'.

Many attend NA and pay no attention to the steps. The organization is used on a number of levels, from enhancement of social contact to what is sometimes seen as 'obsessive' preoccupation with the process of recovery and growth.

## Who attends?

'Very simply an addict is a man or woman whose life is controlled by drugs'. 'There is only one requirement for membership, the honest desire to stop using'.

In practice NA membership comprises a variety of persons who have experienced problems relating to drugs. Many have been dependent upon opioids, alcohol, stimulants, and sedatives. Some describe a history of chaotic polydrug misuse, whilst others have become concerned over heavy recreational use of cannabis. The attending population varies with geographical location and local drug taking practices. Central London meetings are likely to include teenagers as well as elderly people dependent upon prescribed benzodiazepines. The atmosphere is variable and it is suggested that newcomers should 'shop around', looking for meetings to which they are attracted.

## Affiliation with NA

Initial impressions suggest that those with social confidence and verbal fluency are more likely to affiliate with NA. Whilst further research is needed, it is often surprising that the 'least likely' candidates sometimes become active and valuable NA members. The converse is also true with those 'tipped as likely to succeed' sometimes seeming quite unable to internalize the basics of the programme.

People find NA through mutual friends, old using acquaintances, prisons, counsellors, parents and wives who begin attending family fellowships, or sometimes by just wandering in off the street. Sometimes people are simply 'just not ready' to engage. They often return, however, perhaps 2 years later having 'tried it out their own way' eventually deciding to 'come around'. Anecdotally the most powerful influence seems to be that of peer group persuasion and attraction as found in the fellowship itself and as used more formally in 12-step based treatment.

## Treatment

The most common form of treatment in the USA is abstinence-based and makes use of AA/NA principles. In the USA there are literally thousands of 28-day residential programmes that encourage problem drug users/drinkers to understand themselves as people with an illness who need to get well, via abstinence and attendance at 12-step fellowships. In the UK this has become known as the Minnesota Model (see Wells 1986; Cook 1988).

Such treatment centres are to be found in the private and charitable sectors, whilst a diluted version is sometimes practised in National Health Service (NHS) alcohol and addiction treatment units. Minnesota Model centres may be residential, with programmes lasting from 21 to 56 days. They may be out-patient or day-care with a number of 'half-way houses' available. Some centres offer a family programme in which family members spend a residential period, followed by attendance at family fellowships to deal with their own difficulties. Most centres ask the family to attend at weekends, to be part of the addict's recovery programme both during and after treatment.

An entire book is being written (by an NA member) about the development of the Minnesota Model treatment centres. From Broadway Lodge which opened in 1974, a plethora of centres have developed. The issue of funding has been a constant and sometimes fatal area of difficulty, with some centres having been forced to close within weeks of having opened. Different centres have different styles, with some being purely available to fee-paying patients or those with insurance. Others have registered as nursing homes and take patients on 'assisted places', receiving DSS payment, often as well as providing two or three completely free beds (for those not entitled to DSS payments).

In March 1991 there were some 30 treatment centres offering Minnesota Model style treatment in the UK and Ireland. They all have a history that contains amusing and tragic anecdotes. They all see themselves as struggling against 'the establishment' for recognition and credibility. Some have excellent training programmes and good relationships with local health authorities, all are concerned about future funding, NHS reforms, and the contract culture.

Controlled research is needed to evaluate these treatment centres, some of which make extravagant claims as part of a marketing strategy.

## Some problems

NA is far from perfect. It is a self-help group organized and run by people in varying stages of recovery. Relapse does occur, being treated constructively as a 'learning experience', with individuals being welcomed back.

Some groups are immature, some members are more interested in romantic relationships than recovery, and sometimes bad advice is given, for example by dogmatic individuals who may suggest that drugs such as naltrexone, lithium, and disulfiram should be stopped in order to participate in a totally drug-free programme.

Some members describe adverse experience of hospitals and previous help-seeking. Psychiatrists and other professionals are often ridiculed in meetings (sometimes with justification). Mature members, however, in general have a healthy respect for professionals and often make appropriate referrals when things go wrong or problems occur.

## Conclusion

NA started in Britain in 1979. It grew rapidly throughout the 1980s, and continues to grow as it develops a good reputation and relationships With professional staff. Whilst there are some problems, it remains an important, freely available adjunct to therapy and after-care for persons and their families suffering drug-related problems. Any such clients may usefully be encouraged to attend. Professionals are invited to attend open meetings themselves, many of whom enjoy doing so, often acquiring a list of useful contacts in the process.

NA has much collective wisdom to offer both client and professional. It contains an array of relatively untapped research material and remains a source of energy, enthusiasm, humour, and positive feedback to those in the caring professions who deal with problem drinkers and drug takers.

## References

Robinson, D. (1979). *Talking out of alcoholism*. Croom Helm, London.
Wells, B. (1987). Narcotics Anonymous (NA): the phenomenal growth of an important resource. *British Journal of Addiction*, **82**, 581–2.
Cook, C. (1988). The Minnesota Model in the management of drug and alcohol dependency: miracle, method or myth? Part I The philosophy and the programme. *British Journal of Addiction*, **83**, 625–34. Part II Evidence and conclusions. *British Journal of Addiction*, **83**, 735–48.
NA (Narcotics Anonymous) (1988). *The NA big book*, 5th edn. World Service Office Inc., Van Nuys CA.
NA (1989). For the newcomer. *Information Pamphlet No. 16*. UK Service Office, PO Box 704, London SW10.

# 19. Minimizing harm from drug use

*Gerry V. Stimson*

It has taken the threat of acquired immune deficiency syndrome (AIDS) to legitimize and concretize a set of loosely related ideas and practices around the reduction of harm from drug use.

Since 1987 English drugs policy has been preoccupied with the problem of drug injecting and the consequent risk of the transmission of human immunodeficiency virus (HIV). Prominent has been the idea that many people who inject drugs are unable and unwilling to stop injecting and therefore ways must be found to help them reduce their risks of infection with HIV and of transmitting it to others. There are various ways in which this may be achieved; for example in the United States, dominant approaches have been prescribing methadone in order to help people stop injecting, and reaching out to drug injectors and persuading them to use bleach to decontaminate syringes. In England HIV risk reduction has centred predominantly around the idea of 'syringe-exchange'.

## Schemes for the exchange of needles and syringes.

Syringe-exchanges are agencies which provide sterile injecting equipment to injecting drug users on an exchange basis. The equipment will include needles and syringes and may also include swabs for cleaning skin, and safe containers for the eventual return of equipment. Syringe-exchange has become a figurehead for the new response to drug problems. Within 2 years of pilot schemes being established in 1987, there were over 120 schemes throughout England and Wales, with over one in three of all drugs agencies now running some form of syringe-exchange (Lart and Stimson 1980). At the same time there has been a less well publicized expansion in the provision of syringes by retail pharmacies.

Syringe-exchanges have had a considerable impact on drugs services, and have been demonstrated to reach drug injectors and to help them change their behaviour (Stimson *et al*. 1988). They are important because they provide the means for drug injectors to change their behaviour, but they are also important because they epitomize a new set of ideas about the nature of problem drug use and what can be done to respond to it.

## Looking beyond the exchange

Syringe-exchanges are symbolic of what many drug workers are now hoping to achieve. However, they should be seen as only one part of a reorientation to drug problems that has occurred since 1987. Of equal significance is the harm minimization literature which has been produced with hints and tips for safer drug use, much of this produced in a format (for example, comics) which is thought to be accessible to drug injectors. Also important is the growth of a 'user friendly' ethos by drugs workers and the attempts that some agencies have made to go a long way along the road of meeting drug injectors on their own terms. Finally, the idea of reducing risk of HIV and AIDS has also helped to put the health of drug users on the agenda. For many years drug clinics, being preoccupied with the problem of drug use, did not give much explicit attention to the health problems facing their clients (although in practice advice on health hazards of injection, and practical first aid was often on hand). Harm minimization around injecting drug use—for example, how to avoid complications of drug injecting such as abscesses, hepatitis, and septicaemia, spills over into broader health promotion—such as advising drug injectors on diet and exercise.

## The rapid acceptance of harm minimization

How could harm minimization arrive so swiftly and gain such ready acceptance? As we have discussed elsewhere (Stimson and Lart 1991) there were three important factors. First, there existed a wide range of non-medical drugs agencies which were receptive to new ideas. The majority of drugs agencies currently operating in England and Wales have a very short history, having been established under the Central Funding Initiative (CFI) in the mid-1980s (MacGregor *et al.* 1990). The CFI was a response to the problem that many parts of the country lacked adequate drug services. 'Pump priming' money was made available for the improvement of existing services and the establishment of new ones. A new level of drug advice and information services was established. Whilst most agencies still had a medical input or sought to make links with prescribing doctors, they were freed to a large extent from traditional medical views on the treatment of problem drug users. The consequence was a lessening of the importance of traditional drug dependency clinics in the British response to drugs problems, in comparison with earlier periods (for further discussion see Stimson 1987). It also provided jobs and career opportunities which attracted new people into the drugs field. The result was that there was an array of fresh drugs agencies responsive to new ideas and readily adaptable to the emerging problem of AIDS and HIV in 1986.

The second factor was the framework within which this initiative was undertaken. In policy terms, the CFI provided a central push plus the carrot of new finance for drugs services. At the same time, in a typical British manner, there was little firm direction from central government about the way these new services would be run. The central push has been combined with a high degree of autonomy at the local level. A similar thing happened when the drug dependency clinics were first established in 1968. The clinics were established from the centre, but if we look back to the commentaries at the time, we can see that there was a high level of uncertainty about what the clinics would actually do (Stimson and Oppenheimer 1982). At that time this was probably due to the British Government's reluctance to interfere with the clinical autonomy of the new drug dependency consultants. In the 1980s and early 1990s, the emphasis on market forces under the Thatcher Government coupled with the philosophy of local accountability has led central government to claim reluctance to specify the content of local services. Such a policy framework can have detrimental effects. In the case of drug clinics, the clinical freedom claimed by individual consultants means that it is difficult for a general policy (for example methadone prescribing) to be uniformly pursued, or for there to be common standards of service. On a beneficial side, it means that drugs agencies can (if they wish) respond quickly and creatively to new problems, as was the case with the response to AIDS and HIV. This particularly British way of doing things indicates that the English drugs policy shares much in common with many other areas of policy making. (These issues are further discussed in Chapter 26.) In consequence, the response to drug problems has been particularly flexible, tolerant, pragmatic, and adaptable.

The third factor was the existence of a discourse on harm minimization. Constant themes within English drugs policy indicate that reducing the problems that occur from drug use are appropriate aims for clinicians and others. In clinical work with drug users the ideas can be traced back to the recommendation of the Rolleston Committee Report in 1926, that in certain circumstances it was legitimate medical practice to prescribe drugs of addiction to those addicted to them. It was thought this enabled people to lead relatively normal social lives. This has found greater or lesser currency at different phases, sometimes being seen as good practice, and sometimes the work of the heretic. It first finds some quasi-official recognition in the Advisory Council on the Misuse of Drugs report *Prevention* (1984), which argued that 'prevention' included both the prevention of drug use and the prevention of drug related harm.

## Changing ideas about harm minimization

Tracing the precursors of contemporary ideas should not be taken as suggesting that the ideas have remained constant and have been used in the same way in different periods. Ideas surface, are reproduced, and are changed in their use in different historical contexts. (See for example, Stimson and Lart 1990, for a discussion of the different ways in which the concept of 'public health' has been employed in drugs policy.) It would be unwise therefore to attribute current ideas of harm minimization to ideas of the 1920s. It would, however, be legitimate to argue that similar structural relationships between the state and the medical profession in the 1920s, and the state and drugs agencies in the 1980s, allowed such ideas to proliferate (see Chapter 26).

The antecedents of today's ideas about harm minimization are more likely to be have arisen initially not in professional discourse about the drugs problem, but in the undergrowth of ideas that grew up around drug use from the mid 1960s through to the early 1970s. Here was an example of an indigenous drug using culture which produced guidelines on how to use drugs safely and enjoy them. Book shops selling 'alternative' literature were replete with manuals on the production, use, and enjoyment of drugs, and advice on how to avoid problems associated with them. Similar advice was found in the columns of 'underground' newspapers. For example, in the late 1960s in London, New York and San Francisco and many other Western centres, there was a comprehensive folk science concerning the use of LSD. This included attention to the particular setting in which it was to be taken, advice that the novice should be accompanied by someone more experienced, and that someone should be present who did not take the drug. The mental set, or preparedness, of the person was also considered important: for example, it was soon discovered that LSD could enhance existing mood states and that 'bad trips' could arise from taking the drug when the person was anxious or depressed. It included advice for talking people through 'bad trips'. There was also an active debate about the pros and cons of medication with tranquillizers for those undergoing unpleasant LSD experiences. At the same time, there was an underground campaign against the use of methylamphetamine under the slogan 'speed kills', along with warnings of the potential 'horrors' that came with over-indulgence (this was the condition known in medical parlance as 'amphetamine psychosis' after the work of Connell 1958).

This folk science or, in anthropological terms, ethnoscience of drug experiences, had its own theoreticians. Timothy Leary's work put some intellectual stamp on this project. Quasi-scientific journals appeared, such as the *Psychedelic Review*. Huxley's works, along with those of Blake, were widely read as guides to mystical experiences. From a slightly different direction, some of Laing's work drew parallels between schizophreniform episodes, voyages of mystical discovery, and drug-induced experiences. In short, the 1960s drug literature aimed to maximize pleasure and minimize harm.

The sociological protagonist was Howard Becker. In a series of publications which had a major impact on the new deviancy theorists of the late 1960s, he explored the inter-relationship between society and drug use. An early paper on 'Becoming a marijuana user' emphasized the importance that drug cultures play in teaching people how to use and enjoy drugs. Becker argued that the novice needed to be taught both the technology of drug use (in the case of marijuana, and how to prepare and smoke it), and to be taught to identify both the positive and negative effects (Becker 1963). Because drugs have a multiplicity of effects, it is through taking drugs with others that people learn to identify what is pleasurable. In other words, Becker suggested that people learn how to be 'high'. Becker also proposed a 'moral career', in that the novice user also had to learn how to cope with the negative moral esteem that others associated with smoking marijuana. The argument is pursued in later articles in which he argued that cultures adapt to drug effects: the more familiar a drug becomes within a community, the fewer problems that will be encountered. Thus he predicted that when a drug was newly introduced into a society, problems would arise until members of that society learnt ways to manage use of that drug (Becker 1967, 1974). He also argued that if individuals in specific societies were prevented from acquiring knowledge about a drug—an example would be the medical profession's attempt to control and limit knowledge about the effects of prescribed medications—the harmful side-effects might not be identified or appropriately managed. Becker's theory is about the importance of knowledge in the way subcultures can develop an expertise in drug use, and the role of knowledge in guiding subjective positive and negative effects. All cultures, he proposes, develop indigenous ways of regulating drug use.

## Harm minimization and its relationship to the promotion of pleasure

The underground literature on minimizing drug-related harm and promoting of drug-related pleasure, and the intellectual proponents of these views, found little favour amongst the mainstream academics and policy makers of the time. The suspicion surrounding the pleasurable uses of non-traditional drugs meant that proposals for new forms of control for these drugs—as in the Wootton report on cannabis, were rejected by politicians on all sides. Becker's proposal, at an Anglo-American conference on drug problems held at a stately home in England in 1967, that drug dependence problems could be solved by a scientific effort to produce pleasure-making drugs that lacked a dependence liability, met with a silence as empty as the fake leather-bound volumes on the surrounding library shelves.

The lack of enthusiasm for the pleasure-promoting side of this argument is understandable. Less so the lack of enthusiasm for harm minimization. Harm minimization continued as a minority point of view throughout much of the 1970s and early 1980s. It was practised in some drug clinics, particularly in their early days when some had 'fixing rooms' where clients could inject. But it was never prominent on the agenda. Attempts to put it back on the agenda were often met by a hostile reception. For example, there was the problem of what advice could be given concerning the use of glues and solvents. Here were substances which were quite legally obtainable, and it was inconceivable that manufacturers would readily accept legislation which would limit or prohibit their availability. This was a clear opportunity for harm minimization, given the general failure of drug prevention campaigns and the absence of legal controls. The Institute of the Study of Drug Dependence (ISDD) produced the harm minimization guide *Teaching about a volatile situation* in 1980. Described by the *London Evening Standard* as the 'Good glue guide', this suggested health education strategies for minimizing casualties associated with solvent sniffing. But some time later one advocate of harm minimization for solvent abuse was attacked in the media when he repeated an ISDD suggestion that to prevent people from suffocating when inhaling solvents from large polythene bags, he would advise them to use a smaller bag.

Throughout much of this period, the clinical equivalent of harm minimization, the prescription of drugs of dependence to those dependent on them, continued, but outside of mainstream treatment philosophy which, from the mid-1970s to the mid-1980s tended to be abstinence oriented. Although it has not been made explicit, harm minimization also contradicts the centrality of reaching 'rock bottom' in the Alcoholics Anonymous and Narcotics Anonymous approaches (K. Dolan, personal communication 1990).

## AIDS breaths new life into harm minimization

Such was the situation when AIDS came to the fore in 1986. Considerable prominence was given to the reports from Scotland of the rapid spread of HIV infection amongst injecting drug users in Edinburgh and elsewhere on the east coast of Scotland, and to the circulation of the Scottish Home and Health Department (1986) report on HIV infection and intravenous drug use. That report suggested making sterile needles and syringes available to people who inject drugs in order to reduce the spread of HIV infection. When the Advisory Council on the Misuse of Drugs was asked to consider this proposal in early 1986, the suggestion was rejected on the grounds that there was little evidence that drug injectors shared because of a shortage of syringes, and that the provision of syringes was probably not a viable solution to the problem of the spread of HIV.

## The experiment of needle and syringe exchange schemes

In the event, despite the cautious negativity of the Advisory Council, a decision was made late in 1986 that there should be a limited experiment in the provision of syringes to people who inject.

Three important factors influenced this position. First, there was the strong evidence from Scotland that a shortage of syringes had facilitated the transmission of HIV, and the fear by English politicians that what had occurred in Scotland could occur in English cities. Second, there was the political arena within which the debate on AIDS was developing. The then Secretary of State for Health, Norman Fowler, had taken on AIDS as a special issue and had made prominent visits to San Francisco to look at the response to AIDS amongst gay men and by health service and other providers there, and had also visited Amsterdam, where there had been syringe distribution since 1984.

The third important feature in the scenario of the mid 1980s was the evidence of the indigenous gay response to the threat of AIDS, which put safer sex on the agenda as a way of maximizing pleasure and minimizing harm in face of the risk of HIV. If it worked with gay men, would it work with drug injectors?

These new factors then came together with the three features that were identified earlier in this essay—the proliferation of drugs agencies under the CFI, a situation which allowed for high levels of autonomy at the local level, and the emerging discourse on harm minimization.

Many of the 'Gurus' of harm minimization are themselves products of the 1960s, whilst many of the acolytes in drugs agencies were re-cruited into this new situation in the mid-1980s and were unencumbered by earlier medical professional views of the importance of abstinence in the care of problem drug takers. Many drugs workers will themselves have used illegal drugs at some time in the past, and believe harm mini-mization policy to be an honest way of dealing with potential drug problems in others.

That harm minimization is a viable option has been demonstrated in the evaluation work conducted by the Monitoring Research Group which showed, first, that syringe-exchange is a workable strategy, in that agencies can set-up and efficiently run such a service and success-fully attract clients, and second, that it helps some people sustain lower risk behaviour and others to adopt it (Stimson *et al.* 1988). There are some limitations: syringe-exchanges are not very good at retaining contact with clients and are not very good at attracting women and younger drug injectors. There are also limits to the numbers of people who can be reached. This has led to the suggestion that from a public health point of view, the aim should be to maximize the distribution of syringes through a proliferation of outlets in addition to syringe-exchanges.

## Conclusion

In conclusion, the idea of harm minimization has now been established as a key area of work with drug users. However, the situation remains somewhat in flux and the position has not been achieved where the seal can be set on yet another stage in the development of English drugs policy. Four contradictions suggest that this is still a developing situation. First, there is the tension between a drugs agency oriented harm minimization service and a public health HIV prevention strategy. The drugs agency approach focuses on individual counselling for drug users in the truest traditions of English social work. From this perspective, syringe-exchange is a useful bait for attracting drug injectors into contact with services in order to then offer them other forms of help. Syringe-exchange in this context is thus seen as a low threshold contact. An alternative perspective derives from the imperatives of a public health response to HIV, where drug problems and providing help for them are less important than the public health issue of the prevention of HIV, which calls for the major distribution of syringes to drug injectors.

The second tension is that whilst the threat of HIV has legitimized risk reduction and harm minimization measures *vis-à-vis* drug injecting, there has been little parallel development concerning harm minimization with other (that is, non-injectable) drugs. Even in the present favourable climate, it is likely that those who advocate harm minimization for the use of Ecstasy or other commonly used drugs, will find short shrift from the drugs and political establishments. Witness the government and police response to rave or 'Acid House' parties.

Thirdly, there is the tension created by the fact that although harm minimization developed in the 1960s as an indigenous response to potential problems with drug use, it has now been co-opted by and developed as a professional response. In this, the drugs response to HIV is unlike the gay response. Drugs agencies have co-opted an indigenous idea, but few agencies have concomitantly developed an adequate theory or practice of engendering indigenous cultural change amongst people who inject drugs.

Fourthly and finally there is the nagging link between harm minimization and the promotion of pleasure. In several quarters (and in particular in the United States) harm minimization has been rejected because it is thought to condone drug use. The argument in this chapter, with the historical examples from the 1960s, suggests that the unexplored corollary of harm minimization is in enabling safe pleasure from drugs. Whilst harm minimization has been legitimized in response to the threat to individual and public health posed by HIV, the promotion of pleasurable drug use has not. Ideas about drug use are in a creative turmoil and some surprises are still in store from those pushing the boundaries of harm minimization.

## Acknowledgements

I would like to thank Kate Dolan, Robert Power, Adam Crosier, Alan Dean, and Nick Dorn for perceptive comments and some useful insights.

## References

Advisory Council on the Misuse of Drugs (1984). *Prevention*. HMSO, London.
Becker, H. (1963). Becoming a marijuana user. In *Studies in the sociology of deviance*. Macmillan, New York.
Becker, H. (1967). History, culture and subjective experience: an exploration of the social basis of drug induced experiences. *Journal of Health and Social Behaviour*, **8**, 163–76.
Becker, H. (1974). Consciousness, power and drugs. *Journal of Psychedelic Drugs*, **6**, 67–76.
Connell, P. (1958). *Amphetamine psychosis*. Maudsley Monograph 5. Institute of Psychiatry. Oxford University Press, London.
ISDD (1981). *Teaching about a volatile situation* (pamphlet). ISDD, London.
Lart, R. A. and Stimson, G. V. (1990). National survey of syringe-exchange schemes in England. *British Journal of Addiction*, **85**, 1433–43.
MacGregor, S. *et al.* (1990). *Drug services in England and the impact of the Central Funding Initiative*. Report. ISDD, London.
Scottish Home and Health Department (1986). *HIV infection in Scotland*. Report of the Scottish Committee on HIV infection and intravenous drug misuse.
Stimson, G. V. (1987). British drug policies in the 1980s. *British Journal of Addiction*, **82**, 477–88.
Stimson, G. V. and Lart, R. A. (1991). HIV, drugs and public health in England: new words, old tunes. *International Journal of the Addictions*, **26**, 1263–7.
Stimson, G. V., Alldritt, L., Dolan, K., Donoghoe, M. C. and Lart R. (1988). *Injecting equipment exchange schemes: final report*. Goldsmiths' College, London.
UK Advisory committee on Drug Dependence (1968). *Cannabis*, HMSO, London.

# Part III

Other responses

# 20. Promoting new services: the Central Funding Initiative and other mechanisms

*Susanne MacGregor*

## Introduction

The central funding initiative (CFI) was part of an increase in resources to extend and improve drugs services in England, which characterized the 1980s. It involved an injection of £17.5 million in grants, normally covering a 3 year period. These were followed by central government allocations to Regional Health Authorities (RHAs) based on the number of 15–34-year-olds in their populations. RHAs were given discretion over the dispersal of these earmarked funds, subject to general guidelines. The overall funding process thus combined a 'kick-start' with a steady flow of funds thereafter to maintain the system.

Rather like Topsy, the CFI had just seemed to grow. Initially, the sum made available to agencies was £2 million during 1983–84, announced officially in December 1982. In January 1983, the total fund was increased to £6 million over 3 years. In June 1984, in response to the 'overwhelming' number of applications for funds, a further £1 million became available. Following the publication of the Advisory Council on the Misuse of Drugs (ACMD) report on *Prevention* in July 1984, yet another allocation (£3 million) was made and announced in February 1985.

The total CFI sum finally allocated was £17 558 020 (£14 479 561 revenue: £3 078 459 capital).

## The objectives

The CFI was presented as part of the government's response to the ACMD report on *Treatment and rehabilitation*, which had been published in December 1982. This report recommended *inter alia* the injection of new monies on a pump-priming basis to ensure the development of an adequate treatment and rehabilitation service. A comprehensive response, including both statutory and non-statutory, specialist and non-specialist, agencies was said to be needed. The emphasis on 'pump-priming' was judicious since this reflected the government's view that funding for drugs services should come primarily from local sources, and it would have been 'spitting in the wind' at that time to argue for long-term central funding. Throughout the period, the tension between the need for central funding and a rhetorical preference for local funding was a major theme in policy debate.

The objectives of the CFI set out in 1983 were:

1. To provide for regional and local assessments of the nature and spread of drug misuse problems.

2. To improve levels of awareness of the problems of drug misuse and increase the ability of professionals and others working in this area to help people with drug-related problems.

3. To improve links between health service provision and other community-based services.

4. To improve the effectiveness of services and to provide value for money.

It was hoped that the CFI would be a way of remedying 'old problems' such as lack of service co-ordination, inadequate treatment and rehabilitation resources and absence of training for staff, while also rising to 'new challenges' such as providing a more comprehensive response, generating public awareness at the local level and promoting better joint planning. It should also be able to respond to changes in the shape of the needs associated with drug misuse. As it turned out, this was to be particularly important. When the CFI was initiated, there were no references to AIDS, at that time not recognized as the spectre on the horizon it turned out to be. In the event, services had to respond rapidly to new demands, especially those resulting from the growing problem of HIV disease (ACMD 1988, 1989).

The services set up as a result of the CFI reflected the 'new orthodoxy' of the 1980s. Bids were made for services largely characterized as multidisciplinary, community-based, and accessible. Special attention was given to establishing provision in areas of the country where there was little, and to developing new services which were responsive to the needs of women and of parents with children. Notably excluded from this structure were services concentrating on alcohol and solvents and there was no specific mention of services devoted particularly to the needs of either ethnic minorities or people in prison.

The first year of the allocation exercise saw more approvals than rejections, 74:18. Thus those who got their applications in in this first year had a much better chance of success than those applying later, although the actual amount of money available increased over time. The following year was a 'catching-up' year preparing the way for what was to be the peak year of allocations, 1985/86 (judged in terms of the total funds distributed rather than the number of grants). In this year, the balance changed with 67 approvals but 137 rejections, that is the majority of applications were unsuccessful this year, a clear contrast with the first year of the scheme. (In the first year, 80 per cent of bids were successful; in the third year only 33 per cent were successful.) Clearly, the timing of applications affected success and thus favoured those who were quicker off the mark.

## Related developments

In December 1985, an additional £5 million was made available to health authorities for 1986–8 for the expansion of treatment services. Part of this allocation might be made available to voluntary organizations and to local authorities' social services departments under joint finance arrangements. Funds made available to local authorities under this scheme would continue in full for 10 years, instead of the usual 3 years for joint finance projects. This £5 million (later increased to £6.5 million per annum) became built-in to health authority allocations each year thereafter. These funds were further increased by an additional £3 million per annum, first made available in 1988–89 to provide for services designed to cope with the link between injecting drug misuse and the spread of HIV infection (Circulars HC(86)3/LAC(86)5; HC(88)26/LAC(88)7; and HC(88)53/

**Table 20.1** Shape of services funded through CFI grants (the proportion of total funds allocated to different types of service)

| Type of service | Total funds (£) | % of total |
| --- | --- | --- |
| Community services<br>  statutory and non-statutory | 9 868 426 | 56.2 |
| DDU/hospital services | 2 560 074 | 14.6 |
| Support for existing<br>  non-statutory services, self-help, CVS, etc. | 1 752 427 | 10.0 |
| Training, research | 1 719 509 | 9.8 |
| Residential rehabilitation | 1 657 584 | 9.4 |
| Total | 17 558 020 | 100.0 |

**Table 20.2** Shape of services funded

| Nature of activity | Number of grants |
|---|---|
| Community centres | 42 |
| Additional support for existing voluntary organizations | 36 |
| Community workers | 32 |
| Developments in general medicine or psychiatry | 22 |
| Developments at drug dependency units | 19 |
| Training and education | 11 |
| Residential rehabilitation | 9 |
| Information-gathering/research | 7 |
| Self-help groups | 4 |
| Community detoxification/aftercare | 1 |

**Table 20.3** Type of service funded

| Purpose of grant | Number of grants |
|---|---|
| New projects | 64 |
| Extension to project | 36 |
| Drug screening equipment/capital grant | 67 |
| Training/education | 11 |
| Information-gathering | 7 |
| Other | 1 |

**Table 20.4** Overall expenditure (in £)

| | Total | Revenue | Capital |
|---|---|---|---|
| NHS/District Health Authority | 9 059 930 | 8 166 248 | 893 682 |
| NHS/RHA | 1 419 948 | 1 241 482 | 178 466 |
| Total (statutory health) | 10 479 878 | 9 407 730 | 1 072 148 |
| Rehabilitation | 471 574 | 7 432 | 464 142 |
| Other non-statutory | 347 741 | 4 813 886 | 1 533 855 |
| Total (non-statutory) | 6 819 315 | 4 821 318 | 1 997 997 |
| Local authority | 258 827 | 250 513 | 8 314 |
| Grand total expenditure | 17 558 020 | 14 479 561 | 3 078 459 |

**Table 20.5** Average amount of grants to different types of approved CFI projects

| Type of service | Average amount of CFI grant (£) |
| --- | --- |
| Residential rehabilitation | 223 542 |
| Community project | 131 579 |
| Drug dependency units | 85 218 |
| Hospital services | 40 910 |

LAC(88)18). To the £5 million announced for 1986/87 was added £132 000 for an experimental programme of syringe-exchange schemes and drug counselling in 1987/88. By 1988/89 total additional earmarked funds from all three circulars then operational were £9.5 million. A Drug Advisory Service was established in December 1985 to advise district health authorities on the need for services and the most effective ways of establishing them. The reports of this service, together with guidelines on good clinical practice circulated to all general practitioners and hospital doctors in Great Britain and to the Prison Medical Service (Department of Health and Social Security; DHSS 1984), played an important part in increasing the extent of central advice and monitoring of service development, which with the earmarking of funds had a major impact on the drugs field in this period (see also DHSS 1985; DHSS *et al.* 1985; Home Office 1986, 1988; Social Services Committee 1984–85, 1987–88).

A commitment to monitoring was endorsed by the Department of Health (DoH) circular HC (89)30 which asked 'regional health authorities to set up a database to monitor trends in drug misuse and the use of drug misuse services and to introduce a system for providing this information to the Department of Health'. This database should be fully operational by 31 March 1991.

## The role of research

This belated interest in systematic monitoring with the decision to fund regional databases could in itself be seen ironically as a by-product of the CFI. Throughout that pump-priming phase, the comment had often been made that the information base on which to assess the initiative was inadequate.

It is worth recalling that the CFI on drugs was one of a number of such initiatives that came out of the DHSS in the 1980s. Others were projects concerned with the under-5s, intermediate treatment, helping the community to care, care in the community, opportunities for volunteers, and the children's initiative. By 1986, there were 11 CFIs, all monitored in different ways. The extent of research involvement in each varied considerably, as did the proportion of research expenditure within the total budget. The CFI (drugs) was the least well resourced as regards research of any of the CFIs.

Although many of the projects funded within the CFI had their own built-in evaluation study, these were often rudimentary. The distinctions between information-gathering, monitoring, evaluation and research often went unrecognized. It is important to realize that there are different audiences for the results of different types of research, ranging from local funding authorities, national policy networks, various kinds of practitioners and the research community, to the general public.

All evaluation studies face the common problem of a lack of clarity about the goals of programmes. However, there was an added although not unusual issue in the case of the CFI. One aim of the CFI was to diffuse innovation and help work on the ground by providing information on problems and on examples of good practice. The question of future funding confused the issue, however; it was unrealistic to expect completely detached and disinterested assessment reports to be produced in these circumstances.

Many of the other DHSS initiatives included a built-in research element, funded from the start of the programme, with funds top-sliced from the overall budget. In the case of the drugs CFI, it was only after the programme had been in operation for almost 3 years that it was realized that there was no provision for independent assessment. The research on which this chapter is based began in 1986 and was funded independently by the DHSS from its general research budget to rectify this ommission; partly this was because it became clear that the House of Commons Social Services Committee would want to know the outcome of the CFI. Alarmed civil servants quickly moved to fill the gap and rather belatedly commissioned research on the central funding initiative from a team based at Birkbeck College, University of London and directed by Susanne MacGregor (research which forms the basis of this chapter). However, by this time, projects had set up their own information gathering systems, generally ignoring the rather inadequate guidelines with which they had been issued, and a wide variety of different systems and measures were in operation (where there were any at all). Although the Birkbeck research on the central funding initiative provided some measures of the activity of agencies, for example through a series of censuses of clients at the CFI funded agencies, and other questionnaires formed part of this research exercise, on the whole the opportunity to collect standardized information on an ongoing basis in all agencies was missed by not being built in from the beginning and seen as part of the requirements of receipt of funding.

All projects were required to submit a report to the DoH at the end of their period of CFI funding. These reports were said to provide an evaluation of the work of the agency. (The likely final outcome appears to be that 60 per cent would fulfil this requirement.) The reports varied enormously in form and content. They do not form a consistent evaluation either of the CFI itself or even of each agency. The information included is neither consistent nor standardized. Although some of these reports might individually prove useful for critical self-evaluation, as information for local decision-makers, or occasionally as contributions to understanding of clinical practice and service development, overall they do not add up to a useful body of information.

The reason for this lost chance was the great speed with which the initiative had to be devised, implemented, and administered. Basically, the need for research was simply forgotten in the first instance. Although the Birkbeck research went some way to rectify this (MacGregor *et al.* 1991), a lot of effort was wasted through a lack of co-ordination and planning. Other attempts were made to establish some order, such as ISDD's setting up a network of researchers, but they were working against the odds.

A related factor which helps to explain the failure to accord a prominent role to research (one not unique to the CFI but a feature of the 1980s as a whole) was the general undervaluing of social research as a professional activity. When local administrators realized that they needed information for planning purposes, they appointed people to posts as evaluators or information-gatherers. But often these people had had no training whatsoever in social research; some even lacked a background in a relevant discipline. The attitude prevailing in some quarters that anyone could do evaluation led to a serious underestimation of what was required: the results were sometimes nonsensical findings and reports.

## Take-up of funding at the local level

Future funding was a key issue for the CFI agencies. The majority (80 per cent) of projects had end dates in 1987, 1988, or 1989.

For the voluntary sector, funding is an endemic worry. For all the services funded on a pump-priming basis, the knowledge that their time was limited affected their activities, even where in the end they did secure future funding. Projects reported that it was often difficult to convince the local statutory bodies, who were the largest providers of funds, that there was a continued need for their service; they also said that they found it hard to find the time to fund-raise in addition to carrying out their service function; some staff had little or no fund-raising experience and did not know how to go about this.

It should be recalled that 100 agencies were available to continue beyond the end of CFI funding. Of these 100, 76 secured future funding. At the time of our survey, 18 were still negotiating and six had closed. The pattern was much the same between the statutory and non-statutory sectors. However, whereas statutory services were overwhelmingly re-funded on an 'indefinite basis' (itself an ambiguous term), services in the non-statutory sector were often limited to between 2 and 5 years or guaranteed funds for only 12 months, having to reapply annually. Thus we must be cautious before concluding that the CFI established through its pump-priming operations a set of services which would form a firm basis for future service development.

Further differences between the statutory and the non-statutory sectors emerge when patterns of funding are considered. The majority of new CFI projects in the statutory sector which secured funds post-CFI secured all their funding from one source; the majority of those in the non-statutory services had to call on a number of funders to meet their target budgets.

Moreover in the majority of the cases where statutory services are funded by two sources, those two are the district and the regional health authorities. By contrast, the non-statutory services rely largely on local authorities and charities to supplement funds from the health authorities.

## Conclusions

In the 1980s, the standard type of service developed was a more access-ible and less expensive one than had prevailed before, most frequently staffed by between one and five people and located across the country. While the overall balance between the number of statutory and non-statutory services is exactly even, the CFI can be seen to have particularly encouraged the development of statutory services.

The allocation exercise seems to have been successful in targeting areas of need. North West Thames and Mersey RHAs are the regions which on key indicators had at this time the most serious problems of drug misuse and these were the regions which were most successful in bidding for CFI funds. These two regions are also interesting to compare in terms of the different pattern of allocations and the different shape of services that resulted from this expenditure, a pattern which was affected by the pre-existing shape of service provision.

The degree of central direction over the allocation of funds, a process which was closely controlled by a very small team of experts in the DoH, allowed firm control over the design of services which developed nationally.

The agencies which got in on the act earlier ended earlier and were more likely to have secured future funding by 1989—they continued to be ahead in the race for funds. This process has tended to favour the longer established names in the field, the elite, in both the statutory and the non-statutory sectors, who have grown in size and power as a result of their opportune exploitation of CFI funds. They had plans and ideas worked out well in advance, were able to act quickly, knew whom to approach for money, knew the procedures involved in bidding for public money, and anticipated what would be needed in order to secure further funding once CFI funds ran out. However, some newcomers to the field also did very well, mobilizing local support, media stars, and politicians to their cause.

The early fear that the pattern of services that developed would be haphazard and not reflect need does not appear to have been borne out by developments. The current assumption is that following the expansion of services in the 1980s, there is now sufficient awareness and expertise at the local level to devolve these decisions, which was thought not to be the case in the early 1980s.

Those who benefited from this service development appreciated the additional injection of funds but also had some criticisms to offer. They commented that the short-term nature of the exercise meant that it encouraged a different response from those organizing the services than would have been the case if they were sure that good services would be secure. They also commented that the stress on drugs conflicted with some practitioners' views on service development, especially those who favoured integrated services for people with problems related to misuse of a range of substances, including alcohol. Although the CFI was seen as a useful start, there were those who would have preferred allocations on a revenue basis, ring-fenced as at present, to have been introduced earlier. Some criticized the rush to provide advice and counselling services, commenting that these might even be over-supplied while treatment services had been relatively poorly developed. Specifically, some felt that the CFI had failed to expand the traditional drug dependence clinic services for injecting drug users: they felt that the doctor's role had been diminished too far, and with that there had arisen a shortage of prescribing services.

The decision to make further funds available to the regions, in addition to the CFI, for an expansion of services, for training and for harm-minimization efforts seemed to secure the future of the services which were funded on a short-term basis with CFI money. Some of these adapted their response and incorporated, for example, needle and syringe exchange schemes in order to qualify for funding under the later circulars. Other new services were also developed. However, it could be asked whether firmer central control on the later allocation exercises could have ensured that the total number of services expanded proportionately, rather than responsibility for funding being shifted from general accounts to earmarked funds for drugs services with less overall expansion of services. But this should all be seen in the context of resource constraints in the NHS in this period. Given the pressure on funding, it could well have been the case that without earmarked funds from central government, services for drug misusers, rather than managing to keep pace with rising demand, would have been reduced in the competition for funds from more 'deserving' patients and stronger specialist groups. The survival of these services appears also to be partly the result of the HIV epidemic rather than of rational evaluation of the benefit derived from services at the local level.

## Acknowledgements

The research on which this chapter is based was funded by a grant from the DoH, which is gratefully acknowledged. I should also like to acknowledge the contribution made to the research by other members of the research team at Birkbeck College Department of Politics and Sociology between 1986 and 1990: Ross Coomber, Adam Crosier, Betsy Ettorre, and Harriet Lodge. A fuller account of the findings reported in this chapter can be found in *Drugs services in England and the impact of the Central Funding Initiative* (Susanne MacGregor, Betsy Ettorre, Ross Coomber, Adam Crosier, and Harriet Lodge) ISDD Research Monograph Series no.1, ISDD 1991.

## References

ACMD (Advisory Council on the Misuse of Drugs) (1982). *Treatment and rehabilitation*. HMSO, London.
ACMD (1984). *Prevention*. HMSO, London.
ACMD (1989). *AIDS and drug misuse, Part 1*. DHSS, HMSO, London.
ACMD (1989). *AIDS and drug misuse, Part 2*. DHSS, HMSO, London.
DHSS Medical Working Group on Drug Dependence (1984). *Guidelines on good clinical practice in the treatment of drug abuse*. DHSS, London.
DHSS (1985). *Drug misuse: prevalence and service provision—a report on surveys and plans in English NHS regions*. DHSS, London.
DHSS (1986). *Health Service development: services for drug misusers*. Circular HC (86)3/LAC(86)5. DHSS, London.
DHSS, DES, Home Office, MSC (1985). *Misuse of drugs: Government response to the Fourth report from the Social Services Committee session 1984–85*. HMSO, London.
Home Office (1986). *Tackling drug misuse: a summary of the Government's strategy*. HMSO, London.
Home Office (1988). *Tackling drug misuse: a summary of the Government's strategy* (3rd edn). HMSO, London.
Social Services Committee (1984–85). *Misuse of drugs with special reference to

*the treatment and rehabilitation of misusers of hard drugs* (4th Report). HMSO, London.

Social Services Committee (1987–88). *Resourcing the NHS and short term issues* (1st Report). HMSO, London.

# 21. Notification and the Home Office

*Joy Mott*

The suggestion that doctors might be obliged to notify their addict patients to the Home Office was first examined by the Departmental Committee on Morphine and Heroin Addiction set up by the Ministry of Health in 1924. The Committee of doctors under the chairmanship of Sir Humphrey Rolleston, then President of the Royal College of Physicians, was asked to provide advice on 'the circumstances in which the supply of morphine and heroin to persons suffering from addiction to these drugs may be regarded as medically advisable'. Notification was considered as a means of reducing the opportunities for patients 'to whom morphine or heroin is being administered continuously without other necessity than for the relief of the symptoms of addiction' to obtain supplies of the drugs from more than one doctor at a time. The Committee thought that a requirement of notification would

no doubt tend also to diminish doubtfully justifiable supplying or ordering of the drugs. Moreover, it would assist practitioners to exercise firmer control over their patients, and would tend to relieve practitioners who were acting in good faith from suspicion, and from the liability to irksome inquiries, which at present are unavoidable.

In the event, the Rolleston Committee did not recommend notification, mainly because it believed that the disadvantage of impairing the confidential relationship between doctor and patient outweighed the benefits. Berridge (1980) notes that this reflected the views of the British Medical Association, which was particularly opposed to the notification of addict doctors. The Committee also understood that the small number of addicts known at the time was not expected to increase and the Home Office did not consider notification was essential to detect persons who were obtaining drugs of addiction from more than one doctor at a time (Ministry of Health 1926).

Doctors have been liable to what the Rolleston Committee called 'irksome inquiries' from the Home Office about their prescribing of certain drugs since 1916. Regulations made under the Defence of the Realm Act 1914 permitted only authorized people (members of the medical profession, persons holding special permits, or persons who had received the drug on a doctor's prescription) to possess cocaine and required persons authorized to supply cocaine and opium to keep records of all transactions in the drugs. Pharmacists could only supply cocaine on a doctor's prescription which could be dispensed once, and had to record the details of persons receiving such prescriptions in a separate book. Similar records had to kept of sales of raw or powdered opium but a doctor's prescription was not required. Home Office officials and, from 1917, police officers above the rank of inspector were empowered to examine the records from time to time to ensure that the requirements were being observed. The provisions of these Regulations, extended to heroin, morphine, and other preparations of opium, formed the basis of the Dangerous Drugs Act 1920 and of all subsequent drug control legislation.

Although the police have been empowered to inspect pharmacists' records of their sale and dispensing of controlled drugs since 1917 it was not until 1939 that they were asked to inform the Home Office Drugs Inspectorate of individuals found to be receiving unusually large or regular prescriptions of the drugs. The Inspectorate may investigate whether the drugs have been prescribed in the course of medical treatment or, as the Rolleston Committee put it, 'simply to enable persons who had become addicted to satisfy their craving' in contravention of the intention of the legislation that doctors should supply controlled drugs only so far as is necessary for the practice of their profession. Until the notification procedure was introduced in 1968 the relatively few doctors who treated addicts, in order to safeguard themselves, usually voluntarily reported their addict patients to the Drugs Inspectorate who maintained an informal index of named addicts since the mid-1930s.

## Reports of the Interdepartmental Committee on Drug Addiction 1961 and 1965

It was not until 1958 that the Government next sought advice on drug addiction 'in the light of more recent developments' when an Interdepartmental Committee, consisting of seven doctors and a pharmacist, was set up by the Ministry of Health and the Department of Health for Scotland under the chairmanship of Sir (later Lord) Russell Brain, an eminent neurologist and then President of the Royal College of Physicians. The 'recent developments' included the availability of new analgesic drugs which were capable of producing addiction, and innovations in the treatment of addiction.

The Committee was satisfied that 'the incidence of addiction to drugs controlled by the Dangerous Drugs Act 1951 is still very small and traffic in illicit supplies is almost negligible, cannabis excepted'. It considered that 'the existing administrative arrangements continue to ensure that nearly all addicts to dangerous drugs are known to the Home Office ...' (that is, the informal index) and made no reference to notification (Ministry of Health 1961, the first Brain Report).

In 1964 the Interdepartmental Committee was reconvened as a result of Home Office anxiety about the continuing increases in the number of young heroin and cocaine addicts coming to notice who had become addicted to the drugs other than as a result of treatment for physical illness or injury. The Committee concluded that their major source of supply had been 'a very few doctors who, while acting within the law and according to their professional judgement, had prescribed the drugs excessively'. The Committee was concerned to retain a doctor's right to prescribe 'dangerous drugs' without restriction for ordinary patients' needs while achieving 'better control of prescribing and supplying'. It made four recommendations for this purpose: the notification of addicts by doctors to a central authority, the provision of advice when addiction was in doubt, the provision of treatment centres, and restrictions on the number of doctors who could prescribe heroin and cocaine to addicts.

The Committee provided a definition of an addict, 'a person shall be regarded as being addicted to a drug if, and only if, he has as a result of repeated administration become so dependent upon the drug that he has an overpowering desire for the administration of it to be continued'. It recommended that 'all addicts to drugs controlled under the Dangerous Drugs Act should be formally notified to a central authority and this authority should keep an up-to-date list of such addicts with relevant particulars' with provision 'that any registered medical practitioner can refer to the list promptly and at any hour of the day or night if there is need to check whether or not a particular addict has been notified, or to obtain further particulars about an addict's history'. The Committee was at pains to stress that 'notification' was used as in 'the Public Health Act which lays upon doctors the duty to notify patients who are suffering from infectious diseases' and suggested that 'the analogy was apt because addiction is after all a socially infectious condition and its notification may offer a means for epidemiological assessment and control'.

The Committee recommended that it should become a statutory duty for doctors to notify their addict patients and that disciplinary action should be taken against those who failed to do so. It further recommended that, if evidence were found by the Drugs Inspectorate of a doctor's failure to notify without a satisfactory explanation, the doctor would most appropriately be dealt with by the Disciplinary Committee of the General Medical Council rather than by the criminal courts since 'the issues involved were primarily those of professional judgement and conduct' (Ministry of Health 1965, the second Brain Report).

The recommendation that doctors should notify their addict patients to a central authority was apparently greeted with approval by the medical profession at the time. A leading article in the *British Medical Journal* (1965) commented

Notification of addicts is the basis—sound and acceptable—of the committee's proposals. Drug addiction is a disease, and a disease which spreads by contagion in a community. Once a disease is notifiable a number of consequences follow, of which statutory provision of treatment centres is one ...

The *Lancet* (1965) was rather less enthusiastic, and its leading article raised an issue of continuing concern by noting

The nature and site of the proposed central authority for notification is perhaps deliberately left vague. On the one hand, the Home Office has done well for a long time with overseeing this exceedingly difficult problem; on the other, it does use policemen for the purpose.

## The Notification Regulations 1968 and 1973

The notification procedure was introduced on 22 February 1968 by Regulations made under the Dangerous Drugs Act 1967. After consultations with the medical professional organizations the Chief Medical Officer at the Home Office was named as the central authority to whom doctors were required to notify their addict patients. The Chief Medical Officer of the Department of Health is an adviser to the Home Secretary. The Regulations restricting the prescribing of heroin and cocaine to addicts to doctors specially licensed by the Home Secretary came into force on 16 April 1968. The Act allowed the Home Secretary to refer the cases of doctors contravening the notification or prescribing Regulations to a tribunal consisting of one senior lawyer and four doctors. The General Medical Council had declined to accept the disciplinary role proposed by the Brain Committee.

The 1968 Regulations used the definition of an addict provided by the Brain Committee and required doctors to notify patients whom they considered to be addicted to any drug in Part 1 of the Schedule to the 1965 Dangerous Drugs Act. These included heroin and morphine, other potent analgesics, cocaine, cannabis and all the drugs brought under strictest control by the United Nations 1961 Single Convention on Narcotic Drugs.

The notification requirement was retained by the Misuse of Drugs Act 1971 and the Misuse of Drugs (Notification of and Supply to Addicts) Regulations 1973 came into force in July of that year. At present the Regulations apply to 14 of the most strictly controlled drugs (Class A drugs) including cocaine, diamorphine (heroin), dipipanone (Diconal), methadone (physeptone), morphine, opium, pethidine, and seven other powerful analgesics. They do not apply to other controlled drugs with a high dependence or addictive potential such as the amphetamines, barbiturates, and benzodiazepines. The Home Secretary, after consultation with the Advisory Council on the Misuse of Drugs, may amend the Regulations and the drugs to which they apply. By 1993 no new drugs had been added to the list of notifiable drugs. The Advisory Council (1991) recently considered and rejected the suggestion that the amphetamines should become notifiable drugs on the grounds that few amphetamine misusers came to medical notice and there was doubt that habitual amphetamine misuse could result in addiction as defined in the Notification Regulations.

The 1973 Regulations retained the Brain Committee's definition of an addict. Thus, it is for doctors to use their clinical judgement to decide whether a patient who is taking notifiable drugs fully meets the criteria of 'repeated administration' and 'overpowering desire' to merit notification. Edwards (1981) noted that the Regulations provide a useful 'simple and commonsense case definition' of an addict. When they consider, or have reasonable grounds to suspect, that a patient meets the criteria for notification doctors are required to provide, within 7 days, in writing to the Chief Medical Officer at the Home Office, the name, address, sex, date of birth, national health service number of the patient together with the date of attendance, and the name of the drug or drugs concerned.[1] Doctors usually also volunteer details of the drug/s prescribed in treatment. In September 1987 the Chief Medical Officer asked them to record whether the addict injects any drug, irrespective of the type of drug, so that information may be collected on those at risk of human immunodeficiency virus (HIV) infection. Until March 1989 they were asked to record the nationality of the addict, if known, and since then to record their ethnic group instead.

## Doctors' compliance with the Notification Regulations

There has been evidence of poor compliance ever since the Regulations were introduced. Woodside (1973) found that 25 per cent of eligible patients attending the Edinburgh Drug Dependence Unit between 1968 and 1971 had not been notified. Smart and Ogborne (1974) found that patients attending London Drug Dependence Units in 1972–73 were unlikely to be notified unless they were taken on for treatment. Ghodse

---

[1] Doctors are not required to notify those patients for whom they consider the continued administration of notifiable drugs is required for the purpose of treating organic disease or injury (but they should do so if the patient has become addicted as the result of such treatment and when the doctor considers that there no longer any medical need for them to receive the drugs) or those patients who have already been notified from that general practice or hospital within the past year.

(1977) found that 77 per cent of eligible patients attending London hospital accident and emergency departments in 1975 had not been notified. Strang and Shah (1985) found that 75 per cent of patients referred to a regional Drug Dependence Unit in 1983 had not been notified by the referring doctor, with doctors working in general hospitals the least likely to have done so. Robertson and Bucknall (1985) found that about two-thirds of eligible patients attending an Edinburgh general practice in 1984 had not been notified strictly in accordance with the Regulations. Horn *et al.* (1987) found that over 80 per cent of apparently eligible patients admitted to a Glasgow general hospital between 1980 and 1984 had not been notified. Glanz (1986), from a survey of a national sample of general practitioners in mid-1985, found that only a third said they had notified the addict they had most recently attended.[1]

More recent research suggests compliance is improving in some areas at least. Neville *et al.* (1988) found that 30 of 36 (83 per cent) of heroin users known to one or other of three general practices in Dundee in 1986 had been notified. Mott *et al.* (1993) found that 90 per cent of the eligible patients reported to the North-West Drug Misuse Database during a 4-month period in 1988/89 had also been notified to the Home Office, with doctors working in hospitals rather than general practitioners the least likely to notify their addict patients.

Only one study has investigated the validity of addict notifications. Mott and Macmillan (1979), studying men first notified as addicts in 1969, found that there was convincing evidence of addiction during a 5-year follow-up period for at most 30 per cent of those notified by prison medical officers compared with 95 per cent of those notified from hospitals.

The reasons most often advanced for doctors' failure to notify their addict patients are ignorance or misinterpretation of the Regulations, oversight, pressure of work, and fears that the information will not be held in confidence by the Home Office. Unwillingness to breach the generally accepted rule of medical confidentiality that a doctor should not pass on information about their patients to a third person without the consent of the patient has also been cited as a reason, but it would seem to be good clinical practice for the doctor to discuss notification with their addict patients with an explanation of the purpose and with reassurance that the information is held in strictest confidence. Doctors who are in doubt about these matters may discuss them with Chief

---

[1] Doctors who fail to notify their addict patients may be subject to a direction made under S13 of the 1971 Act. The Home Secretary, after referring the matter to a tribunal, may make a direction prohibiting the doctor from prescribing, administering, or supplying specified controlled drugs. A contravention of a direction is a criminal offence. To date only one doctor has been brought before a tribunal solely for failure to notify his addict patients. He was admonished and no further action was taken.

Inspector of the Home Office Drugs Branch or with a member of the local Inspectorate.

From time to time the Home Office and the Department of Health remind doctors of their obligation to notify addicts, for example, in the *Guidelines of good medical practice in the treatment of drug misuse* (1993) and in the medical journals (Acheson 1990). There may have been failures to notify because a prescribed form was not introduced until September 1987, although any written communication continues to be accepted. In an attempt to increase compliance, and to collect information of any drug misuse by injection because of the major risk of HIV transmission, the Chief Medical officer wrote to all doctors in England in July 1987 to remind them of their duty to notify addicts and to introduce the form to use for the purpose. Similar letters were sent to doctors in Scotland and Wales from the Scottish and Welsh Offices. These forms are available to all doctors together with post-paid labels. The increase in the number of notifications of both new and former addicts in 1988 as compared with 1987 was thought to be due, in part at least, to the introduction of the new form (Home Office 1989).

Increasing numbers of notifications may reflect improved compliance by doctors and/or increasing numbers of addicts in the population and/or greater willingness on the part of addicts to seek medical treatment. There is some evidence that some misusers of notifiable drugs may be reluctant to approach doctors because they fear being notified (Bennett and Wright 1986; Drug Indicators Project 1989). The latter study found that women were particularly anxious about being notified because of fears that they could lose the care and custody of their children as a result, although another found that 'fear of becoming known to the Home Office' was not a major source of anxiety among addicts seeking treatment for the first time (Sheehan *et al.* 1986).

## The Addicts Index

An informal index of named addicts had been maintained by the Drugs Branch Inspectorate since the mid-1930s as a convenient means of keeping records about addicts who came to their notice. It was used to compile the annual statistics of known addicts for the Opium Board of the League of Nations until 1945 and subsequently to the United Nations Commission on Narcotic Drugs. The informal index contained records of named addicts (and the drugs to which they were addicted, the name of the doctor who was treating them and the drugs he was prescribing). Most came to the notice of the Inspectorate from their own and police inspections of pharmacists' records of dispensed dangerous drugs and others as a result of voluntary reporting by doctors of their addict patients. The index also contained the names of persons convicted of offences involving opioids or cocaine (obtained from police records) where there was also evidence of addiction, of addicts identified by prison medical officers and of addicts who approached the Home Office seeking to become 'registered' (Spear 1969).

In the late 1950s and early 1960s there was considerable interest in North America in the 'British System' of treating addiction and there was a widespread belief that there was a system of registration in the United Kingdom which entitled addicts to a regular supply of heroin. A number of Canadian addicts were known to have arrived in the early 1960s in the expectation of becoming 'registered' (Spear and Glatt 1971). The first report of the Brain Committee (1961) was at pains to point out that no such system existed, although the use of the term 'registered addict' persists.

The Addicts Index was formally established by the Home Office Drugs Branch in 1968 to store the information about individuals specified in the 1968 and 1973 Notification Regulations. The Index is the Brain Committee's 'up-to-date list of addicts with relevant particulars' to which doctors can refer in order 'to check whether or not a particular addict had been notified, or to obtain further particulars about an addict's history' so that addicts' opportunities to receive supplies of drugs from more than one doctor at a time are reduced.

When a notification is received it is acknowledged in writing on behalf of the Chief Medical Officer and the notifying doctor is told whether or not the individual has been previously notified and if they have, are informed of the name and address of the most recent notifying doctor. Doctors are also able to make telephone enquiries to the staff of the Index about the notification histories of their addict patients and whether another doctor is known to be currently treating them for addiction. Enquiries may be made during office hours on weekdays, with a telephone recording service operating at other times for later reply. A 24 hour service, as recommended by the Brain Committee in 1965, would be very costly to maintain and it is unlikely that enough enquiries would be made after the usual consulting hours of general practitioners or hospital out-patient departments to justify the expense.

In 1987 the Addicts Index was computerized and it now contains summary records of all addicts notified to the Chief Medical Officer at the Home Office since 1968. An earlier attempt at computerization, in 1984/85, at a time when the number of addicts being notified was increasing dramatically, was unsuccessful and resulted in a substantial backlog of unprocessed notifications. There was a suggestion that doctors' compliance with the Regulations suffered as a consequence of being unable to obtain up-to-date information from the Index (Home Office 1987).

At present the computerized Index contains the details specified in the Regulations about each addict's first and three most recent notifications, and the names of the notifying doctors, together with the volunteered information about the drugs the addict was prescribed in treatment for addiction by the most recent notifier, and whether or not the addict was described as injecting any drug by the most recent notifier. The location of the addict's home address is coded by national police force area and the professional address of the notifying doctor is coded by regional and district health authority or Scottish hospital board.

In addition to the information stored in the computerized Index there are also paper files for each addict containing the records of all their notifications and any further information about them which comes to the notice of the Drugs Inspectorate, for example, records of prescriptions from police checks of pharmacy records, correspondence from notifying doctors, death certificates. At present the files are retained for 3 years after it is known an addict has died.

When the Index was established in 1968 it was expected that the great majority of addicts would be treated by the newly opened National Health Service drug treatment centres (now called Drug Dependence Units) and that they would continue to receive treatment for some time, by being prescribed notifiable drugs, at the same Unit. In order to collect regular information on the treatment of addicts by the Units a procedure was established whereby the consultant in charge was asked to complete 2-monthly returns to report to the Index whether each addict notified from the Unit was still attending and to indicate which drugs they were being prescribed in treatment and, if an addict was no longer attending, whether or not they were regarded as still addicted at the time of their last attendance. A small number of doctors who treated substantial numbers of addicts privately also completed 2-monthly returns. The procedure began to fall in abeyance during 1985 because, as a result of the considerable increase in the number of addicts attending, it placed too great a burden on the staff of the Drug Dependence Units and has not been revived.

For addicts notified by general practitioners a different procedure was followed. If an addict had not been re-notified by a different doctor within 12 months, and if the original notifier had indicated that a notifiable drug had been prescribed to the addict in treatment of addiction and had not provided a repeat notification on the anniverary date, a reminder was sent asking if the addict was still attending and being treated for addiction.

By the end of 1988 it had become plain that the accuracy of an addict's record of treatment depended upon how recently he or she had been notified (Home Office 1989). It had also become apparent that in some cases an addict may have been recorded in the Index as re-notified when a doctor had informed the Home Office that he or she was no longer treating the addict for addiction. To overcome these difficulties, from January 1991, the doctor who most recently notified an addict has been sent a note on the anniversary of that notification asking whether or not the addict is still being treated, and if they are, what drugs are being prescribed in treatment of addiction.

In order to collect information on addict deaths the names of all new addicts (that is, those being notified for the first time) are passed to the National Health Service Central Register where they are assigned a study marker so that a copy of their death certificate can be sent to the Home Office. The Register is the main source of information about the deaths of known addicts although about a third usually cannot be identified, either because they are not registered with a general practitioner or because they are recorded in the Register under a different name and/or date of birth from that in the Addicts Index. Other sources of information about addict deaths include the doctors who have notified them, police reports, coroners reports, press cuttings, special studies, and copies of death certificates when the underlying cause of death was drug-related from the Office of Population Censuses and Surveys Vital Statistics Unit and the General Register Office for Scotland (Home Office 1991).

## The confidentiality of the Addicts Index

Great care is taken by the Home Office and the Department of Health to ensure that the information about individuals in the Index is held in strictest medical confidence. Staff appointed to the Index are individually authorized by the Chief Medical Officer as having achieved a satisfactory appreciation of the importance of maintaining the highest standards of medical confidentiality and a Senior Medical Officer of the Department of Health takes part in their training (Advisory Council on the Misuse of Drugs 1991).

Index staff are instructed not to release information from the Index to any other person or body other than a *bona fide* doctor without authorization. When a doctor telephones to enquire whether a named patient is recorded in the Addicts Index they will be asked to give their name, professional address, and telephone number. If the doctor is not already known to the staff, their name and address will be checked in the Register of the General Medical Council. (All medical practitioners in the United Kingdom must be currently registered with the Council in order to practice.) When the doctors' *bona fides* have been checked they will be called back and told whether or not their patient has been notified previously and the name of the doctor who most recently notified them. A similar procedure is followed when the written notifications are acknowledged. Any further information about individuals and their medical management is exchanged on a doctor-to-doctor basis at their discretion, but there is no obligation for the enquiring doctor to make contact with previous notifiers. At present, doctors make some 200–300 telephone enquiries a month to the Index.

The computerized Index is subject to the terms and conditions of the Data Protection Act 1984. Anyone who wishes to know if information about them is held in the Index may apply for disclosure on the prescribed form with acceptable proof of identity and on payment of a fee. On receipt of such an application, and if the person is recorded on the Index, it is the practice to check with the doctor who has most recently notified the addict whether disclosure would cause undue suffering and distress. By March 1991 disclosure had been requested by three individuals.

During the passage of the Dangerous Drugs Act 1967 and the Misuse of Drugs Act 1971 the Government announced on several occasions in Parliament that the names of notified addicts would be passed to the police to assist them in their inspections of pharmacists' records. In 1975 the arrangements for doing so were suspended following complaints from a number of doctors that some police officers had used the information for purposes other than those for which it was intended. (There is, however, no reason why police forces should not keep their own records of persons identified as receiving supplies of notifiable drugs from their checks of pharmacy records.) The arrangements have not been reinstated despite requests from some Chief Officers of Police. Assurances were given to the House of Commons Social Services Committee in 1985 by the Chief Inspector of the Drugs Branch that there had been no further evidence that confidentiality had been breached and that the General Medical Council was satisfied with the arrangements to ensure the confidentiality of the Addicts Index (House of Commons 1985).

It was suggested to the Social Services Committee that both doctors and addicts would be reassured about the confidentiality of information in the Addicts Index if the Index was located in the Department of Health. However, the Committee agreed that such a transfer might result in the public losing sight of the penal aspects of the drug control legislation ('over-medicalizing' the problem of addiction), would not be worth the upheaval, and would not necessarily reduce anxiety about confidentiality.

In very exceptional circumstances the name of an addict might be disclosed to the police in the interests of public policy or the welfare of the addict. A recent example of exceptional disclosure was the help given to the police in identifying the body of a murder victim who had been notified which, in turn, led to the identification of the person charged with the murder.

## Other uses of the Addicts Index

### *Detection of addicts obtaining dual supplies of notifiable drugs*

Information supplied to the Index by the police from their inspection of pharmacy records enables addicts who obtain dual supplies of notifiable drugs to be identified. It is an offence for addicts to be in possession of supplies of notifiable drugs obtained simultaneously from more than one doctor (Regulation 10(2) of the Misuse of Drugs Regulations 1973). In recent years since most of the notifiable drugs misused, particularly heroin and cocaine, have come from illicit sources, the number of addicts who have been identified as obtaining dual supplies has been very small and it has become rare for proceedings to be instituted for the offence.

### *Monitoring the prescribing of notifiable drugs*

The information in the Addicts Index provides the Home Office Drugs Inspectorate with the means of monitoring doctors' prescribing of notifiable drugs. For this purpose it is essential that addicts and notifying doctors can be identified by name. When the police inspections of pharmacy records show that prescriptions for unusual or regular supplies of notifiable drugs have been dispensed to an individual the Inspectorate can check if they have been notified as an addict. If they have not, the doctor supplying the prescriptions will be visited by an inspector and reminded of their obligation to notify addicts and of the powers of the Home Secretary to deal with irresponsible prescribing. When a doctor who has not previously notified addicts begins to do so, or when a doctors' practice in prescribing notifiable drugs gives rise to concern, the Inspectorate will take similar action.

### *Statistics of addicts known or notified to the Home Office*

Both the informal and formal Addicts Index have been used to compile statistics of addicts known or notified to the Home Office since 1934. Spear (1969) published an invaluable table showing the number of addicts known to the Home Office each year between 1935 and 1968, the drugs to which they were addicted, the number of 'professional addicts' (that is, persons working in medical or allied professions) and, from 1958 to 1968, the number of persons whose addiction was of non-therapeutic origin (that is, had not arisen as the result of treatment for organic illness or injury). The latter are no longer routinely available because the 1973 Notification Regulations do not require doctors to record the occupation or profession of addicts or the origin of their addiction, although such information may be volunteered. Doctors are not required to notify patients if they are receiving notifiable drugs in the course of treatment for organic illness or injury. Edwards (1981) published a table showing the number of 'professional' and 'therapeutic' addicts known between 1958 and 1979 but cautions that the post-1968 figures are unreliable.

The Home Office has published addict statistics annually under various titles since 1969 and the *Statistics of the misuse of drugs: addicts notified to the Home Office, United Kingdom* have been published in the spring since 1989. The computerized Index has been used to provide the statistics since 1986. Statistics on deaths of addicts previously known to the Home Office by year of death since 1979 were first published in 1991 (Home Office 1991).

The definition of, and the basis for counting, addicts notified for the first time has never changed. Nor have individuals notified as suspected addicts been counted unless the suspicion was later confirmed. But there have been changes in the definition and counting rules for addicts who had been notified in a previous year and who are again notified in the current year.

Tables were published until 1988 which showed the number of addicts being notified for the first time (described as 'not previously known' until 1983 and as 'new addicts' since 1984), the number of addicts 'known in previous years' (1970–83) or 'former addicts' (1982–88), and the number who were recorded as receiving notifiable drugs in the treatment of addiction on 31 December. Addicts were counted as 'known in previous years' or as 'former addicts' only if they were not known to be receiving notifiable drugs in treatment of addiction on 31 December of the previous year.

Until 1988 the total number of addicts notified during the year was calculated by adding together the number of addicts recorded as receiving notifiable drugs in the treatment of addiction on 1 January (which was the same as the number recorded as receiving notifiable drugs in treatment of addiction at 31 December of the previous year), the number of new addicts, and the number of former addicts.

The number recorded as receiving notifiable drugs in treatment of addiction on 31 December was intended to provide a census figure of active or current addicts and to provide information about the drugs they were being prescribed in treatment. In order to arrive at the 'year end' figure, the statistics showed the number of addicts recorded on 1 January but not recorded on 31 December as receiving notifiable drugs in treatment of addiction (that is, not current addicts) because they had died during the year, or been admitted to a penal institution, or were never recorded as receiving notifiable drugs in treatment of addiction or because a period of treatment had ended. Until the early 1980s rather more attention was paid to this 'year end' number than to the number of new addicts notified during the years (for example, Home Office 1979).

The 'year end' figure was published for the last time in the 1988 addict statistics. It was clear that this figure had become increasingly unreliable since 1985 because many of the Drug Dependence Units were unable to provide regular updated information on the number of addicts they were treating or of the numbers who were no longer attending. No information had been received during 1987 and 1988 about the treatment during the year for about half the number recorded as receiving treatment at the beginning of the year (Home Office 1989).

Since 1989 the annual statistics have shown the number of new addicts (that is, addicts being notified for the first time) and the number of re-notified addicts (that is, those who were first notified in a previous year) (Home Office 1990). The definition of re-notified addicts includes those defined in the earlier statistics as 'former addicts' as well as addicts thought to be receiving treatment for addiction on 1 January who were notified during the year. The 1988 statistics anticipated the changes to be introduced in 1989 and included figures for each of these groups for 1987 and 1988 (Home Office 1989).

Supplementary statistics have been published since 1981 with tables showing the number of new and re-notified addicts from each police force area, and since 1986 from regional health authority or health board areas. Since 1988 the Department of Health has prepared half-yearly analyses of the addict statistics by English regional and district health authorities together with charts showing the numbers attending hospitals and drug treatment centres as out-patients in each regional health authority.

Table 21.1 shows the number of addicts known to the Home Office at 5-yearly intervals between 1935 and 1967 and Table 21.2 shows the number notified to the Chief Medical Officer at the Home Office at 5-yearly intervals between 1970 and 1992. Table 21.3 shows the types of drug to which new addicts were reported to be addicted at 5-yearly intervals between 1976 and 1992. Until 1985 the addict statistics showed the drug to which addiction was reported at the time of an addict's first notification during the year, since 1986 the figures refer to drug of addiction at the last notification during the year (Home Office 1991).

**Table 21.1** Numbers of addicts known to the Home Office during the year 1935–67

| 1935 | 1940 | 1945 | 1950 | 1955 | 1960 | 1965 | 1967 |
|------|------|------|------|------|------|------|------|
| 700  | 505  | 367  | 306  | 445  | 437  | 927  | 1729 |

*Source:* Spear (1969). Until 1945 the practice was to retain cases in the total for 10 years after the last information except for those who were known to have died. Figures from 1958 include only those persons known to have been taking drugs during the year in question.

**Table 21.2** Numbers of addicts notified to the Home Office during the year, 1970–92

| 1970 | 1975 | 1980 | 1985 | 1990 | 1992 |
|------|------|------|------|------|------|
| 2657 | 3425 | 5107 | 14 688 | 17 755 | 24 703 |

*Sources:*

1970: Statistics of the misuse of drugs United Kingdom 1977. Home Office.
1975, 1980, 1985: Statistics of drug addicts notified to the Home Office: United Kingdom. Home Office Statistical Department.

1992: Statistics of the misuse of drugs: addicts notified to the Home Office: United Kingdom. Home Office Statistical Department.

*Note:*

From 1970 to 1985 the total number of addicts notified during the year has been calculated by adding together the number recorded as receiving notifiable drugs in the treatment of addiction on 1 January, the number of new addicts and the number of previously known or former addicts notified. For 1990 the total consists of the number of new addicts plus the number of renotified addicts.

**Table 21.3** Percentages of new addicts notified to the Home Office during the year by type of drug to which addiction was reported, 1976–92

|  | 1976 | 1980 | 1985 | 1990 | 1992 |
|---|------|------|------|------|------|
| Heroin | 62 | 72 | 93 | 84 | 79 |
| Methadone | 31 | 22 | 10 | 21 | 26 |
| Dipipanone | 13 | 22 | 3 | 2 | 2 |
| Cocaine | 11 | 9 | 8 | 9 | 12 |
| Total number notified during the year | 894 | 1600 | 6409 | 6923 | 9663 |

*Sources:*

Statistics of the misuse of drugs, United Kingdom, 1986.
Statistics of the misuse of drugs: addicts notified to the Home Office, United Kingdom, 1992.

*Notes:*

1. Since 1976 all the notifiable drugs to which addiction is reported have been counted so that the figures for individual drugs cannot be added together to produce a total. The number of addicts reported as addicted to other notifiable drugs not shown in the table appear in the relevant Home Office Statistical bulletins.

2. Between 1976 and 1985 the drug/s to which addiction was reported refer to the addict's first notification during the year. Since 1986 the drug/s to which addiction was reported at the time of their last notification during the year are counted.

**Table 21.4** Addicts notified to the Home Office by source of notification (%)

|  | 1970 | 1975 | 1980 | 1985 | 1989 | 1990 | 1992 |
|---|---|---|---|---|---|---|---|
| New addicts |  |  |  |  |  |  |  |
| General practitioners* | 15 | 29 | 49 | 51 | 52 | 48 | 43 |
| Hospitals/treatment centres | 45 | 42 | 36 | 31 | 37 | 41 | 44 |
| Prison Medical Officers | 40 | 29 | 15 | 18 | 11 | 11 | 13 |
| Re-notified addicts |  |  |  |  |  |  |  |
| General practitioners* |  |  |  |  | 55 | 50 | 38 |
| Hospital/treatment centres |  | Not available |  |  | 39 | 43 | 54 |
| Prison Medical Officers |  |  |  |  | 6 | 6 | 9 |

* Includes police surgeons.

*Sources:*
1970, 1975 and 1980: Advisory Council on the Misuse of Drugs (1982) Appendix F, Table 4.
1985, 1989 and 1992: Statistics of the misuse of drugs: addicts notified to the Home Office: United Kingdom.

*Note:*
Re-notified addicts are those who have been notified in a previous year and notified again in the current year. These data are only available from 1987.

**Table 21.5** Drug addicts notified to the Home office by injecting status at last notification during the year (%)

|  | 1988 | 1989 | 1990 | 1992 |
|---|---|---|---|---|
| New addicts |  |  |  |  |
| Injecting any drug | 54 | 57 | 56 | 50 |
| Not injecting | 28 | 30 | 31 | 39 |
| Not recorded | 18 | 13 | 13 | 12 |
| Re-notified addicts |  |  |  |  |
| Injecting any drug | 53 | 55 | 52 | 45 |
| Not injecting | 24 | 26 | 27 | 39 |
| Not recorded | 23 | 20 | 21 | 16 |

*Source:*
Statistics of the misuse of drugs: addicts notified to the Home Office, United Kingdom, 1992.

*Note:*
The Notification Regulations 1973 do not require doctors to provide information on whether or not their addict patients inject drugs. In September 1987 the Chief Medical Officer asked doctors voluntarily to record when notifying an addict whether they injected any drug whether or not the drug/s were notifiable.

Since 1981 figures have been published of the number of new and re-notified addicts notified by general practitioners (including police surgeons, doctors to the armed forces), doctors working in hospitals (including National Health Service general and psychiatric hospitals, designated drug treatment centres, private hospitals), and prison medical officers (see Table 21.4).

In September 1987 doctors were asked to record whether or not the addicts they notify inject any drugs. From 1988 the number of new and re-notified addicts who were described as injecting any drug at the time of their last notification during the year have been published (see Table 21.5).

## Research

Access to information in the Index may be given to *bona fide* research workers for approved research projects, in consultation with the Department of Health, and with appropriate safeguards. These include requiring everyone who will see the information to sign the Official Secrets Act declaration, and to give undertakings that they will hold the information securely and in confidence, not to use the names of any addict or doctor in any report, and to give the Home Office the opportunity to comment on any report using the information before it is submitted for publication.

Researchers have had access to the Index for local epidemiological studies (for example, Hartnoll *et al*. 1985; Parker *et al*. 1988), and since it contains individuals' histories of notifications, the Index has been used to follow-up treatment outcome (for example, Wiepert *et al*. 1978; Stimson and Oppenheimer 1982), to enumerate addict deaths (Spear 1983; Ghodse *et al*. 1985), to study the validity of notifications (Mott and Macmillan 1979) and to investigate the relationship between addiction and crime (for example, Mott 1986).

## Notifications and estimating the prevalence of addiction

The annual notification statistics do not, and cannot, provide precise figures of the number of persons in the population who are addicted to the drugs specified in the Regulations. Some will not come, or choose to bring themselves, to the attention of the medical services and, if they do, the doctor they attend may fail to notify them. The number of addicts seeking treatment may increase as a result of changes in the treatment practice of doctors in local areas (for example, increased willingness to prescribe notifiable drugs or the prescribing of notifiable drugs in the treatment of addiction to a non-notifiable drug), or changes in the availability of treatment (for example, more general practitioners being willing to treat addicts).

National estimates of the number of notifiable opioid addicts in the population have been calculated by multiplying the number of addicts notified in a particular year by five or 10 (for example, Advisory Council on the Misuse of Drugs 1988). These 'multipliers' were derived from the findings of two local prevalence studies conducted in the early 1980s. Hartnoll *et al.* (1985), working in north London, tentatively suggested that the number of opioid addicts notified from the area underestimated the number of regular misusers by a factor of five while less rigorous research in Glasgow in 1981 suggested a factor of 10 (Ditton and Speirits 1981). More recently, Chadwick and Parker (1989), found that almost half the opioid users known to local social agencies and drug services in 1986/87 had been notified as addicts.

Since the late 1980s there may have been improvements in many doctors' compliance with the Notification Regulations as the result of exhortations by the Chief Medical Officer and the Drugs Branch Inspectorate, with the provision of special forms and post-paid envelopes, increased appreciation of the need to collect information on whether or not addicts inject drugs to estimate the numbers at risk of HIV infection, and from the introduction and promotion in 1990 of the regional drug misuse databases.

## Discussion

The notification procedure was introduced in 1968 when the number of known heroin and cocaine addicts was relatively small and when they were often treated by being prescribed the drugs over long periods, with spillage from doctors' prescriptions providing the main source of illicit supplies. It was one of a package of measures aimed at achieving better control over doctors' prescribing of 'dangerous drugs', and of reducing addicts' opportunities to obtain supplies of such drugs from more than one doctor at a time. The procedure was also seen as a means of collecting national epidemiological and statistical information about addiction.

The Addicts Index was established by the Home Office to store the information about individual addicts specified in the Notification Regulations and is used to enable doctors to make contact with the previous notifiers, if any, of their addict patients thus helping to ensure that the patients do not simultaneously obtain supplies of notifiable drugs from more than one doctor. The Index, which includes information from the police inspections of pharmacists' records of prescriptions, continues to provide the Home Office with the essential means of checking that the drugs to which the Regulations apply are responsibly prescribed and of detecting addicts who are receiving dual supplies of the drugs.

After 1968, with the opening of National Health Service hospital out-patient drug treatment centres (now Drug Dependence Units) and the restriction of the prescribing to addicts of heroin and cocaine to specially licensed doctors, virtually all of whom work in the Drug Dependence Units, the prescribing of heroin and cocaine in the treatment of addiction declined. Glancy (1972) reported that by the end of 1970 cocaine was very seldom prescribed and methadone was rapidly replacing heroin. From the early 1970s increasing numbers of addicts were notified as addicted to dipipanone (Diconal) and the *Lancet* later (1982) criticized the liberal prescribing of the drug by private practitioners. Spear (1982) noted the revived concern about the role of prescribing as a source of supply of drugs for the illicit market. He commented that many doctors prescribed the drug, often to temporary patients, without realizing that it was a notifiable drug. In 1984 the prescribing of dipipanone to addicts was restricted to specially licensed doctors and the number of new addicts notified as addicted to the drug subsequently declined.

From the late 1960s until the mid-1970s illicit supplies from Hong Kong of heroin diluted with caffeine and prepared for smoking, known as 'Chinese heroin', were available in London (Spear 1982). In the late 1970s illicitly imported supplies of cheap good quality heroin became readily obtainable in many parts of the UK and, after a period of relative stability, the number of addicts notified as addicted to heroin began to increase. From the mid-1970s there there were also indications that illicit supplies of cocaine were becoming more readily available. Thus, since the dipipanone phenomenon, spillage from prescriptions of notifiable drugs has not provided much in the way of supplies for the illicit drug market and the role of the notification procedure in limiting their availability has become less significant. As a result it has become most valued for providing national statistics of the extent of addiction to the drugs to which it applies. As injecting drug misusers are at high risk of HIV infection the procedure has, since 1987, provided a convenient vehicle for collecting statistics of addicts who inject any drug whether or not it is notifiable.

The annual addict statistics are used by the Government as one of the major indicators of the extent of the most harmful drug misuse. Although the statistics do not and cannot provide precise estimates of the number of persons in the population who are addicted to the drugs covered by the Notification Regulations they are the best regular source of information presently available of trends in the incidence and pre-valence of addiction to the drugs both nationally and for small areas. Recent research suggests that, in some areas at least, the extent to which the statistics more accurately reflect the number of addicts in the popu-lation seeking medical treatment is improving.

The value of the addict statistics for planning drug services is limited since the Notification Regulations apply only to doctors and to a limited number of drugs. The Department of Health announced in 1989 that, in order to plan services for all types of 'problem drug taker', each regional health authority in England would be setting up a drug misuse database modelled on an existing system (Donmall 1990). Similar databases have been set up in Wales, Scotland, and Northern Ireland. All the medical and non-medical agencies in the area are asked voluntarily to provide the databases with anonymized information about the drug misusers they see, while doctors will continue also to notify named addicts to the Home Office. When all the databases are fully operational it is likely that the continued utility of the notification procedure will be reviewed.

## Acknowledgements

I am grateful to John Buckle for explaining the operation of the computerized Addicts Index, and to Pat Dowdeswell for guiding me through the addict statistics.

## References

Acheson, D. (1990). Notification of drug addicts. *British Medical Journal*, **300**, 1343.

Advisory Council on the Misuse of Drugs (1988). *AIDS and drug misuse, Part 1*. HMSO, London.

Advisory Council on the Misuse of Drugs (1991). *Interim Report of the Addicts Index Working Group*. Home Office, London.

Bennett, T. and Wright, R. (1986). Opioid users' attitudes to and use of NHS clinics, GPs and private doctors. *British Journal of Addiction*, **81**, 757–63.

Berridge, V. (1980). The making of the Rolleston Report. *Journal of Drug Issues*, Winter, 7–28.

*British Medical Journal* (1965). Control of drug addiction. *British Medical Journal*, **2**, 259–60.

Chadwick, C. and Parker, H. (1989). *Three thousand in three years: a profile of known drug users in Wirral 1984–88*. University of Liverpool.

Department of Health, Scottish Office Home and Health Department, Welsh Office (1991). *Drug misuse and dependence. Guidelines on clinical management*. HMSO, London.

Ditton, J. and Speirits, K. (1981). *The rapid increase in heroin use in Glasgow during 1981*. Background Paper No. 2, Department of Sociology, University of Glasgow.

Donmall, M. (1990). Towards a national drug database. *Druglink*, **5**, 10–12.

Drug Indicators Project (1989). *Study of help-seeking and service utilization by problem drug takers*. Institute for the Study of Drug Dependence, London.

Edwards, G. (1981). Monitoring and the Home Office Index. In: *Drug problems in Britain* (eds G. Edwards and C. Busch), pp. 25–50. Academic Press, London.

Ghodse, H. (1977). Casualty departments and the monitoring of drug dependence. *British Medical Journal*, **1**, 1381–2.

Ghodse, H., Sheehan, M., Taylor, C., and Edwards, G. E. (1985). Deaths of drug addicts in the United Kingdom, 1967–81. *British Medical Journal*, **290**, 425–8.

Glancy, J. E. McA. (1972). The treatment of narcotic dependence in the United Kingdom. *Bulletin on Narcotics*, **XXIV**, 1–10.

Glanz, A. (1986). Findings of a national survey on the role of general practitioners in the treatment of drug misuse: dealing with the opiate misuser. *British Medical Journal*, **293**, 486–8.

Hartnoll, R., Lewis, R., Mitcheson, M., and Bryer, S. (1985). Estimating the prevalence of opioid dependence. *Lancet*, **i**, 203–5.

Home Office (1979). *Statistics of the misuse of drugs United Kingdom 1977*. Home Office, London.

Home Office (1987). Statistics of the misuse of drugs, United Kingdom 1986. *Home Office Statistical Bulletin Issue 28/87*. Home Office, London.

Home Office (1988). Statistics of the misuse of drugs, United Kingdom, 1987. *Home Office Statistical Bulletin Issue 25/88*. Home Office, London.

Home Office (1989). Statistics of the misuse of drugs: addicts notified to the Home Office, United Kingdom 1988. *Home Office Statistical Bulletin Issue 13/89*. Home Office, London.

Home Office (1990). Statistics of the misuse of drugs: addicts notified to the Home Office, United Kingdom, 1989. *Home Office Statistical Bulletin Issue 7/90*. Home Office, London.

Home Office (1991). Statistics of the misuse of drugs: addicts notified to the Home Office United Kingdom 1990. *Home Office Statistical Bulletin Issue 8/91*. Home Office, London.

Home Office (1993). Statistics of drug addicts notified to the Home Office, United Kingdom, 1992. *Home Office Statistical Bulletin Issue 15/93*. Home Office, London.

Horn, E. H., Henderson, H., and Forrest, J. (1987). Admission of drug addicts to a general hospital. *Scottish Medical Journal*, **332**, 41–5.

House of Commons (1985). *Fourth Report of the Social Services Committee*. HMSO, London.

*Lancet* (1965). Drug addiction. *Lancet*, **ii**, 1113–14.

*Lancet* (1982). Drug addiction: British System failing. *Lancet*, **i**, 83–4.

Ministry of Health (1926). *Report of the Departmental Committee on Morphine and Heroin Addiction*. HMSO, London. (The Rolleston Report).

Ministry of Health and Department of Health for Scotland (1961). *Drug Addiction. Report of the Interdepartmental Committee*. HMSO, London. (The first Brain Report).

Ministry of Health and Scottish Home and Health Department (1965). *Drug Addiction. The Second Report of the Interdepartmental Committee*. HMSO, London. (The second Brain Report).

Mott, J. (1986). Opioid use and burglary. *British Journal of Addiction*, **81**, 264–8.

Mott, J. and Macmillan, J. (1979). The validity of addict notifications. *British Journal of Psychiatry*, **134**, 264–8.

Mott, J., Caddle, D., and Donmall, M. (1993). Comparing doctors' practice in notifying addicts to the Home Office and reporting them to the North Western drug misuse database. *Addiction*, **88**, 249–56.

Neville, R. G., McKellican, J. F., and Foster, J. (1988). Heroin users in general practice: ascertainment and features. *British Medical Journal*, **296**, 755–8.

Parker, H., Bakx, K., and Newcombe, R. (1988). *Living with heroin*. Open University Press, Milton Keynes.

Robertson J. R. and Bucknall, A. (1985). Heroin users: notifications to the Home Office Addicts Index by general practitioners. *British Medical Journal*, **291**, 111–4.

Sheehan, M., Oppenheimer, E., and Taylor, C. (1986). Why drug users sought help from one London clinic. *British Journal of Addiction*, **81**, 765–76.

Spear, H. B. (1969). The growth of heroin addiction in the UK. *British Journal of Addiction*, **9**, 745–55.

Spear, H. B. and Glatt, M. M. (1971). The influence of Canadian addicts on heroin addiction in the United Kingdom. *British Journal of Addiction*, **66**, 141–9.

Spear, H. B. (1982). British experience in the management of opiate dependence. In *The dependence phenomenon* (eds M. M. Glatt and J. Marks). MTP Press, Lancaster.

Spear, H. B. (1983). Drug abuser deaths. *British Journal of Addiction*. **78**, 173–80.

Smart, R. and Ogborne, A. (1974). Losses to the addiction notification system. *British Journal of Addiction*, **69**, 225–30.

Stimson, G. V. and Oppenheimer, E. (1982) *Heroin addiction: treatment and control in Britain*. Tavistock, London.

Strang, J. and Shah, A. (1985). Notification of addicts and the medical practitioner. *British Journal of Psychiatry*, **147**, 195–8.

Wiepert, G. D., Bewley, T. H. and d'Orban, P. T. (1978). Outcomes for 575 British opiate addicts entering treatment between 1968 and 1975. *Bulletin on Narcotics*, **30**, 21–32.

Woodside, M. (1973). The first 100 referrals to a Scottish addiction treatment centre. *British Journal of Addiction*, **68**, 231–42.

## 22. The power behind practice: drug control and harm minimization in inter-agency and criminal law contexts

*Nicholas Dorn and Nigel South*

### Introduction

The conventional view of drug misuse policy in Britain is that it is dominated by medical or health concerns. In reality, however, British policy has been shaped by an accommodation between medical and criminal justice concerns, with the latter in the ascendance for the post-war period. Criminal law was and remains the framework of British drug policy. Within a recognition of this, three specific issues are addressed: the structures of inter-agency co-ordination; the processes of diversion of drug users out of the criminal justice system; and the meaning of prevention work (including minimization of social, legal, and physical harm) in a criminal law context. It is concluded that it is realistic to recognize that 'drugs work' occurs within a criminal justice context and that, in this context, harm minimization is not only possible but increasingly important.

### Policing, punishment, and prevention

Until very recently, most British books on drug misuse and control perpetuated a myth—that there is or at least was a uniquely British system of drug control, in which treatment and rehabilitation were to the fore, with the medical profession dominant. In this vision, the criminal law was seen variously as absent, as epiphenominal or as an irrational distraction from treatment.

Historically, this delusion has been reinforced by the well-intentioned attentions of North American visitors and commentators, who have for many decades fed back to the British a picture of their circumstances as the opposite of the criminal law-based approach of the USA (for example, see Schur 1963, 1964; Trebach 1982). Today, this mis-recognition is being further advanced by contrasts being drawn between US and UK responses to the human immunodeficiency virus (HIV) and the acquired immune deficiency syndrome (AIDS), with British syringe exchange schemes being contrasted with a general lack of such provision in the USA and regarded as further evidence of a British System in which criminal law responses are subordinated to health considerations.[1] The most deluded visitors refer to this as the Liverpool or Merseyside approach, the idea having got into their heads that exchange schemes are not supported elsewhere. The final touches are put to this pastiche when multi-disciplinary panels of welfare, medical and treatment personnel declare that their collective aim is to encourage drug users into treatment—in contrast to a perceived North American emphasis upon criminal prosecution.

Yet, if the 'medicalization of drug use' thesis has any validity at all, it can be seen to apply to the USA as or more readily than to the UK. It was, after all, in the USA particularly that medical and para-medical (eg pharmacists) interest groups contributed to the campaign for regulation and then prohibition of the public sale of drugs, with a view to enhancing their own professional monopoly of control over prescribing and dispensing practice (Nadelman 1990, p. 505). The power of the medical profession—including the rise of psychiatry—and of the pharmaceutical companies, has been as influential in shaping the legal and illegal availability of drugs in the USA as much as in the UK.

Thus, it takes only a moment's pause and consideration to see that this neat dichotomy (UK = treatment; US = law) fits the facts of neither country. In Britain, the lead government department is the Home Office, with over 100 directly employed staff working on drug control at central and regional levels, much more than those employed by the Department of Health and Regional Health Authorities. In terms of budgets the money applied to law enforcement is in excess of that applied to drug treatment and rehabilitation. And the numbers of persons formally processed annually through the criminal justice system in relation to drugs (about 30 000 per year in the early 1990s) exceeds those going through treatment or rehabilitation programmes.

Thus, looking at things from the point of view of how policy is implemented, the 'British System' revolves around criminal justice (and this is before we go on to consider anti-trafficking measures). Within this general framework, differing agencies recruit a different client profile. The greatest number of arrests are in relation to cannabis possession.

---

[1] For contemporary evidence of this pervasive mis-recognition see for example the overall tenor of any early 1990s issue of *The International Journal on Drug Policy*, especially the regular column of Ernie Drucker ('Notes from the drug wars').

By contrast, few cannabis users require the services of advice or counselling agencies. Heroin users—who are generally multidrug users—have traditionally constituted the main clientele for the drugs agencies; many others are in the prison system. It is only recently that British agencies have recognized the lack of services for stimulant users. Though from the late 1980s onwards the stimulant most talked about was cocaine, the stimulant most used for the past three decades has been amphetamine, it being social concern over use of this drug in particular by working class youth that led to its criminalization in the 1960s and, subsequently, more attention from the police than from the health sector. Indeed the manner in which Britain responds to amphetamine may be seen as symptomatic of its general drug policy; here is a drug that can certainly be associated with a range of health and social problems (overdose, psychosis, accidents, and HIV transmission when overexcited users of it in its injectable form share injection equipment). Yet the typical British response is to process the user as an offender. British System?

Turning from drug possession to drug dealing, it is important to remember that these offences were not originally distinguishable as regards maximum penalties before the 1971 Misuse of Drugs Act. By the middle 1980s, however, dealing had become the focus of special censure, punishable by up to life imprisonment and asset confiscation [Controlled Drugs (Penalties) Act 1985; Drug Trafficking Offences Act 1986]. Furthermore, during the 1980s, drug dealing became such an emotive issue that it contributed to a discursive re-definition of the lexicon of drugs enforcement: from 'drug squads' and 'user-dealers' to 'international mutual assistance' against 'major traffickers' (Dorn and South 1991; Dorn *et al.* 1992).

In the wake of these latter developments, and particularly the intentions and implementation of the Drug Trafficking Offences Act 1986, it has been harder for any commentator on the 'British System' to ignore the power and influence of the criminal justice system in responding to contemporary drug problems. This is not to deny the importance of continued support for health and social work initiatives, as exemplified by the 1982/83 Central Funding Initiative and related policy debates and service development (cf. MacGregor 1989, pp. 1–3 and *passim*; MacGregor *et al.* 1991). Rather, it is to emphasize that such a dual track response has always characterized the British response to drug problems and their containment and control. Furthermore, it is to assert that not only have medical practice and health service responses always been in a partnership with the state rather than exercising the autonomy often attributed to them, but additionally, the agenda of Government response has always accorded high priority to intervention through the criminal justice system.

# A revisionist history of drug control

During the nineteenth and early twentieth centuries, the power of the medical profession grew considerably and its construction of a new realm of scientific discourse brought within its concerns many new 'aberrations' of the body (Turner 1982, 1987)—for example, deviant sexuality, criminal behaviour, and drug use—inventing new diseases of body and mind, such as morphomania and morphinomania (Berridge and Edwards 1981). But such developments did not themselves lead to significant legislative control over drugs (the 1868 Poisons and Pharmacy Act merely introduced the requirement that opium derivatives and similar drugs be sold only from registered pharmacy shops). It was provisions within the Defence of the Realm Acts (Regulation 40 B), passed to introduce 'emergency powers' during the First World War, that first prohibited the possession of a drug—cocaine. Whatever the alarmist or misconceived nature of such a measure (the issue was largely a construction of public and press panic) a significant step had been taken. The phrase 'the die was cast' is overworked, yet it may accurately be applied here. With this legislative development, the Home Office moved from 'watching in the wings' to a 'centre-stage' position, and subsequent drug control policy was to be influenced by a tendency to criminalization as much as one favouring medicalization (cf. Berridge 1978).

The influence of American prohibitionist pressures, seeking to introduce international agreements concerning restrictions on drug supply and consumption (cf. Bruun et al. 1975) encouraged further domestic legislation in the form of the Dangerous Drugs Acts of 1920 and 1923. These Acts made it a criminal offence to be in unauthorized possession of opiates and cocaine (that is, if they were not supplied by a medical practitioner) and the Home Secretary was given powers of regulation over their processing, manufacture, distribution, and sale. The criminalization tendency exerted its influence and, as Stimson and Oppenheimer (1982, p. 25) have observed, the Home Office 'had successfully claimed the problem as a criminal and policing one'.

The subsequent report and recommendations of the Rolleston Committee (Ministry of Health 1926) are often seen as the key staging post in the development of a system of responses to drug problems dominated by the medical and public health perspectives. The focus of the Report was indeed on a rethinking and reorganization of what medical practitioners could and should do in relation to diagnosis of, and prescribing for, addicted patients in their care. Yet acceptance of and action on the proposals of the Report did not take place in a context empty of other influences. Possession of drugs deemed 'illegal' was an important criminal offence—important because then, as now, drugs attracted sensationalist press coverage and the fascination of the public. Furthermore, the Home

Office retained and has developed over the years its administrative control and influence over the system of drug dispensation, and over the reporting and recording of drug 'addicts' . Some may argue that it may not have done so with particular efficiency, but at the same time, it may be argued that the role of the later Home Office Drugs Inspectorate, particularly in the years when it was headed by Bing Spear, represented a Home Office-led or, at least, tacitly approved, 'harm minimization' strategy long before such an approach was identified as 'radical' and 'new' (see Chapter 1).

The perception of the Rolleston Committee report as the 'blueprint for the British System' and the reification of this view into a 'conventional wisdom' of quite staggering proportions has had an influence far beyond the bounds which cautious or critical thought would advise. As Berridge (1979, p. 85) observes, post-Rolleston, doctors 'henceforth were in partnership with the state'. And the principal office of the state remains the Home Office. To forget its influence and its remit, as the government body responsible for providing the criminal justice framework in which issues of social concern are handled, seems a form of historical amnesia.

To return to the present, a balanced judgement of the British System of drug control must be that heroin/methadone prescribing and anti-HIV measures constitute islands of exception within the framework of historically hegemonic criminal law responses. The criminalization of the great bulk of users goes beyond this country's international obligations and beyond the control measures adopted by some other countries. The relevant international agreements only require that countries set up some kind of control, they do not require criminalization of users. Interpreted by other countries, this may mean regulated outlets (for example, cannabis in Holland), or civil/administrative laws encouraging users into treatment (Italy), or partial decriminalization of small amounts for personal use in some US States.[1] In so far as the 'British System' in its contemporary theory and practice goes beyond what is required internationally and beyond the control measures adopted by some other countries, it may fairly be characterized as a criminal law-based system of control of the user (as well as the trafficker). This is the background against which key issues for practitioners can be understood today.

---

[1] Eleven US states instituted nominal fines no greater than $200 for possession of small amounts of marijuana, and Alaska made possession legal. Thus whilst formal decriminalization was restricted to the one state, a decriminalization of a looser kind—the substitution of a misdemeanour for a felony—was rather more widespread. Nevertheless the majority of states made no such move and the tendency from the early or mid 1980s onwards has, if anything, been in the opposite direction in the United States.

## Issue 1: structures of inter-agency co-ordination (health care/police/democracy)

Thinking about the proper division of labour in management of drug problems in Britain has gone through three phases in recent decades. In the 1960s, there arose a bifurcation in controls, with criminalization for users of most drugs and for dealers, and specialist medically supervised prescribing for a minority of opiate injectors (see other contributors to this volume). In the 1970s, the 'voluntary sector' expanded in an attempt to meet the limitations of provision for what can be seen as a multidrug and social work-type problem (Dorn and South 1985). By the 1980s, there were attempts to introduce some element of inter-agency liaison (if not co-ordination) through Regional Drug Problem Teams (based on Drug Dependency Units) and health district-located Drug Advisory Committees (DACs) [Advisory Council for the Misuse of Drugs (ACMD) 1982, 1984]. Social concern over heroin smoking and injection and, sub-sequently, cocaine and crack, together with an enlargement of the pool of cannabis users available for arrest, fuelled increases in numbers of drug offenders processed through the criminal justice system in England and Wales.[1] Alleged targeting of black people became a controversial issue in many localities (Dorn *et al.* 1992, chapter 7).

Meanwhile, multi-agency co-operation on drugs issues remained little more than a pious hope in most parts of Britain. The formal structure of liaison reflects the ideological bias towards health issues and does not engage well with criminal justice concerns. Liaison is supposed to be facilitated at local level by Regional Drugs Problem Teams [RDPTs (based on the staff of Drug Dependency Units)] and at local level by rather broader DACs (ACMD 1982, 1984 including Minority Report). Neither body has real 'clout' when it comes to questions of resources or inter-agency strategy, and the system encouraged by the ACMD has not weathered well (cf. Baker and Runicles 1991). There has been a tendency for police forces to be represented on DACs by sometimes junior and frequently bemused officers from 'community involvement' units, rather than operational Regional Crime Squads 'Drugs Wings' or Force Drug Squads. Such real communication and horse-trading as did occur between local health and police agencies has tended to take place outside these structures of inter-agency liaison.

There appear to be three potential responses to the ineffectiveness of health-focused structures of multi-agency liaison. The first is to re-affirm RDPTs and DACs as the proper focus for liaison and to en-

---

[1] The escalation in criminalization was particularly marked in Scotland, where the advent of HIV was perceived as another reason for policing the user.

courage senior uniform branch or drug squad officers to participate; in some areas, energetic officers have themselves taken initiatives in this direction. A second option is to go further, setting up an integrated framework of inter-agency liaison managed by Home Office staff and/or regional/force drug squads, reflecting recognition of the Home Office as lead government Department. This occurred in an increasing number of areas from 1990, as the Home Office set up its local Drug Prevention Units. A third path is for Local Authorities (that is, of cities and counties) to set up new structures, under the general oversight of elected members, drawing in participants from health and welfare, Local Authority services (for example housing), and the police. Such initiatives exist in some areas (Kensington and Chelsea in London; Manchester in northern England) and may emerge more widely. Lacking any clarification by government, inter-agency liaison seems set to wobble between forms which might be characterized as based on principles of health care, policing of criminality, and democratic representation. Perhaps by the year 2000 we shall have sorted this one out—or will 'drugs' continue to act as a metaphor for a broader confusion about the way society should be regulated?

## Issue 2: suction into/diversion from the criminal justice system

The provisions of the 1991 Criminal Justice Act encourage a whole raft of tendencies toward diversion out of the Criminal Justice system. The Act concerns itself with encouraging non-custodial sentences by the courts for the middle range of criminality—including minor trafficking by drug users, possession of larger amounts of heroin or cocaine, or repeated offences of possession of cannabis—which currently may attract custodial sentences. At the time of writing, there were a number of unanswered questions about the financing of the non-custodial disposals, and we can only assume that government will at some point have to make provisions to finance 'punishment in the community', perhaps using funds to be saved from a reduction in prison places (or are we being naive here?). Leaving aside such questions, and looking forward to the full implementation of the Criminal Justice Act from 1993 onwards, it can be seen that it will come into force against a background of other diversion and sentence-reduction practices. These include the use of police discretion (informal warnings); cautioning (a process which involves formal admission of guilt); and 'plea bargaining' (in which a lesser charge may be brought, and/or a reduced sentence imposed, in recognition of information given about traffickers or other criminals). Although plea bargaining is a less recognized and more sensitive issue in Britain than in the USA, it is acknowledged by police officers to be a routine option in drugs and other cases. It represents one aspect of 'conditionality' in diversion from the criminal justice system.[1]

A second aspect of conditionality relates to the idea that a less punitive or non-punitive method of disposal of drug offenders is justified if they agree to accept some kind of drug treatment, rehabilitation and/or opportunity for reflection about their deviance. So-called 'treatment packages' are devised by the probation service and presented to the court as a means of disposal alternative to imprisonment or fine. The term 'treatment package' may help to convince magistrates of the justification for diversion, but there are a series of problems. The possibilities include:

(1) that 'treatment' may be taken literally and narrowly construed to mean immediate or rapid cessation of all drug consumption;

(2) that drug testing would be a standard condition of diversion, when relapse might lead to lengthier and potentially more punitive disposal than previously considered legitimate;

(3) and that the availability of disposal options perceived as 'soft' or 'welfarist' may encourage criminal justice system personnel to attend to more offenders than they would otherwise.

The latter process, called 'net widening' (Cohen 1979), may also surface in pre-court diversion schemes, as police officers use their discretion— to agree not to press charges, or to caution, or to charge for a minor offence—on condition that offenders agree to attend a local drugs agency. Some specialist drugs workers may welcome any tendency for the criminal justice system to do 'outreach' work for them, accepting that drug users brought to them on a less than fully voluntary basis may require an approach rather different from that appropriate for self-referrals. Clearly, there are also unresolved issues of funding, as police expectations of agency co-operation meet agency expectations of specific funding for what may become a wider and more demanding work-load.

These two aspects of conditionality:

(1) diversion in return for information received; and,

(2) diversion only on acceptance of attendance at a drug agency

are focal points for negotiation at individual and inter-agency levels in the early 1990s. Drug workers will distinguish between, on the one hand, the dangers represented by net widening and the subordination of

---

[1] To caricature the speech of an officer attempting to induce a prisoner to give information: 'You help us, and we'll help you. Otherwise it could go difficult for you, know what I mean? After all, you're in a lot of trouble . Here, have a cigarette? Go on, sometimes you feel better after you've had a little cry'. (At this point, reassuring physical contact may be helpful.) 'I'm trying to help you, but you've got to help me too. After all, we're in this together—we're mates, you and me'.

welfare networks to criminal justice system aims; and, on the other hand, positive aspects of diversion and the good intentions which it represents. It seems likely that one fruitful contribution of drugs agencies to diversion schemes will be their insistence that clients may require access to a wide variety of educational, occupational, housing, health and welfare services, and income-generation opportunities—not just 'drug counselling' or 'treatment'. There remains the danger that such a contribution may be squeezed by, on the one hand, magistrates' stereotypical ideas about drug addicts and the need for specialist treatment and, on the other hand, drug agencies' desire for contracts and funding for their drug specialist services. Time will tell.

## Issue 3: the meaning of prevention in a criminal law context

Within Europe, drug policy has been informed by various notions of prevention and intervention which include reduction of levels of drug distribution and consumption, and also minimization of the various forms of harm (health, social, legal, financial etc.) that may be associated with drug use. British workers are comfortable with this dual notion of prevention: for some, minimization of harm is seen as the primary goal, with reduction in consumption as secondary (that is, as one amongst many methods of achieving the primary goal). Hence, for example, syringe exchange schemes (minimizing harm to health). At the same time, various approaches to diversion out of the criminal justice system (informal warnings, cautioning, non-custodial sentences, etc.) may be seen as attempts to minimize social and legal forms of harm (which are by no means inherent in drug use *per se*, rather a side-effect of controls). There are many ways in which drug policy may seek to reduce harm to the individual, friends and relatives, and the community at large.

On the other side of the Atlantic, however, the concept of harm minimization is not widely understood, and this lack of understanding had a resurgence in Britain in the late 1980s. Politicians, in particular, were seized by the idea that some drugs, such as cocaine, are so dangerous that the only way to minimize harm is to reduce consumption. Following the 1989 crack panic in Britain, plans were laid for new local Home Office Drug Prevention Teams to develop and financially support local prevention activities other than those with harm minimization aims. The then Home Secretary gave his opinion that cautioning was an inappropriate disposal in cases of simple possession of heroin or cocaine—rather against the grain of the police response, which continues to favour cautioning as an option to be considered in relation to possession of any drug.

Where then do the British stand on the issue of harm minimization, especially in relation to the application of the criminal law? This is an issue on which every drug worker and every agency will have a view, and workable compromises must be argued out, made explicit, and preferably committed to paper and signed by representatives of each agency, including the police. Our own view is that it is dangerous to rely on cosy 'understandings' with individual police officers, since not only may individual officers change their postings, but also the same officer may *volte face*, shrugging off informal understandings, according to the changing demands of his or her hierarchy (itself responding to shifting political imperatives). A formal and written agreement, made public as a commitment between various agencies (subject, say, to annual review) is rather more binding—though correspondingly more difficult to achieve [Institute for the the Study of Drug Dependence (ISDD) 1991]. Failing this, the police should be encouraged to make public their own Force Policy on Drugs, and to consult widely in drawing it up. This may result in a (formal) stance that is acceptable to many other agencies and which may include a committment to harm minimization. In the case of the Metropolitan Police, for example, the recommendation of Territorial Operations 30, the responsible policy-making branch, is that the Force should fashion a policy (Metropolitan Police 1990, p. 6).

To reduce the use of drugs locally through multi-agency cooperation and co-ordination by tackling the drugs problem on three main fronts:
A) Enforcement of the criminal law;
B) Reducing the harm caused to the individual and society as a whole;
C) Reducing the demand for drugs.

An appendix suggests that (B) above can be pursued by facilitating offenders' access to independent advice through 'referral schemes' (cf. Dorn *et al.* 1990 and Dorn 1994); by supporting the establishment of syringe-exchange schemes; and by considering the social side-effects of enforcement operations (Metropolitan Police 1990, appendix B).

This is only a formal statement, and it is symptomatic that it has a broadly advisory status rather than being directive or instructional. Many senior Met officers have either never heard of it or, if they heard of it once, would have difficulty in recalling its content. In the real world, actual procedure will vary enormously according to the views of individual officers and other contingencies. But, still, such statements of purpose represent a benchmark against which the actual police practice may be judged. There are clear indications that police support for syringe exchange schemes in England and Wales and their agreement not to mount surveillance or engage in harassment of their customers has been crucial for their successful operation. This is a step in the right direction.

Present circumstances may be quite propitious for the development of harm minimization in its legal and other forms—if those in favour of such reform actively seek to influence and shape the agenda for the 1990s. Such action should, if it is realistic, start from a recognition that the drugs arena is and will no doubt remain that of the criminal law.

# References

ACMD (Advisory Council on Misuse of Drugs) (1982). *Treatment and rehabilitation*; and (1984). *Prevention*. HMSO, London.

Baker, P. and Runicles, D. (1991). *Coordinating drugs services: the role of regional and district drugs advisory committees*. London Research Centre and NLAFDM, London.

Berridge, V. (1978). War conditions and narcotics control: The passing of the Defence of the Realm Act Regulation 40 B. *Journal of Social Policy*, 7, 285–304.

Berridge, V. (1979). Morality and medical science: concepts of narcotic addiction in Britain, 1820–1926. *Annals of Science*, **36**, 67–85.

Berridge V. and Edwards, G. (1981). *Opium and the people*. Allen Lane, London.

Bruun, K., Pan, L., and Rexed, I. (1975). *The Gentlemen's Club: international control of drugs and alcohol*. University of Chicago Press, Chicago.

Cohen, S. (1979). The punitive city: notes on the dispersal of social control. *Contemporary Crises*, **3**, 339–63.

Dorn, N. (1994). Three faces of police referral: welfare, justice and business perspectives on multi-agency work with drug arrestees. *Policing and Society*. (In press.)

Dorn, N., Murji, K., and South, N. (1990). Drug referral schemes in Britain. *Drugs Arena* (National Drugs Intelligence Unit), 10 (Autumn), 28–32. (Copy from authors.)

Dorn, N., Murji, K., and South, N. (1992). *Traffickers: drug markets and law enforcement*. Routledge, London.

Dorn, N. and South, N. (1985). *Helping drug users*. Gower, Aldershot.

Dorn, N. and South, N. (1991). Profits and penalties: new trends in legislation and law enforcement concerning illegal drugs. In *Policing and prescribing: the British system of drug control* (ed. D. Whynes and P. Bean). Macmillan, London.

ISDD (1991). *High policy: drugs and youth work pack*. ISDD, London. (especially page 20 of Manual therein.)

MacGregor, S. (1989). The public debate in the 1980s. In *Drugs and British society* (ed. S. MacGregor), pp. 1–19. Routledge, London.

MacGregor, S., Ettorre, E., Coomber, R., Crosier, A., and Lodge, H. (1991). *Drugs services in England and Wales and the impact of the Central Funding Initiative*. Research Monograph One. ISDD, London.

Metropolitan Police (1990). 'Force strategy for a drug dependency reduction programme—an integrated approach, part II', TO30, Scotland Yard, unpublished photocopy.

Ministry of Health (1926). *Report of the Departmental Committee on morphine and heroin addiction*. HMSO, London.

Nadelman, E. (1990). Global prohibition regimes: the evolution of norms in international society. *International Organisation*, **444**, 479–526.

Schur, E. (1963). *Narcotic addiction in Britain and America: the impact of public policy*. Tavistock, London.

Schur, E. (1964). Drug addiction under British policy. In *The other side: perspectives on deviance* (ed. H. Becker), pp. 67–83. Free Press, New York.

Stimson, G. and Oppenheimer, E. (1982). *Heroin addiction: treatment and control in Britain*. Tavistock, London.

Trebach, A. (1982). *The heroin solution*. Yale University Press, New Haven.

Turner, B. (1982). The government of the body: medical regimens and the rationalisation of diet. *British Journal of Sociology*, **33**, 254–69.

Turner, B. (1987). *Medical power and social knowledge*. Sage, London.

# 23. The growth of information. The development of Britain's national Drug Misuse Information Resource

*Jasper Woodcock*

## Amateur beginnings

Drugs were matters of great public concern in 1967. Legislation to control the prescribing of heroin and cocaine to addicts was passing through parliament, the debate over the appropriate legal status of cannabis was as vigorous as it ever has been in the UK; in August, *The Times* published an advertisement signed by some very unexpected people describing the laws in relation to cannabis as 'immoral, unworkable, and unjust'. But there was an acknowledged absence of factual information to support all the rhetoric. An early day motion in the House of Commons, which received support from the leaders of all three political parties, asked for sound objective information on drug abuse to be made available (*Brentford and Chiswick Times* 1967).

That this was easier said than done became apparent to Frank Logan, former Home Office and UN Division of Narcotics Official, when he looked for bibliographical support for an article he wished to write on drugs and found no library able to retrieve relevant material that he knew must exist. (The difficulty stems from the fact that material on drug misuse was—and still is—to be found scattered among the pages of journals covering an extraordinarily wide range of academic disciplines.) Not a man to be easily thwarted, he conceived the idea of an institution where one would be able to gain access to what had been published about drug abuse. Having just retired from a second career at the Royal Institute of International Affairs, the very British idea of an independent non-governmental institute was the paradigm for his solution. A working group was established, the idea of an interdisciplinary institute refined, a letter written to *The Times* soliciting support, and on the strength of a single donation of £5000 from a property magnate the Institute for the Study of Drug Dependence (ISDD) was formed.

There was debate in the working group about the Institute's name and objectives. Logan wanted to call it the Institute for the Prevention of Drug Addiction, but others (notably Dr C. R. B. Joyce) took the view that nothing should take precedence over the Institute's main target, the amassing of a solid corpus of information on drug misuse that might serve as a foundation on which effective policy responses could be developed by all and any who cared to make use of the Institute's resources. So 'Institute for the Study of Drug Dependence' won the day (at that time 'drug dependence' was the latest attempt to find a less value-laden term for 'drug addiction'—nowadays it might have been called the 'Institute for the Study of Drug Misuse' or 'of Drugs in Society'). Another principle established from the beginning was that ISDD must not only be wholly independent but clearly seen to be so. Financial support from government, or alcohol, tobacco, or pharmaceutical interests would have been refused if it had been offered (which it was not), in those formative years.

With Logan as Director (part-time, drawing no salary), a full-time secretary, a part-time Information Officer, a team of medical students from the London Hospital Medical College to index the material in the library in their spare time, a part-time typist, and a relatively sophisticated manual information retrieval system based on that at the UN Division of Narcotics Library in Geneva, ISDD opened its doors to the public from an attic in the Royal Society of Medicine's Chandos House near Oxford Circus on 1 April 1968.

Assembling a reference library organized so as to be able to produce articles relevant to any enquiry about the misuse of drugs, however specific or however general, has remained ISDD's central activity ever since. Begun perforce from lack of funds in an amateur way, the operation has been professionalized over the years and now ranks not only as the world's best information resource on drug misuse, but also is highly regarded as a specialized library *qua* library.

During its first years, ISDD's only other activity was holding three seminars on cannabis at that time the centre of much controversy inflamed by the Wootton report (Advisory Committee on Drug Dependence 1968). These seminars had an information remit also. The object was to gather a select group of the world's leading authorities at a time when sufficient work had been done to make an exchange of experience fruitful. The first seminar confined its subject to the botany and chemistry of cannabis, this being the only area where sufficient solid advances were felt to have been made (Joyce and Curry 1970). Two others, on the pharmacology of cannabis (Paton and Crown 1972) and on human use of cannabis (Connell and Dorn 1975) followed.

Another subject of controversy in the working group that set up ISDD centred around whether research should be included among the ISDD's objectives. A majority thought that the process of answering enquiries from the existing published literature might reveal gaps in knowledge, questions that were being asked where no answers were to be found, and that ISDD should be empowered to promote or undertake research to remedy the lack. One area that quickly emerged as lacking researched information was drug education in schools. At the time, there was a division of opinion among authorities as to whether school-children should be given instruction about drug abuse. Some said that they must be warned of the dangers that drugs could present, others (including the World Health Organization and the UK Department of Education and Science) maintained that this would only arouse curiosity and encourage experimentation. There was, however no good research to indicate who was right—whether drug education 'turned them on' or 'turned them off'. Teachers wanting help with drug education materials and methods formed a significant proportion of ISDD's early enquirers, and it was felt to be necessary, though scarcely helpful, to tell them of this unresolved debate about whether they should be teaching about drugs at all.

This was a clear example of a gap in research. Given ISDD's rudimentary organization, the way to fill it seemed clear—find a source of funds and interest an established centre of educational research to conduct the study. A source of funds was quickly identified, The Sir Halley Stewart Trust, but surprisingly no educational research establishment was interested in mounting a study to evaluate the effect of drug education on schoolchildren. Fortunately, the Trust was not deterred and proposed that ISDD set up its own Education Research Unit to do the job.

## Growing professionalization

So in 1972 a team of three researchers, headed by a social psychologist with experience in evaluating the effects of TV on children, was set up; to compensate for ISDD's lack of managerial expertise, the Trust also retained a firm of management consultants to advise and monitor progress. Thanks to this initial grounding in good habits, ISDD's Research Unit thereafter acquired an excellent record of completing its research projects on time and within budget.

This ushered in the first phase of ISDD's expansion and professionalization. In the same year, 1972, the Drug Abuse Council (a US non-governmental body funded by Ford and other large US foundations) was sufficiently impressed by ISDD's library to give ISDD a substantial 3-year grant to enable the Council to model its own library on it with bibliographical support from ISDD, and to enable ISDD to explore the prospects of international exchange of drug abuse information. At the same time, the Department of Health offered an equally substantial 3-year grant to enable ISDD to staff its library with professional librarians and information specialists; ISDD by then felt sufficiently secure in its independence to accept.

The attic in Chandos House was by now overflowing and in July 1973 ISDD moved to a converted Victorian house in north-west London. The full-time staff had grown to 12. A number of new developments were initiated over the next 2 years. As part of the Drug Abuse Council contract, all the world's drug abuse documentation centres were surveyed (ISDD 1974), and with ISDD advice a documentation centre was established in the Centro Mexicano de Estudios en Drogodependencias in Mexico City. The first steps towards ultimate computerizing of the library were taken, most importantly the construction of a proper thesaurus to replace the simple list of keywords that was being used for indexing, were taken. The Research Unit began a long and fruitful period of collaboration in the development of drug education materials and strategies with the Danish Ministry of Education.

In 1975, Frank Logan retired as honorary Director and was replaced by a full-time paid successor (Logan remained active on ISDD's Council as Vice-Chairman until 1979) thus erasing the last vestige of ISDD's boldly amateur beginnings. However, all these developments were soon threatened by the impact of inflation rates of nearly 30 per cent, which eroded the value of the grants on which ISDD depended. Staff began to leave because they could not survive on the salaries that ISDD was able to pay. In the autumn of 1976, ISDD's managing Council decided that any further reduction in activity would render the library useless—so ISDD would close its doors within 6 months when its small reserve fund ran out. Like many organizations before and since ISDD seemed about to fall victim to the inexorable consequences of trying to exist on hand-to-mouth project grants without adequate core funding.

## Consolidation

At this point, the Department of Health and Social Security came to the rescue and in 1977 began providing ISDD with funding related to the actual core costs of its library and administration. This enabled the library to be brought back up to its establishment of four professionals, and began the third phase of ISDDs development. This involved among other things clarification of exactly what clientele ISDD was seeking to satisfy. At the beginning, lacking knowledge of what the demands would be, ISDD tried to be all-embracing; information was collected on alcohol and tobacco as well as illicit drugs, on dependence on prescribed drugs such as benzodiazepines, on solvent abuse, the use of drugs for social control, to enhance athletic performance, etc.; all scientific disciplines were covered, including chemistry and pharmacology. Nine years' practical experience, however, had made it clear that ISDD's users were almost exclusively interested in the human aspects of drug misuse. Consequently, chemistry and pharmacological studies on animals (except for major literature reviews) were dropped. Much earlier, the collection of material on alcohol and tobacco had been given over to other organizations that claimed to serve the needs of ISDD enquirers about these substances. This more precise delimitation of ISDD's scope was a necessary prelude to computerization.

While the library was narrowing the area of its remit, the Research Unit was defining its area of interest more broadly than simply drug education to include social research into any aspects of prevention, including public policy and law enforcement.

So from 1977, ISDD was enabled to develop on the basis of secure (though not always adequate) funding and stable staffing (most of the senior staff have been at ISDD more than 14 years, giving them an un-rivalled pool of experience), ideal conditions for the deployment of the painstaking attention to detail required to set up a pioneering database.

During the next 7 years, the library completed and published the thesaurus. The entire collection of by then 35 000 documents was uniformly indexed and catalogued, expunging the last evidence of the lack of professional library skills of the original part-time staff. The Research Unit (now named Research and Development Unit) began to expand its area of interest beyond education to topics such as the significance of the activity of drinking alcohol to teenagers (alcohol and tobacco have never ceased to figure in the work of the Research Unit). This period also saw a considerable expansion in the number and range of ISDD publications aimed at providing useful information to professionals with a less than central interest in drug misuse—teachers, family doctors, social workers, probation officers, and so on. A newsletter *Druglink* began to be published irregularly.

In 1983 a major injection of government money (the Central Funding Initiative) expanded services for drug users throughout the UK and produced a consequentially large increase in the demand for ISDD's services. Lack of space prevented the necessary expansion of staff and technical support, so in 1984 ISDD moved yet again to its present address on the fringe of the City. The final stages of the preparation of the library for computerization were completed by the next year, but it took another 2 years before the money could be found to purchase the necessary hardware and software, finally installed in October 1987. Setting up the database occupied a further year before the first records were loaded in November 1988. By 1993, the most recently acquired third of the

60 000 documents in the library were retrievable by computer. The rapidity of computerized searches has also enabled the library to keep pace with the constantly growing number of enquiries, running at the rate of 5000 specialist searches per annum.

The fastest growing area of ISDD's work during this period was its publications. What had begun as an adjunct to the library's enquiry-answering function—a few thousand copies of a handful of informative broadsheets—had become a sizeable mail-order publishing enterprise with a list of 100 titles generating 3500 orders a year and a turnover of £300 000. This necessitated the setting up in 1986 of a separate Publications Unit and the renting of additional office space nearby to accommodate it and the expanded administration needed to service an organization with an annual budget of £500 000 (by 1993 this had become £1 000 000).

*Druglink* whose publication had lapsed because of lack of resources, was relaunched as a regular bi-monthly journal and is currently produced entirely with in-house desktop publishing facilities. With a circulation of 1400 and a readership many times that, it has established itself as the 'trade' journal of the drugs field.

The Research and Development Unit extended its work to encompass criminological research into the UK drug market and enforcement strategies, development of innovative materials for youth workers and managers, and research and development in the field of women and AIDS.

By 1993, ISDD had a staff of 25, and was embarking on a new phase of outreach both nationally and internationally. It has taken a lead in promoting liaison and collaboration among drug abuse documentation centres in Europe. Its library (so far as it has been loaded into the computer) is currently accessible through a comparable institute in Madrid, the Instituto de Documentacion e Informacion sobre Drogodependencias.

## Conclusions

What are the factors that have enabled ISDD to develop from a tiny amateur enterprise to become the world's leading documentary resource on drug abuse and the authoritative source of information on drug abuse in the UK? First, it was established to remedy a real lack of reliable information, and all its subsequent developments have been undertaken to remedy other real lacks. ISDD has consistently avoided areas where others were already active, on the principle that there are so many unmet needs in the drug abuse field that duplication is an unaffordable luxury. Little of ISDDs energies has been absorbed in competitive rivalry.

So the pace of development at ISDD has been dictated by the exigencies of the task in hand and the availability of funding. The difficulties in acquiring the latter certainly added some delay, but in the context of setting up a pioneering information resource in as uniquely multi-disciplinary a field as drug abuse, this was probably no bad thing; it helped to ensure there was ample time for forethought. All of ISDD's senior specialist staff have been with the Institute for a long time— from 14 to 23 years. This continuity in personnel has been important in several ways. First, the sheer accumulation of knowledge and experience has incalculable benefits in an information-based organization. Secondly, it has been significant in generating and supporting the self-confidence that has enabled ISDD to maintain its independence despite receiving over 40 per cent of its income from the Department of Health. Thirdly, it has enabled the technical development of ISDD's resources and activities to be undertaken by the same staff that is responsible for the day-to-day work. So instead of the possible alternative process of bringing in 'experts' in various techniques, such as computer data handling, the staff have themselves with the aid of training and outside consultancies, acquired the technical accomplishments that were needed to expand the effectiveness of what they were already doing. This has assured a sound marriage between ISDD's work and the technical resources deployed to implement it.

## References

Advisory Committee on Drug Dependence (1968). *Cannabis*. HMSO, London.

*Brentford and Chiswick Times* (1967). Editorial: A 'teach-in' on drugs. 13 October, p. 8.

Connell, P. H. and Dorn, N. (eds) (1975). *Cannabis and man: psychological and clinical aspects and patterns of use*. Proceedings of the 3rd international cannabis conference organised by the Institute for the Study of Drug Dependence at the Ciba Foundation, London. Churchill Livingstone, Edinburgh.

ISDD (1974). *International directory of centres for documentation and information on the non-medical use of drugs*. ISDD, London.

Joyce, C. R. B. and Curry, S. H. (1970). *The botany and chemistry of cannabis*. Proceedings of a conference organized by the Institute for the Study of Drug Dependence at the Ciba Foundation, 9–10 April 1969. Churchill Livingstone, London.

Paton, W. D. M. and Crown, J. (ed.) (1972). *Cannabis and its derivatives: pharmacology and experimental psychology*. Proceedings of a symposium arranged by the Institute for the Study of Drug Dependence, London, May 1972. Oxford University Press, London.

# 24. Media- and school-based approaches to drug education

*John B. Davies and Niall Coggans*

## Media anti-drug campaigns

The past decade has seen a substantial increase in the use of the media, and especially of television, to disseminate messages concerning health. Particular attention has been attracted by a number of campaigns aimed at discouraging illicit use of drugs, and more recently fears about the spread of human immunodeficiency virus (HIV)/acquired immune deficiency syndrome (AIDS) have led to similar media campaigns focusing on needle-sharing amongst intravenous drug users, and safer sex in the general population. The association between HIV infection and intravenous drug use makes the two issues inseparable for certain purposes.

Media anti-drug and AIDS campaigns in the UK have been dominated by negative, stereotypical imagery; with drug users portrayed as helpless, unhealthy and immoral. For example, in the 1985–86 'Heroin screws you up' campaign the strong impression was conveyed that use of heroin would very quickly and inevitably lead to serious if not fatal consequences. An even more pejorative tone was communicated by the 1987 'Smack isn't worth it' campaign with its message of moral corruption amongst drug users. Another streotypical assumption utilized in media anti-drug campaigns is the belief that drugs compel people to steal (Hammersley *et al.* 1990), as in the 'Smack can leave a scar on your whole family' poster. At the time of writing another fear arousal campaign is under way, based around the message 'Drugs—the effects can last forever'.

With some notable exceptions, it is fair to say that the methods favoured for media campaigns, and the ideology that lies behind them, are generally opposite to the methods and ideology that underlie health education initiatives concerning drugs and AIDS at the school and community level. For the most part, the former are characterized by messages which arouse fear of illness and/or death; that is, so-called 'fear arousal' messages. On the other hand, the state of the art in health education specifically avoids fear arousal, and concentrates on group dynamics, social influences and the 'life-skills' approach. Furthermore, health education theory and research which underlies most of the school-based initiatives, specifically rules out fear arousal as a legitimate means of promoting healthy behaviour in these areas. Research evidence suggests that fear arousal is ineffective; but it also suggests that drug education based simply on the presentation of factual material is either ineffective or even counter-productive (de Haes and Schuurman 1975; Kinder *et al.* 1980; Schaps *et al.* 1981). On the other hand, other evidence suggests that a life-skills approach, broadly based rather than concentrating on specific substances, and integrated into a more general health curriculum, offers the best route forward, at least so far as young people are concerned (Coggans *et al.* 1991; Davies and Coggans 1991).

In addition, there is a strange irony about the fact that some of the most eye catching, frightening and it should be said, costly campaigns deal with drug problems which account for some 400 deaths per annum; whilst major causes of death in the population at large (alcohol, tobacco, road traffic accidents, heart disease) appear to attract less intensive coverage. Smoking, for instance, is said to account for some 100 000 deaths per annum (Royal College of Psychiatrists 1987). Given that media anti-drug campaigns seem so much out-of-step with good educational practice, and that the scale of the response seems out of proportion to the scale of the problem, it is not surprising that in some quarters there is scepticism about the real function of media anti-drug campaigns.

This scepticism is evidenced by a recent public exchange between a drugs researcher and the government's Central Office of Information (COI). The view was put forward that media anti-drug campaigns of the sort described above had simply served to reinforce stereotypical perceptions of drug users on the part of non-users and to undermine the effectiveness of other initiatives in combating the spread of HIV, by alienating drug users (Rhodes 1990). Evidence was adduced, both by Rhodes and by the COI in a reply (Stubbington 1990), from evaluations of these campaigns carried out by government sponsored consultants to support their relative positions (Andrew Irving Associates Ltd 1986; Cragg, Ross and Dawson Ltd 1989). On the one hand Rhodes suggested that evaluation had demonstrated such campaigns were counter-productive to the extent that they reinforced drug users' negative self-perceptions. On the other hand, however, the COI felt that the same reports supported their view that the campaigns concerned had avoided alienation of drug users, and that the reports commissioned by the Department of Health had been quoted out of context. However, the argument hinged on the interpretation placed on data which were primarily qualitative in nature. Such qualitative data are misused when they form the basis for statements about the way the world 'really is' rather than the way people see it or believe it to be. In the absence of hard outcome measures the issue remains unresolved.

## The effects of anti-drug campaigns

The first point which it is necessary to grasp is that, in terms of stopping or preventing people from taking drugs, many anti-drug campaigns have simply not worked or have sometimes made things worse. For example, in a major review of prevention programme evaluations Schaps *et al.* (op. cit.) found that of the 127 programmes they reviewed, the majority (74) had no effect on average ratings of drug use, intentions to use, and/or attitudes towards use. In addition, while 45 had a positive effect on drug-related outcome ratings, seven programmes had a negative effect. Those that had a negative effect were information based while those with a positive effect involved either affective or counselling components.

Another review of outcome studies also identified problems with drug and/or alcohol education programmes. Kinder *et al.* (op. cit.) reported that such programmes had mostly been ineffective in achieving the goals of decreasing substance use or preventing future use, and also found in some instances that drug education could lead to increased use. As most of the programmes reviewed by Kinder *et al.* were information based it can be concluded that an information-only approach tended not to reduce drug use and sometimes had effects counter to those intended. Finally, for those who would advocate a simple message based on coercion and punishment, Engs and Hanson (1989) produced data from a sample of 3375 American College students after introduction of a new age limit of 21 years for purchase of alcohol. There was an immediate increase in the numbers drinking under 21 years of age, and more of these were heavy drinkers compared with those of legal age. According to Engs, the findings support 'reactance theory', which suggests that people seek to regain control whenever they perceive that their freedom is unjustly threatened, and do so via reduced compliance.

It seems therefore that, in general, drug education strategies emphasizing either information-giving or fear arousal have had little or no effect on drug-using behaviour. Moreover, reliance on a single educational strategy is increasingly criticized in the light of a growing awareness that there is a need to tailor educational programmes to take account of local cultural and social factors relevant to the target population (Reid and Massey 1986); something which television despite its vast potential as an educational tool is singularly ill-equipped to do.

Precisely because television is ideally suited for the dissemination of a common message to all sections of the community, its use has to be restricted to situations where such global coverage represents the best strategy. This is not the case with messages about drugs, due to the problems raised by antecedent probabilities, as discussed in Davies (1986). Briefly, the advantages of any preventive health strategy can only be assessed by careful examination of the relative likelihood of positive and negative outcomes, and the prevalence of the condition in the parent population. For example, whooping-cough vaccine prevents the illness in the majority of cases, but there is a risk involved in so far as a small number of those injected actually develop the disease. In the same way, small numbers of young people are probably attracted to, or have their interest aroused in, drugs as a result of anti-drug campaigns. Nonetheless, it is still sensible to continue with the prevention strategy on a population scale up to the point where the false-positive rate exceeds the natural prevalence. In simple terms, if most people were abusing drugs, then the advantages of disseminating a message broadly would outweigh the risks. However, most people are not using drugs, and data suggest that amongst young people only a small percentage overall have anything resembling a regular habit (Coggans *et al.* op. cit.; Davies and Coggans, op. cit.; Swadi 1988). Consequently, if the education arouses an interest in more than that percentage of recipients, there is a possibility that effects opposite to those intended may result. In a similar way, a vaccine which is 99 per cent safe and successful is not usable on a population scale if the condition in question has less than a 1 per cent prevalence, other things being equal.

The problem with television is that in circumstances where there are doubts about antecedent probabilities, it is the most effective way of maximizing any harm as well as any benefits that might result. By contrast, campaigns targeted at areas where local prevalence of drug use is high run less risk of creating more problems than they solve. But national television campaigns simply do not 'target' in this way.

## Problems of evaluation

Ill-advised and inappropriate messages can thus make things worse; and the fact that the intentions behind a campaign are good is neither here nor there. On the other hand, the fact that some approaches are unhelpful does not mean that all approaches are unhelpful; and similarly, it is possible to argue that extent of use is only one criterion by which success in this area can be measured. For example, even if use is more widespread after a campaign, it is possible to argue that there might be desirable changes in attitudes and knowledge, or that use is generally safer than previously.

What is certain, however, is that the success or otherwise of mass-media campaigns is singularly difficult to measure. Because of this difficulty, many evaluations of media campaigns have concentrated on a variety of process measures, that is measures of people's awareness of various aspects of the campaigns, and their beliefs and opinions about the likely effectiveness. From such data, it is a short but quite un-warranted step to claim that a campaign was 'successful' on the grounds that many people were aware of it, and a majority thought it was a good idea.

In fact, quite a lot is known about what is likely to constitute an effective drug message. For example, in a study by de Haes and Schuurman (op. cit.), three types of message were compared. One used the classic 'fear arousal' approach; the second was information based, deriving from the assumption that people do harmful things because they lack knowledge; and the third was a more loosely constructed life-skills approach concentrating on self-image and interpersonal relationships. Of the three approaches, only the latter had any beneficial effect in terms of changes in attitudes and drug-use. Nonetheless, it is an established fact that most people outside the drug-education area believe that fear arousal is the essential ingredient in drug education. For example, during the National Evaluation of Drug Education in Scotland (Coggans *et al.* 1989; Davies and Coggans 1991) discussion groups with secondary-school children revealed that they felt much of the Scottish Health Education Group's (SHEG's) health propaganda was lacking in what they saw as the essential fear ingredient; this despite the fact that SHEGs approach was based on the best principles and knowledge. In a similar vein, Finnigan (1988) asked members of the public to choose one of two messages as a model for tackling drug problems. One message used fear arousal, and concentrated on stressing terrible health consequences for drug users; the other used a social message, stressing the consequences of excessive drug use on family, friends, and children. Whilst the lay public almost unanimously favoured the fear-arousing health consequences message, a group of drug users reported that the message stressing social consequences was the one that made them think most seriously about changing their behaviour.

The message is clear. Lay perceptions of what is effective are quite simply out of step with research evidence. Consequently, one can neither design nor evaluate effective drug-education messages by reference to public opinion, and it is surprising that anyone should imagine that this is the case. Road-networks, power stations, space shuttles, bridges, are not designed according to public perceptions of what is likely to be effective, and it is difficult to see why drug-education should be any different.

## Drug education in schools

The first part of this chapter discussed the form that media campaigns have taken, with some exceptions, and the shortcomings that have been identified with fear arousal. One area of drug and AIDS education in which some attempt has been made to take account of research findings is in schools. In contrast to media campaigns, most drug education in schools eschews explicit fear arousal and has adopted the life-skills approach. Throughout the latter part of the 1980s school-based drug education developed from *ad hoc* approaches involving, if anything, leaflets, stern homilies and/or the occasional video. Most schools now have access to one or more standard drug education packages, which have advantages over more idiosyncratic attempts. These packages vary to some extent in their content, in their target age groups, and to a lesser extent in their educational approach; and there are a lot of them. Unfortunately, development of package-based drug education has taken on the appearance of the search for the Holy Grail; the perfect package which works all the time in all circumstances. While having drug education material available is convenient for teachers, packages have the disadvantage that insensitive or inexperienced teachers may feel that all they have to do is open the box and let prevention fill the room.

The success of a package depends on the dynamic interaction between teachers and pupils. This interaction seems best catered for in the life-skills approach. Life-skills type programmes include cognitive, affective, and behavioural components that attempt to:

(1) equip people with the interpersonal skills to resist direct social pressure to try/take drugs; and

(2) to positively influence affective or cognitive factors presumed to mediate likelihood of drug use, such as self-confidence or self-esteem, self-assertion, decision-making, and communication skills.

In addition, emphasis is often given to increasing awareness of alternatives. While some such programmes are based on social or personal inadequacy models of drug use, most accept that peer pressure or the desire to gain the social 'benefits' of becoming involved in local drug scenes are potent motivations towards drug use.

The rationale underlying the life-skills approach stems from the perspective which sees smoking, drinking, and other drug use as behaviour that is learned in a social context and is functional, rather than a sign that something is necessarily wrong. Furthermore, such behaviour results from a complex interaction between characteristics of the individual and characteristics of his or her social environment; (Jessor and Jessor 1977). Development of the life-skills approach has provided the theoretical and practical framework for new educational processes in drug education. Didactic, content heavy presentations in which young people were expected to passively assimilate anti-drug messages have been replaced by more dynamic, interactional methods involving role-play.

In addition, drug and AIDS education is increasingly integrated within the general curricular area of health and social education and, in more progressive schools, permeates the broader curriculum.

## The national evaluation of drug education in Scotland

This evaluation is the most recent large-scale study of the effects of drug education on the attitudes, knowledge, and behaviour of young people. Because of the timing of the evaluation it was possible to include subsamples whose exposure to drug education ranged from none to full coverage of drug education courses based on standard packages. In addition, young people were included whose drug education experience was based on some non-standard material such as leaflets or videos, and others who had taken part in drug education which consisted of partial use of standard packages. This range of drug education experience made it possible to test the hypothesis that more drug education would be more effective, in terms of various process and outcome measures.

In the Scottish evaluation 1197 pupils completed questionnaires concerning attitudes to drug use, perceptions of drug users, drug-related knowledge, and reports of drug use. (Other aspects of the evaluation addressed the effectiveness of in-service training of teachers in drug education, which is reported elsewhere (see Coggans *et al.* 1989, op cit.)

A series of process measures completed by pupils suggested that they had some positive perceptions of drug education. However, the outcome measures showed little impact of drug education. Nonetheless, it is worth noting that for the bulk of the pupils in the study illegal drug use was not part of their lives. Only low levels of use were reported, with higher levels for alcohol and tobacco. It is also important to note that drug education was not associated with increased drug use on any measure.

The actual impact of drug education, in terms of outcome, was assessed on a number of measures, including drug-related knowledge, attitudes, and self-reported drug use. Other background variables were taken into consideration: age, sex, and social class. Using regression analysis, the direct effect of each possible predictor was assessed while controlling for the confounding effects of the other background variables. The factors that had an effect on the outcome variables examined were, in descending order of importance, age, sex, social class, and drug education. Drug education only had an effect on drug-related knowledge.

The impact of drug education on drug use was neutral. However, levels of illegal drug use in the sample were very low. On the other hand, use of alcohol and tobacco was higher and, given that the intention of drug education in general was to have a broad impact in terms of all drugs, legal and illegal, it is of some interest that drug education did not have an effect on consumption of these (legal) drugs either.

The finding that drug education had a positive influence on levels of drug-related knowledge supported the views of most teachers that pupils knew more about drugs as a consequence of drug education. In the case of drug-related attitudes, however, the outcome did not support teachers' beliefs that pupils were more anti-drugs as a result of drug education.

Where self-reported drug-use was concerned the findings were again at variance with teachers' beliefs that pupils would be less likely to take drugs as a result of drug education. In summary, there was no detectable effect of drug education on reported levels of drinking, smoking, solvent abuse, or illegal drug use.

## Factors associated with good drug education practice

The evaluation nonetheless showed that there were important differences between schools and between individual teachers, in terms of their approach to health education issues. On the basis of case studies, which formed part of the overall project, it appeared that a number of factors were associated with good drug education practice. Overall, it seemed that effective teachers involved in drug and AIDS education would need:

(1) to show sensitivity to the importance of their role as credible sources of information; and

(2) to be aware of the importance of eschewing opinionated or moralizing input.

They would also need to be aware that the assumption that most young people who take drugs do so because they are in some way lacking in self-esteem, unusually susceptible to peer group influence, or are otherwise socially deficient is an inadequate explanation for a variety of reasons. While there is some evidence that people with positive health practices have higher self-esteem, neither of these attributes necessarily preclude an interest in or even use of drugs. These types of 'inadequacy' explanations of drug use sometimes look very much like stereotyping in disguise.

When teachers or parents endeavour to educate young people about the harm associated with drugs it is important that they avoid the mistake of presenting prejudice as fact. Young people, whether they take drugs or not, will possess a certain amount of factually based knowledge and/or some misconceptions. Furthermore, in some areas young people will be quite sophisticated in the their level of drug awareness. Irrespective of the degree of drug-related knowledge on the part of the young people concerned, when teachers or parents attempt to pass off misleading assertions about drugs as fact it will only detract from the success of their educational intervention. In some cases the effect may even he such as to negate sound information or advice previously presented.

One of the key concepts in much of todays drug and AIDS education is 'decision-making', intended to help young people to make the decision not to take drugs or to engage in unsafe practices. In reality decision-making sessions can easily degenerate into decision-implementation sessions, with the decision to say 'no' supplied by the teacher. Even in certain drug education packages emphasizing the life-skills approach, there were cases in which the message to simply say no to drugs was implicit or explicit in the package content. This can be counter-productive in two ways. First, and particularly in the hands of an insensitive teacher, telling young people not to do something that they find attractive runs counter to good educational practice. In other words, it will not work. Many young people will simply reject, or even resent, being told what to do. If this sort of insensitive approach is coupled with misleading information then the whole enterprise would be a waste of everybody's time. Second, this sort of drug education has nothing to offer young people who are already experimenting with drugs. If the guiding criterion of good drug education is to prevent people from coming to harm from drugs then simplistic 'just say no' type drug education does not have a place as part of a flexible range of drug education approaches.

Schools should be seen as systems in which individual young people will be influenced by different aspects of school life, directly or indirectly. In education generally there is a trend amongst forward looking teachers to recognize the importance of the whole-school as a caring and health promoting system. The role of the school as 'a caring community' and the importance of guidance as a whole school responsibility was extensively discussed in a recent document *More than feelings of concern* (Scottish Consultative Council on the Curriculum or, SCCC 1986). More recently the SHEG (recently replaced by HEBS—Health Education Board for Scotland) and the SCCC have produced a wide ranging set of proposals for the promotion of good health emphasizing the need for a whole-school approach which co-ordinates policy and permeates health education throughout the curriculum, including various aspects of the 'hidden curriculum' such as teacher/pupil interactions and the codes, standards, and values implicit in the way the school operates (Munn 1977; SHEG/SCCC 1990).

The whole-school perspective sees the school as a system in which different aspects of the institution can affect the success of health education. For example, success would be hindered by lack of clear policy to which all members of staff are party and by the lack of a management structure designed for the implementation of this policy. School policy in relation to drug and AIDS education must reflect the needs of young people to develop attitudes and to make the choices that are both relevant to their present circumstances and the basis for developing healthy lifestyles. Just as with alcohol education, which is generally approached from a harm-reduction perspective, we need to move towards 'all-drug' education that reflects the fact that for some people choosing to try drugs is both a rational and a positive choice. Perhaps the most important point to grasp is that young people who experiment with drugs, or use occasionally, will probably not encounter serious health consequences. Furthermore, the realization that in all likelihood illicit drug use will continue to be a feature of our society, has given rise to a growing body of support for policies that address the problems of living with drugs rather than vainly pursuing the ideal of a drug-free world. Perhaps until these issues are taken into account it is unrealistic to expect more from drug education than its current limited impact.

## References

Andrew Irving Associates Ltd (1986). Anti-misuse campaign: qualitative evaluation research report.

Botvin, G. J., Baker, E., Renick, N. I., Filazzola, A. D., and Botvin, E. M. (1984). A cognitive–behavioural approach to substance abuse prevention. *Addictive Behaviours*, **9**, 137–47.

Coggans, N., Shewan, D., Henderson, M., Davies, J. B., and O'Hagan, F. (1991). *National Evaluation of Drug Education in Scotland* (Research monograph no. 4). Institute for the Study of Drug Dependence (ISDD), London.

Cragg, Ross, and Dawson Ltd (1989). Misuse of drugs anti-injecting campaign: qualitative research report.

Davies, J. B. (1986). Unsolved problems with mass media drug education campaigns: three cautionary tales. *Health Education Research*, **1**, 69–74.

Davies, J. B. and Coggans, N. (1991). *The facts about adolescent drug abuse*. Cassell, London.

De Haes, W. and Schuurman, J. (1975). Results of an evaluation study on three drug education models. *International Journal of Health Education*, **18**, 4 (Supplement).

Engs, R. and Hanson, D. J. (1989). Reactance theory: a test with collegiate drinking. *Psychological Reports*, **64**, 1083–6.

Finnigan, F. (1988). Stereotyping in addiction: an application of the Fishbein-Ajzen theory to heroin using behaviour. PhD Thesis, University of Strathclyde.

Hammersley, R., Morrison, V., Forsyth, A., and Davies, J. B. (1990). *Heroin use and crime: a comparison of heroin users in and out of prison*. HMSO, London.

Hopson, B. and Scally, M. (1980). *Lifeskills teaching*. McGraw-Hill.

Jessor, R. and Jessor, S. (1977). *Problem behaviour and psychosocial development: a longitudinal study of youth*. Academic Press, London.

Kinder, B. N., Pape, N. E., and Walfish, S. (1980). Drug and alcohol education programs: a review of outcome studies. *International Journal of the Addictions*, **15**, 1035–54.

Rhodes, T. (1990) The politics of anti-drugs campaigns. *Druglink*, **5** (3), 16–18.

Royal College of Psychiatrists (1987). *Drug scenes*. The Royal College of Psychiatrists, London.

Schaps, E., Di Bartolo, R., Moskowitz, J. M., Palley, C., and Chugrin, S. (1981). A review of 127 drug abuse prevention program evaluations. *Journal of Drug Issues*, **11**, 17–44.

Scottish Central Committee on Guidance (1986). *More than feelings of concern: guidance and Scottish secondary schools*. SCCC, Edinburgh.

Scottish Education Department (1977). The structure of the curriculum in the third and fourth years of the Scottish secondary school. *The Munn Report*. HMSO, London.

SHEG/SCCC (1990). *Promoting good health: proposals for action in schools*. SHEG, Edinburgh.

Stubbington, C. (1990). Letter. *Druglink*, **5** (6), 19.

Swadi, H. (1988). Drug and substance use among 3333 London adolescents. *British Journal of Addiction*, **83**, 935–42.

## 25. HIV and drugs services— the challenge of change

*Steve Cranfield, Charlotte Feinmann, Ewan Ferlie, and Cathy Walter*

### Introduction: the organizational context

It must be remembered that although there is an innovative and vigorous non-statutory sector delivering British drugs services, many services are also delivered through the statutory sector [that is, the National Health Service (NHS)]. Changes in the drugs services can only be understood in relation to the changing context of the NHS as a whole throughout the 1980s, for example, the introduction of general management which by the late 1980s had cascaded down to service level.

The advent of the human immunodeficiency virus (HIV) posed a number of fundamental challenges to NHS drugs services. It raised the question of how major changes in the structure and style of services were to be achieved especially in institutional settings [Drug Dependence Units (DDUs)] seen as resistant to change. Although drugs services were increasingly seen as 'strategic', and able to attract more finance and attention, this also raised some more difficult issues. The traditional autonomy of drugs services was eroded: they were asked to collaborate more with other specialties; become part of a wider planning process; and were increasingly held to account for the large sums of earmarked finance which they managed to attract. The advent of HIV thus poses a number of fundamental organizational and managerial issues for NHS drugs services.

This article reports the experience of one high caseload District Health Authority (DHA) which developed as a leading centre for HIV/AIDS (acquired immune deficiency syndrome) services in the 1980s. The general picture was that the DHA rapidly and effectively developed a range of services for HIV/AIDS in the 1980s. Indeed, HIV/AIDS was seen as one of the District's success stories and there was a feeling of excitement and panache around in HIV work.

However, the response within drugs services was seen as the weak link in the chain and there was a danger that drugs services would become 'labelled' as the poor performers in the District because of continuing internal dissension and lack of clear leadership and an inability to seize the opportunity to influence their own future. Why should this flawed response have been apparent? What, in particular, are the ideological and organizational dynamics which help explain this disappointing outcome? These are the two key questions which this chapter addresses.

## HIV/AIDS and changing drug treatment policies

The advent of HIV/AIDS has presented a major challenge to drug treatment policies which had often been abstinence orientated. The Advisory Council on the Misuse of Drugs' (ACMD 1988) unambiguous declaration:

The spread of HIV is a greater danger to individual and public health than drug misuse. Accordingly, services which aim to minimise HIV risk behaviour by all means should take precedence in development plans.

accorded much more emphasis than hitherto on risk reduction and also attraction into treatment. Previously discarded policies such as maintenance and the prescription of injectable drugs are now being re-examined in the light of their potential to reduce HIV risk behaviours (Brewer 1990), although they remain highly controversial and difficult for established centres to accept.

DDUs are the institutions which have been central to the formulation of British drug policy and continue to sit, often uneasily, at the centre of the debate around drugs and AIDS. Like other psychiatric institutions, they sometimes resist attempts to move to a more community-based approach. So the adaptation of the DDU from a site-based psychiatric service to one which is more community orientated, and which incorporates HIV prevention, has proved problematic. Established staff often feel deskilled and threatened by proposed changes in role and become identified with particular treatment philosophies. A lively debate on prescribing policy is now evident (Strang 1990).

The emphasis is often now on an eclectic approach and 'flexibility.' However, some evidence suggests that in contrast to the changes evident in the development of a new generation of outreach, health care, and syringe-exchange services, real changes in DDU prescribing policies have been minimal (Ashton 1989), with the possible exception of preferential treatment of drug users with HIV.

The sudden advent of HIV/AIDS as a health care 'crisis' locally in 1982–84 posed difficult questions for two specialties, both of which could be regarded as equally marginal to the traditional concerns of acute medicine and as lacking organizational power: drug dependency and genito-urinary medicine (GUM). Yet GUM services were seen as responding rapidly and effectively; while drug services were seen as confused and fragmented. There were perceived to be special problems in drugs services which prevented an effective and coherent response.

## Case history

This case history describes one District's response to the HIV/AIDS epidemic by its drugs services in the mid- and late 1980s. The chronology is summarized in Table 25.1.

### Background

At the beginning of 1985, the drug dependency services were largely based on the DDU. This DDU was if anything seen as relatively innovative and open to research. There was an eclectic variety of out patient treatment activities including: prescribing, counselling, casework, rehabilitation, and social work support. In the mid-1980s and using central government funding, services were extended to meet the needs of younger polydrug users and drug using parents with childcare responsibilities. An Easy Access Centre (akin to a satellite clinic) was set up, and a Day Programme for families at the DDU. Staff were recruited from a mix of different professions and there was a strong ideology of multi-disciplinary working.

This consensual form of decision making was perhaps going to be difficult to make work effectively even under favourable circumstances. However, the well-established consultant psychiatrist, an adept fundraiser, left at a crucial time. His post was not effectively filled for 2 years, leaving a considerable power vacuum. Decisions were not taken, and there was great anxiety among staff who had come into the dependencies to work on a broader psychosocial model about possible 'remedicalization' of drugs services.

### The initial response

However, there were still proposals for post-HIV service development (for example, a needle exchange) coming up from nursing staff and a part-time Senior Lecturer working in the DDU. The role of nursing staff —as well as consultants—as would be innovators in drugs services is noticeable. However, these staff were on short-term contracts, not centrally placed within the organization's decision-making structure and still relatively inexperienced in committee work and lobbying (although they were rapidly to learn the tricks of this new trade). The newly introduced general management was also slow to see the potential of these proposals.

While there was support within the DDU for the value of such initiatives, it was also felt any needle exchange should be sited away from the DDU in order to attract clients and also to preserve the existing treatment patterns of the DDU.

**Table 25.1** Chronological summary of events

---

**1985**

May  Discussions with GUM clinic about HIV screening: DDU decides not to proceed.

June  DDU consultant leaves and is not replaced for a further 2 years.
Day Programme and Easy Access Centre open to clients.

Oct.  Visits from drug workers in New York increase DDU's urgency about AIDS prevention.
All assessments of clients now include AIDS information and limited risk reduction counselling.
Easy Access Centre institutes methadone prescribing.

**1986**

Feb.  DDU AIDS working party set up.
More intensive health education initiatives: concoms made available to clients but not needles and syringes.

March  Community pharmacists invited to DDU to discuss selling clean works to drug users.
Senior nurse at DDU helps set up Drugs Education Group at Terrence Higgins Trust.

May  Meetings with GUM clinic to operate clinical service at DDU.

July  Proposals for needle exchange and health team begin.

Nov.  GUM clinic starts up service at DDU.
Easy Access Centre builds up substantial caseload of drug users with HIV.

Dec.  Proposals for new services to AIDS committee by both DDU and GUM.

**1987**

Needle exchange started up at local A and E department.

Feb.  Dependencies Care Planning Team (DCPT) minutes: 'AIDS not on the agenda'. DCPT requires DDU to undertake major internal exercise to determine agency aims and objectives: this takes almost 1 year to complete.

June  Needle exchange opens to clients. Conflicts between Exchange and DDU over prescribing. Haemorrhage begins of staff from senior management in Mental Health Unit.

Sept.  GUM service withdraws from DDU and moves to Exchange.
New staff at MHU attempt to reconcile Exchange and DDU with little success.

Oct.  Health Improvement Team in post but premises take a further 4 months to complete.
Local authority freezes all social work posts at DDU.

**1988**

Feb.  Day Programme not refunded by Region and majority of clinical staff leave.
Continued friction between parts of service.

Oct.  Appointment of co-ordinator to DDU.

**1989**

Community Drug Team and Methadone Holding Programme set up but several delays in becoming operational.

---

Slowly links with power centres were being forged. A proposal was forwarded to the District AIDS Committee—in effect the key budget holder—in late 1986 requesting funding for an off-site needle exchange and a peripatetic health improvement team to replace the GUM team. But 'bottom up' innovation was also occurring spontaneously. For example, a 'pilot' needle exchange facility was set up in early 1987 at a local Accident and Emergency (A and E) Department by a drugs and alcohol liaison nurse, not managerially accountable to the DDU. This evolved into a big 'stand alone' needle exchange, again not managed by DDU staff.

Soon ideological conflict began to emerge between the two services. The needle exchange staff, feeling they were at the cutting edge of prevention, insisted on their right to assess appropriate treatment options for their clients and began putting pressure on the DDU to prescribe injectables. Staff at the DDU refused to devolve their function of independent assessment and blocked any move towards injectable prescribing. Consequently the exchange began to forge links with general practitioners (GPs) in the area and refused to refer clients to the DDU. The Exchange, far from acting as a conduit for new referrals to the DDU, appeared to have become a rival service. The Exchange quickly established a clear identity as well as a large number of clients (Carvell and Hart 1990). By comparison, the new Health Improvement Team (HIT), also funded from AIDS monies but sited next to the DDU, found itself providing a back up service to the DDU (Datt and Feinmann 1990) and did not establish any comparably clear aims and objectives.

## The careers of innovations: which services survived?

As the dependency services fragmented into a series of competing initiatives chasing the same clients, an eventual shake out was likely. The presence or absence of a strong team leader—often a nurse—was one important predictor of survival. The Easy Acccss Centre and the needle exchange were championed by nurses with good political links, and both established a reputation for an effective response. The Day Programme and HIT, by contrast, had no clear leaders or were unwilling to allow one to emerge. The Day Programme lobbied ineffectively at District level for refunding and by 1988 a majority of the staff employed on the Programme had left in the face of job uncertainty.

Indeed there often seemed to be a recurring cycle of intense staff effort, burn out and departure from the District. The rate of both clinical and managerial staff turnover was extremely high. A condition of organizational amnesia set in and valuable experience was lost. For example, the debate over prescribing was discussed without conclusion by a staff group unaware that it was rehearsing arguments which had taken place 10 years previously. The Exchange—even with its strong 'champion'—was also experiencing a high level of staff turnover and burnout.

Two further initiatives, a Community Drug Team (to encourage GPs to take on treatment of drug users and prescribe methadone) and a 'Low Threshold' Methadone Programme were initiated by the DDU in 1989. Money was once again made available at short notice, so the proposal was hurriedly routed to a special drugs/HIV allocation held at region and hence not integrated with the District's AIDS strategy.

Despite the appointment of a 'Co-ordinator' to the DDU in 1988, no accepted drugs and HIV strategy emerged. Teams had developed their own identity and loyalty: both the Exchange and HIT refused to communicate about clients to each other or to the DDU on the grounds that this would breach confidentiality. By 1990 pressure was emerging from general management for dependency services to identify their aims: the DDU was by now two-thirds funded by AIDS money and HIT and the Exchange completely dependent on AIDS money. The rest of the AIDS services began to question openly whether they were obtaining value for money.

## Who should be managing?

Although it was introduced as early as 1984/85 at District level, general management was slow to cascade down the Mental Health Unit and reach the drugs services. The DDU in turn was suspicious of 'management' (hence the number of 'Co-ordinators' employed), perhaps echoing the radical values of many of its staff and the difficulties of a multidisciplinary setting. However, by the late 1980s, general management was beginning to arrive on the scene. At operational level, new clinical manager posts were being created. At a more senior level, the apparent incoherence in drugs services increasingly signalled a strategic problem. Top down pressure for change began to be applied on drugs services for the first time, although the short length of management's attention span was a problem in the District, given the number of competing issues on management's agenda. So top down pressure was sometimes short lived, and failed to grasp many of the underlying difficulties.

## Case analysis—some emerging themes

This case study also throws up some more general themes in the management of change in drugs services.

How does change or innovation come about in organizations? One way—common throughout the 1980s—is from the top putting pressure on the periphery to change. But changes may also be bottom up in nature, emerging from front-line service providers (the development of community-based psychiatry in the 1970s might be an example of this).

Perhaps the most effective combination is a marriage between top down pressure and bottom up concern (Pettigrew *et al*. 1992): here the task facing managers is to allow or encourage innovation while preventing chaos.

One suspects that much of the ideology of front line workers in drugs services favours the bottom up model of innovation. Indeed, the case study suggests that the top tier seemed relatively inert throughout the period and disengaged from the issues. But perhaps the weakness of bottom up innovations was fragmentation, as the different innovations were not pulled together. So drugs workers may be wise to engage their managers to ensure that there is interest at this higher tier.

Paradoxically, an insistence on consensus based forms of decision making often coexisted with complaints about the lack of 'leadership'. What sort of 'leadership' was evident in the case study? Often the initiative passed to 'product champions' based at the periphery. Stocking (1985) has found the concept of a 'product champion' to be important in explaining why new schemes are taken up locally in the NHS. A 'product champion' may not be the same as a primary innovator or the conventional view of a 'strong leader' but rather someone with enthusiasm, stamina, and skill in working an organization. They may also need to have a position of status within the organization. Effective product champions do not need to be the people who invent an idea or product, or be the formal leaders of the organization, but they need to know how to get the idea through the system. The possession of organizational power is a critical factor here as there were clear examples of 'powerless' product champions in the case study unable to get proposals for change accepted.

Clearly and despite the multi-disciplinary setting, the consultant psychiatrist continues to play a crucial role as a holder of organizational power and in the absence of a full-time appointment a power vacuum emerged. In many schemes, nurse 'product champions' emerged instead. Several new teams, staffed largely by nurses, were created with their own distinctive working methods and aims. But the greater the number of teams, the greater the number of distinctive ideologies that have emerged and the greater the number of boundaries that became difficult to cross. Particular innovations sprang up, but such *ad hoc* innovation did not result in coherent strategic change. Nor was a real 'team' created who could act across service boundaries.

Clearly the advent of HIV/AIDS presented much more profound ideological issues for staff in drugs settings than, say, GUM settings. The tension between different ideological models is as apparent here as in previously studied psychiatric settings (Strauss *et al*. 1964). For long-standing staff, in particular, who had grown up with the abstinence based models of the 1970s, a switch to offering maintenance or injectables was a difficult act to perform. Meanwhile new groupings of staff were emerging outside the DDU, often younger and more radical, who rejected medically led models and had a firm attachment to harm minimization. Given these value conflicts, it was always going to be difficult to achieve coherence. Managing change in such circumstances is less about the re-drawing of structural boundaries and more about the aligning of values and models of practice.

Finally, we want to speculate whether this case study alerts us to the need for more study of DDUs as an organizational form. A number of organizational pathologies may be evident: the development of long-term patient 'careers'; the institutionalization of staff as well as patients; an emphasis on rules and procedures; the displacement of ends by means; and a reluctance to engage in real as opposed to apparent innovation. There may here be parallels with Goffman's work (1961) which in many ways is general rather than specific to 'asylums', notably in his develop-ment of a theory of 'total institutions' and of a model of doctor—patient interaction which can be applied in a number of different settings.

While it is obviously impossible to generalize from one case study such as this, it does provide interesting pointers. External forces (a perceived health care need and generous external funding) were not enough to force an effective response, and the micro politics of the organization played a key role. There may be some implications for localities which are considering how best to develop services in the 1990s.

The case study has highlighted the internal organizational barriers which blighted attempts to introduce new service strategies. It demon-strates the danger of fragmentation and of incoherence in service delivery, springing from the different value systems which may be in conflict and possibly also the nature of the DDU as an institution. It suggests ways of launching and managing innovation, especially the importance of combining top down pressure and bottom up concern.

'Leadership' may be more than the conventional view of a single leader (perhaps a charismatic consultant) or a strong general management hierarchy, although these may have an important role. Front-line workers such as nurses emerged as important 'product champions' in the case study but their talents were not pooled. There might be a case for collective as well as individual leadership in such complex settings, taking the form of a mixed (but purposeful) team which could cross conven-tional boundaries. There is also a need for active strategic management across HIV/drugs services as a whole.

Finally, the case study highlights the need for particular organizational and managerial competencies in the management of such change, which may have implications not only for management training but also the medical curriculum, given the key role of the consultant and the need to bring on the consultants of the future. These might include: the ability to build a team; management of change skills; the capacity to think strategically; and a competence to act as a motivator and animator of patients and staff.

## References

Advisory Council on the Misuse of Drugs (1988). *AIDS and drug misuse, Part 1*. HMSO, London.

Ashton, M. (1989). HIV fails to galvanise clinics. *Druglink*, **4** (3), 5.

Brewer, C. (1990). Intravenous methadone maintenance: maximising the benefit, minimising the disadvantages, presentation at the First International Conference on the Reduction of Drug Related Harm. Liverpool, April 9–12 1990.

Carvell, A. M. and Hart, G. J. (1990). Help seeking and referrals in a needle exchange: a comprehensive service to injecting drug users. *British Journal of Addiction*, **85**, 235–40.

Datt, N. and Feinmann, C. (1990). Providing health care for drug users? *British Journal of Addiction*, **85**, 1571–5.

Goffman, E. (1961). *Asylums: essays on the social situation of mental patients and other inmates*. Penguin, London.

Pettigrew, A. M., Ferlie, E. B., and McKee, L. (1992). *Shaping strategic change*. Sage, London.

Stocking, B. (1985). *Initiative and inertia: case studies in the NHS*. Nuffield Provincial Hospitals Trust, London.

Strauss, A., Schatzman, L., Bucher, R., Elrich, D., and Sabstin M. (1964). *Psychiatric ideologies and institutions*. Free Press, London.

Strang, J. (1990). The roles of prescribing. In *AIDS and drug misuse: the challenge for policy and practice in the 1990s* (ed. J. Strang and G. V. Stimson), pp. 142–52. Routledge, London.

# 26. The relationship between the State and local practice in the development of national policy on drugs between 1920 and 1990

*Gerry V. Stimson and Rachel Lart*

There never was such a thing as the 'British System' for dealing with drug problems. There was never a 'system' in that there was no grand idea, no grand plan, and no systematic practice. Instead, there was a loose and shifting collection of ideas and practices, at times appearing firm and definite, becoming elusive on closer examination. It was not 'British', because although policy documents and legislation applied throughout the United Kingdom, this hid a distinctive and growing national and regional diversity.

What was distinctive was not the overall plan, the idea or the practices, so much as the relationship between the state in the form of central government, and the various professions and groups which have claimed an interest in drug problems. What came to be called the 'British System' was really a reflection of the way social and health policy emerged within the United Kingdom. As such, we have to understand drugs policy, not as an entity in its own right, but as part of the broader trends in social policy.

## From the 1920s to the 1960s

The 'British System' was created by its commentators. The term was coined by E. W. Adams, who had served as secretary to the Rolleston Committee and helped draft its report in 1926 (Adams 1937). But in the United Kingdom, we really discovered that we had a 'system', when our approach to drug problems became useful ammunition for protagonists in the United States. Between the late 1940s and the early 1960s, they strongly argued against the criminalization of addiction and looked favourably at the supposed medicalization of drug addiction in the

United Kingdom. A series of UK watchers and visitors, including Rufus King (1972), Alfred Lindesmith (1965), and Edwin Schur (1963), thought that we did things better. In essence they argued that we had only a minor problem with the major drugs of abuse such as heroin and cocaine, because our addiction problems had been contained within a system of medical treatment. We were justly proud and flattered by their comments and complacently and inaccurately agreed with their wisdom.

Their, and our, interpretations exaggerated the significance of the report of the Rolleston Committee, which had legitimized the medical treatment of addiction (Departmental Committee on Morphine and Heroin Addiction 1926). The Rolleston Committee considered that it was appropriate, in certain circumstances, for doctors to prescribe drugs of addiction to those addicted to them. The Rolleston Committee Report set the scene for the next 40 years, and remained the only point of reference for those seeking to understand the formal underpinnings of our approach. There was no other document to read: this is not to suggest that many in fact read it.

There is a certain irony that sociological commentators from the United States argued for the benefits of the medicalization of drugs problems, when a few years later other sociological commentators would argue so strongly against medical dominance.

There is a second irony in that the description of the 'British System' as primarily a medical (and hence many would claim benign) approach, was only a partial description of United Kingdom policy. As Berridge has pointed out, the medical response to drug problems always operated within a penal and legal framework (1984). Since the 1920 Dangerous Drugs Act, we could, and did, send people to prison for the unauthorized possession of dangerous drugs. However, many commentators on the 'British System', in focusing on the medical involvement, rarely gave much attention to the penal response.

The approach outlined by Rolleston was class-based. It was designed for the respectable and deserving addict. It was geared to the therapeutic addict—the iatrogenic victim—whose addiction was an accidental side-effect of medical treatment, and to the 'professional' addict, which was official euphemism for doctors, nurses, and veterinary surgeons who had become addicted through raiding their drugs cabinet or writing false prescriptions.

The medical approach outlined by Rolleston began to fall apart during the 1960s with the emergence of the unrespectable and undeserving addict, who had started to use drugs for fun and excitement, and who continued for self-gratification. Hedonistic drug use did not fit easily into the image of drug addict as victim of medical practice or of occupational hazard.

The policy disintegrated in face of the rising numbers of youthful heroin and cocaine users in the 1960s (Stimson and Oppenheimer 1982). Forty years after Rolleston, it was time to lock again at British Drugs Policy. Of the two reports produced by the Brain Committee in the 1960s, the second was the new landmark (Interdepartmental Committee on Drug Addiction 1965). The Brain Committee did not abandon a medical approach to the treatment of drug addiction, but argued that there were some flaws in allowing general medical practitioners to pre-scribe heroin and cocaine to people addicted to these drugs. Whilst general practitioners may have been willing to treat the respectable addict, only a handful would take on the youthful heroin addict. Some of those who did were dedicated and deserved the respect of their colleagues who shunned this work; others were of more doubtful motivation and judgement, and quite clearly some were being conned by their patients.

The problem for the Brain Committee was how to maintain medical interest but introduce some control over medical practice. This it did by taking the treatment of addiction out of the hands of the general practi-tioner, and into the hands of, for the most part, psychiatrists. This 'psychiatrization' of the problem fitted well with the growth of psychiatry in the 1960s.

On paper this was still a medical approach. The caveat as always, was the continuing role of the penal and legal system. But medicine remained centre stage by dominating the discourse on the nature of drug problems. Just as in the 1920s, the experts of the 1960s were doctors.

## Distinctive features of the medical involvement in drug problems

Both US and UK commentators pointed to the significance of a medical involvement. For some it was a particular medical practice that was important, specifically the ability to prescribe drugs such as heroin to addicts. This was not—and is still not—allowed in many countries. Trebach (1984) indicated how matter-of-factly the British medical pro-fession was allowed to use a drug which invited horror and condemna-tion in the United States. It has always been possible for any medical practitioner to prescribe heroin in the treatment of normal medical conditions (and is still so today). Although prescribing heroin to addicts was a British claim to fame, such prescribing was all but over by about 1970. The major period of prescribing heroin was in the 1960s and during the first couple of years of the drug dependency clinics which had been established post-Brain in 1968. From then on methadone was the drug of choice.

For other commentators it was not prescribing *per se* that was im-portant, but a distinctive relationship between doctor and patient. Rather than being required to treat all addict patients the same way, the British medical practitioner could use his or her discretion in the kind of treatment offered. Patients were treated as individuals, rather than slotted into an inflexible programme. It is indicative in this period that the United Kingdom did not have treatment 'programmes', and that there was little administrative and legal guidance on the treatment of addiction. Contrast this with the United States, where methadone programmes were subject to compendious regulation.

Commentators who pointed to the relationship between doctor and patient were perhaps more accurate in their assessment than those who pointed to the actual practices. Any visitor to a British Drug Dependency Clinic would have been bewildered by the array of treatment regimens and the inability of the consultant to describe the treatment approach in simple terms. Eclecticism and pragmatism rule the day. The other side of the coin was that in this flexible situation, no one would force a medical practitioner to prescribe for addicts. As a result there were parts of the country where there was no prescribing.

## Drug policy, the State, and the medical profession

This special relationship with the patient is the clue to understanding what was distinctive about the approach to drug problems in this period. It was not that doctors were able to prescribe heroin, but the fact that they had the choice to do so or not.

The medical approach to drug problems resulted from an accommodation between the state and a powerful profession. The claim that the medical profession made to be free from control by the state or by patients, and to be a self-regulating occupational body, meant that as an occupation it had extremely high levels of autonomy. In the tussle between the State's desire to do something about the drug problem, and the medical profession's desire to retain its power, clinical freedom emerged unscathed.

It was doctors who were called on as experts on their own behalf in the 1920s and again in the 1960s and to give judgement on legitimate medical practice, and later to produce guidelines for good medical practice.

That this was the case in the 1920s should not be surprising, given the dominance of private medical practice. It might seem surprising in the post-1948 nationalized National Health Service (NHS), where there would appear to be more opportunity for central regulation over clinical activity.

However, this was not the case until very recently. Up to the introduction of general management in 1984–85, there was no real mechanism for central control of peripheral activity within the NHS. Indeed such mechanisms were explicitly rejected at the start, with Bevan's view that the NHS was there to provide the framework which would leave doctors free to do their work. The only means of regulation that central government had was that of overall budgetary control. Prior to the 1974 reorganization, management was conspicuous by its absence; administrators' and treasurers' roles were to administer and keep financial order, not to take a proactive line in the development of services. Clinical autonomy, the medical practitioner's right to exercise his or her professional judgement in the choice of treatment for any individual patient was not only protected within the NHS, but enhanced by the removal of concern over the immediate financial consequences of decisions. Professional judgement meant the application of medically accepted knowledge, but left a wide margin for individual variation in practices and techniques. What actually happened within the NHS was the sum total of individual consultants' decisions, rather than a result of defined policy aims.

The period of consensus management following the 1974 reorganization of the NHS tended to reinforce rather than curb this medical dominance, with the real locus of power frequently being outside the management team and in the hands of individual clinicians (Royal Commission on the National Health Service 1978). It was only in the mid-1980s that there was serious attempt, with the introduction of the Griffiths-style general managers, to 'shift the frontier of control' between central government and the medical profession (Harrison 1988).

In the field of addiction, this emphasis on clinical autonomy allowed for the variety of treatments (including no treatment at all) through the whole period from the 1920s through to the late 1960s. There was no Department of Health or Home Office policy-making body to plan a British strategy. The Home Office Drugs Branch played an important behind the scenes role from the 1930s and had powers under various dangerous drugs legislation to call aberrant doctors to order, but in practice it rarely invoked formal sanctions, preferring instead, a gentlemanly British nudge and a nod.

Policy making in this period was done by calling together committees of 'the great and the good'. At times of crisis, the unpaid volunteer professional class was called on to make judgement and steer the country in the right direction. The period is marked by *ad hoc* committees— first Rolleston and later Brain. There was no politicization of drugs problems, indeed in true gentlemanly British fashion, politics were excluded from debate.

Jeffery Weeks, in discussing the wider social reconstruction of morality that went on in the 1950s and 1960s, illustrates this with a comparison of the debates over issues such as homosexuality and abortion in the United States and Britain. In the United States the debate was politicized and employed the language of rights and of appeals to justice within the framework of a defined constitution. In this the State had a role in positively affirming an individual's rights. In Britain the debate was about privacy; defining the boundaries between private and public behaviour, and limiting the State's interference. The US style demanded 'drama and national campaigns', while the British style was one of 'delicate manoeuvring, parliamentary persuasion and political stealth' (Weeks 1985), an essentially private world where policy was made by accommodation between experts and civil servants.

The establishment of the Advisory Council on the Misuse of Drugs (ACMD) in 1971 continued in this vein. Although meeting on an ongoing basis rather than convened in response to crises, its composition reflected that tradition of British Committee membership and its debate was characterized by a lack of politics and an ethic of politeness. The fact that it was an 'Advisory' committee also indicates the loose British approach to policy making. The Advisory Committee could advise, but Ministers did not have to listen.

The first conclusion is that drugs policy emerged from a particular relationship between the State and the medical profession. What has been identified *vis à vis* the medical profession and drugs reflected more generally the relationship between the State and the medical profession and thus what was possible in medicine in Britain. It also reflected, as is argued below, particular relations between the Centre and periphery in social and health policy.

## Drug policy in the 1980s

There were several changes in policy and practice in the period from the beginning of the 1980s. The first significant feature was the decline in centrality of medicine in the response to drug problems, in comparison with earlier times. Drug Dependency Clinics and the medical treatment of drug problems continued, but there was a shift in balance and doctors no longer dominated the discourse on drug problems (Stimson 1987).

Throughout the 1980s there was the growth of new drugs agencies, funded under the Central Funding Initiative. In fact, the majority of drugs agencies started work from the mid-1980s onwards (MacGregor *et al.* 1991). As indicated elsewhere (Stimson and Lart 1990; also see Chapter 00) this resulted in many new occupational groups being drawn into working with drug users, freed to some extent from preoccupations with medical treatment and abstinence. The multiplicity and diversity of institutional sites enabled the rapid development of a new discourse on drug problems, which came to be seen as 'harm minimization'. Although much of the medical work done from the 1920s could also be described as harm minimization, it was not so described at the time. This concept is a key to understanding a new way of viewing drug problems and dealing with drug users.

The multiplicity of institutional sites, and the prevailing discourse on harm minimization, were important precursors to the response to the acquired immune deficiency syndrome (AIDS) and the human immuno-deficiency virus (HIV) (Stimson and Lart 1990). In the period from 1986 when AIDS became a prominent issue, many drugs agencies were able to respond readily and rapidly to the problem (Stimson 1990). The willingness to discuss and adopt many new strategies—such as syringe distribution and syringe exchange, new ways of working with methadone, an hierarchy of objectives, and innovative educational approaches—could only have emerged given these pre-conditions. It is significant that much of what came to be considered commonplace in the current British response to AIDS and drugs misuse was considered anathema in the United States. It would not be possible for a government committee in the United States to make a statements such as those made by the ACMD, and to retain its credibility. The guiding statement from ACMD was that AIDS was much more of a threat to individual and public health than drugs (ACMD 1988).

## Drug policy, the State, and the new drugs strategy

There was considerable flexibility in response to HIV and AIDS, much innovation, and adaptability to local circumstances. At first sight, this might seem to be a repetition of the story of professional autonomy and practical freedom. Indeed, the 1980s allowed for a high level of freedom for workers in these new agencies. However, we would suggest that this has to be understood in terms of the new relationship between the State and health and social welfare in the 1980s. There was a new balance between central direction and local activity. The new situation reflected the ideas of market-place Thatcherism, coupled with a claim to non-interference at a local level in order to encourage local account-ability. The claimed demise of the 'nanny state' in fact hid a new, and perhaps stronger, form of centralism which operated mainly through control of resources.

This balance, made up of new and complex central/peripheral relations has been noted by several commentators. In the early 1980s the emphasis was on devolving responsibility for managerial decisions, as outlined in the policy document *Care in action* [Department of Health and Social Security (DHSS) 1981], and exemplified by the abolition of the Area Health Authority tier of management and the creation of the District Health Authorities. Smaller and smaller units were to make more deci-sions about implementation of policy. Allsop (1984) commented that 'the strategy is to diffuse responsibility for policy change to the periphery', while Parston (1988), more positively, noted a 'sense of local determination' on the part of the new Health Authorities. The NHS was no longer a monolithic structure with uniform patterns of administration, but demonstrated local variations. For example with the implementation of the Griffiths' Management Inquiry, each District was free to determine its own structure and pattern of units and management. This period, the early 1980s, was one of fragmentation.

Following this, there was the development of a new kind of centralism. The District Health Authorities and then the Griffiths' general managers were supposed to be close enough to local services and local needs to make decisions in a way that was sensitive to local variations and conditions. However, the pressures of financial constraints and the use of controlling techniques such as individual performance review and performance-related pay tended to make management more upward than outward looking. Devolved responsibility turned out in practice to mean increased accountability, and particularly financial accountability. There was also a growing tendency for central government to tell the periphery how to carry out this 'devolved responsibility' by the issuing of guidelines, directives, and circulars. An American commentator noted this trend, describing how, over a 6 week period, the paper thus distributed to each District amounted to a stack eight inches high (Light 1990).

This new relationship between the central State and local practice in health care had three elements. First, the power of medicine was challenged and the extent to which the medical profession would act as *de facto* policy makers was curtailed. Secondly, the unified structure of the NHS was broken and, below District level, structures and power relations varied, resulting in diversity and a degree of local autonomy. Finally, the state found more sophisticated ways to exert central control than its former method of overall budgetary limits; the issuing of directives and exhortations, coupled with tighter mechanisms of accountability.

In the drugs field these three elements unravelled in particular ways.

First, as noted above, there was the displacement from centre stage of a purely medical perspective on drug use and the drug user. Second, fragmentation and local diversity in service provision were especially characteristic of drug services. The nearest thing to national plans for service provision were the various reports of the Advisory Council on the Misuse of Drugs [(ACMD 1982; ACMD 1984; ACMD 1988; ACMD 1989)] and the health circulars following them which, in true British style, 'drew attention to' their recommendations.

Linked to this was a third element; increased centralism. In the drugs field this was exemplified by the fact that the government began to play an active role in drugs policy making and drugs strategy. This could be seen in the establishment of the Ministerial Group on the Misuse of Drugs, an inter-ministerial committee with representatives from all government departments who had some interest in the drugs problem. It was only under the Conservative administration that a British government has produced a strategy document on tackling drug misuse. Prior to this period, there were no formal planning mechanisms. It was also found in the funding mechanisms, such as the Central Funding Initiative, and the earmarked allocation of money given for AIDS and drugs. In both, the approach was to encourage local activity by the allocation of resources, coupled with a central but brief statement about the desirability and nature of certain services, but then with a lack of oversight and control over the actual nature and day to day work of those services.

This centralism in drugs services and policy did not, yet, involve the financial constraints that constituted its coercive element elsewhere in health services. While services could have operated better and reached more clients if they had more money, it has also to be acknowledged that drug services did, in the 1980s, receive unprecedented levels of finance. The nature of that finance is crucial to this discussion. It was delivered in the form of the Central Funding Initiative and, since 1986, earmarked allocations. The use of these was intended to reinforce the view that drug services were regarded at central level as a national priority; money for them was to be protected from the local politics of allocation. In the wider view then, finance for drug services reflected the increasing centralism within health policy. At the level of practice, the diverse nature of services as they developed reflected the lack of central control over day to day work and procedures.

Thus, the setting for the new drugs policy was a particular social policy framework that allowed for strong central direction accompanied by local autonomy. How this balance between central control and local activity was to be affected by the next stage of NHS reforms from 1990 onwards must form part of a further analysis.

## In conclusion

It is not the particular ideas and practices which are the key to understanding the British response to drugs, so much as the framework in which these ideas and practices are allowed to emerge.

For much of the time from the 1920s through to the 1980s drugs policy was shaped by a particular relationship between the State and medicine. The general high levels of autonomy accorded to the medical profession in this period allowed doctors to hold centre stage as experts on addiction, to define drug problems in medical terms (as some kind of disease), and allowed them to choose suitable treatments. In the 1980s, drugs policy was shaped by the new relations that developed between the State and medical and social services, with robust central influence, accompanied by an emphasis on local expertise and decision-making.

Future students should cease to abstract drugs policy from the wider stream of British social policy and the structures in which that policy is produced. Policy about and services for drug users are not a special arena with a unique set of relations between central government and Health Authorities, professions and agencies in the field. The nature and style of relations between the State and the medical profession, and of central/peripheral relations would appear familiar, if somewhat exaggerated, to many general commentators on the NHS.

## References

ACMD (Advisory Council on the Misuse of Drugs) (1982). *Treatment and re-habilitation*. Report. HMSO, London.

ACMD (1984). *Prevention*. Report. HMSO, London.

ACMD (1988). *AIDS and drug misuse, Part 1*. Report. HMSO, London.

ACMD (1989). *AIDS and drug misuse, Part 2*. Report. HMSO, London.

Adams, E. W. (1937). *Drug addiction*. Oxford University Press, London.

Allsop, J. (1984). *Health policy and the National Health Service*. Longman. London.

Berridge, V. (1984). Drugs and social policy: the establishment of drug control in Britain 1900–1930. *British Journal of Addiction*, **79**, 17–29.

Departmental Committee on Morphine and Heroin Addiction (1926). *Report*. HMSO, London.

DHSS (1981). *Care in action*. HMSO, London.

Interdepartmental Committee on Drug Addiction (1961). *Report*. HMSO, London.

Interdepartmental Committee on Drug Addiction (1965). *Second report*. HMSO, London.

King, R. (1972). *The drug hang-up: America's fifty-year folly*. Norton, New York.

Light, D. (1990). Biting hard on the research bit. *Health Service Journal*. 25 October, 1604–5.

Lindesmith, A. R. (1965). *The addict and the law*. Indiana University Press, London.

MacGregor, S., Ettorre, B., Coomber, R., Crosier, A., and Lodge, H. (1991). *Drug services in England and the Impact of the Central Funding Initiative*. Report. Institute for the Study of Drug Dependence, London.

Parston, G. (1988). Evolution—general management. In *Reshaping the National Health Service* (ed. R. Maxwell). Policy Journals, Berkshire.

Royal Commission on the National Health Service (1978). *Research Paper No. 2: Management of financial resources in the National Health Service*. HMSO, London.

Schur, E. M. (1963). *Narcotic addiction in Britain and America*. Tavistock, London.

Stimson, G. V. (1987). British drug policies in the 1980's: a preliminary analysis and suggestions for research. *British Journal of Addiction*, **82**, 477–88.

Stimson, G. V. (1990). AIDS and HIV: the challenge for British drug services (Fourth Thomas James Okey Lecture). *British Journal of Addiction*, **85, 3**, 329–39.

Stimson, G. V. and Lart, R. A. (1991). HIV, drugs and public health in

England: new words, old tunes. *International Journal of the Addictions*, **26** **(12)**, 1263–77.

Stimson, G. V. and Oppenheimer, E. (1982). *Heroin addiction, treatment and control in Britain*. Tavistock, London.

Trebach, A. S. (1982). *The heroin solution*. Yale University Press, New Haven.

Weeks, J. (1985). *Sexuality and its discontents*. Routledge and Kegan Paul, London.

## 27. The 'British System': visionary anticipation or masterly inactivity?

*John Strang and Michael Gossop*

The plain truth of the matter is that there is no British System. There is no explicit set of rules or central policy underpinning an organized system to which observed benefits can be attributed. So one might conclude that there is no point in any further examination of 'the British System'. However, despite the lack of formal structure over the years, there may nevertheless be certain characteristics of the British approach, and certain components within the British responses which deserve special study. There may be no clear system; it may not be particularly British; but there may well be benefits to be accrued from an examination of policy in Britain—even if the policy has often been policy by default.

In looking back at Britain's national response to its drug problems during the twentieth century it is difficult not to look across the Atlantic and to make comparisons with US drug policy which has been so influential on the international scene. It is not only that US government expenditure on drug policy far exceeds UK expenditure, it is also that the governing ideas behind the different policies have often been remarkably different. This was evident during the early years of the century when the courses of British and US drug policy diverged with the passage of the 1916 Harrison Act in the USA and the 1926 Rolleston Report in the UK. These differences have surfaced again recently with the British interest in identifying harm-reduction measures which are directed towards improving the well-being of the ongoing drug user. This harm-reduction approach stands in stark contrast to the 'zero tolerance option', 'user accountability', and the US goal of a 'drug free America' (Kleber 1993).

Much attention has been focused upon the differences between British and American approaches in the period between the 1920s and the 1960s, when the USA pursued a policy reliant solely on control measures. Over these years, the UK, with its much smaller injecting drug problem, pursued the path of medicalization of the condition of drug dependence, even though the Home Office used its influence to try to push Britain towards a similar system as the USA and a reliance upon an entirely penal approach with criminal sanctions against both users and prescribing doctors (Berridge 1984).

During the 1960s, both the UK and the USA re-examined and revised their policies. America 'discovered' methadone maintenance through the work of Dole and Nyswander, and methadone maintenance programmes were established. Such substitution programmes found acceptance from practitioners, politicians, and the general public, on the basis that they represented a 'treatment' of the underlying 'disease' (the manifestations of which included social, economic, and criminal disturbances). In the UK, a different re-examination was taking place, with the prescribing of drugs being seen as a 'bait' with which to 'capture' the addict into the treatment programme. The prescription of heroin or methadone was seen more as a pragmatic and instrumental measure and not in the same narrow 'treatment' light as in America. At the same time, US programmes developed in a more business-like manner and were largely constructed along the lines of public policy or public health measures, whereas UK treatment was still delivered in the paradigm of individual treatment negotiated between doctor and patient.

Such differences have tended to become more clearly evident with the review prompted by the advent of the human immunodeficiency virus (HIV) and the acquired immune deficiency syndrome (AIDS). In the UK, a great deal of attention has been paid to the development of strategies which may lead the drug user into less harmful patterns of drug use— and many of these approaches have been covered by the broad term 'harm reduction'. The concept of the health-conscious addict has been considered (Stimson 1990) and it has been possible to consider health care interventions in the context of a 'well users clinic' in a way similar to consideration of a 'well woman's clinic' (Strang *et al.* 1989). In such a therapist/client or doctor/patient relationship, the provision of methadone is not seen as the treatment in itself but as part of a package which is designed to encourage the patient/client to approach and continue to attend the treatment service. In contrast, in the USA, the entirety of drug-taking behaviour is seen increasingly within an illness paradigm, which not only lends legitimacy to treatment measures and increases the likelihood of public and political support, but also leads to drug prescribing (such as methadone) being seen again as 'treatment', even though there is clear acknowledgement of the considerable extent to which the context of treatment delivery has such a considerable effect on the benefit of the treatment.

It has not been the way of things in the UK to construct formal drugs policy. Policy changes are often seen to have occurred only with the benefit of hindsight. Paradoxically, the most distinctive characteristic of the British System over the years may be the lack of any defining characteristic. Amongst the (probably unintended) benefits of this approach may be the avoidance of the pursuit of extreme solutions and hence an ability to tolerate imperfection, alongside a greater freedom, and hence, a particular capacity for evolution (Addiction Research Unit 1976).

Policy and practice have certainly changed over the years. Whilst there are some points of change which relate to new legislation (such as the introduction of the new drug laws in 1967), a distinctive feature of the evolution of policy in the UK is that it has more often been achieved through the preparation of closet policy. For example the Rolleston Committee, the Brain Committee, the Wayne Committee and, for the last 20 years, the Advisory Council on the Misuse of Drugs (ACMD) have prepared recommendations for consideration by the Government through their special reports. Often these do not become official policy, but nevertheless they inform the process of development of services in the years that follow. Thus the 1982 *Treatment and rehabilitation* Report from ACMD expressed the views that led to the development of community services and community drug teams throughout the 1980s; and the *AIDS and drug misuse* Reports from the ACMD (1988, 1989) played a similar role in relation to the new HIV-conscious drug services of the late 1980s and 1990s.

## The different ages of the 'British System'

Perhaps with the benefit of that most useful of scientific devices, the *retrospectoscope*, it may be possible to discern certain distinct periods during which different variations of the 'British System' have been evident.

### The Rolleston era

A relationship certainly existed between opium and the people long before the 1920s (cf. Berridge and Edwards 1981), but it was probably not until the publication of the Rolleston Report in 1926 that a distinctly 'British System' can be identified. At a time when the early prescribing clinics in the USA had all been closed down, Britain was moving along an altogether different path, with opiate addiction becoming the legitimate domain of medical practice (and hence prescribing). As much as anything else, it is perhaps this contrast between the British and American paths which defines the 'British System' of this time.

It is clear that the numbers of opiate addicts in the UK were extremely low during these years. Typically a few hundred cases came to official attention each year, of whom a substantial proportion were either health care professionals or 'therapeutic addicts' (a term used to describe

individuals who became addicted to the drug during a period of therapeutic use—for pain relief, for example). What is far less certain is
whether any causal relationship can be identified between the post-
Rolleston 'British System' and the absence of an opiate drug problem.
Some commentators have confidently attributed many of the benefits to
the policy and practice approaches of the day (for example, Schur 1966;
Trebach 1982), whilst others have referred to this 'period of non-policy'
(Smart 1984) or to a period during which '... there was no system, but
as there was very little in the way of misuse of drugs, this did not
matter' (Bewley 1975). Downes (1977) concluded that the 'British System'
had been '... well and truly exposed as little more than masterly inactivity
in the face of what was an almost non-existent addiction problem'.

## Crisis and review in the 1960s

With the migration of North American (mostly Canadian) injecting
opiate addicts to the UK in the late 1950s and early 1960s, and with the
emergence of a new and youthful drug-taking culture, the structural
timbers of the old 'British System' began to creak. Substantial numbers
of young injecting drug takers began to be seen for the first time, and
the existing 'British System' was failing to limit the spread of this new
pattern of heroin addiction, and actually appeared to be making matters
worse. The second Brain Report put forward three linked proposals—
restrictions on the prescribing of heroin and cocaine, the establishment
of drug treatment centres, and the introduction of the notification system.

New guidelines from the Ministry of Health defined the role of the
drug treatment centres as the provision of appropriate treatment to drug
addicts, whilst also '... containing the spread of heroin addiction by
continuing to supply this drug in minimum quantities where this is
necessary in the opinion of the doctor; and where possible to persuade
addicts to accept withdrawal treatment' (Ministry of Health 1967). Thus,
as Stimson and Oppenheimer (1982) subsequently commented, the new
treatment centres were given the twin responsibilities of medical care
and social control.

In their early days, the new clinics prescribed injectable heroin in
doses which were similar to the private prescribing doctors whom they
replaced, although the average daily dose of prescribed heroin then fell
steadily over the next few years. In their first flush of clinical practice,
the clinics also prescribed injectable cocaine, but stopped this quite
quickly within the first year of operation. Gradually injectable forms
of heroin were replaced by injectable methadone as the preferred drug
of prescription (preferred by the clinic doctors, for whom injectable
methadone was perhaps more closely aligned with treatment and could
also be taken at less frequent intervals). The original intention had been
to draw all addicts into treatment, thereby containing the 'epidemic'.

However, even during these early years of the clinics, there was evidence of a large population of drug users who remained out of contact with the new treatment centres. Blumberg *et al*. (1974) reported that, even by 1970/71, addicts attending the new treatment centres were reporting that only half of their drug-using friends were in treatment.

## The middle years of the clinics: care or control?

The optimistic original view had been that, as a result of frequent contact with the new treatment centre, the drug user would be led to the realization that they should give up using drugs. However, in practice the effect of the regular contact and a secure supply of pharmaceutical injectable drugs often led to an institutionalization of drug use, with the addict becoming confirmed in their addiction, albeit a clinic-maintained addiction. As Edwards commented as early as 1969, 'the result of such a humane policy may sadly be the reverse of that intended: the drug taker is protected from all adverse social consequences of his addiction, and all motivation for withdrawal is sapped'. During the 1970s the clinic staff and especially the psychiatrists who were responsible for prescribing drugs lost enthusiasm—first for prescribing heroin and then for prescribing any injectable preparations (Gossop 1990). As the initial optimism was replaced by realism or even rebound pessimism, the London drug clinics appear to have undergone a collective existential crisis in the mid-1970s. Was their prime responsibility care of the individual patient, or the social control of addiction?

The hope that the prescribing of supplies of National Health Service injectable drugs would prevent the development of any black market appeared to be flawed, and was consequently largely abandoned—certainly at the broader policy level, although probably not at the individual level. Individual treatment or care came to be the dominant raison d'être of the drug treatment centres, whose work was increasingly managed by the multidisciplinary teams employed in the drug clinics. Oral methadone became the most commonly prescribed drug for new patients, and thus a therapeutic apartheid was created between small numbers of patient who had attended in the early years of the clinics (many of whom continued to receive injectable drugs) and the more recent addicts who were usually offered only oral methadone. It would appear that this combined shift in prescribing practice and the introduction of therapeutic contracts served to give disillusioned clinic staff a new sense of purpose and direction—perhaps with their energies being directed towards helping the drug addict to become abstinent.

## Community-orientated services

A new community orientation to the delivery of care was introduced in the early 1980s, particularly following the publication of the *Treatment and rehabilitation* Report from the ACMD (1982). Perhaps coinciding with the move away from prescribing as the focus for the intervention, and alongside a presumption that this prescribing would be of oral-only medication, the general practitioner was encouraged to be a readily available and local provider of care to the increasing numbers of heroin users in the community, many of whom had never had any contact with formal treatment services.

The era of the specialist was over. Provision of care to the drug user was now seen as part of the everyday work of all general practitioners. However, despite the central promotion of this model for at least a decade, the continued reluctance of many general practitioners remains evident. Whilst the gains which have been made represent a significant improvement in the local availability and provision of care, it is nevertheless still the case that the majority of family doctors are hostile to their proposed key involvement in looking after drug users—especially when this may involve the prescribing of substitute drugs such as methadone (Tantam *et al.* 1993; ACMD 1993; see also Chapter 11, this volume).

## The need to develop a new AIDS-conscious 'British System'

AIDS has forced a fundamental re-examination of British drug policy, and this reappraisal is continuing. The urgency of the need to respond to the threat of HIV infection has created an understandable (if unfortunate) temptation to seize upon proposals as possible total solutions. In reality, the new 'British System' is better understood as a collection of attempts to secure multiple small gains rather than a search for hoped-for master-strokes (Drummond *et al.* 1987; ACMD 1988). In their policy analysis, Drummond *et al.* (1987) identified the need for separate consideration of higher policy and responses of the individual level. At the higher policy level, a balance must be struck between strategies aimed at preventing infection and strategies geared towards providing care for the increasing number of HIV-positive drug users. 'More into treatment' and 'earlier into treatment' warrant particular consideration.

A number of recent developments of clinical practice have been given the term 'harm reduction strategies', though interventions aimed at the reduction of drug-related harm have been evident for many years in British responses (see, for example Gossop 1982; Gossop *et al.* 1982). In harm reduction strategies, the driving force is not the drug taking or abstinence of the drug user, but the extent to which harm has been reduced as a result of the intervention. This may occur at the level of harm for the individual, or harm for the broader population. Consideration of harm reduction interventions also requires an estimation of the likely course that the drug use would otherwise have followed, and must therefore be reviewed regularly—both for individuals and for systems.

This harm reduction perspective runs through the three reports on *AIDS and drug misuse* from the ACMD (1988, 1989, 1993). As the second report states, the decision of whether or not to prescribe to the drug taker may be influenced by consideration of four criteria:

We see no reason to depart from the principle that prescribing should never be undertaken without an identified goal ... (such as) ...

a) to attract sero-positive drug misusers into regular contact with services;
b) to promote behaviour change away from practices which carry a risk of transmitting HIV infection;
c) to promote behaviour change in such a way as to maximise personal health and stability;
d) to encourage compliance with medical treatment including regular check-ups
   ...

However, as the report points out, the first of these goals is not an end in itself, but rather the platform on which the others are founded.

Three particular developments in the policy debate may warrant special consideration.

First, needle and syringe exchange schemes have been introduced across much of the UK, and information is now widely distributed (for example, in guidance to general practitioners) on methods for the emergency cleaning by a drug injector of a contaminated needle and syringe. The introduction of needle and syringe exchange schemes in particular has required an acceptance of the limited impact of any prevention or control initiative; and this more modest and realistic appraisal of efficacy legitimizes consideration of other interventions which may reduce the harm of the continued drug use, without necessarily interfering with the pre-existing prevention, control, or treatment efforts.

Secondly, a reappraisal has taken place with regard to the prescribing of injectable drugs, and several specialist centres now include this within the armamentarium at the disposal of the prescribing doctor (see Chapter 14). However, the prescription of injectable drugs (whether of methadone or of heroin) is not widespread in Britain as is sometimes inaccurately suggested and recent considerations of the efficacy of this renewed injectable prescribing have not found this option to be as encouraging as had originally been hoped (Battersby *et al.* 1992; ACMD 1993).

Thirdly, in the light of the encouraging data on reduced needle sharing amongst methadone maintenance programmes, there is a renewed examination of the role of oral methadone maintenance within the 'British System'. This latter consideration comprises of at least two parts: one part relating to the chosen oral methadone prescribing policy (for example high dose versus low dose; long term versus short term; etc.) and the other part relating to the context of delivery of the treatment (that is whether prescribing occurs within a well structured and diverse programme, or whether it is little more than a prescribing and dispensing service).

The changes in methadone prescribing in the early post-AIDS years might be considered more in the first of these two areas, that is, that more methadone has been prescribed and with a higher average daily dose, and it is disappointing how little consideration has been given to the nature of the service associated with the substitute prescribing.

## Conclusion

In conclusion, then, it might appear that there is no 'British System' —certainly no single 'British System'. However, there have been some distinctively British ways of addressing and dealing with the problems of drug use in society. Whether by the absence of a policy in any other direction, or by the identification of the covert policy document, the shape of the 'British System' can be seen behind the responses to the changing drug problem in the UK. It is not a constant system, and its lack of tight definition is sometimes exasperating; but on occasions this same characteristic enables a prompter response to changing circumstances (such as the advent of HIV, for example).

One of the most significant omissions within the 'British System' has been the failure to take advantage of the capacity of research methods to inform and guide national responses. Many questions that are centrally important to the national response can be stated in terms which permit empirical investigation. As such the effectiveness of many components of the national response could have been (and still can be) investigated by properly designed research procedures. The reliance upon policy-by-committee or policy-by-default may sometimes work, but without research support it provides the most fallible and perilous foundation for an enterprise as momentous as the formulation and implementation of a national drugs policy.

Future policy under the 'British System' may be determined either by changes in the process of overt or covert policy formation, or by the resolve not to pursue a different path. Whatever the mechanism of future policy formation, an appreciation of our recent and more distant past will increase the likelihood that we are able to preserve those features of the 'British System' which we wish to preserve, whilst not being shackled to an old and inflexible framework of diverse policy products. At the end of the day, it may be that pragmatism and the capacity to change and respond to changing circumstances are the most distinctively British features of the 'British System'.

## References

ACMD (Advisory Council on the Misuse of Drugs) (1982). *Treatment and rehabilitation*. HMSO, London.

ACMD (1988). *AIDS and drug misuse, Part 1*. HMSO, London.

ACMD (1989). *AIDS and drug misuse, Part 2*. HMSO, London.

ACMD (1993). *AIDS and drug misuse, Update*. HMSO, London.

Addiction Research Unit (1976). Appraisal. In *Drugs and drug dependence* (ed. G. Edwards, M. A. H. Russell, D. Hawks, and M. MacCafferty), pp. 176–8. Saxon House, Farnborough.

Ball, J. C. and Ross, A. (1991). *The effectiveness of methadone maintenance treatment: patients, programs, services and outcome*. Springer-Verlag, New York.

Battersby, M., Farrell, M., Gossop, M., Robson, P., and Strang, J. (1992). 'Horse trading': prescribing injectable opiates to opiate addicts. A descriptive study. *Drug and Alcohol Review*, **11**, 35–42.

Berridge, V. (1984). Drugs and social policy: the establishment of drug control in Britain 1900–1930. *British Journal of Addiction*, **79**, 17–29.

Berridge, V. and Edwards, G. (1981). *Opium and the people*. Penguin Books, Harmondsworth.

Bewley, T. H. (1975). Evaluation of addiction treatment in England. In *Drug dependence—treatment and treatment evaluation* (ed. H. Bostrom, T. Larsson, and N. Ljungstedt), pp. 275–86. Almqvist and Wiksell International, Stockholm.

Blumberg, H. H., Cohen, S. D., Dronfield, B. F., Mordecai, E. A., Roberts, J. C., and Hawks, D. (1974). British opiate users: I—People approaching London drug treatment centres. *International Journal of the Addictions*, **9**, 1–23.

Downes, D. (1977). The drug addict as folk devil. In *Drugs and politics* (ed. P. Rock), pp. 89–97. Transaction Books, New Jersey.

Drummond, C., Edwards, G., Glanz, A., Glass, I., Jackson, P., Oppenheimer, E., *et al.* (1987). Rethinking drug policies in the context of acquired immunodeficiency syndrome. *Bulletin of Narcotics*, **39**(2), 29–35.

Edwards, G. (1969). The British approach to the treatment of heroin addiction. *Lancet*, **i**, 768–72.

Gossop, M. (1982). *Living with drugs*. Temple Smith, London.

Gossop, M., Strang, J., and Connell, P. H. (1982). The response of out-patient opiate addicts to the provision of a temporary increase in their prescribed drugs. *British Journal of Psychiatry*, **141**, 338–43.

Gossop, M. (1990). Prescribing for drug addicts in Britain. In *Proceedings of Netherlands Institute of Mental Health Conference*, 29 June 1990, Utrecht (ed. F. Kok and J. Derks).

Kleber, H. (1993). The US anti-drug prevention strategy: science and policy connections. In *Drug, alcohol and tobacco: Making the science and policy connections* (eds. G. Edwards, J. Strang, J. Jaffe), pp. 109–20. Oxford University Press, Oxford.

Ministry of Health (1967). *Treatment and supervision of heroin addiction*, HM67/16. Ministry of Health, London.

Schur, E. M. (1966). *Narcotic addiction in Britain and America: the impact of public policy*. Associated Book Publishers, London.

Smart, C. (1984). Social policy and drug addiction: a critical study of policy development. *British Journal of Addiction*, **79**, 31–9.

Stimson, G. V. (1990). AIDS and HIV: the challenge for British drug services. *British Journal of Addiction*, **85**, 329–39.

Stimson, G. V. and Oppenheimer, E. (1982). *Heroin addiction: treatment and control in Britain*. Tavistock, London.

Strang, J., Orgel, M., and Farrell, M. (1989). Well users clinic for illicit drug users. *British Medical Journal*, **298**, 1310.

Tantam, D., Donmall, M., Webster, A., and Strang, J. (1993). Can general practitioners and general psychiatrists be expected to look after drug misusers? Results from an evaluation of a non-specialist treatment policy in the North West of England. *British Journal of General Practice*, **43**, 470–4.

Trebach, A. S. (1982). *The heroin solution*. Yale University Press, New Haven.

Ward, J., Darke, S., Hall, W., and Mattick, R. (1992a). Methadone maintenance and the human immunodeficiency virus: current issues in treatment and research. *British Journal of Addiction*, **87**, 447–53.

Ward, J., Mattick, R., and Hall, W. (1992b). *Key issues in methadone maintenance treatment*. University of New South Wales Press, Sydney.

# Index

Bold numbers denote reference to tables and illustrations.